EDUCATION
IN INDONESIA

The **Indonesia Project**, a major international centre for research on the Indonesian economy and society, is housed in the **Crawford School of Public Policy**'s **Arndt-Corden Department of Economics**. The Crawford School is part of the **ANU College of Asia and the Pacific** at **The Australian National University (ANU)**. Established in 1965, the Project is well known and respected in Indonesia and in other places where Indonesia attracts serious scholarly and official interest. Funded by the ANU and the Australian Agency for International Development (AusAID), the Indonesia Project monitors and analyses recent economic developments in Indonesia; informs Australian governments, business and the wider community about those developments and about future prospects; stimulates research on the Indonesian economy; and publishes the respected *Bulletin of Indonesian Economic Studies*.

The College's **Department of Political and Social Change (PSC)** focuses on domestic politics, social processes and state–society relationships in Asia and the Pacific, and has a long-established interest in Indonesia.

Together with PSC, the Project holds the annual Indonesia Update conference, which offers an overview of recent economic and political developments and devotes attention to a significant theme in Indonesia's development. The *Bulletin of Indonesian Economic Studies* publishes the conference's economic and political overviews, while the edited papers related to the conference theme are published in the Indonesia Update Series.

The **Institute of Southeast Asian Studies (ISEAS)** was established as an autonomous organization in 1968. It is a regional centre dedicated to the study of socio-political, security and economic trends and developments in Southeast Asia and its wider geostrategic and economic environment. The Institute's research programmes are the Regional Economic Studies (RES, including ASEAN and APEC), Regional Strategic and Political Studies (RSPS), and Regional Social and Cultural Studies (RSCS).

ISEAS Publishing, an established academic press, has issued more than 2,000 books and journals. It is the largest scholarly publisher of research about Southeast Asia from within the region. ISEAS Publishing works with many other academic and trade publishers and distributors to disseminate important research and analyses from and about Southeast Asia to the rest of the world.

Indonesia Update Series

EDUCATION
IN INDONESIA

EDITED BY

DANIEL SURYADARMA
GAVIN W. JONES

ISEAS

INSTITUTE OF SOUTHEAST ASIAN STUDIES
Singapore

First published in Singapore in 2013 by
ISEAS Publishing
Institute of Southeast Asian Studies
30 Heng Mui Keng Terrace
Pasir Panjang
Singapore 119614

E-mail: publish@iseas.edu.sg
Website: http://bookshop.iseas.edu.sg

The responsibility for facts and opinions in this publication rests exclusively with the authors and their interpretations do not necessarily reflect the views or the policy of the Institute or its supporters.

ISEAS Library Cataloguing-in-Publication Data

Education in Indonesia / edited by Daniel Suryadarma and Gavin W. Jones.
   (Indonesia update series)
   This book emanates from the 30th Indonesia Update Conference organized by the Australian National University Indonesia Project on 21–22 September 2012.
   1. Education—Indonesia—Congresses.
   2. Education and state—Indonesia—Congresses.
   3. Islamic education—Indonesia—Congresses.
   4. Education, Higher—Indonesia—Congresses.
   5. Teachers—Training of—Indonesia—Congresses.
   I. Suryadarma, Daniel.
   II. Jones, Gavin W.
   III. Australian National University. Indonesia Project.
   IV. Indonesia Update Conference (30th : 2012 : Canberra, Australia)
DS644.4 I41 2012   2013

ISBN 978-981-4459-86-0 (soft cover)
ISBN 978-981-4515-04-7 (hard cover)
ISBN 978-981-4459-87-7 (e-book, PDF)

Cover photo: A senior high school class in South Central Timor, East Nusa Tenggara. Photo by Gavin W. Jones.

Edited and typeset by Beth Thomson, Japan Online, Canberra
Indexed by Angela Grant, Sydney
Printed in Singapore by Mainland Press Pte Ltd

CONTENTS

Tables   vii
Figures   ix
Contributors   xiii
Acknowledgments   xxi
Glossary   xxiii

1   Meeting the Education Challenge   1
    Daniel Suryadarma and Gavin W. Jones

2   Trends in Education in Indonesia   15
    Suharti

3   Teacher Training, School Norms and Teacher
    Effectiveness in Indonesia   53
    Christopher Bjork

4   Integrating Islamic Schools into the
    Indonesian National Education System:
    A Case of Architecture over Implementation?   68
    Robert Kingham and Jemma Parsons

5   Early Childhood Education and Development
    Services in Indonesia   82
    *Hafid Alatas, Sally Brinkman, Mae Chu Chang, Titie Hadiyati,
    Djoko Hartono, Amer Hasan, Marilou Hyson, Haeil Jung,
    Angela Kinnell, Menno Pradhan and Rosfita Roesli*

6   Where Did All the Money Go?
    Financing Basic Education in Indonesia   109
    Samer Al-Samarrai and Pedro Cerdan-Infantes

7   An Assessment of Policies to Improve Teacher
     Quality and Reduce Teacher Absenteeism   139
     Asep Suryahadi and Prio Sambodho

8   Indonesian Universities:
     Rapid Growth, Major Challenges   160
     Hal Hill and Thee Kian Wie

9   Beating the Odds: Locally Relevant Alternatives
     to World-class Universities   180
     Rivandra Royono and Diastika Rahwidiati

10   Financing Higher Education: The Viability of
     a Commercial Student Loan Scheme in Indonesia   203
     Bruce Chapman and Daniel Suryadarma

11   The Transformation and Internationalization of
     Higher Education: The Malaysian Experience   216
     Khong Kim Hoong

12   Role of the Education and Training Sector in
     Addressing Skill Mismatch in Indonesia   236
     Emanuela di Gropello

Index   267

TABLES

1.1   Share of the workforce with a primary school education
or less, selected Asian countries   6

2.1   Average years of schooling of population aged 15 or over
by urban/rural area and gender, 1993–2010   20

2.2   Number of schools by school level and type of provider,
1993–2008   32

2.3   Educational attainment of teachers by school level and
type of provider, 1999/2000–2009/10   39

2.4   Total public spending on education in selected countries,
1999–2008   47

2.5   Breakdown of local government expenditure on education
by level of government, 2007–10   48

5.1   Types of ECED services by ministry   88

5.2   Child development instruments and the developmental
domains to which they are related   94

5.3   Mean scores of children aged 4–5 on Early Development
Instrument, 2009–10   95

5.4   Share of children aged 4–5 deemed developmentally
vulnerable based on their Early Development Instrument
scores, 2009–10   96

5.5   Mean scores of children aged 4–5 on Strengths and
Difficulties Questionnaire, 2009–10   97

5.6   Performance of children aged 4–5 on Dimensional
Change Card Sort task, 2009–10   99

5.7   Mean scores of children aged 1–5 on child ability tasks,
2009–10   100

5.8   Mean scores of children aged 1–2 on child ability tasks
as rated by mothers, 2009–10   101

5.9	Mean scores of children aged 4–5 on drawing tasks, 2009–10	102
5.10	Share of children aged 1–2 correctly answering questions testing receptive and expressive language skills	103
7.1	The middle-income trap	141
7.2	Comparison of teachers' salaries in selected Southeast Asian countries	145
7.3	Average remuneration of tertiary graduates in the private and government sectors by age group, 2006	146
7.4	Forecast of costs associated with teacher certification, 2007–15	147
7.5	Rates of teacher absenteeism in Indonesia and Papua	153
8.1	Higher education enrolments in Indonesia, 2005–10	163
8.2	Higher education institutions in Indonesia by type, 2009/10	165
9.1	Expenditure per student by selected tertiary education institutions	188
A10.1	Age–earnings profiles, ordinary least squares and unconditional quantile regression estimations	215
11.1	Students enrolled in higher education in Malaysia by type of institution and level of study, 2011	222
11.2	Countries of origin of foreign students enrolled in higher education in Malaysia by sector and gender, 2011	231
11.3	Main destinations of Malaysian students studying abroad, and whether sponsored or self-supporting, 2011	233
12.1	Main characteristics of firms in the employer module of the survey	238

FIGURES

1.1 Secondary school gross enrolment rates, selected Asian countries, 1990–2010   4

2.1 Population aged 19 years or over by highest level of educational attainment and gender, 1990–2010   19

2.2 Average years of schooling by province, and the district within each province with the maximum/minimum years of schooling, 2010   20

2.3 Adult illiteracy rate by age group, 1993–2010   21

2.4 Adult illiteracy rate by province, 2010   22

2.5 Gross enrolment rate by school level, 1968–2010   24

2.6 Age-specific enrolment rate for students aged 13–15 and 16–18 by household expenditure quintile, 1993–2009   25

2.7 Ratio of net enrolment rate of females to net enrolment rate of males by school level, 1994–2010   26

2.8 Flow of students through primary school, academic year 1988/89–2008/09   28

2.9 Flow of students through junior secondary school, academic year 1988/89–2008/09   29

2.10 Education survival probability of population aged 13–15 ever enrolled in school by household expenditure quintile, 1993 and 2009   30

2.11 Education survival probability of population aged 16–18 ever enrolled in school by household expenditure quintile, 1993 and 2009   31

2.12 Number of primary schools constructed under the Presidential Primary School (Inpres SD) program, academic year 1973/74–1998/99   33

2.13 Number of teachers by school level, academic year 1999/2000–2009/10   35

2.14   Index of growth in the number of teachers and students,
        and trends in the student–teacher ratio, academic year
        1999/2000–2009/10   36
2.15   Educational attainment of teachers by school level   38
2.16   Share of teachers with a four-year degree or higher by
        school level and province, academic year 2009/10   40
2.17   Distribution of average scores for junior secondary
        schools in the 2010 national examination by subject   43
2.18   Share of junior secondary school students with
        mathematics scores above six and eight points in the
        2010 national examination   44
2.19   International comparison of performance of year 8
        students in the TIMSS mathematics test, 2011   46
4.1   Institutional architecture of the national education
        financing system   75
5.1   Share of 26–28-year-olds in poorest and richest 20 per
        cent of urban/rural households who have completed
        each year of schooling, 2010   84
5.2   Performance in reading of children from poorest and
        richest 10 per cent of households, Programme for
        International Student Assessment (PISA), 2003–09   85
5.3   Provision of ECED services by intended age group   89
5.4   Enrolments in ECED services of children from poorest
        and richest 20 per cent of households, 2004–10   91
5.5   Characteristics of rural households and ECED sample
        households by income quintile   93
5.6   Effect of Indonesia ECED Project participation on child
        development outcomes for 4-year-olds, 2009–10   105
6.1   Expenditure on education, Indonesia, 2001–10   111
6.2   Public expenditure on education as a share of total
        government expenditure, GDP and GDP per capita,
        selected countries   113
6.3   Composition of government expenditure on education
        in 2008, and of additional resources in 2009, by level of
        education   114
6.4   Share of education budget spent on non-basic education,
        selected countries   115
6.5   Share of total government budget spent on BOS grants
        program, universities, teacher certification, teacher salaries
        and other major programs, 2006–08 and 2009   116

6.6   Share of children enrolled in school by age and
      consumption quintile, 2006 and 2010   118

6.7   Indonesian students' PISA scores in mathematics and
      reading by socio-economic decile, 2003 and 2009   120

6.8   Student–teacher ratios in primary and junior secondary
      schools, 1995–2010   122

6.9   Correlation between primary schools' student–teacher
      ratios and year 5 students' average mathematics scores,
      2010   122

6.10 Impact of teacher certification on teacher motivation/
      welfare, teacher competency and student learning   123

6.11 Impact of teacher certification program on the 2015
      education budget   125

6.12 Correlation between average local government
      expenditure per primary or junior secondary student
      and education outcomes, 2009   128

6.13 Indicators of quality of local governance in 50 Indonesian
      districts, 2009   130

7.1   Gross enrolment rates by school level, 1970–2010   140

7.2   GDP by sector, 1971–2010   140

7.3   Gross enrolment rates in Indonesia and the developing
      countries of East Asia and the Pacific, 2000–10   143

7.4   Performance of year 8 students in TIMSS mathematics
      test, selected Southeast Asian countries, 1999–2011   143

7.5   Educational attainment of teachers, 2006   144

8.1   Public expenditure on tertiary education in East Asia   164

9.1   Proposed alternative framework for high-quality
      small TEIs   200

10.1 Repayment schedule for a hypothetical loan of
      Rp 30.4 million   207

10.2 Age–earnings profiles by area and gender   209

10.3 Loan repayment burden for the hypothetical loan
      scheme   211

11.1 Enrolments of foreign students in public and private
      higher education institutions, and annual growth in
      enrolments, 2001–11   229

12.1 Employers' perceptions of the importance of education,
      knowledge and experience among managerial/
      professional and skilled workers   241

12.2   Employers' perceptions of the importance of core
       subject-based and generic skills among managerial/
       professional and skilled workers   242

12.3   Employers' perceptions of the importance of
       behavioural skills among managerial/professional
       and skilled workers   243

12.4   Employees' perceptions of the importance of on-the-job
       skills   243

12.5   Employers' perceptions of the importance of education,
       knowledge and experience by sector   244

12.6   Employers' perceptions of the importance of
       behavioural skills among managerial/professional
       and skilled workers, by sector   245

12.7   Employers' perceptions of the difficulty of filling
       vacancies by sector   247

12.8   Employers' perceptions of the difficulty of filling
       vacancies by export orientation   248

12.9   Employers' perceptions of gaps in core subject-based
       and generic skills among managerial/professional
       and skilled workers   248

12.10 Employers' perceptions of the quality of secondary
       graduates hired within the 12 months preceding the
       survey   252

12.11 Employers' perceptions of the quality of tertiary
       graduates hired within the 12 months preceding
       the survey   253

12.12 Employers' perceptions of main strengths of
       secondary options   254

12.13 Employees' perceptions of main weaknessses of
       general secondary schools   255

12.14 Employees' perceptions of main weaknessses of
       vocational secondary schools   255

12.15 Employers' perceptions of main strengths of
       tertiary options   257

12.16 Employees' perceptions of main weaknessses of
       universities   258

12.17 Employees' perceptions of main weaknessses of
       formal vocational tertiary institutions   258

12.18 Employees' perceptions of main weaknessses of
       informal vocational post-secondary institutions   259

CONTRIBUTORS

Hafid Alatas holds a master's degree in development practice from the University of Queensland. He is a consultant with the Education Unit of the Human Development Sector, East Asia and Pacific Region, at the World Bank in Indonesia.

Samer Al-Samarrai is a senior education economist, East Asia and Pacific Region, at the World Bank. He currently coordinates the research and analytical work of the Education Unit in Indonesia. Before joining the World Bank in 2011, he worked for UNESCO and co-authored the annual 'Education for all global monitoring report'. Between 2003 and 2008, Dr Al-Samarrai managed a governance project in Bangladesh that supported the Ministry of Finance's efforts to improve the financing and quality of service delivery in the health and education sectors. He has also been a research fellow at the Institute of Development Studies in the United Kingdom and has undertaken research and advisory work in many countries in sub-Saharan Africa and South Asia. He has published widely on gender, finance and governance issues in the education sector. Dr Al-Samarrai holds a PhD in economics from the University of Sussex.

Christopher Bjork is associate professor and chair of education at Vassar College in New York. His research interests include educational reform in Asia, educational decentralization, and teaching cultures in Indonesia and Japan. He is the author of *Indonesian Education: Teachers, Schools, and Central Bureaucracy* (Routledge, 2005), the editor of *Educational Decentralization: Asian Experiences and Conceptual Contributions* (Springer, 2006) and the co-editor of *Education and Training in Japan* (Routledge, 1997) and *Japanese Education in an Era of Globalization: Enduring Issues in New Contexts* (Teachers College Press, in press). He is currently working on a book that will examine the effects of *yutori kyoiku*, a set of reforms to reduce academic intensity in Japanese schools.

Sally Brinkman is a social epidemiologist at the Telethon Institute for Child Health Research and holds adjunct positions with the University of Western Australia and the University of Adelaide. She brings internationally recognized epidemiological skills to her work, particularly in relation to the monitoring of child development and early education. She has a commitment to practical, pragmatic and translatable research.

Pedro Cerdan-Infantes is an education economist, East Asia and Pacific Region, at the World Bank in Indonesia. Currently based in the World Bank's Jakarta office, he has managed several studies on Indonesian education, most recently the report 'Spending more or spending better: improving education financing in Indonesia'. Before going to Indonesia, he spent four years in the Latin America and Caribbean region, working for the World Bank and the Inter-American Development Bank. He holds a master's degree in public administration in international development from the Kennedy School of Government at Harvard University.

Mae Chu Chang is lead education specialist at the World Bank in Indonesia, where she heads the Human Development Sector, East Asia and Pacific Region. She has worked intensively to help governments develop comprehensive education reform strategies in countries in the Middle East, East Asia and South Asia. Dr Chang also manages a research program that has produced about 100 titles covering a wide range of topics, including early childhood development, basic education and teacher development, and higher education and skills development.

Bruce Chapman AM (PhD, Yale) is a professor of economics at the Crawford School of Public Policy at the ANU. He has published over 200 articles in the areas of applied economics, education policy, the economics of crime, the economics of cricket and the role of income-contingent loans in public policy. His main area of current research relates to micro-econometric analyses in the economics of higher education, an area in which he is considered to be a world expert. He has had extensive direct policy experience, including with the motivation and design of Australia's income-contingent charge system for higher education (HECS) in 1988; as a senior economic advisor to Prime Minister Paul Keating (1994–96); and as a researcher/consultant to the governments of around 15 countries, mainly in the area of student loan policy (1992–2012). He is currently the president of the Economic Society of Australia.

Emanuela di Gropello is a World Bank sector leader in the Africa region, and previously lead economist in the East Asia region. She has led several regional studies on education and skills in Latin America and East

Asia, and has published extensively on the governance and financing of education systems. She has extensive operational experience in managing education projects in Latin American, East Asian and more recently African countries. She holds a PhD in economics from the University of Oxford.

Titie Hadiyati is one of the task team leaders for the Early Childhood Education and Development Project, Human Development Sector, at the World Bank in Indonesia. She holds degrees in civil engineering and education evaluation.

Djoko Hartono is a consultant on monitoring and evaluation with the Education Unit of the Human Development Sector, East Asia and Pacific Region, at the World Bank in Indonesia. He holds a PhD degree in demography from the ANU.

Amer Hasan is an education economist with the Human Development Sector, East Asia and Pacific Region, at the World Bank in Indonesia. He holds a PhD in public policy from the Irving B. Harris School of Public Policy Studies, University of Chicago.

Hal Hill is the H.W. Arndt Professor of Southeast Asian Economies, Arndt-Corden Department of Economics, Crawford School of Public Policy, ANU. His general research interests relate to the ASEAN economies. He is the author or editor of 16 books and has written about 140 academic papers and book chapters. Current and recent book projects include a textbook on the ASEAN economies, and edited volumes on regional development dynamics in the Philippines, the Malaysian economy, Indonesian economic development, middle-income Asian developing economies after the global financial crisis, and foreign investment in the Asia–Pacific. He serves on the editorial board of 13 academic journals, and has held visiting academic appointments at 10 universities and research institutes. He has worked as a consultant for AusAID, the Asian Development Bank, the World Bank and various UN agencies.

Marilou Hyson holds a PhD in child development and early childhood education from Bryn Mawr College. She is a consultant in early child development and education for the World Bank and other organizations, and an adjunct faculty member in the Graduate School of Education at the University of Pennsylvania.

Gavin W. Jones is the director of the JY Pillay Comparative Asia Research Centre at the National University of Singapore. He has been with the university for 10 years, serving earlier as research leader of the Changing Family in Asia cluster in the Asia Research Institute. After completing his PhD degree at the ANU in 1966, he joined the Population Council, where he worked first in New York, then in Thailand and Indonesia, before returning to Australia. He was with the Demography and Sociology Program at the ANU for 28 years, including eight as head of the program. His current research interests include very low-fertility regimes in Asia; delayed marriage, non-marriage and cross-boundary marriage; urbanization issues; and the equity aspects of educational development. He has served as consultant to many international agencies. Professor Jones has published about 25 books and monographs and some 170 refereed journal articles and book chapters.

Haeil Jung is an assistant professor at the School of Public and Environmental Affairs at Indiana University. His research focuses on applied econometrics and social policy evaluation. He received his PhD from the Irving B. Harris School of Public Policy Studies at the University of Chicago.

Khong Kim Hoong has served as the academic director of HELP University College since 1991. He is now deputy vice chancellor. He graduated from the University of Malaya in 1969, winning the Gold Medal for Best All Round Student for his excellent academic performance and leadership. Dr Khong completed his PhD in political science in 1975 at the University of Pittsburgh. He taught at the University of Malaya, where he was the chairman of the Public Administration Division. Dr Khong's international appointments include visiting fellowships at Ohio University, the University of Sydney, the East-West Center, the Japan Institute of International Affairs and the Institute of Southeast Asian Studies. He was a visiting professor at the Helsinki School of Economics in Finland (2001–09). His publications include *Merdeka: British Rule and the Struggle for Independence in Malaya*; *The 1990 Malaysian Elections: Continuity, Change and Ethnic Politics*; and *The Politics of Japan–Vietnam Relations*.

Robert Kingham is an Islamic education specialist who has been working in and with Islamic schools in Indonesia since the mid-1980s, including several years at the Darul Da'wah wal Irsyad *pesantren* in Pinrang, South Sulawesi. He was also the coordinating trainer for Program Pembibitan Calon Dosen IAIN se-Indonesia from 1989 to 1993. He worked in Asian program development for the Overseas Service Bureau, specializing in assignments for Australian volunteers in Islamic-majority countries. He was assigned by AusAID to develop and direct the Learning Assistance Program for Islamic Schools (LAPIS) in 2004, and continued to work as its senior technical advisor until the completion of the program in 2011. He is currently the Islamic education specialist for Australia's Education Partnership in Indonesia, placed in the Ministry of Religious Affairs in Jakarta, and for AusAID's BEAM–ARMM program in the Autonomous Region of Muslim Mindanao (ARMM), Philippines.

Angela Kinnell is a research fellow at the Telethon Institute for Child Health Research and holds adjunct positions with the University of Western Australia and the University of Adelaide. She has a PhD in psychology from the University of Adelaide. Her research examines the factors contributing to child health, development and well-being.

Jemma Parsons is a senior consultant for Cardno Emerging Markets Jakarta, and is currently working on a number of AusAID development projects in Indonesia and East Timor. From 2009 to 2011 she was principal researcher at the Asian Law Centre, University of Melbourne, and associate director of the Asian Law Group, a law and justice-focused development consultancy at the university. In 2011 she conducted a socio-economic impact assessment of the *madrasah* accreditation support activity delivered under AusAID's Learning Assistance Program for Islamic Schools (LAPIS).

Menno Pradhan is a professor of project and program evaluation for international development at VU University Amsterdam and the University of Amsterdam. He is also a fellow of the Tinbergen Institute and the Amsterdam Institute for International Development.

Diastika Rahwidiati leads AusAID Indonesia's Tertiary Education and Knowledge Sector Unit. She has been working in international development for the past 11 years. Her professional interests include education, policy-related research and the design of development programs. She led the design of AusAID's new knowledge sector initiative. Together with Rivandra Royono, she is currently working on designing options for a potential investment by AusAID in Indonesia's tertiary education sector. She holds a master's degree in international development and environmental analysis from Monash University.

Rosfita Roesli is an education specialist with the Human Development Sector at the World Bank in Indonesia, and one of the task team leaders of the Early Childhood Education and Development Project. She holds a master's degree in development studies from the University of Leeds.

Rivandra Royono is the principal designer of a planned AusAID initiative to support Indonesia's tertiary education sector. Before joining AusAID, he worked for the World Bank in Jakarta, focusing on teacher management in basic education, and contributed to the 2012 World Bank report on 'Citizens and service delivery'. His professional interests cover a range of education-related themes, including early childhood education, curriculum reform, learning assessment, teacher management and tertiary education. He holds a bachelor's degree in engineering physics from the Bandung Institute of Technology and a master's degree in public policy from the University of Indonesia.

Prio Sambodho is a researcher at the SMERU Research Institute in Jakarta. He holds a master's degree in public policy from Lee Kuan Yew School of Public Policy, National University of Singapore. His research interests include asset-based poverty reduction policies, poverty mainstreaming in public policy and urban poverty reduction. He is currently involved in the SEADI–SMERU poverty mainstreaming toolkit project. He is a principal writer for the Indonesian government's Masterplan for the Expansion and Acceleration of Poverty Reduction (MP3KI).

Suharti is a staff member at the Directorate of Education, National Development Planning Agency (Bappenas). She holds a master's degree in applied economics from the University of Michigan and is currently studying for her PhD at the ANU, where her research focuses on inequality in education performance in Indonesia. She has been involved in the formulation of a number of development policies in Indonesia, including the government's scholarship program, conditional cash transfer program and school operational subsidy scheme. Before taking official leave to pursue her PhD, she was a member of the Indonesia Education for All Working Group and was actively involved in the Gender in Education Working Group.

Daniel Suryadarma (PhD, ANU) joined the Indonesia Project at the ANU as a research fellow in 2010. An applied econometrician, his research focuses exclusively on development issues in Indonesia, mainly in the areas of education, labour, poverty and social protection. His work has appeared in many peer-reviewed academic journals, including the *Journal of Development Economics*, the *World Bank Economic Review*, *Food Policy* and *Education Economics*. His research encompasses child labour, human capital accumulation, the quality of education, higher education financing, migration, corruption, rural index insurance, local elections, targeting mechanisms of social programs and an evaluation of the Indonesian government's community-driven development program. He has also provided advice to the Indonesian Vice President's Office, AusAID and the World Bank.

Asep Suryahadi is the director of the SMERU Research Institute in Jakarta. He holds a PhD in economics from the ANU. His research interests cover the areas of poverty, social protection, labour, education, health and economic development in general. His current research topics include the impact of unconditional cash transfers on social welfare, the impact of the spread of television on fertility, and the consequences of poor health and informal coping mechanisms. His latest publications include articles for *Education Economics,* the *Journal of Development Economics, Food Policy* and the *Bulletin of Indonesian Economic Studies.*

Thee Kian Wie is a senior economist at the Economic Research Centre, Indonesian Institute of Sciences, and also a member of the Commission for the Social Sciences, Indonesian Academy of Sciences (KIS–AIPI). Born in Jakarta in 1935, Dr Thee received his first degree from the Faculty of Economics, University of Indonesia, in 1959, followed by a PhD in economics from the University of Wisconsin, Madison, in 1969. In 2004, the ANU awarded him an honorary doctorate. His major research interests are economic, industrial and technological development in East Asian countries, with particular reference to Indonesia. His latest book, *Indonesia's Economy since Independence,* was published by the Institute of Southeast Asian Studies in May 2012.

ACKNOWLEDGMENTS

This book is based mainly on papers given at the Indonesia Update conference, held at the Australian National University (ANU) in September 2012. We are especially grateful to Richard Woolcott, former Australian ambassador to Indonesia and former head of the Department of Foreign Affairs, and a great friend of the Indonesia Project, for opening the conference. We also sincerely thank all the speakers, many of whom came from Indonesia, but also from places farther away, including the United States. We acknowledge the important contribution of the session chairs, who managed the limited time with efficiency and provided enough opportunities for the audience to ask questions.

The conference would not have taken place without the efforts of those who worked tirelessly behind the scenes. Preparation took nine months, and we are grateful for the unwavering commitment shown by many individuals. First and foremost, we would like to thank the Indonesia Project administration: Cathy Haberle, Nurkemala Muliani and Trish van der Hoek. They were helped by Allison Ley and Thuy Thu Pham from the Department of Political and Social Change. We would also like to thank Umbu Reku Raya and Dewa Wisana for providing IT support and for producing high-quality video documentation. Finally, but definitely not least, we are grateful to the student volunteers.

In addition to the papers presented at the conference, the book contains articles contributed by non-presenters. These include a chapter on early childhood education, one on basic education financing and a chapter on the role of the education and training sector in addressing skills mismatch. We thank the authors of those chapters for taking the time to contribute to the book. We also thank Cynthia Lai Uin Rue for providing research assistance.

The editors and also Beth Thomson, who has edited and typeset nearly every Indonesia Update book since 1994, have reviewed all chapters contained in this book. Beth's work has significantly improved the quality of each chapter, and as editors we are grateful for her professionalism.

As has been the case for many years, the conference and the book were funded by the Australian Agency for International Development (AusAID) as part of a generous grant to the ANU and the Indonesia Project. The Department of Political and Social Change also provided some funding for the conference. Finally, we would like to thank the head of the Indonesia Project, Budy Resosudarmo, for his vote of confidence in letting us organize the conference.

We hope that the book contains enough of substance to do justice to the broad and important topic of education in Indonesia, and to provide feasible recommendations to policy makers in Indonesia.

Daniel Suryadarma and Gavin W. Jones
Canberra and Singapore, March 2013

GLOSSARY

ACCA	Association of Chartered Certified Accountants (United Kingdom)
ANU	Australian National University
ASEAN	Association of Southeast Asian Nations
AUQA	Australian Universities Quality Agency
AusAID	Australian Agency for International Development
BAN-PT	Badan Akreditasi Nasional Perguruan Tinggi (National Accreditation Agency for Universities)
BAN-S/M	Badan Akreditasi Nasional Sekolah/Madrasah (National Accreditation Board for Schools and Madrasah)
Bappenas	Badan Perencanaan Pembangunan Nasional (National Development Planning Agency)
Bidik Misi	Beasiswa Pendidikan untuk Mahasiswa Miskin ('targeted mission' program for university students from poor households)
BKB	*bina keluarga balita* (toddler family group)
BKKBN	Badan Koordinasi Keluarga Berencana Nasional (National Family Planning Coordination Agency)
BLK	Balai Latihan Kerja (Vocational Training Centre)
BOS	Bantuan Operasi Sekolah (Schools Operational Assistance)
BPS	Badan Pusat Statistik (Statistics Indonesia, the central statistics agency)
BSNP	Badan Standar Nasional Pendidikan (Board of National Education Standards)
DAK	Dana Alokasi Khusus (Specific Purpose Fund)
DAU	Dana Alokasi Umum (General Purpose Fund)
DCCS	Dimensional Change Card Sort (task)
DID	Dana Insentif Daerah (Regional Incentive Fund)

DKI	Daerah Khusus Ibukota (Special Capital Region)
dosen inti	special lecturer
ECED	early childhood education and development
EDI	Early Childhood Instrument
EMIS	Education Management Information System
EU	European Union
EYE	Education for Youth Employment
GDP	gross domestic product
GER	gross enrolment rate
Golkar	orig. Golongan Karya (the state political party under the New Order, and one of the major post-New Order parties)
golongan miskin	group of poor people
GTT	*guru tidak tetap* (school-hired non-permanent teacher)
GTY	*guru tetap yayasan* (school-hired permanent teacher in a private school)
guru	teacher
HECS	higher education contribution scheme
ICL	income-contingent loan
Inpres	Instruksi Presiden (Presidential Instruction, a program of special grants from the central government)
Inpres SD	Inpres Sekolah Dasar (presidential program to construct primary schools)
IPS	Indeks Prestasi Sementara (Preliminary Achievement Index)
IDI	Ikatan Dokter Indonesia (Association of Indonesian Physicians)
IT	information technology
KB	*kelompok bermain* (playgroup)
KKG	Kelompok Kerja Guru (Primary School Teachers Working Group)
KPP	Kursus Para Profesi (Para Professional Course)
KUM	academic credit system in Indonesian higher education
LIPI	Lembaga Ilmu Pengetahuan Indonesia (Indonesian Institute of Sciences)
LPEM-FEUI	Lembaga Penyelidikan Ekonomi dan Masyarakat, Fakultas Ekonomi, Universitas Indonesia (Institute for Economic and Social Research, Faculty of Economics, University of Indonesia)

LPMP	Lembaga Penjamin Mutu Pendidikan (Education Quality Assurance Institute)
madrasah	Islamic school
manajemen berbasis sekolah	school-based management
MGMP	Musyawarah Guru Mata Pelajaran (Secondary School Subjects Teachers Working Group)
MQA	Malaysian Qualifications Agency
NIE	newly industrialized economy
NUPTK	*nomor unik pendidik dan tenaga kependidikan* (personal identity number for teachers and educational support staff)
OECD	Organisation for Economic Co-operation and Development
OLS	ordinary least squares
PAD	Pendapatan Asli Daerah (locally derived revenue)
Pancasila	the five guiding principles of the Indonesian state: belief in God, humanitarianism, nationalism, democracy and social justice
PDII-LIPI	Centre for Scientific Documentation and Information at the Indonesian Institute of Sciences
Pemberian Sertifikat Pendidik secara Langsung	direct certification of teachers
Pendidikan dan Latihan Profesi Guru	retraining of teachers
Penilaian Portofolio	portfolio assessment of teachers
PGRI	Persatuan Guru Republik Indonesia (Indonesian Teachers Union)
PhD	doctor of philosophy
PIRLS	Progress in International Reading Literacy Study
PISA	Programme for International Student Assessment
Podes	Potensi Desa (Village Potential, a BPS survey of village economic status)
Pos PAUD	*pos perkembangan anak usia dini* (ECED post)
posyandu	integrated health service unit
PP	Peraturan Pemerintah (Government Decree or Regulation)
PSG	Pendidikan Sistem Ganda (Dual Education System)
pribumi	indigenous, not of immigrant stock
QAA	Quality Assurance Association for Higher Education (United Kingdom)
RA	*raudhotul atfal* (Islamic kindergarten – formal)

Sakernas	Survei Angkatan Kerja Nasional (National Labour Force Survey)
SDQ	Strengths and Difficulties Questionnaire
sekolah tinggi	advanced school
SIKD	Sistem Informasi Keuangan Daerah (Regional Financial Information System)
SPS	*satuan PAUD sejenis* (early childhood unit)
Susenas	Survei Sosio-Ekonomi Nasional (National Socio-Economic Survey)
TEI	tertiary education institution
TIMSS	Trends in International Mathematics and Science Study
TK	*taman kanak-kanak* (kindergarten)
TPA	*taman penitipan anak* (childcare centre)
TPQ	*taman pendidikan quran* (Islamic kindergarten – non-formal)
UIN	Universitas Islam Negeri (Islamic State University)
UNICEF	United Nations Children's Fund
UQR	unconditional quantile regression
US	United States

Currencies

$	US dollar
A$	Australian dollar
RM	Malaysian ringgit
Rp	Indonesian rupiah

1 MEETING THE EDUCATION CHALLENGE

Daniel Suryadarma and Gavin W. Jones

1.1 INTRODUCTION

If well-informed persons anywhere in the world were asked about what they knew about education in various countries, they would be likely to have something to say about countries such as India or South Korea. On India, they would be likely to mention the striking contrast between the production of top-flight statisticians and IT professionals on the one hand, and the failure, on the other hand, of millions of Indian children, especially girls, to complete primary school. On South Korea, they would be likely to mention the brilliant performance of Korean students in objective tests, but also that this is achieved at considerable cost, represented by the prevalence of cram schools and the unrelenting pressure on children to succeed.

The same informed persons would be unlikely to have ready answers if asked about education in Indonesia, however. There appear to be few distinctive images of Indonesian education that are widely known internationally. Yet in Indonesia, as elsewhere in Asia, education will inevitably play a key role in the trajectory of national development as the twenty-first century unfolds. Indonesian education may lack a clear image – benign or otherwise – in the international community, but that is not because nothing is happening. The past decade has seen major changes in the structure of the education system and in the schooling trajectories of Indonesian children and adolescents. It has also seen major policy discussions and initiatives. The purpose of this book is not to build an image, but to explore the reality of the current state of education in Indonesia.

Before addressing Indonesian education specifically, we should set the scene by emphasizing just why attention to educational trends and issues should be a key concern for any country pursuing a development agenda. What is the role of education in development?

The literature on this topic is vast and covers a wide range of aspects, including the connections between education and overall economic development, health, fertility, sustainable population growth, workforce productivity and the development of democratic systems of governance.[1] The general import of this literature is that education is of crucial importance, almost across the board, in advancing both workforce and non-workforce-related aspects of development. Equally important is the timing of investments in education; earlier is better, because of the long lead times in translating increased levels of schooling into a more productive workforce.

1.2   PRIMARY AND SECONDARY EDUCATION

There is fairly general agreement among economists interested in rates of return to education that poor countries starting from a low human resource base should invest heavily in primary education, because of the evidence of higher social rates of return to education at this level (Psacharopoulos and Patrinos 2004, and the references cited therein). That is what Indonesia did with the windfall gains from the oil price increases of the 1970s. The result was a striking rise in primary school enrolment rates continuing into the 1980s. Indonesia is generally considered to have achieved universal enrolment in primary school education around 1983. This was true in the sense that almost all children were spending some time in primary school. But as Suharti shows in Chapter 2 of this book, even a decade after that, only about 66 per cent of pupils entering primary school actually graduated from grade 6 (Figure 2.8). This figure reached 81 per cent in academic year 2007/08 – a great improvement, but still well short of universal completion of primary schooling.

A great deal of work still needs to be done, then, to ensure that all primary school-aged children complete their primary education, even leaving aside the quality of the educational experience of those that do. It is a tragedy that in the second decade of the twenty-first century, some children in Indonesia are not completing primary school and are turned out into the workforce as functional illiterates. By the middle of this

---

1   See, for example, Cochrane (1979), Caldwell and Caldwell (1985), Hannum and Buchmann (2005), Glaeser, Ponzetto and Shleifer (2007), Hanushek and Woessmann (2008), Lutz (2009), Lutz, Cuaresma and Abbasi-Shavazi (2010), Baker et al. (2011) and Pamuk, Fuchs and Lutz (2011).

century, such children will still be in the workforce as poorly educated older workers, dragging down overall productivity levels.

Despite the problems with primary school retention rates, Indonesia, like many other countries, has now shifted its attention to the second phase of basic education – the first three years of secondary school – on the grounds that primary schooling is now close to universal. The junior secondary level of education is pivotal to Indonesia's efforts to raise productivity by developing the country's human resources, not only because it forms part of an essential basic education, but also because it is the bridge between primary education and upper secondary and higher education, for those students who proceed to these levels. As an economy develops, changes in the structure of employment mean more job opportunities in middle-level technical fields such as trades, administration and various kinds of services. Such work requires at least a junior secondary education. Farmers, who traditionally were not considered to need an education, do in fact need, at the very least, to be literate and numerate in order to make optimal use of fertilizers and pesticides, agricultural extension activities and increasingly complex marketing arrangements. Moreover, there is evidence that workers with more years of education deal better with the increasing pace of change, and that getting some secondary education makes people more confident in dealing with officialdom (Colclough 1982; Jamison and Lau 1982). In short, primary schooling alone cannot provide the insights, skills and competencies needed by workers in Indonesia's evolving economy (Lewin and Caillods 2001: Ch. 1).

Senior secondary and tertiary education were formerly reserved for the select few in Indonesia, but are now considered by most parents to be necessary to secure a reasonable job. Enrolments at these levels are therefore expanding rapidly. The quality of junior secondary education has a crucial bearing on performance at these higher levels. Where its availability is limited or its quality unsatisfactory, as is often the case in more isolated rural areas, the opportunities for advancement of large numbers of young people are blocked. This has unfortunate repercussions, not only for the young people themselves, but also for the economy as a whole, because the distribution of talent in a population is not restricted to urban dwellers or those whose parents are more prosperous.

Quantitative gains in education at both the junior and senior secondary levels in Indonesia have been impressive. As shown in Figure 1.1, Indonesia's secondary school gross enrolment rates (GERs) have increased roughly in line with those in China and Thailand, and in recent years even appear to have closed the gap with those in Thailand. Indonesia's rates remain well above those in India. From a GER of around 50 per cent in the mid-1990s, Indonesia's secondary school enrolment rate was approaching 80 per cent in 2010.

Figure 1.1   Secondary school gross enrolment rates, selected Asian countries, 1990–2010 (%)

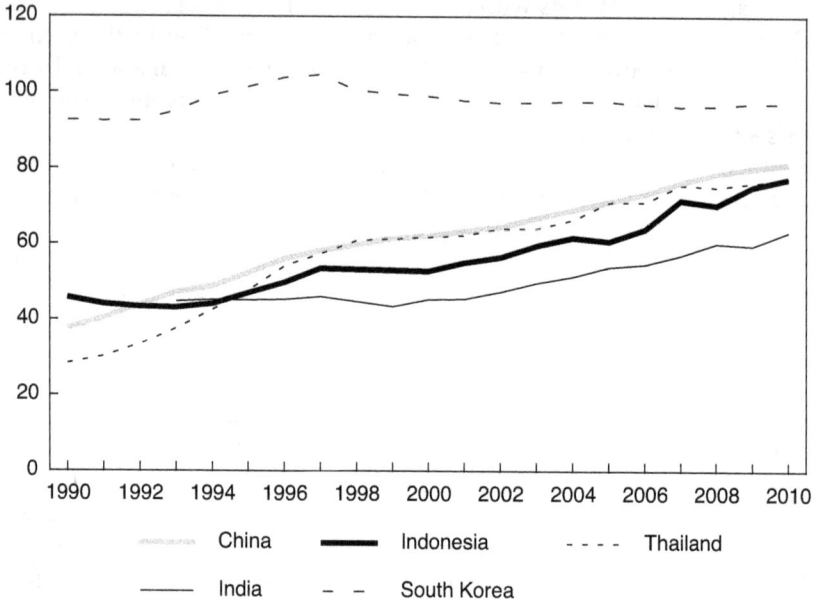

Source: World Development Indicators.

Issues of equity of access to education, however, remain very serious in Indonesia, as is clear from Figures 2.10 and 2.11 in Chapter 2. Happily, there is no longer much evidence of the inequity of access by gender that used to characterize Indonesia and that continues to characterize South Asian countries. But the figures on continuation of education by socio-economic background are of great concern. There is a need to lower the actual costs of education borne by poor families, to improve the quality of the schools serving them and to subsidize the brightest of the students from poor backgrounds, not just to complete primary school but to achieve the key transfers from primary to junior secondary and higher levels of education.

It is noteworthy that recent studies tend to suggest that rates of return to primary education may now be lower than rates of return to the post-primary levels of education (Colclough, Kingdon and Patrinos 2009). One concern is that this might

> ... reduce the incentives for poor households to send their children to school if they believed that the prospects for their progressing upwards through secondary schooling and beyond (where the higher returns accrue) were small (Colclough, Kingdon and Patrinos 2009: 2).

Such issues need to be considered seriously in the Indonesian context.

The weight of evidence indicates that the quality of education in Indonesia is very poor. The catalogue of qualitative defects in Indonesian primary schools is long, and includes poorly trained teachers, high rates of teacher absenteeism, an emphasis on rote learning, insufficient textbooks, poor-quality buildings and a lack of toilets and running water. The effect of such factors on the cognitive abilities of students is very important; as Hanushek and Woessmann (2008) observe, studies of the impact of education on economic growth that do *not* take into account cognitive skill differences arising from variations in school quality are highly biased in the direction of underestimating the impact of schooling.

This would seem to be a particularly important challenge for Indonesia in view of the evidence of poor student results in international standardized tests. As Samer Al-Samarrai and Pedro Cerdan-Infantes point out in Chapter 6 of this book, Indonesia consistently performs more poorly than neighbouring Malaysia, Thailand and Singapore on the Programme for International Student Assessment (PISA) and Trends in International Mathematics and Science Study (TIMSS) tests, measuring performance of students in reading and mathematics (see also Suryadarma and Sumarto 2011: Figures 7, 8 and 9). Not only are the average scores of Indonesian students low, but the share of students achieving the highest levels of performance is far less than in Thailand and Malaysia. Moreover, there has been no significant improvement in learning outcomes over the last decade, except in reading. To round off this rather dismal story, disaggregating the PISA data by wealth reveals that children from poor families who manage to stay in school perform worse than children from richer families (Figure 6.7).

Deficiencies in both the quantity and quality of education in Indonesia in recent decades have long-term implications. There is an 'inertia' factor built into educational turnover of the labour force. The majority of those in the labour force today were of school age at a time when enrolment rates were much lower than they are now. This accounts for the very low average educational levels of the workforce at the present time (Table 1.1). Looking ahead, most of those entering the labour force in 2010 will still be in the workforce mid-century. If they have no secondary education, this will hold down productivity in the economy for decades to come. The contrast between Indonesia and South Korea is telling; for the workforce as a whole, the gap between the two countries in the proportion with a primary education or less is very large; but for the young adult workforce it is even larger, because of the spectacular educational advances made by Korea in recent years.

Indonesia's political leaders have recognized the urgency of raising levels of public expenditure on education. In a series of amendments to

*Table 1.1   Share of the workforce with a primary school education or less,
selected Asian countries (%)*

Country	Year	Total workforce	Young adult workforce (aged 25–34)
Indonesia	2010	50.4	31.8
Malaysia	2008	18.3	9.3[b]
Philippines	2008	31.1	21.1
Singapore[a]	2007	27.7	7.3
South Korea	2007	23.0	2.0[b]
Taiwan	2011	8.5	<5.0
Thailand	2010	52.7	29.8

a   Data refer to the resident population.
b   Young adults aged 25–29.

Source: Indonesia: Susenas; Malaysia: Yearbook of Statistics (2010: Table 95) and 2000 population census; Taiwan: Statistical Data Book (2012: Table 2-10b); Thailand: average of four rounds of Labour Force Survey 2010; other countries: ILO, *Key Indicators of the Labour Market,* sixth and seventh editions.

the Constitution in 2002, a paragraph was inserted in article 31 obliging the central and regional governments to allocate at least 20 per cent of their annual expenditures to education. This was legally enshrined in 2003 in the amended education law (Law 20/2003 on the National Education System). Due to the constitutional and legal trappings surrounding the 20 per cent target, however, the central government was able to achieve the target only in 2009.

The 20 per cent policy and other initiatives have certainly resulted in greatly increased financial resources to support public investments in education. It must be borne in mind, however, that the upper levels of education, where educational expansion is now concentrated, are much more expensive per student than primary, or even junior secondary, education. Moreover, as Asep Suryahadi and Prio Sambodho point out in Chapter 7, teacher salaries are very low – much lower than in comparable countries (Table 7.2). Very considerable increases in educational expenditures will therefore be needed.

The government's attempt to increase salaries by providing certification allowances and remote area allowances will have a big impact on government finances. But even if achieved, the increases in expenditure are no guarantee of success in raising the quality of education. Indeed, as yet there is no evidence that the provision of certification and remote area allowances has had any positive effect on quality (Chapter 7).

Acting on evidence of shortcomings in the certification program, in 2012 the Ministry of Education and Culture introduced competency testing to ensure that teachers were assessed rigorously before receiving certification. The process would be improved further if periodic recertification were also required, to provide incentives for teachers to upgrade their skills (Chapter 6).

The problems in Indonesian education go far beyond the issue of financial resources. The quality of an education system can be thought of as resting on three components: financial resources, policies and governance – the latter referring to the way financial resources are used and policies are implemented. These three components will then determine the intermediate outcomes, for example teacher availability, teacher quality and performance, and school infrastructure and management. The final outcome of the education system is the skills acquired by the students. Therefore, while discussion of financial resources is important, it is equally important to consider the other aspects that determine the quality of the education system.

Many of the obstacles to improving public education in Indonesia relate to the teaching force. In particular, the country has more teachers than it needs. Teacher hiring over the past decade has continued to outpace increases in school enrolments, causing student–teacher ratios to decline below international benchmarks associated with good education quality (Chapter 6). This has led to an increase in expenditure without a commensurate impact on student learning outcomes. The intergovernmental resource transfer system is partly responsible, in effect providing incentives for local government to overhire. Political and other considerations at the local level also contribute to overhiring, along with elements of corruption and lack of transparency in the recruitment of teachers (Chapter 6). The problem is not helped by unacceptably high rates of teacher absenteeism that are not restricted to more remote areas (Chapter 7).

As for modes of teaching, Christopher Bjork (Chapter 3) notes that although the Ministry of Education and Culture has tried to encourage teachers to incorporate innovative instructional techniques into their lessons, the instructors he has observed 'used the vast majority of class time to lecture students and summarize the content of textbooks' (p. 60). He argues that it is not easy to change the culture of teaching from one in which obedience and loyalty as a civil servant trumps any inclination to innovate, to one in which a teacher is expected to make learning more engaging. Quality and accountability of teachers is crucial. What are the causes of the dysfunctional teaching styles, high levels of absenteeism and limited commitment to the teaching role on the part of many teachers? As Bjork argues, the root of the problem lies in the fact that in

Indonesia teachers are part of the civil service. Rather than being evaluated on the quality of their work in the classroom, teachers are judged on the basis of their loyalty to the school principal and the district education office. They therefore have no incentive to improve their teaching quality.

How are these issues to be addressed? Suryahadi and Sambodho (Chapter 7) find that merely increasing teachers' salaries does not appear to have improved the performance of students or reduced rates of teacher absenteeism. Bjork (Chapter 3) argues that the orientation of teachers must be reshaped to enable them to assume leadership roles and view themselves as professionals. This could be initiated through a new evaluation system based on classroom performance, although the shift should start much sooner by providing teachers with more rigorous pre-service education and professional development, and giving them the training to be able to act autonomously. Such reforms are very hard to implement, but it is imperative that the government embark on this path.

Indonesian schools also suffer from serious deficiencies in management. As a striking example, a number of teachers and school principals have been arrested on corruption charges (*Kompas*, 31 August 2012). And the problems are not limited to corruption, with numerous reports of ill-maintained school buildings and inadequate facilities. A strategy that has been implemented to address this problem is school-based management (*manajemen berbasis sekolah*), which involves the community in the running of a school through an institution called the *komite sekolah* (school committee). The idea is that monitoring and pressure from below will improve school management. However, Al-Samarrai and Cerdan-Infantes (Chapter 6) find that school committees tend to be passive participants in school decision making, which is dominated by principals and teachers (see also Pradhan et al. 2011). So far, the attempts to strengthen the committees have largely been unsuccessful. The reluctance of communities to participate more actively in school management could be due to cultural issues, as well as the fact that teachers and principals have more education than the average parent. Unfortunately, despite holding great promise on paper, school committees have yet to prove their worth in practice as a tool to improve school management.

Parents who are not satisfied with the quality of public schools have the choice to enrol their children in privately administered schools. Conceptually, private schools should be able to compete with public schools, in the process forcing them to improve their quality. In reality, however, the majority of Indonesian private schools serve to absorb excess demand for public education, especially at the secondary level where there has not been any massive government school construction program equivalent to that undertaken in the 1970s under the Presidential Primary School program (Inpres Sekolah Dasar, Inpres SD) (Chapter 2). Newhouse and Suryadarma (2011) document that parents still prefer public schools because – with the exception of a relatively small number of elite private schools – they generally offer a better standard of education than the privately administered ones. Since the inferior private schools cater mainly to children from poor families, a vicious cycle of intergenerational poverty may be perpetuated.

Conditions on the ground call for affirmative action, whereby public schools would be required to allocate a certain proportion of places to children from poor families. Another innovation that could be applicable to Indonesia has come from the non-government sector, which is starting to set up low-cost, for-profit but nevertheless high-quality schools specifically targeting poor children (Tooley and Dixon 2005). Departing from the traditional model of relying on donations, these schools are experimenting with a number of different business models that would allow the schools to be financially independent and sustainable. A well-known example is the Omega Schools in Ghana.

1.3 HIGHER EDUCATION

The tertiary education sector in Indonesia has been growing rapidly. Starting from a base of virtually zero, enrolments began to climb in the 1980s. Close to 15 per cent of 18–22 year-olds were enrolled in a tertiary institution by 2001, and over 23 per cent by 2010 (Figure 7.1). Although Indonesia needs more tertiary-educated workers as it shifts its economy from agriculture to services, the system appears to be coming increasingly under strain from the very rapid expansion of enrolments. These strains are most evident in three areas: funding, autonomy and design.

Funding

The first question is how to fund higher education, given that enrolments are outpacing the government's capacity to increase expenditures. Public spending on tertiary education in Indonesia is only 0.3 per cent of GDP, much lower than in Singapore (1.1 per cent), Malaysia (1.7 per cent) and even Vietnam (1.2 per cent). The sector is therefore highly privatized. Of around 3,400 tertiary education institutions in the country, fewer than 100 are operated by the government. Despite the obvious inability of the government to greatly increase tertiary spending, many Indonesians continue to insist that it should play a more substantial role in financing the sector. In addition, there is an unreasonable expectation that every individual must have a tertiary-level education. As Hal Hill and Thee Kian Wie note in Chapter 8 of this volume, recent attempts by the parliament and the government to diversify the funding of the sector were met with lawsuits lodged with the Constitutional Court.

The fact is that tertiary education is expensive – too expensive to expect the government to assume the dominant role in funding the sector. It is nevertheless in the public interest to ensure good access to tertiary-level education. This is especially relevant for the poor, because higher education brings a large private benefit that can help children from poor families break free from intergenerational poverty. Taking all these aspects into consideration, the most efficient way to finance tertiary education may be through a loan system. This would help to address equity issues, by allowing those who cannot afford tuition fees to borrow the necessary funds and repay them after graduation. Currently Indonesia does not have any large-scale higher education loan system.

Two main types of education loan system are operating in other countries. The first involves government-backed loans provided by banks. Under this 'mortgage-type' arrangement, loan repayments are made on the basis of pre-determined amounts over a given time period. This is the collection basis used to help finance higher education in many countries, including the United States, Canada, the Philippines and Thailand. The second type of system is the income-contingent loan (ICL), which takes the form of students committing to repay debts depending on their future incomes. Such schemes are currently operating in Australia, New Zealand, England, Hungary, Chile and South Korea. The critical characteristic of an ICL system is that the maximum repayment burden is set by legislation, to facilitate consumption smoothing and to provide loan default insurance.

Indonesia must soon decide which system it favours. In Chapter 10 of this book, Bruce Chapman and Daniel Suryadarma provide the first analysis on this issue. One key concern in the Indonesian context is whether students from poor families would dare to enter either arrangement, but particularly the first one, because of the daunting size of the repayments involved when viewed from their perspective.

Autonomy

The second issue concerns autonomy. International evidence shows that tertiary education institutions need autonomy and academic freedom in order to thrive. However, the Indonesian government wants to keep a tight rein on its higher education institutions, both public and private. The current draft law on higher education even goes so far as to stipulate that the Minister of Education and Culture has jurisdiction over the statutes of universities and can determine the study programs offered.

Despite some major contextual differences, the Malaysian experience with higher education is very relevant here, as Chapter 11 by Khong Kim Hoong demonstrates. Malaysia has succeeded in lifting the proportion of the relevant age cohort attending tertiary education from 5 per cent in the early 1970s to 40 per cent today, well above the current level of 23 per cent in Indonesia. The range of tertiary offerings is also much wider, owing to significant private sector and foreign involvement. Malaysia has been relatively successful in attracting international students. About 70,000 foreign students are studying in Malaysian tertiary institutions, providing a significant source of revenue and creating a more cosmopolitan environment for Malaysian students. In considering whether to follow a similar path, Indonesia needs to decide whether it would be prepared to allow foreign universities to play as big a role as in Malaysia, and whether it would permit some of its tertiary institutions to use English as the medium of instruction.

Design

The final issue concerns the need for a 'grand design' for the higher education sector. Specifically, what is the right mix between research-intensive universities producing innovations and small tertiary institutions producing individuals with the skill sets in general demand in the economy? The current debate in Indonesia focuses excessively on the research-intensive universities, even though the overwhelming majority of tertiary education institutions are privately administered, small and focused on the local region.

In Chapter 9, Rivandra Royono and Diastika Rahwidiati discuss the findings of their case study of three small regional universities. They find that rather than making a contribution in the form of research, innovation or international recognition, small or regional universities are playing an important part in inducing social transformation and influencing local policy making. A country as large as Indonesia should certainly aspire to have a number of world-class universities. However, the authors conclude that on balance the large number of small and less prestigious tertiary institutions may provide a larger benefit to society. Although market forces will largely determine the eventual mix of tertiary institutions, policy makers should consider supporting the small institutions, not just the more prestigious, research-intensive ones.

1.4 THE ISLAMIC SCHOOL SECTOR AND THE EARLY CHILDHOOD SECTOR

Islamic schools

Indonesia's Islamic school (*madrasah*) system currently has around 6 million students. The *madrasah* cater mainly to children from poor families or those living in remote areas where regular schools do not exist.

Newhouse and Beegle (2006) find that the quality of the *madrasah* is significantly lower than that of the regular public schools. All these facts point to the *madrasah* being the 'poor cousins' of regular schools.

The administrative arrangements for managing *madrasah* are complex and ineffective, and perpetuate the underfunding of the Islamic school system. Unlike the regular schools, whose administration was devolved to the local level of government in 2001, the *madrasah* remain under the jurisdiction of the centralized Ministry of Religious Affairs. This dual education system poses problems for the *madrasah*. For example, even though it is becoming increasingly clear that the religious affairs ministry is unable to manage the *madrasah* effectively, district governments are reluctant to provide funding or other support to the Islamic schools situated within their boundaries. Under the decentralization framework there is no legal basis for a ministry to interact with a local government on matters outside the formal local government jurisdiction. In Chapter 4, Robert Kingham and Jemma Parsons discuss the progress made by the government thus far in addressing the managerial, funding, quality and other problems facing *madrasah*. The chapter also assesses the prospects for an integrated national education system that provides equity of access to funding and resources for the *madrasah*.

Early childhood education and development

In Indonesia, as elsewhere throughout the world, policy makers are taking an increasing interest in early childhood education, for two reasons. First, it is now apparent that many of the factors that determine success in school stem from the period before children enter primary school. Heckman (2008) argues that children are more likely to be engaged, productive and successful in later life if their early learning and development are promoted.

Second, early childhood education can help to level the educational playing field by providing opportunities for children from deprived backgrounds to get the same start in learning that children from better-off families would normally be exposed to in their home environments. As Hafid Alatas and his co-authors point out in Chapter 5, there is a large disparity in access to early childhood education between children from poor families and those from rich families. They cite data from the latest National Socio-Economic Survey (Survei Sosio-Ekonomi Nasional, Susenas) showing that only 36 per cent of 4–6-year-old children from the poorest 20 per cent of families attended early childhood education programs in 2010, compared with 68 per cent of similarly aged children from the richest quintile of families (Figure 5.4). By comparison, access to early childhood programs is close to 100 per cent for children in Singapore.

Given the evidence of high returns to early childhood education programs both in Indonesia and internationally (World Bank 2013), there is a strong case for facilitating the provision of this kind of education. Without government intervention, however, it may be naive to expect it to play much of a role in levelling the educational playing field in Indonesia. Close to 95 per cent of early childhood centres are privately administered, and the socio-economically disadvantaged groups are unlikely to have the resources or the awareness to be able to access these facilities to anything like the extent that more advantaged groups can.

1.5   CONCLUSION

Overall, the state of education in Indonesia provides many reasons to be optimistic. Access to education at all levels continues to increase, the government is showing a strong commitment to investing significant resources in the sector, and a number of public policies aimed at increasing the quality of education are being tested and implemented. Many challenges remain, however. The gap in access to education between the rich and the poor remains wide, the quality of Indonesian education is very poor by international standards, and the significant increases in public resources allocated to the sector have yet to have a discernible impact on quality. There also continues to be a mismatch between the skills produced by the education system and the skills demanded by the labour market, as detailed by Emanuela di Gropello in Chapter 12. If not addressed, this will put a drag on Indonesia's international competitiveness.

The government needs to take the lead in addressing these challenges by implementing sound evidence-based policies. In addition, it may need to give greater acknowledgement to, and start relying more on, privately administered schools, especially given that private institutions are already the dominant providers of early childhood education, Islamic education, senior secondary education and tertiary education in the country.

REFERENCES

Baker, D.P., J. Leon, E.G. Smith-Greenway, J. Collins and M. Movit (2011) 'The education effect on population health: a reassessment', *Population and Development Review*, 37(2): 307–32.
Caldwell, J.C. and P. Caldwell (1985) 'Education and literacy as factors in health', in S.B. Halstead, J.A. Walsh and K.S. Warren (eds) *Good Health at Low Cost*, Rockefeller Foundation, New York, pp. 181–5.

Cochrane, S. (1979) *Fertility and Education: What Do We Really Know?* Johns Hopkins University Press, Baltimore.

Colclough, C. (1982) 'The impact of primary schooling on economic development: a review of the evidence', *World Development*, 10(3): 167–85.

Colclough, C., G. Kingdon and H.A. Patrinos (2009) 'The pattern of returns to education and its implications', RECOUP Policy Brief No. 4, Research Consortium on Educational Outcomes and Poverty, Cambridge.

Glaeser, E.L., G. Ponzetto and A. Shleifer (2007) 'Why does democracy need education?', *Journal of Economic Growth*, 12: 77–99.

Hannum, E. and C. Buchmann (2005) 'Global educational expansion and socioeconomic development: an assessment of findings from the social sciences', *World Development*, 33(3): 333–54.

Hanushek, E. and L. Woessmann (2008) 'The role of cognitive skills in economic development', *Journal of Economic Literature*, 46(3): 607–68.

Heckman, J. (2008) 'Schools, skills and synapses', *Economic Inquiry*, 46(3): 289–324.

Jamison, D.T. and L.J. Lau (1982) *Farmer Education and Farm Efficiency*, Johns Hopkins University Press, Baltimore.

Lewin, K.M. and F. Caillods (2001) *Financing Secondary Education in Developing Countries: Strategies for Sustainable Growth*, International Institute for Educational Planning, Paris.

Lutz, W. (2009) '*Sola schola et sanitate*: human capital as the root cause and priority for international development?', *Philosophical Transactions of the Royal Society B*, 364: 3,031–47.

Lutz, W., J.C. Cuaresma and M.J. Abbasi-Shavazi (2010) 'Demography, education and democracy: global trends and the case of Iran', *Population and Development Review*, 36(2): 253–81.

Newhouse, D. and K. Beegle (2006) 'The effect of school type on academic achievement: evidence from Indonesia', *Journal of Human Resources*, 41(3): 529–57.

Newhouse, D. and D. Suryadarma (2011) 'The value of vocational education: high school type and labor market outcomes in Indonesia', *World Bank Economic Review*, 25(2): 296–322.

Pamuk, E., R. Fuchs and W. Lutz (2011) 'Comparing relative effects of education and economic resources on infant mortality in developing countries', *Population and Development Review*, 37(4): 637–64.

Pradhan, M., D. Suryadarma, A. Beatty, M. Wong, A. Alisjahbana, A. Gaduh and R.P. Artha (2011) 'Improving educational quality through enhancing community participation: results from a randomized field experiment in Indonesia', Policy Research Working Paper No. 5795, World Bank, Washington DC.

Psacharopoulos, G. and H.A. Patrinos (2004) 'Returns to investment in education: a further update', *Education Economics*, 12(2): 111–34.

Suryadarma, D. and S. Sumarto (2011) 'Survey of recent developments', *Bulletin of Indonesian Economic Studies*, 47(2): 155–81.

Tooley, J. and P. Dixon (2005) *Private Education Is Good for the Poor: A Study of Private Schools Serving the Poor in Low-income Countries*, Cato Institute, Washington DC.

World Bank (2013) *Early Childhood Education and Development in Indonesia: Strong Foundations, Later Success*, World Bank, Jakarta.

2 TRENDS IN EDUCATION IN INDONESIA

Suharti

2.1 INTRODUCTION

Indonesia has made notable improvements in education over the past 40 years, in line with the implementation of a number of key policies and programs. In 1973, the country embarked on a program to build a primary school in every village. The government made six years of education compulsory in 1984, and extended this to nine years in 1994. Other major policies to lift the standard of education have included the decentralization of education to the regions, an emphasis on pro-poor initiatives and the introduction of programs to improve teacher quality.

This chapter presents evidence on trends in educational performance in Indonesia using the data described in section 2.2. The analysis covers educational attainment (section 2.3), student enrolments and school progression rates (section 2.4), the provision of educational resources such as schools and teachers (section 2.5), student learning outcomes (section 2.6) and and the budget for education (section 2.7). The data are disaggregated where necessary to show the differences between provinces, between urban and rural areas, between males and females and between rich and poor. The analysis focuses on the past decade but in some cases covers a considerably longer period.

---

* The author is currently completing a doctoral thesis at the Australian National University on the Indonesian education sector. This chapter draws on research for that thesis.

2.2 DATA SOURCES AND EVALUATION

To examine educational performance, this study uses published data on school statistics for academic years 1991/92 to 2009/10 collected by the Center for Education Data and Statistics, Ministry of Education and Culture; online data on educational attainment and school enrolments for 1994–2010 provided by Indonesia's central bureau of statistics (Badan Pusat Statistik, BPS); published data on educational performance for 1967–93 in the presidential reports submitted by the National Development Planning Agency (Badan Perencanaan Pembangunan Nasional, Bappenas); micro data on teachers for the year 2010 from the Ministry of Education and Culture; micro data from the National Socio-Economic Survey (Survei Sosio-Ekonomi Nasional, Susenas) for 1994–2010; and statistics for the period 1993–2008 from BPS's Village Potential (Potensi Desa, Podes) surveys.

The Center for Education Data and Statistics makes its statistics on schools available to researchers upon request. The data provide information on the numbers of students, the numbers and qualifications of teachers and principals, and the physical facilities owned by the schools. However, the statistics do not cover all schools because many of them do not complete the questionnaires sent to them annually; the return rate for junior secondary schools in 2009/10, for example, was only about 50 per cent. According to Sitanggang, a member of the Center for Education Data and Statistics, schools are reluctant to return the questionnaires because they do not feel they gain any direct benefit from doing so, particularly since responsibility for education was devolved to the regions (Directorate General of Basic Education 2010). A second problem is the possibility of data 'fudging', where the data appear to be the same for some or all schools in a particular district or city. Cross-school data assessment therefore needs to be conducted.[1] Also complicating the task of the researcher is the failure to use school codes; each school has a unique serial number, but many do not use those numbers when completing the questionnaires. In 2011, the task of collecting data on schools was transferred from the Center for Education Data and Statistics to each directorate general in the Ministry of Education and Culture. This should improve collection rates and the quality of the data.

The micro data on teachers for 2010 were obtained from the ministry's Directorate General for Quality Improvement of Teachers and Educational Personnel (now called the Office of Education Human Resource Development and Education Quality Assurance). Based on a unique

---

1 These are not new problems. For a discussion of issues in the educational statistics a decade earlier, see Jones, Hagul and Damayanti (2000: Appendix 2).

identity number for each teacher (*nomor unik pendidik dan tenaga kependidikan*, NUPTK), these data are also available upon request. The statistics cover all 2.8 million pre-school, primary, junior secondary and senior secondary teachers in schools administered by the Ministry of Education and Culture, both public and private, but exclude those teaching in the schools administered by the Ministry of Religious Affairs.

The teacher database also suffers from several failings. First, it does not provide information on the subjects taught by teachers, the grades to which they are assigned or their own fields of study. This makes it impossible to establish whether there is a mismatch between teachers and the subjects they are teaching, or an excess or shortage of teachers in certain subject areas. Second, the data suffer from multiple counting, because teachers may be assigned more than one unique identity number. The problem is particularly acute where teachers work in more than one school, but even teachers in the same school can be counted twice if their names appear on different lists with different NUPTKs. Third, the lack of school codes in the data is troublesome, and makes it difficult to analyse data over time. Although teachers do provide the names of the schools in which they work, they sometimes spell the name of the same school in different ways, or abbreviate its name differently. Without the school codes, it becomes very difficult to match individual teachers to individual schools. Finally, the data do not specify the subdistrict in which each school is located. This is an important omission considering that schools are usually supervised by the subdistrict governments.

While the statistics on schools and teachers are compromised by the failure to use school codes, the national examination and other databases may use different coding systems altogether. This makes it very difficult for researchers to merge data from various sources. More importantly, it makes it hard for the Ministry of Education and Culture itself to evaluate the effectiveness of schools in, for instance, improving student performance, or to examine changes in school resources over time.

The micro data from the Susenas are accessed through the Australian Social Science Data Archive at the Australian National University. BPS began conducting its large-scale survey of socio-economic conditions in 1963–64, and has fielded the Susenas annually since 1989. The survey has been nationally representative since 1993, covering all provinces and districts in the country, except where circumstances made this difficult. The sample size has increased over time, from 290,797 individuals living in 66,552 households in 1993 to 1,178,494 individuals living in 293,715 households in 2010. As well as data on individuals, the Susenas provides household-level data on consumption and other characteristics. This makes it possible to link educational performance with household characteristics.

BPS also compiles data on economic conditions in Indonesian villages through its Podes village surveys. The Podes has been conducted every 10 years since 1980 in conjunction with the population census; it is also conducted twice between census years as part of the bureau's periodic surveys of agriculture and the economy. The surveys cover all villages across Indonesia, including transmigration settlements and disadvantaged communities. The census conducted in 2008 covered 73,198 villages in 457 districts. The data on education provide information on the numbers of educational institutions at all levels from pre-school to university, divided into general and religious as well as public and private institutions. These data are used to examine the availability of schools in the absence of complete statistics held by the Ministry of Education and Culture and the Ministry of Religious Affairs.

2.3   IMPROVEMENTS IN EDUCATIONAL ATTAINMENT

The improvement in levels of educational attainment among the Indonesian population can be seen in the population pyramids shown in Figure 2.1. In 1990, of 76.7 million Indonesians aged 19 years or over, 34 per cent had no education at all or had not completed primary school, while 31 per cent had completed junior secondary school or higher. By 2000, the proportion with six years of education or less had fallen to 24 per cent, and the share with a junior secondary education or higher had risen to 37 per cent. Data from the latest population census indicate a better-educated population: only 16 per cent of Indonesians aged 19 years or over had not completed primary school in 2010, while about 50 per cent had completed junior secondary school or higher.

The advancements in educational attainment are also evident in the increase in the average number of years of schooling among the population aged 15 years or over, from 6.2 years in 1993 to 7.9 years in 2010 (Table 2.1). This implies that whereas on average most people did not finish primary school in 1993, by 2010 the majority would have completed year 8 (the second year of junior secondary school). There has always been a gap between the urban and rural populations, but it has narrowed over time. In 2010, those living in urban areas had 2.7 more years of schooling on average than those living in rural areas. A gender gap also exists, but it is very small – on average, males had only around 0.8 more years of schooling than females in 2010.

Nevertheless, there are large differences between regions in the number of years of schooling. Figure 2.2 shows the average number of years of schooling among the population aged 15 years or over in each province, as well as the result for the district within each province with the most,

Figure 2.1   *Population aged 19 years or over by highest level of educational attainment and gender, 1990–2010 (million)*

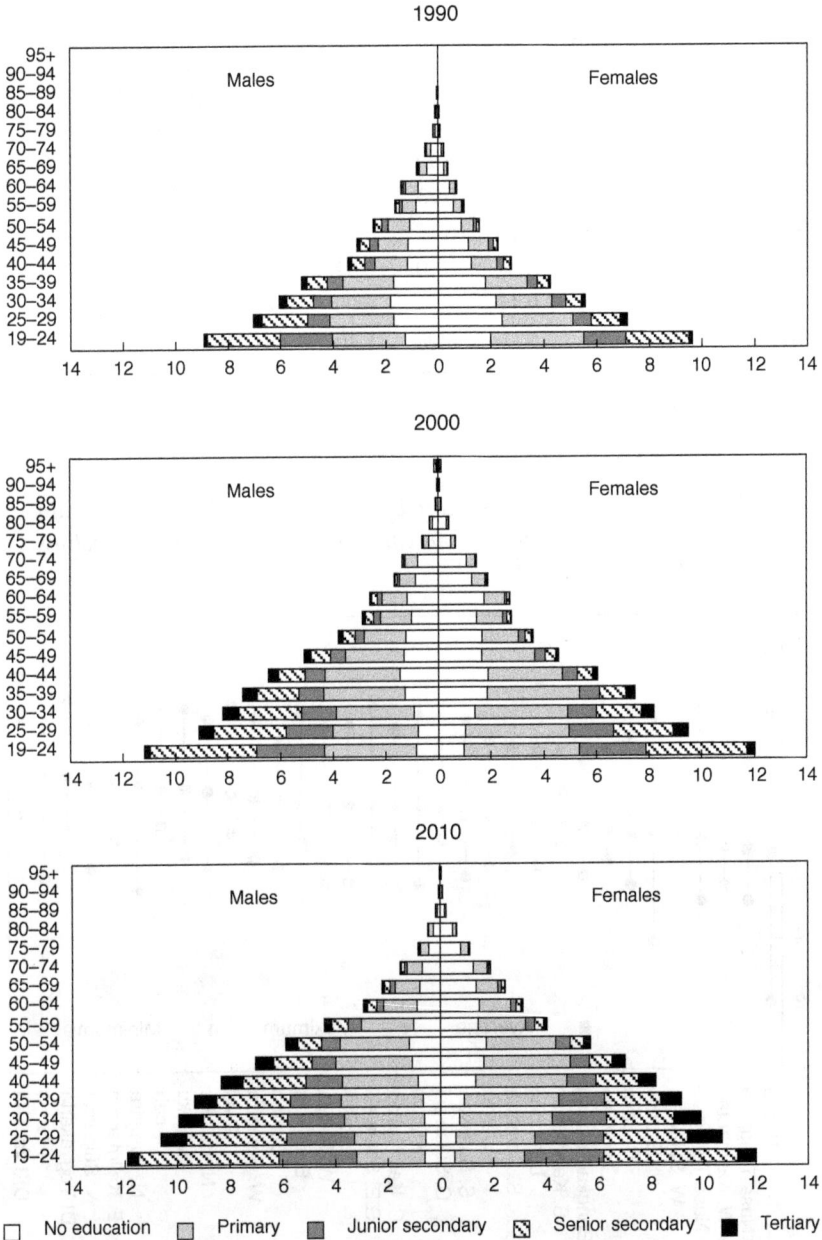

1990

2000

2010

☐ No education   ☐ Primary   ▦ Junior secondary   ⊠ Senior secondary   ■ Tertiary

Source: Population census, 1990, 2000 and 2010.

Table 2.1   Average years of schooling of population aged 15 or over by urban/rural area and gender, 1993–2010

Year	Urban			Rural			Rural + Urban		
	M	F	M + F	M	F	M + F	M	F	M + F
1993	8.73	7.25	7.98	5.40	4.15	4.77	6.84	5.51	6.16
1996	9.07	7.78	8.41	5.73	4.56	5.13	6.84	5.63	6.22
2000	9.15	7.99	8.56	6.17	5.07	5.61	7.39	6.27	6.82
2003	9.36	8.34	8.84	6.50	5.52	6.01	7.70	6.71	7.20
2006	9.55	8.70	9.12	6.86	6.00	6.43	7.87	7.03	7.45
2010	9.68	8.86	9.27	6.98	6.10	6.54	8.35	7.50	7.92

M = males; F = females.
Source: Susenas.

Figure 2.2   Average years of schooling by province, and the district within each province with the maximum/minimum years of schooling, 2010

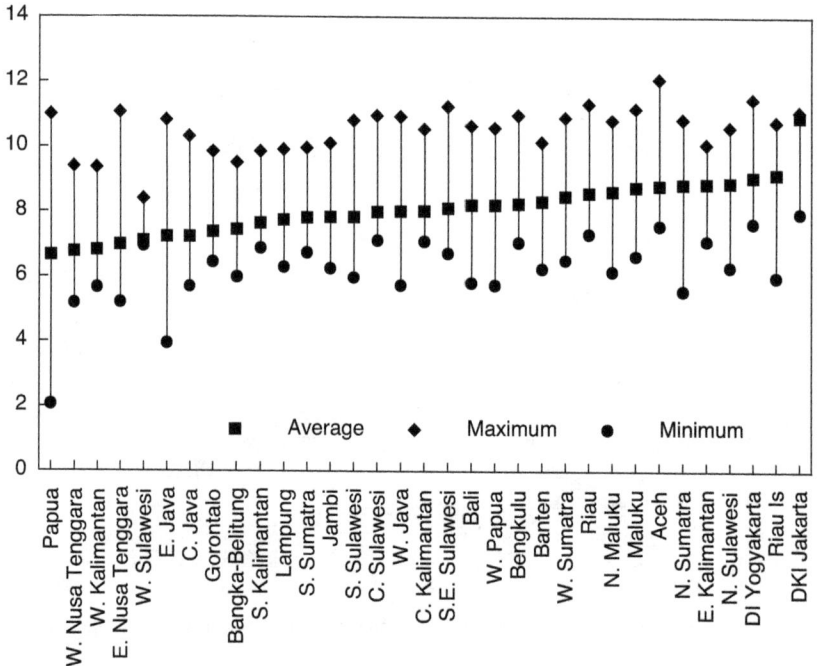

Source: Susenas, 2010.

Figure 2.3   Adult illiteracy rate by age group, 1993–2010 (%)

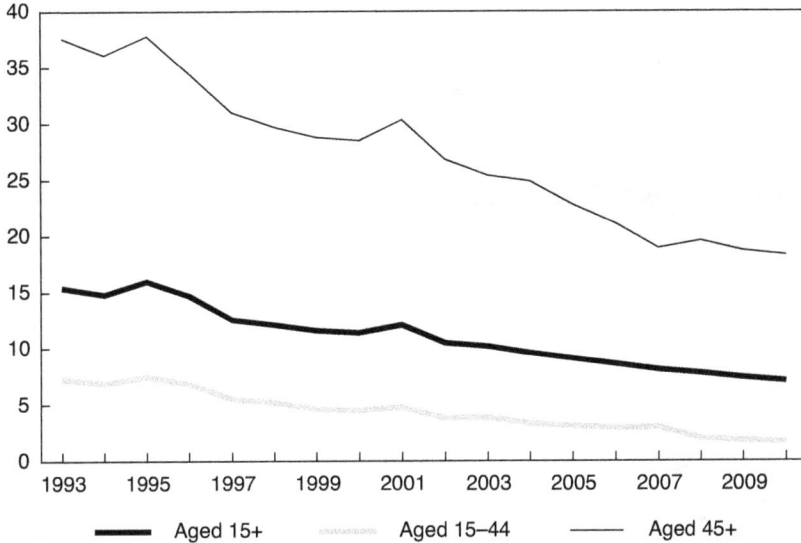

Source: 1993: Susenas; 1994–2010: online data from BPS.

and the least, years of schooling. At the provincial level, the number of years of schooling in 2010 ranged from 6.7 years in Papua to 10.9 years in Jakarta. The differences between districts were even larger, ranging from as little as two years in the worst performing district (in Papua) to as much as 12 years in the best performing district (in North Sumatra). Of Indonesia's 497 districts, 43 recorded an average of less than six years of schooling, and 107 nine years of schooling or more. Districts in the traditionally poor region of eastern Indonesia performed particularly poorly, but several in East Java (Sampang, Bangkalan, Sumenep, Bondowoso, Probolinggo), North Sumatra (West Nias) and Bangka-Belitung (South Bangka) were also among those recording less than six years of schooling.

Another indication of educational attainment is the spread of literacy. Between 1993 and 2010, illiteracy among the population aged 15 years or over fell by 8.3 percentage points, from 15.4 per cent to 7.1 per cent (Figure 2.3). Closer analysis shows that illiteracy is mainly confined to the population aged 45 years or over. In 2010, this cohort had an illiteracy rate of 18 per cent, compared with just 2 per cent for Indonesians aged 15–44 years.

Illiteracy rates are still higher in rural than in urban areas, and higher among females than males, but in both cases the gap has narrowed markedly. The poor continue to have higher illiteracy rates than the rich, although again, the gap has narrowed over time. In 1993, the richest

Figure 2.4   Adult illiteracy rate by province, 2010 (%)

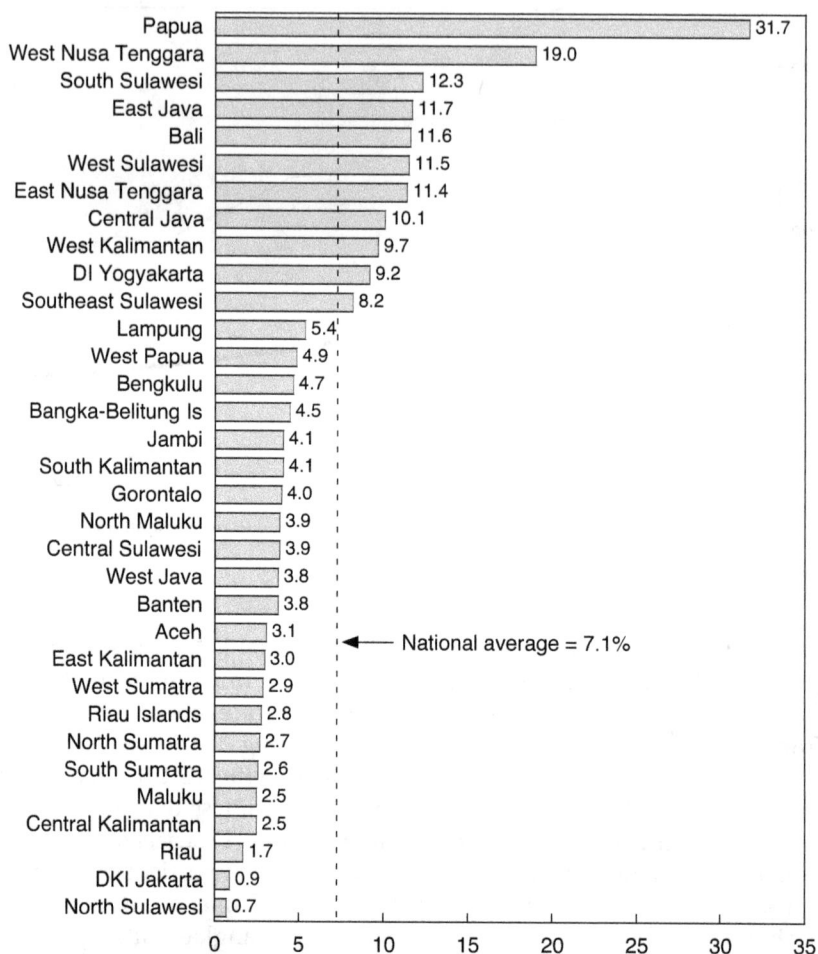

Papua	31.7
West Nusa Tenggara	19.0
South Sulawesi	12.3
East Java	11.7
Bali	11.6
West Sulawesi	11.5
East Nusa Tenggara	11.4
Central Java	10.1
West Kalimantan	9.7
DI Yogyakarta	9.2
Southeast Sulawesi	8.2
Lampung	5.4
West Papua	4.9
Bengkulu	4.7
Bangka-Belitung Is	4.5
Jambi	4.1
South Kalimantan	4.1
Gorontalo	4.0
North Maluku	3.9
Central Sulawesi	3.9
West Java	3.8
Banten	3.8
Aceh	3.1
East Kalimantan	3.0
West Sumatra	2.9
Riau Islands	2.8
North Sumatra	2.7
South Sumatra	2.6
Maluku	2.5
Central Kalimantan	2.5
Riau	1.7
DKI Jakarta	0.9
North Sulawesi	0.7

National average = 7.1%

Source: Online data from BPS.

quintile among the population aged 15 years or over had an illiteracy rate of 4 per cent, while the poorest quintile had a rate of 33 per cent. By 2009, these rates had fallen to 2 per cent and 17 per cent respectively.

Like years of schooling, adult illiteracy rates differ substantially between regions. Figure 2.4 shows that in 2010, the rate ranged from as little as 0.7 per cent in North Sulawesi to as much as 32 per cent in Papua. The differences between districts were even greater, ranging from just 0.1 per cent in the city of Bukittinggi in West Sumatra to 86 per cent in the district of Nduga in Papua. Again Java does not perform in line with expectations; several Javanese districts – all in East Java (Bondowoso, Situbondo, Probolinggo, Sampang, Sumenep) – had adult illiteracy rates above 20 per cent.

2.4 TRENDS IN ACCESS TO EDUCATION

The substantial improvements in educational attainment described in the previous section reflect Indonesia's success over a long period of time in increasing access to education. To describe the changes over time, this section examines enrolments, then school retention and transition rates.

Enrolments

This subsection describes enrolments using both the gross enrolment rate, or GER (the number of students enrolled in school as a percentage of the total population of students in the relevant age group), and the net enrolment rate, or NER (the number of students of official school age enrolled in school as a percentage of the total population of students of official school age in the relevant age group). The GER includes substantial numbers of students who are outside the official school ages, and can therefore exceed 100 per cent.

Figure 2.5 shows the trends in the GER from 1968 to 2010 by school level. Although the data are complete for the country's primary schools, it should be noted that information on Islamic junior and senior secondary schools and religious universities became available only in 1994.

At the primary level, the main improvements in enrolments occurred between 1974 and 1984, when the government constructed 138,940 schools across the country under a presidential program to put a primary school in every village. During that period, the GER increased from about 79 per cent to 119 per cent. It then rose further to reach 123 per cent in 1986 – well above the notional full enrolment rate of 100 per cent because of the many overage students during this period. Since 1990 the rate has been stable at about 107–111 per cent.

The NER is much lower – just 95 per cent at the primary level in 2010, for example, compared with a GER of 112 per cent. The large number of underage students currently enrolled in primary school explains the size of the gap between the two rates. Parents are now allowed to enrol their children at the age of six (rather than the official starting age of seven),[2] but the calculation of the GER is still based on the 7–12 age group. Data from the 2010 Susenas suggest that the proportion of underage students

---

2 This change was introduced in Law 20/2003 (Chapter 8, article 34).

Figure 2.5   Gross enrolment rate by school level, 1968–2010 (%)

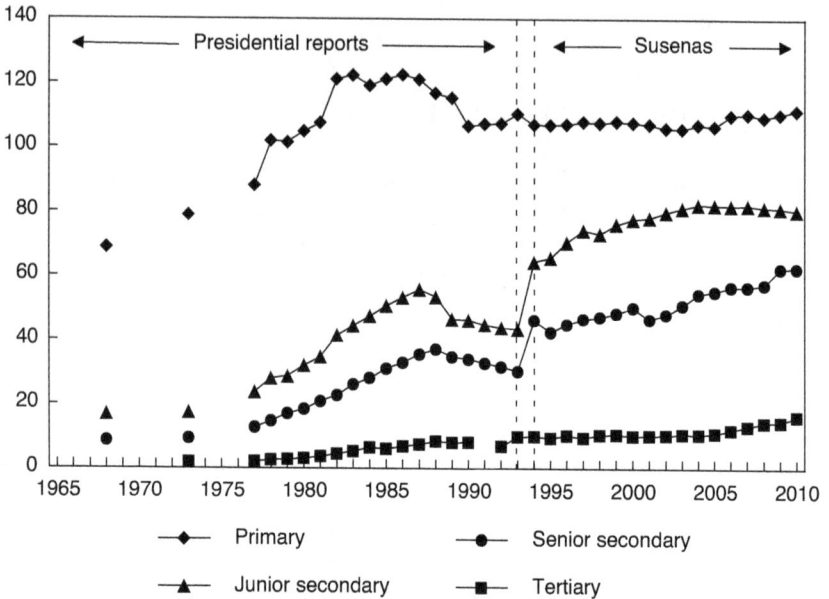

Source: 1968–93: presidential reports, Bappenas; 1994–2010: Susenas.

enrolled in the first year of primary school, including Islamic primary schools, is 47.7 per cent.

With primary enrolment rates high and stable, in 1994/95 the government decided to extend compulsory basic education from six to nine years. The goal was to have all children enrolled in junior secondary school by 2004. But although there have been substantial improvements in junior secondary enrolments, Figure 2.5 shows that the rates have stagnated since the early 2000s. In 2010, the NER and GER for this level of education were only 68 per cent and 80 per cent respectively.

The fact that so many children are unable to advance to junior secondary school after completing their primary education indicates that the program to extend compulsory education to nine years has stalled. One of the main constraints on demand appears to be the financial burden of obtaining an education. Data from the 2009 Susenas (used because of the lack of some variables in the 2010 Susenas) indicate that about 63 per cent of the children aged 13–15 who were not enrolled in school had dropped out for financial reasons: 57 per cent because they could not afford the cost and the other 6 per cent because they had to work to earn a living. The age-specific enrolment rates (ASERs) shown in Figure 2.6 provide further evidence of the role of socio-economic background in

Figure 2.6 *Age-specific enrolment rate for students aged 13–15 and 16–18 by household expenditure quintile, 1993–2009 (%)*[a]

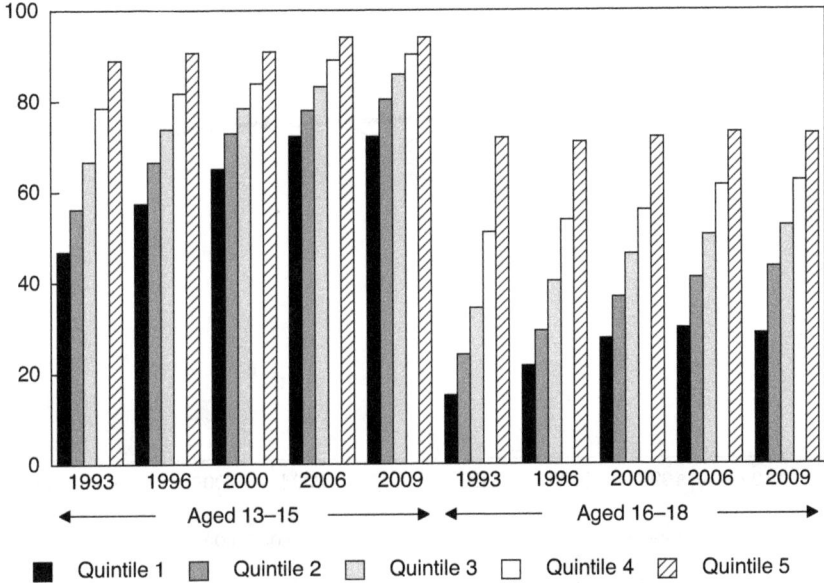

a   Based on per capita expenditure, where quintile 1 is the poorest, and quintile 5 the richest, 20 per cent of households.

Source: Susenas.

gaining access to education. The ASER measures enrolments in a specific age group, irrespective of level of schooling, as a percentage of the total population in that age group. In 2009, the rate among 13–15-year-olds was 72 per cent for the poorest 20 per cent of households, rising to 94 per cent for the richest quintile.

Rosser, Joshi and Edwin (2011: 3) argue that basic education should be free, but believe this can only be achieved if 'pro-UFBE [universal free basic education] coalitions are empowered to influence policy, demand accountability and seek redress against illegal fees'.

Senior secondary enrolments have increased substantially, from 46 per cent in 1994 to 63 per cent in 2010 (Figure 2.5). As might be predicted, inequality is even more pronounced at this level than at the primary and junior secondary levels. The GERs for the individual provinces, for example, ranged from 48 per cent in Papua to 87 per cent in Maluku in 2010. The gap between rich and poor is also large. In 2009, 29 per cent of 16–18-year-olds in the poorest household expenditure quintile, but 73 per cent in the richest quintile, were enrolled in senior secondary school (Figure 2.6).

Figure 2.7   Ratio of net enrolment rate of females to net enrolment rate of males by school level, 1994–2010

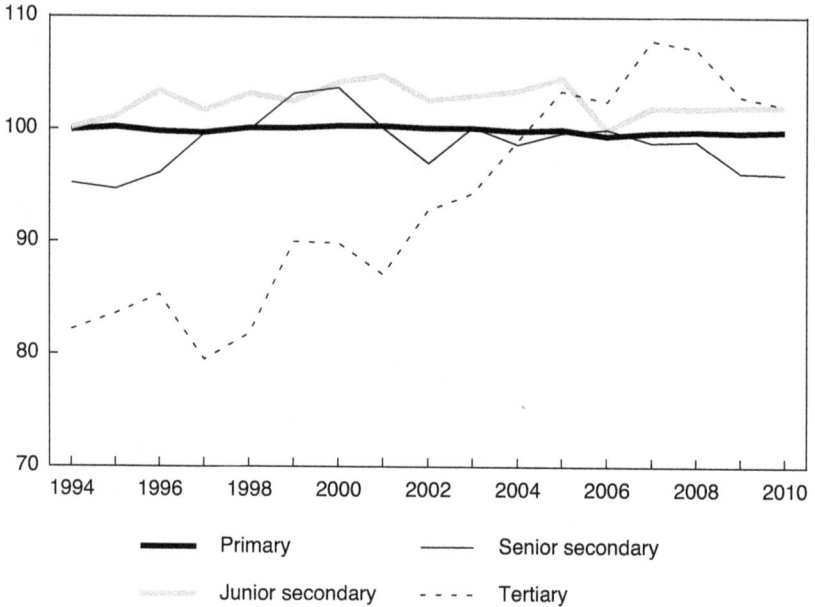

Source: Susenas.

Contrary to the common perception, the gender gap in school enrolments is far less important than the gap between regions and between rich and poor. As Figure 2.7 shows, the ratio of females to males is close to 100 per cent at all levels of schooling, meaning that the female and male populations have similar NERs. The most substantial changes have occurred at the tertiary level, where the ratio of females to males increased from about 80 per cent in the early 1990s to almost 108 per cent in 2007, before falling back to 102 per cent in 2010. With NERs consistently above 100 per cent, more females than males have been enrolled in tertiary education since 2005.

School progression rates

Despite the continuous improvements in school retention and transition rates, some children still do not complete their nine years of compulsory basic education. They either drop out of primary or junior secondary school or discontinue their education after completing primary school. Data from the Ministry of Education and Culture show that about two decades ago, in academic year 1988/89, around 66 of every 100 children enrolled in the first year of primary school completed six years of primary schooling in 1993/94, with about 44 of these advancing to junior secondary school in 1994/95 (Figure 2.8). These numbers imply a school retention rate of only 66 per cent and a transition rate of 67 per cent.

The latest data indicate that of every 100 students enrolled in primary school in 2002/03, around 81 completed six years of primary schooling in 2007/08, and 66 of these went on to junior secondary school in 2008/09 – implying a school retention rate of 81 per cent and a transition rate of 81.5 per cent. This indicates an increase of 15 percentage points in the retention rate, and 14.5 percentage points in the transition rate, since 1988/89. On the other hand, the data also show that around 19 per cent of children still do not complete primary school. The annualized drop-out rate of about 3 per cent may seem small, but because it occurs each year during the six years of primary schooling, the cumulative figure becomes very large.

Retention and transition rates at the junior secondary level are better than those at the primary level. About 75 per cent of students (both new and repeating) enrolled in the first year of junior secondary school in academic year 1988/89 completed their junior secondary schooling in 1990/91, and about 62 per cent of them advanced to either a general or vocational senior secondary school in 1991/92 (Figure 2.9). Twenty years later, in 2007/08, about 87 per cent of students completed their junior secondary schooling, and around 86 per cent of these graduates advanced to senior secondary school in 2008/09. There was a significant decline in the transition rate between 1995/96 and 1999/2000, from 78 per cent to just 59 per cent. This may have been due to the inability of senior secondary schools to accommodate the significant increases in junior secondary graduates, compounded by the Asian financial crisis in 1997–98.

Survival analyses using Susenas data generally confirm the patterns described above. The education survival rate is based on years of schooling, using the approach adopted by BPS to calculate the Human Development Index (BPS, Bappenas and UNDP 2004). The rate of progression from primary to junior secondary school improved significantly between 1993 and 2009. In 1993, more than a quarter of children aged 13–15 who had ever been enrolled in primary school did not advance to junior secondary school. By 2009, that figure had fallen to around 11 per cent.

Further analysis reveals distinct differences in survival rates according to economic status. Most of the children who do not advance from primary to junior secondary school, and from junior secondary to senior secondary school, continue to come from poor families, although the gap has narrowed over time (Figures 2.10 and 2.11). The graphs show that survival rates improved among all quintiles between 1993 and 2009, with the largest increases – perhaps surprisingly – occurring among the poorest group of households.

Figure 2.8   Flow of students through primary school, academic year
1988/89–2008/09 (%)

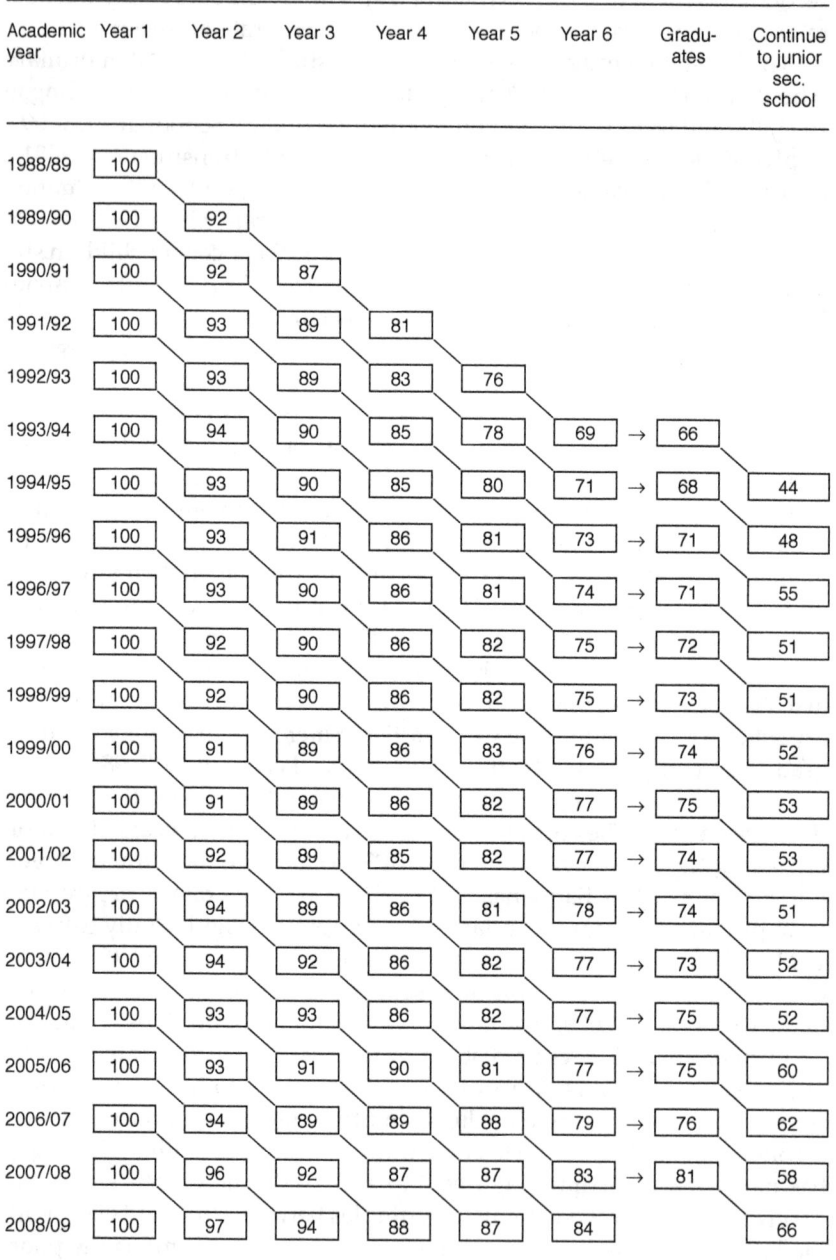

Academic year	Year 1	Year 2	Year 3	Year 4	Year 5	Year 6	Graduates	Continue to junior sec. school
1988/89	100							
1989/90	100	92						
1990/91	100	92	87					
1991/92	100	93	89	81				
1992/93	100	93	89	83	76			
1993/94	100	94	90	85	78	69	→ 66	
1994/95	100	93	90	85	80	71	→ 68	44
1995/96	100	93	91	86	81	73	→ 71	48
1996/97	100	93	90	86	81	74	→ 71	55
1997/98	100	92	90	86	82	75	→ 72	51
1998/99	100	92	90	86	82	75	→ 73	51
1999/00	100	91	89	86	83	76	→ 74	52
2000/01	100	91	89	86	82	77	→ 75	53
2001/02	100	92	89	85	82	77	→ 74	53
2002/03	100	94	89	86	81	78	→ 74	51
2003/04	100	94	92	86	82	77	→ 73	52
2004/05	100	93	93	86	82	77	→ 75	52
2005/06	100	93	91	90	81	77	→ 75	60
2006/07	100	94	89	89	88	79	→ 76	62
2007/08	100	96	92	87	87	83	→ 81	58
2008/09	100	97	94	88	87	84		66

Source: Compiled from school statistics from the Center for Education Data and Statistics,
Ministry of Education and Culture, various years.

Figure 2.9   *Flow of students through junior secondary school, academic year 1988/89–2008/09 (%)*

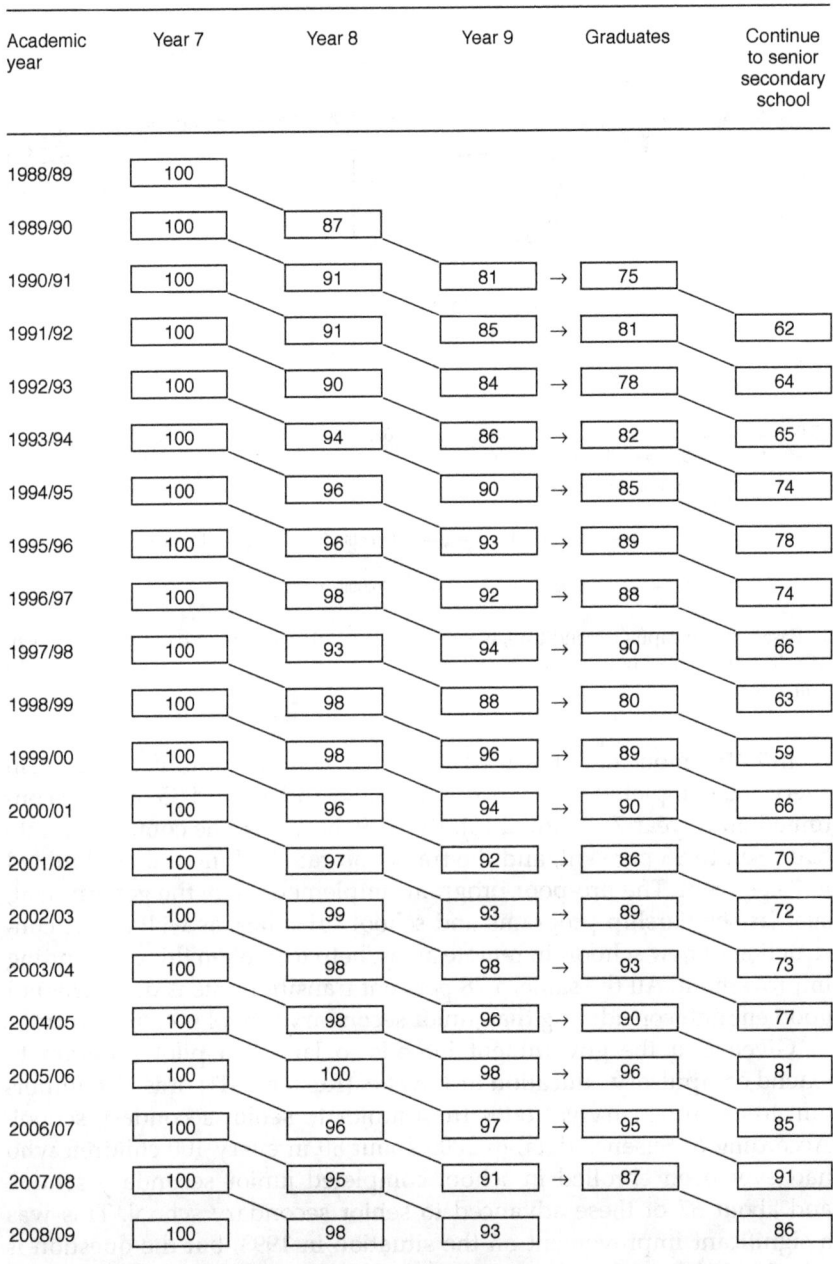

Academic year	Year 7	Year 8	Year 9	Graduates	Continue to senior secondary school
1988/89	100				
1989/90	100	87			
1990/91	100	91	81 →	75	
1991/92	100	91	85 →	81	62
1992/93	100	90	84 →	78	64
1993/94	100	94	86 →	82	65
1994/95	100	96	90 →	85	74
1995/96	100	96	93 →	89	78
1996/97	100	98	92 →	88	74
1997/98	100	93	94 →	90	66
1998/99	100	98	88 →	80	63
1999/00	100	98	96 →	89	59
2000/01	100	96	94 →	90	66
2001/02	100	97	92 →	86	70
2002/03	100	99	93 →	89	72
2003/04	100	98	98 →	93	73
2004/05	100	98	96 →	90	77
2005/06	100	100	98 →	96	81
2006/07	100	96	97 →	95	85
2007/08	100	95	91 →	87	91
2008/09	100	98	93		86

Source: Compiled from school statistics from the Center for Education Data and Statistics, Ministry of Education and Culture, various years.

*Figure 2.10   Education survival probability of population aged 13–15
ever enrolled in school by household expenditure quintile,
1993 and 2009*

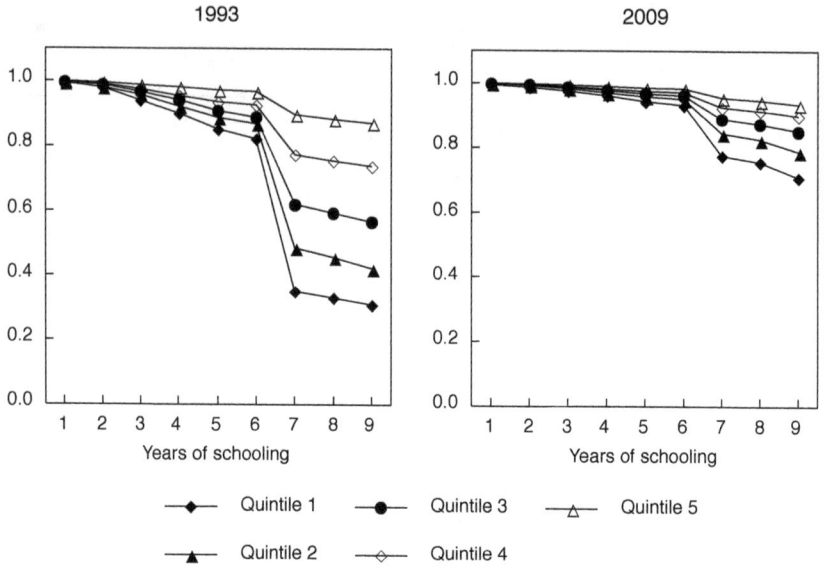

a   Based on per capita expenditure, where quintile 1 is the poorest, and quintile 5 the richest, 20 per cent of households.
Source: Susenas.

In 1993, among children aged 13–15 in the poorest quintile, about 82 in
every 100 completed six years of schooling, and around 35 of these continued on to year 7 (Figure 2.10). By 2009, however, the completion rate
had risen to 93 per cent, and the transition rate had more than doubled
to 78 per cent. The pro-poor programs implemented by the government,
such as scholarship programs and school subsidies, as well as the construction of new schools in remote areas, help to explain this outstanding
improvement. All the same, a 78 per cent transition rate is definitely not
good enough considering that junior secondary school is compulsory.

Given that the government intends to launch a pilot program to
extend compulsory education to 12 years (Ruslan 2011), it is also important to examine survival rates from junior to senior secondary school.
According to Susenas data, in 2009 about 80 in every 100 children who
had ever been enrolled in school completed junior secondary school,
and about 67 of these advanced to senior secondary school. This was
a significant improvement on the situation in 1993, but the question is
whether Indonesia's current performance is good enough to make senior
secondary school compulsory. As Figure 2.11 shows, even the children of

Figure 2.11   *Education survival probability of population aged 16–18 ever enrolled in school by household expenditure quintile, 1993 and 2009*

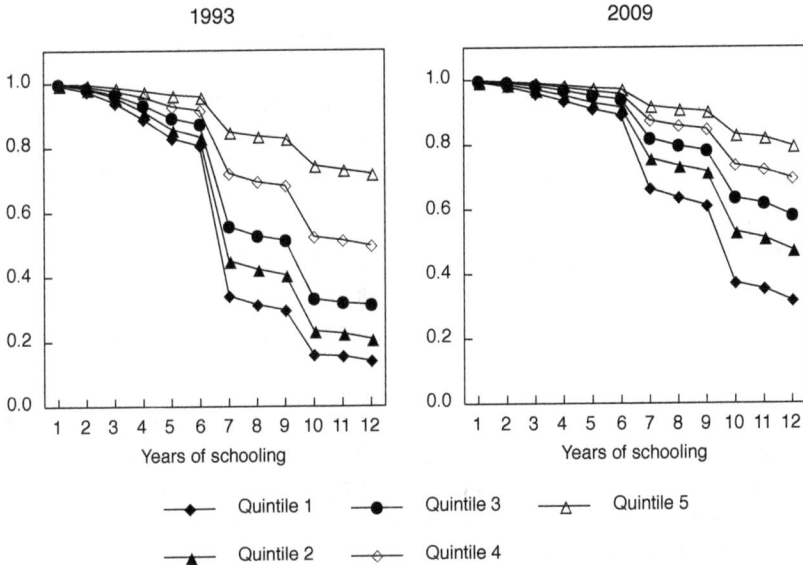

a   Based on per capita expenditure, where quintile 1 is the poorest, and quintile 5 the richest, 20 per cent of households.

Source: Susenas.

wealthy households do not always progress to senior secondary school. In 2009, among children aged 16–18 in the richest quintile who had ever been enrolled in school, about 17 per cent did not reach the first year of senior secondary school (year 10); the corresponding figure for the poorest quintile was a dismal 63 per cent.

Despite the remaining problems, Indonesia can be proud of having only a small gap between its male and female survival rates. In 2009, about 78 per cent of boys and 80 per cent of girls aged 16–18 who had ever been enrolled in school completed nine years of education. This is a good sign of equal treatment of boys and girls, although the pattern varies across regions. Extra consideration may even need to be given to boys, given that their survival rates have been below those of girls since 2000.

2.5   THE SUPPLY OF EDUCATION

The supply of education in Indonesia is described in this section using two main indicators: the availability of schools; and the quantity and

Table 2.2   Number of schools by school level and type of provider, 1993–2008

School level/ provider	1993	1996	2000	2003	2005	2008
Primary						
Public	139,109	145,210	140,158	136,797	134,859	135,974
Private	39,306	35,740	30,383	29,836	30,395	32,246
Total	**178,415**	**180,950**	**170,541**	**166,633**	**165,254**	**168,220**
Junior secondary						
Public	11,316	11,276	12,458	13,395	14,503	18,441
Private	17,445	17,996	18,019	18,067	19,331	22,379
Total	**28,761**	**29,272**	**30,477**	**31,462**	**33,834**	**40,820**
Senior secondary						
Public	3,692	4,168	4,432	5,520	6,345	8,126
Private	10,445	9,815	9,828	11,619	12,627	15,293
Total	**14,137**	**13,983**	**14,260**	**17,139**	**18,972**	**23,419**

Source: Podes village surveys.

quality of teachers. The data on school availability from the early 1990s onwards are from the Podes village surveys conducted by BPS. The data on the quantity and quality of teachers are from school statistics published by the Center for Education Data and Statistics, Ministry of Education and Culture; and from the NUPTK teacher database compiled by the ministry's Directorate General for Quality Improvement of Teachers and Educational Personnel.

School availability

Table 2.2 shows trends in the number of schools from 1993 to 2008. The total number of primary schools actually fell between 1996 and 2005 from around 181,000 to 165,000. It was during this period that the government began to merge schools with small numbers of students if another school was located nearby, in response to a decline in the number of primary school-aged children from 28.8 million in 1994 to 26.8 million in 2005. At the primary level, private schools do not make as big a contribution to the total number of schools as they do at the junior and senior secondary levels. This is because the public system is able to meet demand, leaving private schools to fulfil niche demand for a better-quality, religious or other type of education.

Figure 2.12   Number of primary schools constructed under the Presidential
Primary School (Inpres SD) program, academic year
1973/74–1998/99 (thousand)

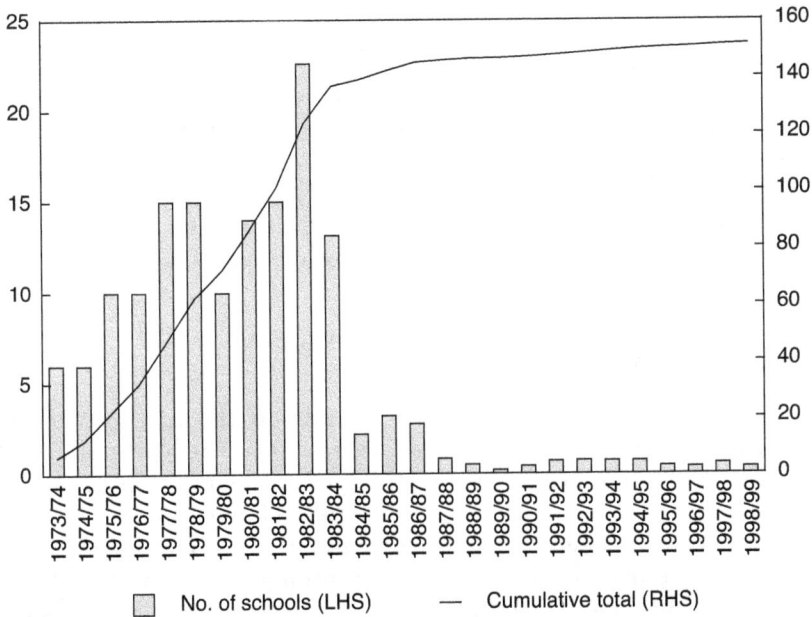

Source: Presidential reports, Bappenas.

Large numbers of primary schools were built between 1973 and 1984 under the Presidential Primary School (Inpres Sekolah Dasar, Inpres SD) program (Figure 2.12). During the first five years of the program, around 47,000 schools were constructed, and by 1984, when President Suharto made it compulsory for children to complete six years of education, 138,940 primary schools had been built. By this time the country's primary schools (including Islamic schools) served about 29.3 million students, leading to a GER of 119 per cent (Figure 2.5).

The total number of junior secondary schools, meanwhile, rose from around 29,000 in 1993 to 41,000 in 2008 (Table 2.2). To provide support for its policy to extend compulsory basic education to nine years, the government increased the number of public junior secondary schools from about 11,300 in 1993 (the year before the policy was introduced) to more than 18,400 in 2008 – an increase of 63 per cent in 15 years. By 2008, 94.4 per cent of the country's 6,425 subdistricts had a public junior secondary school.

The total number of senior secondary schools, consisting of general schools, vocational schools and Islamic schools, rose from around 14,000

in 1993 to 23,000 in 2008. The number of public schools more than doubled during the period, with the biggest increase occurring since 2000.

Despite constructing such a large number of schools, the public sector
has been unable to keep up with the demand for education at the junior
and senior secondary levels. This gap has been filled by the private sector, even though private schools are generally not the first choice of parents when enrolling their children. The quality of the education provided
by private secondary schools is generally considered to be poor, and they
tend to cater to the children of poor families who have been unable to
gain entry to a public school (ADB 1995; Bangay 2005).[3] The challenge
for the government is to lift the quality of private schools, to ensure that
their students enjoy the same quality of education as their peers in public
schools.

The quantity and quality of teachers

In line with the increase in the number of schools, the number of teachers has risen significantly, particularly since 2000. The total number of
teachers in Indonesian schools (excluding Islamic schools) rose from 1.9
million in 1999/2000 to 2.8 million in 2009/10 (Figure 2.13).

In response to a shortage of teachers in the early 2000s, particularly
in rural and remote areas, in 2003 the central government introduced
a scheme to hire more teachers on short-term contracts – the so-called
guru kontrak. Unpublished data from the Ministry of Education and
Culture show that the government hired 190,700 *guru kontrak* in 2003,
and another 79,200 in 2004.[4] In addition to the teachers on the government payroll, schools and the foundations that support them are able
to hire their own 'honorary' teachers. The number of such teachers has
increased significantly since the management of education was decentralized to the regions in 2000. The proportion of honorary teachers is
relatively high even in public schools. Currently the share is about 25
per cent: 27 per cent in primary schools, 20 per cent in junior secondary
schools and 21 per cent in senior secondary schools. This is rather surprising given that public schools would have to cover the cost of honorary (and therefore non-civil servant) teachers using non-salary revenue
from the government, or even parent contributions.

---

3 According to Bangay (2005: 171), three factors limit access to government
   schools: geography (a lack of public schools, particularly in remote rural
   areas); entry based on academic merit (which works against the poor); and
   economics (the widespread but illegal practice of charging fees).
4 These teachers were eventually hired as permanent teachers with civil servant
   status.

Figure 2.13   Number of teachers by school level, academic year 1999/2000–2009/10 (million)[a]

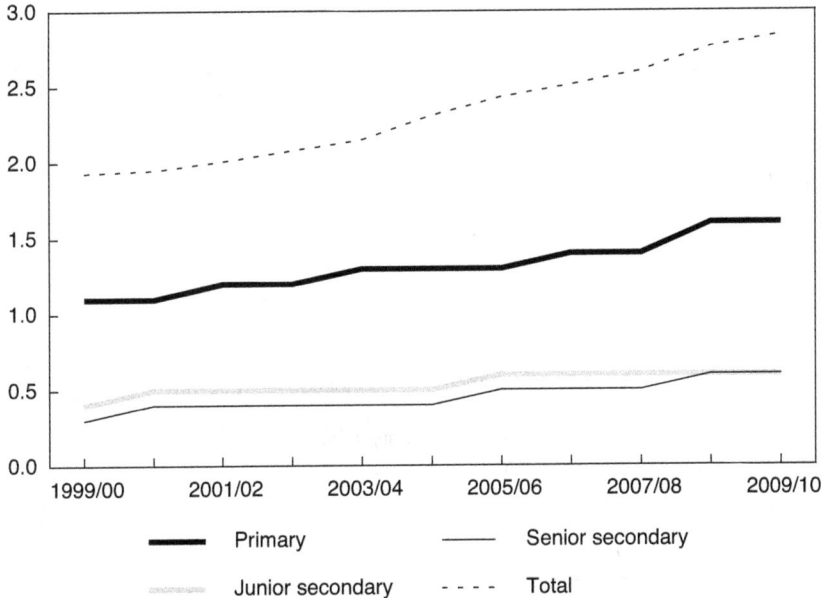

a   Data do not include teachers in Islamic schools.

Source: Compiled from school statistics from the Center for Education Data and Statistics, Ministry of Education and Culture, various years.

As Figure 2.14 shows, there have been sizeable increases in the number of teachers since the decentralization of education in 2000. Between 1999/2000 (the year before the handover) and 2009/10, the number of teachers in all schools (excluding Islamic schools) rose by 51 per cent: 41 per cent at the primary level, 45 per cent at the junior secondary level and 72 per cent at the senior secondary level. During the same period, however, the numbers of primary, junior secondary and senior secondary students went up by only 7 per cent, 22 per cent and 52 per cent respectively. During the previous decade (1989/90–1999/2000), in contrast, the number of teachers actually fell by 5.6 per cent at the junior secondary level and 0.2 per cent at the senior secondary level, despite rises of 30 per cent and 19 per cent respectively in the number of students.

The divergence in the growth rates for student and teacher numbers has led to a significant decline in the student–teacher ratio. On average, the ratio declined from 20:1 in 1999/2000 to 15.4 in 2009/10, with a different figure for each level of education (Figure 2.14). The low student–teacher ratios at the junior and senior secondary levels occur because

Figure 2.14   Index of growth in the number of teachers and students
(1999/2000 = 1), and trends in the student–teacher ratio,
academic year 1999/2000–2009/10

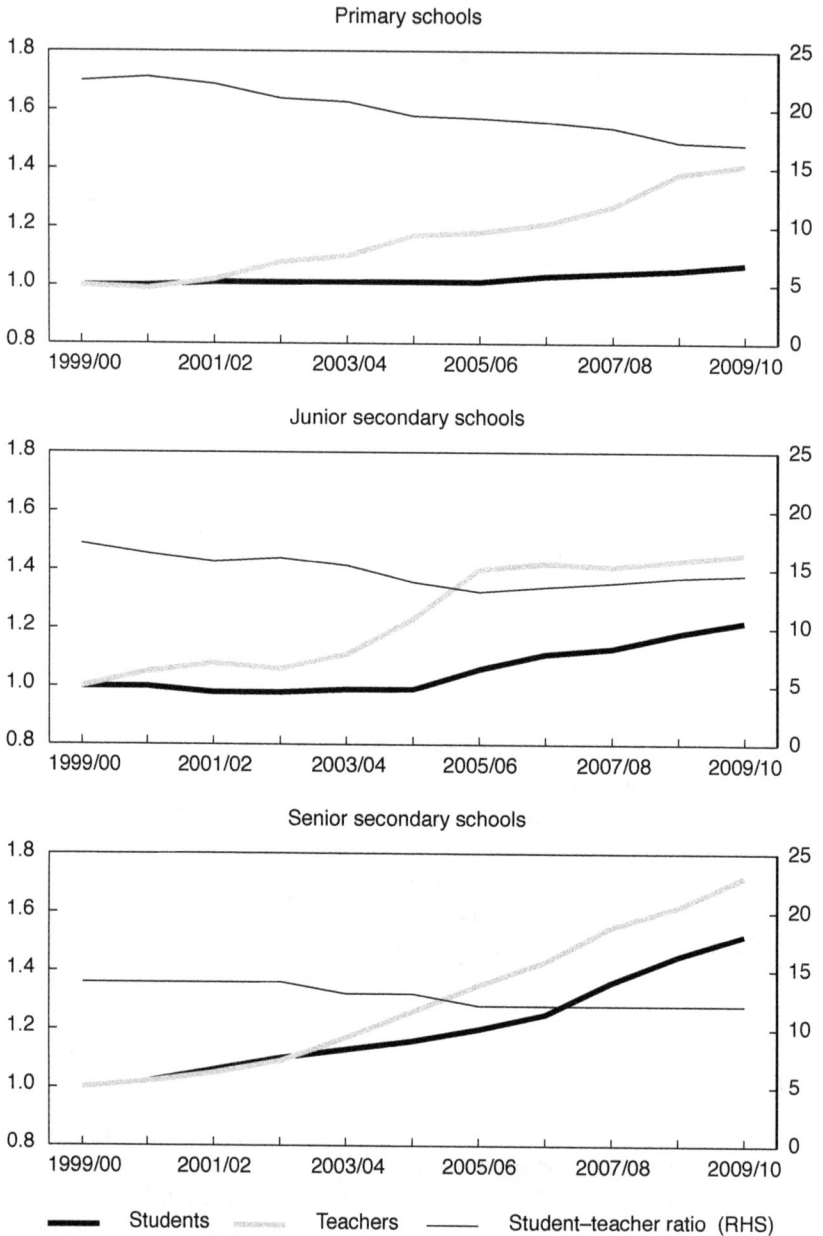

Primary schools

Junior secondary schools

Senior secondary schools

Students ⸻ Teachers ⸻ Student–teacher ratio (RHS)

Source: Compiled from school statistics from the Center for Education Data and Statistics, Ministry of Education and Culture, various years.

teachers are usually assigned to teach one subject, not a cluster of subjects. This practice is inefficient, particularly in small schools where teachers are likely to have fewer teaching hours.

A survey of teacher employment and deployment conducted in 2005 by the World Bank and the Ministry of National Education (2006) found that many teachers worked less than the minimum requirement of 18 hours per week – on average, about 44 per cent of teachers at the junior secondary level, for example. The report found that the problem was particularly acute in rural and remote areas, where schools were more likely to be small: 53 per cent of teachers in rural areas, and 59 per cent in remote areas, worked less than 18 hours per week, compared with 37 per cent in urban areas. The problem of short working hours was not confined to secondary schools, however. The survey found that about 28 per cent of primary school teachers in rural areas worked less than 18 hours per week, compared with 18 per cent in urban areas.

The latest data from the Ministry of Education and Culture show that female teachers are over-represented in the education system, especially at the pre-school level. In academic year 2009/2010, for example, 62 per cent of primary teachers, 54 per cent of junior secondary teachers, 62 per cent of senior secondary teachers and a massive 97 per cent of pre-school teachers were female. Very little research has been done on the causes and effects of the over-representation of female teachers in Indonesia, although research from other countries mainly finds an immaterial association between teacher gender and the educational performance of students.[5] Further research on this topic in the Indonesian context may be needed, however, not just to examine the connection between teacher gender and student performance, but also to explore whether teachers treat male and female students differently, and to provide evidence for future policies to reduce the imbalance between male and female teachers.

As we have seen, Indonesia has made rapid progress in increasing the supply of teachers; the more important issue now is therefore one of quality. This chapter uses two common measures of teacher attributes, educational attainment and years of experience, to assess teacher quality, as well as the results of aptitude and competency tests conducted by the government.

As measured by educational attainment, teacher quality has increased significantly over the last decade. Data from the Ministry of Education and Culture (for general schools only) show that the proportion

---

5   See, for example, Ehrenberg, Goldhaber and Brewer (1995), Marsh and Martin (2005), Carrington et al. (2007), Carrington, Tymms and Merrell (2008) and Skelton et al. (2009).

Figure 2.15   Educational attainment of teachers by school level (%)

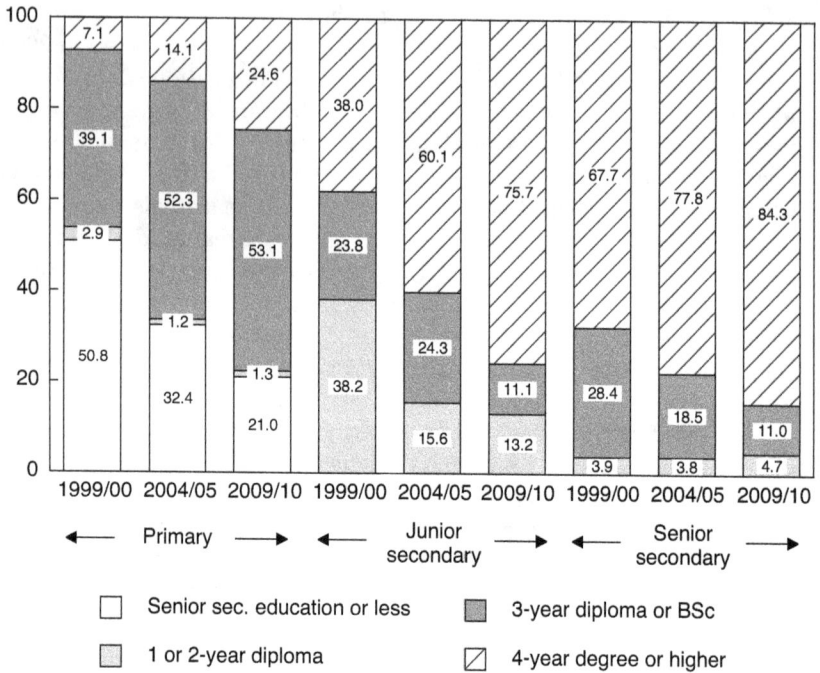

Primary

Junior secondary

Senior secondary

- Senior sec. education or less
- 1 or 2-year diploma
- 3-year diploma or BSc
- 4-year degree or higher

Source: Compiled from school statistics from the Center for Education Data and Statistics, Ministry of Education and Culture, various years.

of teachers holding a four-year diploma (D4) or bachelor (S1) degree – since 2005, the minimum educational qualification – doubled from 24.8 per cent in 1999/2000 to 49.2 per cent in 2009/10. As one would expect, the share is lowest at the primary level; only 24.6 per cent of primary teachers have at least a four-year tertiary degree, compared with 75.7 per cent of junior secondary teachers and 84.3 per cent of senior secondary teachers (Figure 2.15). Primary and junior secondary teachers have the furthest to go to meet the current standard: until the introduction of Law 14/2005 on Teachers and Lecturers, primary school teachers were required to have only two years of tertiary education, and junior secondary teachers three years.

Surprisingly, on average, private school teachers appear to be better educated than public school teachers: about 69.4 per cent have the minimum qualification, compared with just 42.9 per cent of public school teachers. Disaggregated analysis by school level, however, reveals that it is only teachers in private primary schools that are better qualified; in 2009/10, about 42.7 per cent of them had the minimum educational

Table 2.3   Educational attainment of teachers by school level and type of provider, 1999/2000–2009/10 (%)

School level/ educational attainment	Public			Private		
	1999/00	2004/05	2009/10	1999/00	2004/05	2009/10
Primary						
Senior secondary or less	50.5	31.6	20.3	55.2	42.2	26.9
1 or 2-year diploma	2.8	1.1	1.2	3.8	2.3	2.4
3-year diploma or BSc	40.2	54.2	55.9	26.3	29.7	28.0
4-year diploma, bachelor or higher	6.5	13.1	22.6	14.7	25.9	42.7
Junior secondary						
1 or 2-year diploma	39.2	15.8	11.2	36.2	15.2	17.6
3-year diploma or BSc	23.8	21.8	11.6	23.6	29.5	10.2
4-year diploma, bachelor or higher	37.0	62.4	77.2	40.2	55.3	72.3
Senior secondary						
1 or 2-year diploma	2.1	1.9	2.5	5.4	5.3	6.7
3-year diploma or BSc	29.4	17.3	9.8	27.6	19.4	12.2
4-year diploma, bachelor or higher	68.4	80.9	87.7	67.1	75.3	81.1

a   Data do not include teachers in pre-schools and Islamic schools.

Source: Compiled from school statistics from the Center for Education Data and Statistics, Ministry of Education and Culture, various years.

qualification, compared with 22.6 per cent of teachers in public primary schools (Table 2.3). The explanation may be that, at this level of schooling, the private sector must compete on quality, because – as noted earlier – there are enough public primary schools to fully meet demand.

One of the most striking results to emerge from the 2009/10 data on teachers is the large differences across regions in teachers' educational qualifications (Figure 2.16). At the primary level, the proportion of teachers holding the minimum four-year qualification ranges from 6 per cent in Maluku to 50 per cent in Jakarta. Only 10 of the 33 provinces shown in Figure 2.16 exceed the national average, namely all provinces in Java (East, West and Central Java, Banten, Yogyakarta and Jakarta), as well as East Kalimantan, Riau Islands, South Sulawesi and Bali. At the junior secondary level, the share of teachers holding the minimum qualification ranges from 38 per cent in Maluku to 89 per cent in East Java. At the

Figure 2.16   *Share of teachers with a four-year degree or higher by school level and province, academic year 2009/10 (%)*

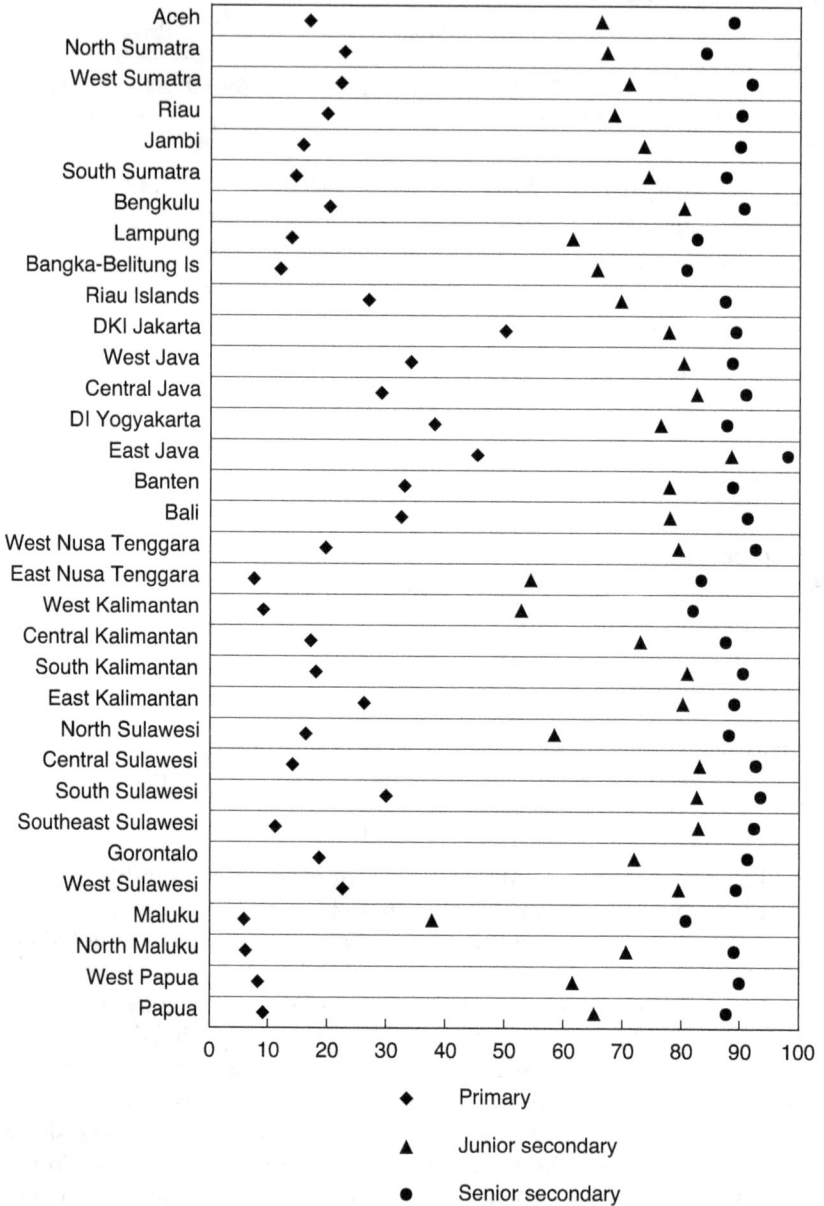

- ◆   Primary
- ▲   Junior secondary
- ●   Senior secondary

Source: NUPTK teacher database, Directorate General for Quality Improvement of Teachers and Educational Personnel, Ministry of Education and Culture.

senior secondary school, where a four-year tertiary degree was required even before the introduction of Law 14/2005, it ranges from 81 per cent in Bangka-Belitung Islands and Maluku to 98 per cent in East Java.

Analysis of the qualifications of teachers at the district level reveals even greater inequality, both across the country and within provinces. Across all districts, the share of primary teachers meeting the minimum requirement ranges from 0.6 per cent in Teluk Wonda in West Papua to 70 per cent in Mojokerto City in East Java. East Java and North Sumatra have the largest within-province variation; the shares range from 18 per cent (in Sumenep) to 70 per cent (in Mojokerto City) in East Java, and from 1 per cent (in North Nias) to 48 per cent (in Medan City) in North Sumatra. Although less pronounced, the cross-country differences between districts even extend to the senior secondary level; across the country, the proportion of senior secondary teachers holding the minimum qualification ranges from 50 per cent in North Nias in North Sumatra to 99.7 per cent in Blitar City in East Java.

In terms of educational qualifications by gender, male teachers tend to be better qualified than female teachers at the pre-school and primary levels, but less well qualified at the junior and senior secondary levels. Statistics for 2009/10 from the NUPTK teacher database indicate that, in pre-schools, about 24 per cent of male teachers but only 15 per cent of female teachers are fully qualified; and that at the primary level, 29 per cent of male teachers, compared with 26 per cent of female teachers, are qualified.

Little research has been done on outcomes among students taught by male or female teachers with equivalent qualifications. Using aggregated data at the school level, however, Suharti (2012) found that students from schools with larger proportions of female teachers tended to perform more poorly in mathematics. It is difficult to explain this result, because no information is available on teachers' academic backgrounds. It could be that female teachers are less likely to specialize in this subject, or that they do not receive as much professional development as their male colleagues.

2.6 STUDENT LEARNING OUTCOMES

The learning outcomes of Indonesian students can be assessed using standardized national examination results as well as standardized international tests such as the Trends in International Mathematics and Science Study (TIMSS), the Progress in International Reading Literacy Study (PIRLS) and the Programme for International Student Assessment (PISA). Individual, cross-school and cross-regional comparisons using national examination data and cross-country comparisons based on international data are all useful.

The scores of about 3.6 million Indonesian junior secondary school students in the 2010 national examination reveal large variations between students. The possible scores for the tested subjects (mathematics, science, Indonesian language and English) range from zero to a perfect 10 points. The average scores for the four subjects are 7.33 points (mathematics), 7.18 points (science), 7.40 points (Indonesian language) and 6.99 points (English). The proportion of students recording a score below five points is 9 per cent for mathematics, 6 per cent for science, 4 per cent for Indonesian language and 9 per cent for English; the share achieving a score above eight is 41 per cent for mathematics, 34 per cent for science, 38 per cent for Indonesian language and 30 per cent for English.

Using data on parental characteristics collected during the examination, Suharti (2012) finds that students whose parents have a better education and a higher-status occupation tend to perform better than students whose parents have less education and a lower-status occupation. On average, students whose fathers are farmers, fishers or blue-collar workers have the worst examination results, while those whose fathers are civil servants or professionals have the highest examination scores in all subjects.

Student performance as measured by examination score varies considerably across schools and districts. Among the 41,812 junior secondary schools participating in the national examination, the average mathematics score ranges from 2.12 to 9.89 points, and the average science score from 2.13 to 9.79 points. The figures do not differ greatly between public and private schools. The distribution of average examination scores for junior secondary schools is shown in Figure 2.17. Across districts, the average scores for the four tested subjects range from 3.97 to 8.87 points for mathematics, 4.68 to 8.90 points for science, 4.25 to 8.72 points for Indonesian language and 4.25 to 8.89 points for English.

The shares also differ across provinces. For example, about 54 per cent of students in Bengkulu, 36 per cent in Gorontalo and 33 per cent in East Nusa Tenggara score below five points in mathematics, whereas over 50 per cent of students score eight points or higher in seven other provinces: North Sumatra, Jambi, South Sumatra, East Java, Bali, North Sulawesi and South Sulawesi (Figure 2.18).

Suharti (2012) finds that school-level factors have only a trivial association with student performance. For example, lower student–teacher ratios and class sizes are not associated with higher student achievement, after controlling for parental characteristics, although the share of teachers with a bachelor's degree or higher does have a small positive association with a school's test score. What matters more in determining student

Figure 2.17   *Distribution of average scores for junior secondary schools in the 2010 national examination by subject*

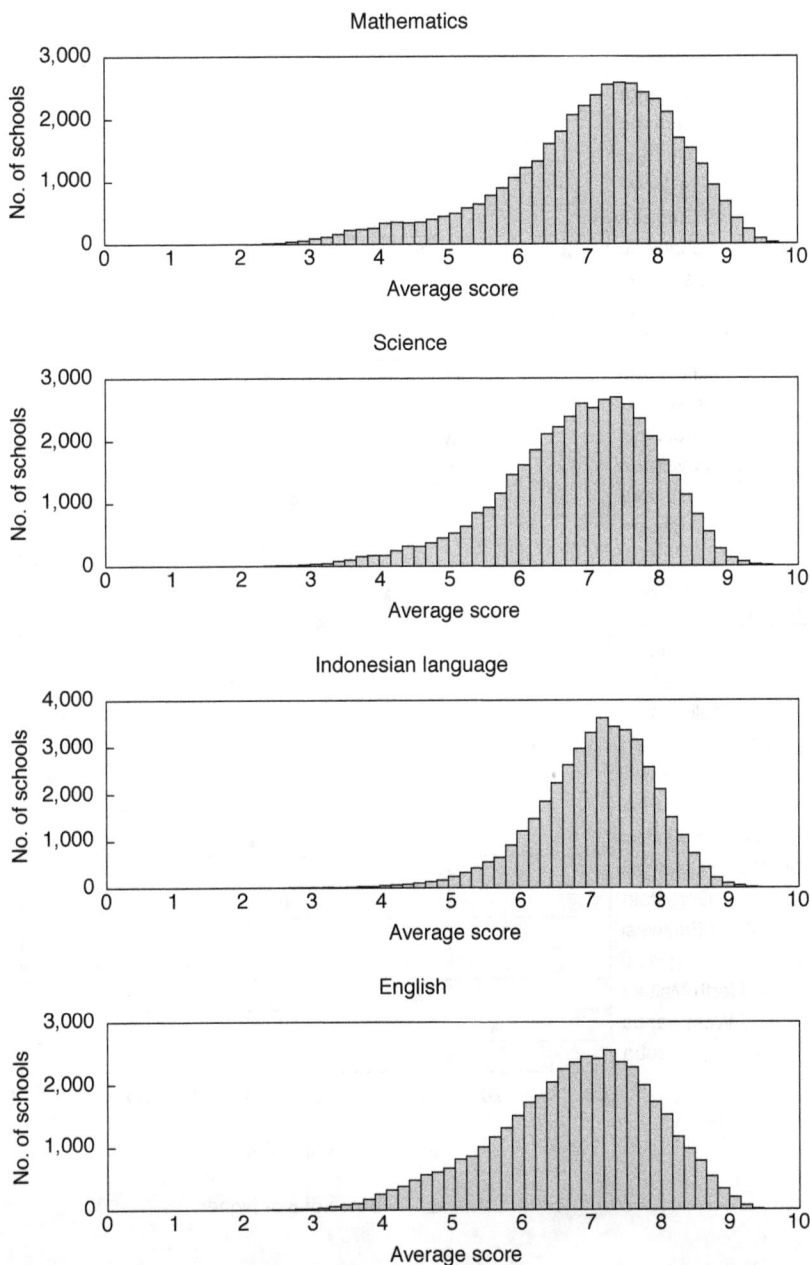

Mathematics

Science

Indonesian language

English

Source: National examination results, 2010.

Figure 2.18   Share of junior secondary school students with mathematics scores above six and eight points in the 2010 national examination (%)

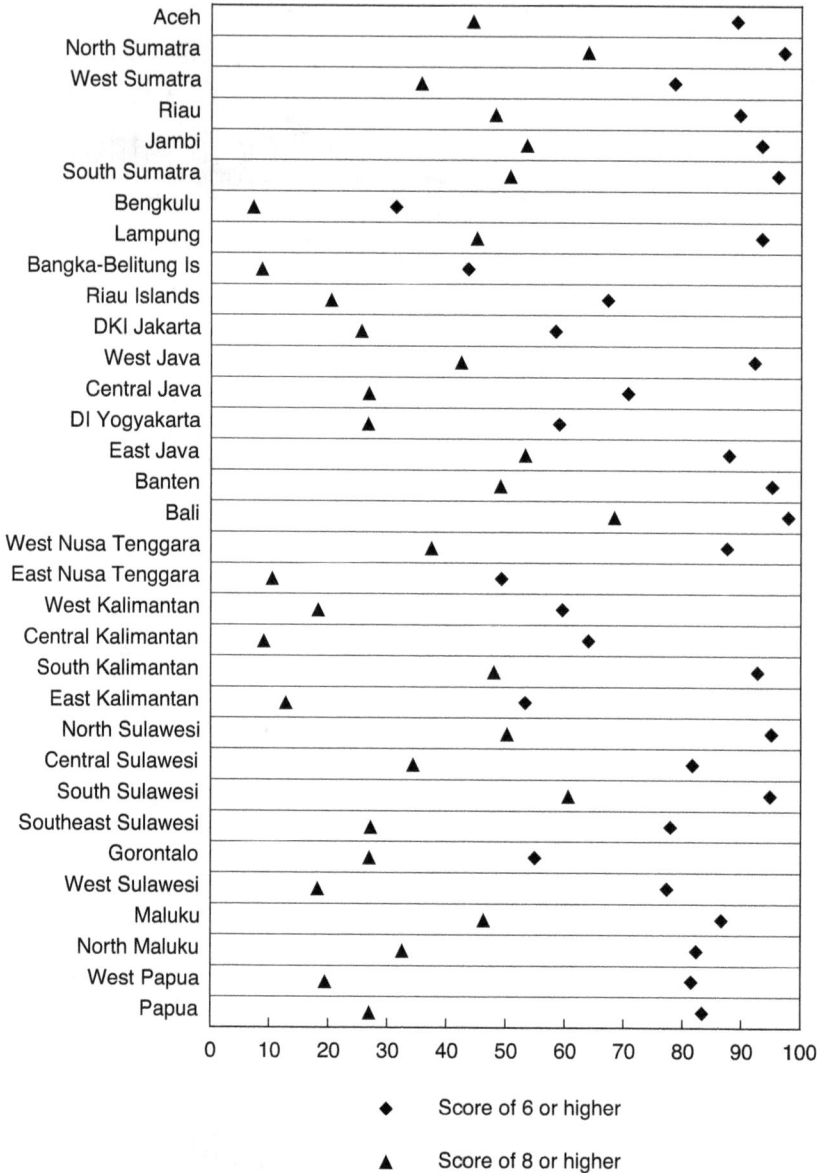

Score of 6 or higher

Score of 8 or higher

Source: National examination results, 2010.

performance is the characteristics of parents. Students perform better if schools have higher proportions of students from families with higher socio-economic status. The better schools, which are able to accept students based on their past results, have disproportionately high shares of bright students. This contributes to the poor correlation between school-based factors and student performance.

At the international level, the results of standardized international tests indicate that Indonesian students perform more poorly than those from many other countries. Data from the 2011 TIMSS show that about 57 per cent of Indonesian students who participated in the mathematics test had scores below 400 points, the lowest benchmark. Only 2 per cent had scores above 550 points, and none achieved the advanced benchmark of 625 points (Figure 2.19). The proportion of Indonesian students reaching the lowest benchmark was actually lower than the proportion in Singapore, South Korea and Taiwan attaining the advanced benchmark.

A similar pattern is evident for the 2011 PIRLS reading achievement test: only 66 per cent of Indonesian 4th grade students had scores above 400 points (the low benchmark), 16 per cent scores above 550 points (the intermediate benchmark) and 4 per cent scores above 550 points (the high benchmark) (Mullis, Martin, Foy and Drucker 2012). As with the TIMSS mathematics test, none achieved the advanced benchmark.[6]

Indonesia also performs poorly in the PISA tests, which assess the competence of 15-year-olds in reading, mathematics and science. Of the 65 countries participating in the tests in 2009, Indonesia was ranked 58th in reading, 63rd in mathematics and 62nd in science (OECD 2010).

2.7 THE FINANCING OF EDUCATION

The financing of education in Indonesia entered a new era when the Constitution was amended in 2002 to require all levels of government to allocate at least 20 per cent of their budgets to education. Ratified in Law 20/2003 on the National Education System, the new policy has definitely made more money available for education. Data from UNESCO show that the government budget for education increased from only 12 per cent of total government spending in 2001 to 16 per cent in 2003 and 18 per cent in 2008 (Table 2.4).

As a share of government expenditure, Indonesia spends more on education than many other countries, including the United Kingdom

---

6 The poor reading skills of Indonesian students may be linked to their lack of interest in reading. Data from the 2009 Susenas show that only 16 per cent of children aged 7–18 read storybooks.

Figure 2.19   International comparison of performance of year 8 students in
the TIMSS mathematics test, 2011 (% achieving benchmark)

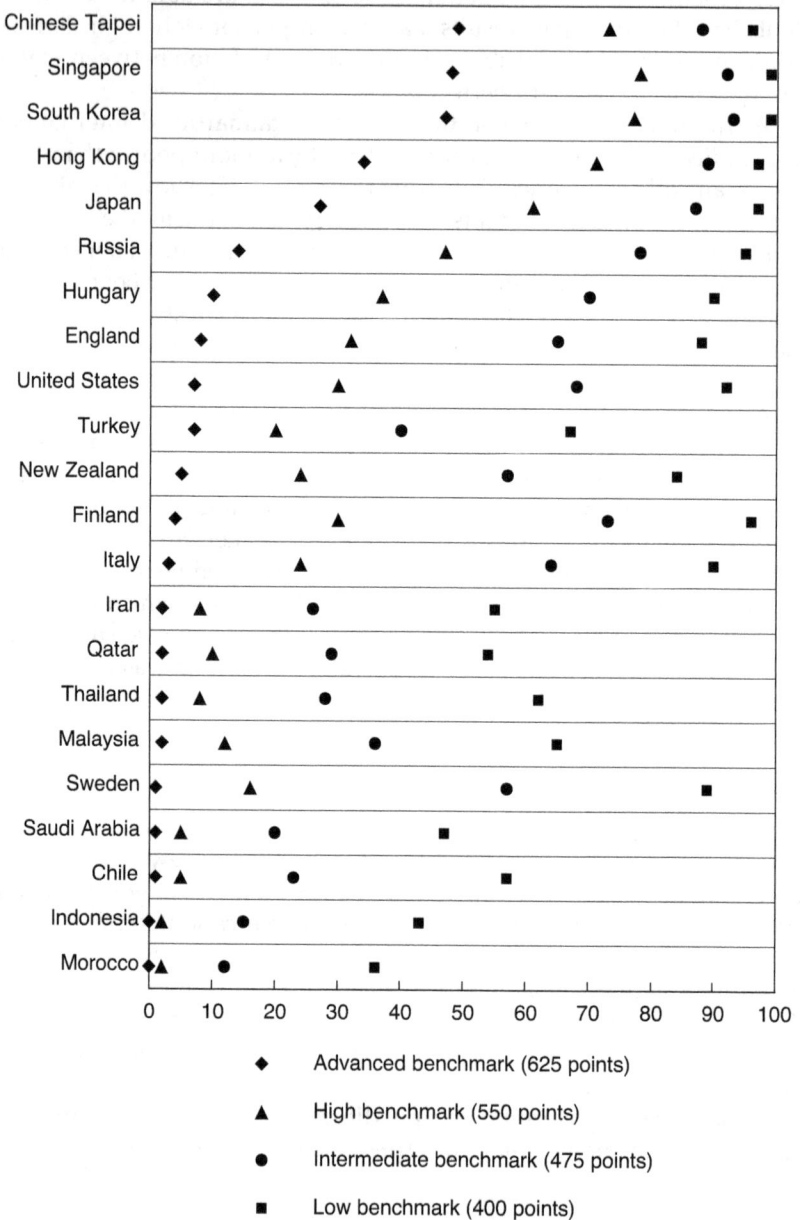

TIMSS = Trends in International Mathematics and Science Study.
Source: Mullis, Martin, Foy and Arora (2012).

*Table 2.4   Total public spending on education in selected countries,
1999–2008 (% of government expenditure)*

Country	1999	2000	2001	2002	2003	2004	2005	2006	2007	2008
Bangladesh	15.3	15.0	15.7	15.8	15.5	14.8	–	14.2	15.8	14.0
Cambodia	8.7	14.6	–	–	–	–	–	–	12.4	–
India	12.7	12.7	–	–	10.7	–	–	–	–	–
Indonesia	–	–	**11.5**	**14.3**	**16.0**	**14.2**	**14.9**	**17.2**	**18.7**	**17.9**
Japan	9.3	10.5	10.5	10.6	9.7	9.8	9.5	9.5	9.4	9.4
Lao PDR	–	7.4	8.8	10.6	–	10.8	11.7	14.0	15.8	12.2
Malaysia	25.2	26.7	20.0	20.3	28.0	25.2	–	–	18.2	17.2
Myanmar	8.1	8.7	18.1	–	–	–	–	–	–	–
Philippines	–	13.9	14.0	17.8	17.2	16.4	15.2	16.7	15.2	16.9
South Korea	13.1	–	14.7	15.5	15.0	16.5	15.3	15.2	14.7	15.8
Thailand	28.1	31.0	28.3	–	–	26.8	25.0	25.0	20.9	20.5
United Kingdom	11.4	11.4	11.4	–	12.0	11.7	12.5	11.9	11.7	11.1
United States	–	–	17.1	–	15.2	14.4	13.7	14.7	14.1	13.8

Source: UNESCO, EdStats Query database, stats.uis.unesco.org/unesco.

and the United States (Table 2.4). Among the countries included in the table, only Thailand spent more on education in 2008. Data from the Ministry of Finance indicate that the central government's expenditure has increased further since then, and now exceeds the goal of 20 per cent set by Law 20/2003.

More than half the government budget for education is transferred to the provincial and district levels of government, mainly to pay for teacher salaries and allowances. A breakdown of provincial and district budgets for education (including transfers from the central government) is shown in Table 2.5. It can be seen that total local government spending on education increased from Rp 73.7 trillion in 2007 to Rp 121.5 trillion in 2010. Adjusted for inflation, this was roughly a 35 per cent increase over three years.

Has the expansion of budgets improved the performance of the education sector? Not enough research has been done to answer this question. Since most of the increase has been allocated to teacher salaries and allowances, the research on the effectiveness of teacher certification may provide a partial answer. Certified teachers currently receive double the salaries of uncertified teachers, but it appears that they do not perform significantly better than their uncertified colleagues. Moreover, Artha et

Table 2.5   Breakdown of local government expenditure on education by level of government, 2007–10 (Rp billion)

Year/ level of government	Personnel expenditure			Capital expendi- ture	Goods & services	Total
	Salaries & allowances	Other	Total			
2007						
Provincial	632	1,089	1,721	1,603	1,193	4,518
District/city	47,961	4,141	52,102	11,160	5,875	69,137
Total	48,593	5,230	53,823	12,763	7,068	73,654
2008						
Provincial	937	1,105	2,042	2,478	2,044	6,564
District/city	60,452	3,818	64,270	12,874	6,565	83,710
Total	61,390	4,923	66,313	15,352	8,609	90,274
2009						
Provincial	990	1,289	2,279	2,314	2,363	6,956
District/city	69,822	3,848	73,671	13,852	6,716	94,238
Total	70,812	5,137	75,949	16,166	9,079	101,194
2010						
Provincial	–	–	–	–	–	19,043
District/city	–	–	–	–	–	102,476
Total	–	–	–	–	–	121,519

Source: Unpublished data from the Ministry of Finance.

al. (2008) find that the increases in real education expenditure at the junior secondary level are negatively associated with changes in Indonesian students' national examination scores.

2.8   CONCLUSION AND RECOMMENDATIONS

Indonesians are becoming increasingly better educated, as indicated by a significant increase in years of schooling and a steady decrease in the illiteracy rate. The government made nine years of basic education compulsory in 1994. It plans to extend this to 12 years, even though many children are still unable to complete their 'compulsory' junior secondary education. Boys and girls have similar levels of access to education, but the children of poor families suffer high discontinuation rates. The problem of low transition rates both from primary to junior secondary school and from junior to senior secondary school requires serious attention, as does the issue of regional disparities in access to education. Without addressing these problems, the goal of nine years of compulsory basic education will never be fully achieved – let alone the target of 12 years.

The government has made significant efforts to lift the quality of education by expanding the teaching force and improving teacher qualifications. In doing so it has encountered two problems. The first is that Indonesia now has a surplus of teachers, which to some extent leads to short working hours. The second is that the improvement in teacher qualifications and levels of certification does not appear to have paid off in better performance among students.

Law 14/2005 requires all teachers to hold the minimum educational qualification and to gain official certification by 2015. With only two years left until 2015, this will not be an easy task. First, most of the remaining unqualified primary school teachers have only a senior secondary education or a one or two-year diploma. It would take them at least two years to obtain a bachelor's degree even if prior learning were taken into account. Two years will not be sufficient to improve the qualifications of more than 1.5 million teachers without abandoning the teaching and learning process in many schools.

The second constraint concerns the capacity of teacher training providers. In 2007, there were only 303 public and private teacher education providers, plus the Open University (World Bank 2007). Even including the new teacher training institutions established since then, it seems unlikely that these providers would be able to meet all of the demand for pre-service and in-service training generated by the new qualification and certification requirements.

If the 2015 goal is not amended, there is a risk that the program to upgrade teachers' qualifications will suffer from compromises in quality. The main purpose of the qualification and certification requirements is to improve teachers' teaching skills, which should lead to better educational performance among students. In-service training should therefore be free of any compromises. The government needs to learn from the failure of similar approaches in the 1990s, when the goal was to have all primary school teachers certified at the post-secondary level (Nielsen 1998). It needs to apply a strategic approach as well to reduce the large differences in teachers' educational qualifications across regions, particularly at the primary school level.

The amendment of the Constitution to guarantee a minimum level of financing for education has led to an improvement in budget allocations across Indonesia. Disappointingly, however, this does not seem to have led to a significant improvement in students' performance. This suggests that it is not just the size of the government budget for education that is important, but also how the money is used.

At present, the financing system lacks incentives for efficiency. For instance, district governments and schools have little incentive to hire only the number of teachers they need, because the central government covers the entire cost of civil servant teacher salaries. This may be the time for the government to consider implementing the 'adequacy' approach to education financing recommended by the National Coordination Forum for Education for All (NCFEA 2003). According to Guthrie and Rothstein (2011: 103), 'adequacy' means 'sufficient resources to ensure students an effective opportunity to acquire appropriately specified levels of knowledge and skills'.

Under this approach, policy makers would estimate an 'adequate' level of financing for education, that is, what it would take 'in terms of textbooks, teaching materials, teacher abilities and qualifications, school libraries, and so forth to produce an educationally adequate education for each child' (NCFEA 2003: VIII3). They would also construct a mechanism to distribute the money equitably to the districts, and provide guidelines on how the money should be spent to produce the outcomes being sought (NCFEA 2003: VIII11). Under the Education for All approach, each district and school would receive only as much money as it needed to provide an 'adequate' level of education.

A final problem is that researchers do not have sufficient access to detailed data on all aspects of education in Indonesia – for example, on the number and quality of schools, the number and quality of teachers, or the results of students in national examinations. The Ministry of Education and Culture and the Ministry of Religious Affairs need to provide better access to their micro data, to enable researchers to complete high-quality studies that can be used to inform future policies on education.

REFERENCES

ADB (Asian Development Bank) (1995) *Report and Recommendation of the President to the Board of Directors on a Proposed Loan for the Private Junior Secondary Education Project*, ADB, Manila.
Artha, R.P., A. Beatty, B. Karyadi, K. Muralidharan, M. Pradhan and F.H. Rogers (2008) 'Can teacher effort be improved? Evidence from Indonesia (preliminary analysis)', presentation by Menno Pradhan to the World Bank Human Development Forum 2008, Washington DC, 3 November.
Bangay, C. (2005) 'Private education: relevant or redundant? Private education, decentralisation and national provision in Indonesia', *Compare: A Journal of Comparative and International Education*, 35: 167–79.

BPS, Bappenas and UNDP (Badan Pusat Statistik, Badan Perencanaan Pembangunan Nasional and United Nations Development Programme) (2004) *Indonesia Human Development Report 2004. The Economics of Democracy: Financing Human Development in Indonesia*, BPS, Bappenas and UNDP, Jakarta.

Carrington, B., B. Francis, M. Hutchings, C. Skelton, B. Read and I. Hall (2007) 'Does the gender of the teacher really matter? Seven- to eight-year-olds' accounts of their interactions with their teachers', *Educational Studies*, 33: 397–413.

Carrington, B., P. Tymms and C. Merrell (2008) 'Role models, school improvement and the "gender gap" – do men bring out the best in boys and women the best in girls?', *British Educational Research Journal*, 34: 315–27.

Directorate General of Basic Education (2010) 'Kendala bukan pada pribadi, melainkan manajemen' [The constraints are not on personnel, but on management], Directorate General of Basic Education, Ministry of Education and Culture, available at http://118.98.166.62/content/berita/utama/ber_912.html.

Ehrenberg, R.G., D.D. Goldhaber and D.J. Brewer (1995) 'Do teachers' race, gender, and ethnicity matter? Evidence from NELS88', NBER Working Paper No. 4669, National Bureau of Economic Research, Cambridge.

Guthrie, J.W. and R. Rothstein (2011) 'A new millenium and a likely new era of education finance', in S. Chaikind and W.J. Fowler (eds) *Education Finance in the New Millennium*, Eye on Education, Larchmont, pp. 99–119.

Jones, G.W., P. Hagul and Damayanti (2000) 'The impact of the scholarships and grants program', Central Independent Monitoring Unit of the Scholarships and Grants Program in Indonesia, Jakarta.

Marsh, H. and A. Martin (2005) 'Motivating boys and motivating girls: does teacher gender really make a difference?', *Australian Journal of Education*, 49: 320–34.

Mullis, I.V.S., M.O. Martin, P. Foy and A. Arora (2012) *TIMSS 2011 International Results in Mathematics*, TIMSS & PIRLS International Study Center, Lynch School of Education, Boston College, Chestnut Hill.

Mullis, I.V.S., M.O. Martin, P. Foy and K.T. Drucker (2012) *TIMSS 2011 International Results in Reading*, TIMSS & PIRLS International Study Center, Lynch School of Education, Boston College, Chestnut Hill.

NCFEA (National Coordination Forum for Education for All) (2003) 'National plan of action: Indonesia's education for all 2003–2015', NCFEA, Jakarta.

Nielsen, H.D. (1998) 'Reforms to teacher education in Indonesia: does more mean better?', *Asia Pacific Journal of Education*, 18: 9–25.

OECD (Organisation for Economic Co-operation and Development) (2010) *PISA 2009 Results: What Students Know and Can Do: Student Performance in Reading, Mathematics and Science (Volume 1)*, Programme for International Student Assessment, OECD, Paris.

Rosser, A., A. Joshi and D. Edwin (2011) 'Power, politics, and political entrepreneurs: realising universal free basic education in Indonesia', IDS Working Paper No. 358, Institute of Development Studies, Brighton, March.

Ruslan, H. (2011) 'Wajib belajar 12 tahun sempat ditolak Kemendikbud, kok bisa?' [12-year compulsory education rejected by the Ministry of Education and Culture, how come?], *Republika Online*, 2 January.

Skelton, C., B. Carrington, B. Francis, M. Hutchings, B. Read and I. Hall (2009) 'Gender "matters" in the primary classroom: pupils' and teachers' perspectives', *British Educational Research Journal*, 35: 187–204.

Suharti (2012) 'Working thesis. Schooling and destiny: behind inequality in education performance in Indonesia', Australian National University, Canberra.

World Bank (2007) 'Indonesia – Better Education through Reformed Management and Universal Teacher Upgrading Project (BERMUTU)', Report No. 39299-ID, World Bank, Jakarta.

World Bank and Ministry of National Education (2006) 'Teacher employment and deployment in Indonesia: opportunities for equity, efficiency and quality improvement', Report No. 45622, joint publication of the World Bank and Ministry of National Education, Jakarta.

3 TEACHER TRAINING, SCHOOL NORMS AND TEACHER EFFECTIVENESS IN INDONESIA

Christopher Bjork

3.1 INTRODUCTION

During one of the first research projects I conducted in Indonesia, I distributed a survey to approximately 100 junior secondary teachers. One of the questions asked instructors how often they used student-centred teaching methods in their classes. Fifty-seven per cent of respondents answered either 'often' or 'always'. Yet when I observed the same people interacting with students in the classroom, I was surprised by what I saw. Teachers tended to lecture from a stationary position at the front of the room or to transcribe large sections from textbooks onto the blackboard. Rarely did I witness the interplay between student and teacher that the teachers' survey responses suggested was a regular part of their instructional repertoires. In an attempt to establish an empirical foundation for my analysis, I recorded the specific pedagogical methods they used. The data indicated that 53 per cent of all lessons involved lecturing, while only 20 per cent involved some sort of hands-on activity and just 5 per cent included a class discussion. The contrast between teachers' reports on their methods and the actual strategies they used with students raised a number of questions. Were the lessons I observed aberrations? Was a typical day in an Indonesian school filled with engaging activities that were put on hold on the days I happened to visit? How did teachers define 'student-centred' methods? Was I missing something?

The follow-up interviews I conducted with educators clarified my thinking and provided valuable insights into the motivations of the individual teachers I had observed. In describing their actions, the teachers told me that they believed they were encouraging their students to take an active role in their studies; but their definitions of what constituted active learning were telling. The three examples of active learning they most often supplied were using workbooks in class; requiring students to complete more review exercises; and assigning homework more regularly. So while I was struck by the static, teacher-centred aspects of the lessons I observed, the people facilitating those activities were firm in their conviction that they were bringing the curriculum to life for their students – and were supporting the Ministry of Education and Culture's efforts to encourage more active engagement of students in the classroom. From their perspective, they were faithfully carrying out the role that had been assigned to them. Yet the disjuncture between central and local perceptions of how to motivate students was undermining reform efforts. As I discovered in subsequent interviews conducted in Jakarta, education officials were unaware of this situation. Very few of the individuals involved in formulating policy had a thorough understanding of conditions in the schools they oversaw.

Indonesian teachers follow many of the same routines as instructors located in Western developed countries: they present lessons from textbooks, assign homework, test student mastery of the curriculum and send report cards home to parents. However, these surface similarities conceal fundamental differences in beliefs about what it means to be a good teacher. The research I have conducted in Indonesia provides convincing support for Fuller and Clarke's (1994: 121) description of teaching as a 'culturally situated' activity. The definition of the teacher in Indonesia has been constructed to fit the unique contours of the nation's social, historical and political landscape. Stress on teachers' membership in a national civil service corps combined with the government's historical concern with national cohesion encourages Indonesian educators to act in ways that might not be rewarded in other contexts. As civil servants, they have learned to follow the directives of upper-level officials, and not to dispute them. The image of the instructor as 'autonomous educator' or 'student advocate' was foreign to most of the teachers I interviewed.

In this chapter I examine the responsibilities assigned to Indonesian teachers, and consider how modifications to their professional profile might lead to more effective policy planning. Drawing on my experiences conducting research on Indonesian education over the past 15 years, I describe the culture of teaching in Indonesia: the evolution of the role of the *guru*, instructors' priorities in the classroom and off-campus, their views of the responsibilities of educators, and the role they have played and can play in reform efforts. This information can enhance our understanding of the influence that teachers have on students and their connections to the broader society.

3.2   THE HISTORICAL CONTEXT FOR TEACHING

To fully understand the actions of Indonesian teachers, it is helpful to examine the evolution of the education system. The goals of the contemporary system, the function of schools within society and the roles ascribed to teachers are all rooted in the past. While this is true of any education system, Indonesia's tumultuous political situation in the years after independence exerted an unusually direct and cogent influence on the structure of the school system. The speed of the expansion of education as well as the political tumult encircling it produced a system with a unique set of priorities.

When Indonesia broke free and became an independent republic in 1945, indigenous Indonesian citizens – the *pribumi* – finally gained the power to oversee the education of their own children. Determined to compensate for the limited opportunities offered by the former colonial rulers, the government declared that all citizens motivated to study would be given access to schooling. It consolidated several independent systems into a single entity, hoping to create an institution that would unite the populace. The freedom to create a new system virtually from scratch proved both liberating and overwhelming. Government leaders were required to compress a process that had unfolded over decades in many other countries into a period of months; they developed guiding principles, built schools, hired teachers and administrators, and tried to convince parents that enrolling their children in school was in their best interests. All of this occurred during a period of great political instability. Social institutions, including schools, were relied on to build national stability and cohesion.

The huge influx of students into the schools placed a strain on a system that had shaky foundations. Education planners tried to provide direction to the swarms of newly appointed bureaucrats while they themselves were attempting to navigate unfamiliar pathways. Individuals with minimal training or classroom experience were drafted into the teaching force and were immediately set to work in the classrooms. Most of the people who had worked as instructors before independence had left the field of education to join the armed forces or to work in government institutions in need of educated labour. In 1951, it was estimated that 140,000 people would have to be trained as teachers to meet the demand for schooling that had been unleashed.

To overcome the shortage, more than 500 emergency teacher training programs were established throughout the country (Djojonegoro 1997). As a result of the combination of heavy demand for new instructors, a limited pool of individuals with a background in teacher education and a shortage of instructional materials, the teacher training institutes tended to emphasize mastery of curricular content rather than instructional methodology. Teacher performance was not closely scrutinized or assessed. Although instructors usually received a teaching schedule and a list of subjects to cover, they had great freedom to translate those documents into learning activities (Djojonegoro 1997). One product of this combination of insufficient training and minimal oversight was a culture of teaching that did not place a high priority on instructional practice. Teachers often had the freedom to invest as much time and effort in their work as they saw fit. Lacking models of effective practice and challenged by large class sizes, they tended to spend most of their time lecturing, and expected pupils to take responsibility for mastering the curriculum.

Although education planners succeeded in rapidly expanding access to schooling, educational considerations often suffered at the expense of political realities. In all societies, individuals in positions of power use the schools to promote their particular values and objectives. This tendency has been especially pronounced in Indonesia because of the constant threats to national stability. Concerned that internal strife would lead to the dissolution of the republic, politicians have frequently used any available means to promote nationalism among the citizenry. Beginning in the 1950s, government officials responded to threats to their authority by curbing the powers of constituencies located outside the inner circle of command. An Anti Subversion Law, which carried a maximum penalty of death, made it illegal to commit any acts that 'distort, undermine, or deviate from' the ideals outlined in Pancasila, the national ideology.[1] Politicians steadily narrowed the limits of politically acceptable cultural expressions and manipulated local rituals, customs and art forms to foster support for the 'national culture' they were attempting to develop (Bowen 1991; Hatley 1994). Local institutions were not trusted to oversee their own affairs, for it was feared that such arrangements might undermine national stability.

The largest and most captive audience available to Indonesian leaders was located in the schools. Regarding schools as fundamental to national integration, politicians went to great lengths to ensure that members of school communities recognized their identity as Indonesians and respected their ties to the central government. Government leaders employed the curriculum, school rituals, uniforms and employment regulations to underline teachers' obligations to the national government. In many cases, the emphasis on nationalism eclipsed the schools' instructional objectives. Educators were rewarded for their ability to loyally follow directives, not for their capacity for independent thought.

---

1 Pancasila's five guiding principles are belief in God, humanitarianism, nationalism, democracy and social justice.

One might have expected the government to loosen the reins after the economy stabilized during the New Order era, but the opposite actually occurred. Under Suharto, the government gradually tightened the leash connecting local schools to the centre. Lacking confidence in the abilities of teachers, the education ministry attempted to make the schools as 'teacher proof' as possible (Shaeffer 1990). The heavy curricular emphasis on nation building signalled to teachers that their primary role was to support the goals for the country articulated by leaders in Jakarta. The national government injected itself forcefully into the schools: ceremonies celebrating the accomplishments of the nation were held more frequently; administrators rated teachers on their displays of obedience; and all public employees were required to support the state political party, Golkar. Even the teachers' union, Persatuan Guru Republik Indonesia (PGRI), was used to monitor the actions of teachers. During the New Order, PGRI became a mechanism for monitoring teachers rather than a forum through which they could express their opinions and concerns. The government succeeded in developing a sense of submissiveness and self-censorship in both the electorate and the civil service (Mackie and MacIntyre 1994; Schwarz 2000). Teachers understood that faithfully supporting policies promulgated by the national government would provide them with job security; devoting themselves to improving the curriculum and pedagogical practice in their schools did not often garner them rewards.

3.3 SHIFTING PRIORITIES

In the 1960s, analysts frequently referred to Indonesia as Asia's 'chronic dropout' and expressed concern about the nation's future (Hill 1995). By 1990, the nation had escaped that label and emerged as one of the region's most striking success stories. Gains in the field of education were impressive: between 1945 and 1984, primary school attendance leapt from 2.5 million to 26.6 million (World Bank 1989). Having achieved nearly universal primary attendance and orchestrated dramatic gains in the number of students advancing to the secondary level, in the early 1990s the Ministry of Education and Culture shifted its attention to improving the quality of instruction provided in the schools. Decentralization became a cornerstone of that effort. Bureaucrats declared that devolving authority to the localities would improve the quality of services delivered to the public and raise the nation's international standing. All sectors of government were affected by the push for decentralization, which the World Bank labelled a 'make or break issue' for the country (Schwarz 2000: 10). A slate of policies designed to delegate authority to the provinces, districts and villages were enacted.

Education planners regarded decentralization as an important strategy for raising the quality and status of the school system. Authorities at the education ministry told me at the time that devolving authority to the localities would encourage teachers to adopt instructional practices that would enhance the quality of teaching and learning in the classroom. In addition, by embracing decentralization, the ministry could expect to garner respect from international organizations. Finally, transferring authority to the local level would lead to reconfigurations of school management structures. A small cadre of experts working in the capital would no longer oversee the entire system. Instead, teachers, parents and other community members would make important decisions about how their schools should operate. Empowering local actors to make those decisions, it was believed, would lead to a more efficient use of resources.

The first significant manifestation of this shift occurred in 1994, when the ministry introduced the Local Content Curriculum. This reform required all primary and junior secondary schools to allocate 20 per cent of instructional hours to locally designed subject matter and to tailor the curriculum to fit the unique environments of the communities they served (Bjork 2004). The schools were directed to develop locally relevant courses that would 'provide students with an understanding of aspects of their local culture, basic life skills and an introduction to income producing skills' (UNDP 1994: 6).

The adoption of two laws in 1999, Law 22/1999 on Regional Government and Law 25/1999 on the Fiscal Balance between the Central Government and the Regions, accelerated the process of decentralization. These laws granted sweeping political powers and revenue-collecting rights to districts and municipalities. In conjunction with this shift, the education ministry implemented a series of reforms that augmented the power of school-based actors. School-based management (*manajemen berbasis sekolah*) was offered as an antidote to the power of central government authorities, and as a means of improving the quality of education provided to children (Raihani 2007).[2] School committees (*komite sekolah*) composed of principals, teachers and community leaders were formed across the nation, grounded in the conviction that 'changes in curriculum and teaching have been found to be more effective if they are linked to efforts to improve school management and governance, making schools and teachers more accountable' (Weston 2008: 1).

Soon after this, in 2004, a new Competency Based Curriculum was implemented. Building on trends set in place with the introduction of

---

2 The school-based management plan adopted by the ministry had five components: management; teaching and learning processes; human resources; administration; and school councils (Jiyono et al. 2001).

the Local Content Curriculum, it gave teachers responsibility for designing syllabuses that would 'provide students with high quality, carefully designed, student-centred activities' in all subject areas (Raihani 2007: 178). Although national and provincial authorities would continue to provide support, responsibility for enacting the plans hinged on the efforts of teachers.

Considering the highly centralized, top-down nature of Indonesian government, the decision to redistribute authority to the local level represented a significant departure from previous practice. A state that had 'embodied centripetal power' (Malley 1999: 72) had indicated that it would transfer key powers to local actors and institutions. That shift had important implications for the way education would be organized and delivered in Indonesia. A system that had previously concentrated authority firmly at the top had signalled that the education ministry's monopoly over the schools would be broken. After a long history of being denied opportunities to participate in the direction of schooling, local educators would be granted unprecedented authority over the curriculum, financial matters and school practice. After decades of following orders delivered from above, they would be encouraged to use their knowledge and creativity to improve the quality of instruction in the schools. Yet it was unclear how actors in the education sector would respond to the reconfiguration of the relationship between state and school (Bjork 2003, 2005).

How would local educators respond to the expanded powers that had been offered to them? What impact would the redistribution of authority to the local level have on school policy and practice? What effects would the steady escalation in power and responsibility assigned to teachers have on the instruction provided to Indonesian children? Policy documents, field reports and published statements by ministry officials tend to emphasize the positive accomplishments flowing from the educational reforms described above. Based on such accounts one might conclude that the government's efforts to empower classroom teachers and enliven instruction have led to a fundamental restructuring of the education system. On the surface, it may appear that local actors now enjoy a degree of autonomy previously denied them, that teachers are using innovative pedagogical approaches to enliven instruction and that students are benefiting from more relevant curricula. But as the anecdote I relate at the beginning of this chapter suggests, self-reports do not always accurately capture the realities of school policy and practice.

When analysing teachers' responses to the reform initiatives, it is essential to balance government reports with first-hand observations of schools. The fieldwork I have conducted in Indonesian schools indicates that education reforms tend to stall after they leave the offices of the education ministry in Jakarta. This finding is confirmed by other scholars who have spent extensive periods of time inside the schools.[3] The mismatch between central expectations and local conditions frequently produces a state of paralysis that prevents meaningful change from occurring.

As noted above, a concerted effort has been made to shift the power to shape the curriculum to the local level. Yet my interviews with teachers, observations of learning activities and review of documents indicate that the topics of study as well as the methods used to introduce that material have changed very little over the past decade. Documents produced by the Ministry of Education and Culture consistently underscore the need to modify teachers' instructional practices to make learning more engaging. Problem solving, discussion, debate and hands-on activities are all encouraged over the transmission-oriented approaches traditionally relied on by Indonesian educators. The ministry has disseminated several manuals designed to help teachers incorporate innovative instructional techniques into their lessons. Interview and survey data I have collected suggest that instructors have absorbed this message and believe that their practice is in line with ministry expectations.

Yet examples of the type of dynamic teaching methods described in the ministry's policy documents are hard to find. Only 5 per cent of the lessons I witnessed included any type of discussion that involved students. Instead, teachers used the vast majority of class time to lecture students and to summarize the content of textbooks. In his study of junior secondary education in Indonesia, Weston (2008: 21) witnessed a similar pattern:

> While revisions of the curriculum have taken place to attempt to make it more relevant to the needs of students, little effort has been made to ensure that teachers understand these changes and are able to translate them into appropriate activities. … As a result teaching in most classrooms remains traditional, dominated by rote learning and intended changes in the curriculum have not been implemented at school level.

In his review of the implementation of the Competency Based Curriculum (CBC), Utomo (2005) also underscored the mismatch between the objectives of reform policies and their translation at the classroom level. He concluded that:

> Teachers claimed to know what CBC is, but in actual classroom implementation of CBC, these teachers were lost, returning instead to the former curriculum, which they were more comfortable teaching (Utomo 2005: v).

---

3 See, for example, Utomo (2005), Sadiman and Pudjiastuti (2006), Raihani (2007), Sumintono (2009), Young (2011) and Dall (2012).

How can we explain the resistance to change displayed by Indonesian educators? Why have they deflected opportunities to increase their power? Are they satisfied with the status quo in schools? Or do they lack the resources necessary to follow reform guidelines?

I believe that a number of factors work against plans to reform instructional practice in Indonesian schools. The first is a scarcity of resources. Lacking adequate support from the government, many schools are forced to solicit contributions of money and materials from parents. In many cases, parents cannot be depended on to provide such support. In such instances, teachers are forced to make do with limited supplies.

Another impediment to reform is inadequate pre-service and in-service training for teachers. As others have noted, the education provided to university students who are planning to become teachers is generally of low quality, focusing on theory rather than instructional practice (Weston 2008; Dall 2012). Education faculty staff rarely have experience teaching in primary or secondary schools; professors tend to rely on the instructional methods that ministry officials are now encouraging teachers to avoid. According to one survey, 93 per cent of parents and teachers believe that standards of teacher training need to be improved (Dall 2012: 109).

The in-service workshops for teachers that I have observed have also been uninspiring. Workshop leaders tend to spend the bulk of their time restating information included in the ministry's manuals, and instructing participants on how to fill out forms. I do not recall ever attending a workshop for teachers that modelled the instructional methods the ministry is currently encouraging teachers to adopt. Not surprisingly, on a survey I distributed to junior secondary school instructors, the education and professional development of teachers was identified as the area most in need of attention if the quality of instruction in Indonesian schools was to improve.

While I acknowledge that these factors create challenges for the educators who are being asked to facilitate change in the schools, I do not believe that giving schools more money or improving the quality of teacher training alone will induce fundamental reform of the education system. If education planners are serious about improving the quality of teaching and learning in Indonesian schools, they need to address the core issue interfering with their initiatives to bring about change. That issue is the culture of teaching.

The primary reason that so many reform policies have failed to meet their objectives is that they assign responsibilities to teachers that the teachers are unprepared or unwilling to accept. One common assumption of the education initiatives implemented in Indonesia over the past two decades is that teachers will take an active role in implementing new programs; eager to act as 'change agents' on their campuses, they will invest the time and energy necessary to realize reform plans. Yet, as I have detailed above, Indonesian educators have been conditioned to repress any inclination they may have to approach their work with a sense of independence. Since the formation of the public school system, teachers' duties to the state have been emphasized over their obligations to students and communities. That stress on teachers' obligations as civil servants has produced a culture of teaching anchored in obedience. Educators are rarely recognized for their instructional excellence or commitment to their craft. Instead, they derive rewards from dutifully following orders from their superiors.

Research on individuals working in large organizations suggests that employees possess multiple co-occurring identities, and that their responses to institutional pressures depend on the relative salience of those identities (Burns and Flam 1987; Kramer 1993; March 1994). According to Kramer (1993), all members of an organization share a common 'superordinate' identity. In addition, they form multiple organizational selves that correspond to job titles, work responsibilities and subgroup memberships. In Indonesia, the government ensured that teachers would treat their civil servant identity as superordinate. That hierarchy continues to guide their relationship with the education system and leads them to prioritize certain responsibilities over all others. When the 'civil servant' and 'autonomous educator' facets of identity conflict, they almost always place a higher priority on conforming to the norms that guide the activities of other government employees. They have been conditioned to pay more attention to the demands of the state than to the requirements of the school or community.

In the junior secondary schools I studied, teachers did not show up for approximately 30 per cent of the classes they were assigned to teach, and were not penalized for their absences. Yet the same individuals almost always appeared on time for the weekly flag-raising ceremony. Following the pattern that Ghazali, Hafidz and Saliwangi (1986) describe in their study of civil servants, teachers tended to carry out the tasks explicitly assigned to them, but were careful not to exceed the established standards – or to behave in any way that set them apart from their peers. In the schools I visited, the tasks that occupied teachers' time were remarkably similar to those of people working in other branches of government. Teachers, like other civil servants, did not feel compelled to fill their hours on the job with work-related tasks. For example, the instructors I observed rarely prepared lesson plans, graded assignments or met with students during their free periods.

Though the teachers I interviewed did not explicitly express feelings of powerlessness, their descriptions of their work downplayed their influence over both institutional structures and student performance. When discussing achievements and problems in their schools, educators hardly ever included themselves among the factors that determined the academic success or failure of their students. This was especially true of veteran teachers. Most instructors with extensive experience in the classroom had learned to channel their energies into activities outside school. Many had part-time jobs they took quite seriously, perhaps because the extra income they generated from those jobs depended on the time and effort they invested in their work; their government salaries, on the other hand, were primarily based on years of service and level of education. Government employees also highly valued family, church and neighbourhood-based activities. In their neighbourhoods and mosques, instructors enjoyed levels of influence that they rarely achieved in the workplace.

Western literature on educational reform would lead us to believe that educators working in public schools are eager to increase their influence. This was not the case in the Indonesian schools I visited. Not being accountable for the academic performance of their students, teachers were generally free from pressure to meet certain instructional standards. The restricted scope of the responsibilities assigned to them reduced the opportunities for them to derive substantial rewards from their work – but also minimized the demands placed on them. In addition, it freed them up to devote themselves to outside obligations and interests. Most teachers deflected opportunities to increase their power and influence, preferring instead to maintain the status quo. This conception of teaching does not mesh with the behaviours that government officials expect teachers to display.

Decades of stress on obedience and loyalty have left individuals located at the lower levels of the hierarchy unprepared to act as leaders in their workplaces. Indonesian teachers, with no history of exercising leadership in educational matters, also lack role models who display the behaviour government officials expect them to adopt. Not surprisingly, when reform initiatives create challenges or additional burdens for them, teachers respond by following the practices that provided them with security in the past. Ignoring pressure to change is the safest, least demanding course of action available to them.

As long as educators continue to view themselves primarily as civil servants, and follow the norms guiding the work of postal workers, tax collectors and the like, reforms that depend on them to assume leadership are likely to fail. Before meaningful change can take place, the culture of teaching needs to be reshaped to fit the ideals undergirding the government's vision for the education system.

3.4   INTERNATIONAL PERSPECTIVES

A number of recently published, cross-national studies of education systems underscore the critical role that teachers play in school reform. They also indicate that it is possible to raise the quality of teaching and learning, even in settings that face formidable challenges (Tucker 2011; Darling-Hammond and Lieberman 2012; Stewart 2012).

Several countries that currently appear at the top of the international league tables previously faced many of the challenges confronting Indonesia today. In many cases, the process of creating reform plans was initiated when economic and social conditions were still quite precarious. Through careful strategic planning, the governments of nations such as Japan, Singapore, Finland and Canada achieved impressive improvements in their schools. In each location, education planners studied practices in other countries and identified those that could be adapted to fit the contours of their own societies. For instance, in the 1970s education was not compulsory in Singapore and only a small percentage of the student population completed secondary school (Stewart 2011). Yet the government's sustained, step-by-step approach to education reform helped the country rise from 'third world to first'. Similarly, education planners in Finland 'worked in a logical way, while governments came and went, in small increments over the same fifty years to take an education system designed to support a small rural economy to world leadership in just five decades' (Tucker 2011: 207).

Two aspects of these success stories merit attention here. First, building on the insights they acquired from studying school systems in other countries, bureaucrats developed long-term reform plans that were implemented in a series of stages. Rather than search for quick fixes, they identified overarching goals and tailored supporting policies to match those goals. That consistency and continuous commitment to improvement gradually yielded positive results. Second, recognizing the vital role that teachers play in any fundamental reform initiative, education officials worked to enhance the abilities and autonomy of those responsible for translating their plans into action at the school level. To accomplish this, they devised multi-pronged reform strategies that targeted teacher recruitment, pre-service education, induction, in-service professional development and performance assessment. At each stage of their careers, teachers were given the support necessary to develop their knowledge base and pedagogical skills. The 'profession-wide approach to the collective improvement of practice' (Darling-Hammond and Lieberman 2012: 166) created a strong foundation for continuous improvement. Individuals working at the national level could depend on school-based actors to realize their plans for change.

The Indonesian government would be wise to follow a similar pathway to reform. As I have described above, in the years after independence, the education ministry facilitated dramatic expansion of the education system. As it shifted its focus from access to instruction, however, the ministry experienced greater difficulty in achieving its goals. Education officials placed large numbers of teachers in schools without adequate training or support. The culture of teaching that subsequently emerged lacked the professional standards and expectations found in settings such as Singapore, Finland, Japan and Canada. Instead, teachers adopted the norms of civil servants, which rewarded obedience rather than initiative.

Over the past decade, the ministry has adopted a number of policies to raise standards and levels of achievement in the schools. These initiatives are usually informed by international trends and have convincing rationales. But they also tend to assign extensive responsibilities to teachers, who are expected to assume leadership for implementing the plans developed in Jakarta. Teachers, however, often lack the skills and dedication necessary to realize those plans. For example, developing a competency-based curriculum that fits the unique needs of students in a particular learning community sounds laudable. But it is also an immense undertaking, likely to prove taxing even to instructors with extensive experience in curriculum design. Few Indonesian teachers have such a background; the institutional contexts in which they work are not likely to encourage them to dedicate themselves to the reform effort. This mismatch between reform demands and school realities has interfered with smooth policy implementation. The education policy-making process in Indonesia has not responded to this disconnect.

When the first national system of education was being established in Indonesia, political leaders focused on creating national cohesion and stability; encouraging teachers to act independently was not a priority. In succeeding years, the government continued to reward employees for their loyalty rather than for any display of initiative. Now that conditions are more stable and the Ministry of Education and Culture is attempting to raise instructional standards in the schools, the culture of teaching needs to be reshaped to fit current ministerial priorities. If teachers are to assume responsibility for improving the quality of the curriculum and instruction in the schools, they need to develop the motivation, skills and sense of collective responsibility required to realize education officials' plans for change. As Darling-Hammond and McLaughlin (1995: 598) have observed:

> Sustained changes in teachers' learning opportunities will require sustained investment in the infrastructure of reform. This means investment in the

development of institutions and environmental supports that will promote the spread of ideas and shared learning about how change can be attempted and sustained.

In the Indonesian case, building such an infrastructure will mean reshaping the individual and collective orientations of teachers. Before instructors can assume leadership in reform initiatives, they will need to view themselves as professionals who have a responsibility to expand the educational opportunities provided to their students. In other words, their superordinate identity needs to change from 'civil servant' to 'educator'. This shift could be initiated by creating a system for evaluating teachers that is based on performance in the classroom rather than adherence to the criteria applied to all civil servants, and ending the requirement for teachers to wear the same uniform donned by postal workers and tax collectors. This delinking of teachers from the civil service should be accompanied by the more demanding task of revising pre-service education and professional development so that teachers acquire the skills necessary to act as instructional leaders. Developing an infrastructure that treats teachers as professionals and gives them the support necessary to act autonomously is an essential antecedent to fundamental reform. Once this foundation has been laid, the outcomes of policy should more closely match the ministry's predictions of change.

REFERENCES

Bjork, C. (2003) 'Local responses to decentralization policy in Indonesia', *Comparative Education Review*, 47(2): 184–216.
Bjork, C. (2004) 'Decentralisation in education: institutional culture and teacher autonomy in Indonesia', *International Review of Education*, 50(3–4): 245–62.
Bjork, C. (2005) *Indonesian Education: Teachers, Schools, and Central Bureaucracy*, Routledge, New York and London.
Bowen, J. (1991) *Sumatran Politics and Poetics*, Yale University Press, New Haven.
Burns, T.R. and H. Flam (1987) *The Shaping of Social Organization*, Sage Publications, London.
Dall, A. (2012) 'A cross-national comparative study of cultural factors underpinning 15-year old students' performance in reading literacy in Finland, Sweden and Indonesia', unpublished doctoral dissertation, University of the Sunshine Coast, Sippy Downs.
Darling-Hammond, L. and A. Lieberman (2012) *Teacher Education around the World*, Routledge, London and New York.
Darling-Hammond, L., and M. McLaughlin (1995) 'Policies that support professional development in an era of reform', *Phi Delta Kappan*, 76(8): 642–5.
Djojonegoro, W. (1997) *Fifty Years' Development of Indonesian Education*, Ministry of Education and Culture, Jakarta.
Fuller, B. and P. Clarke (1994) 'Raising school effects while ignoring culture? Local conditions and the influence of classroom tools, rules, and pedagogy', *Review of Educational Research*, 64(1): 119–57.

Ghazali, A.S., W. Hafidz and B. Saliwangi (1986) *Etos Kerja Pegawai Negeri* [The Work Ethic of Civil Servants], Lembaga Ilmu Pengetahuan Indonesia (LIPI), Jakarta.

Hatley, B. (1994) 'Cultural expression', in H. Hill (ed.) *Indonesia's New Order*, University of Hawai'i Press, Honolulu, pp. 216–66.

Hill, H. (1995) 'Indonesia: from "chronic dropout" to "miracle"?', *Journal of International Development*, 7(5): 665–789.

Jiyono, J., F. Jalal, A. Syamsuddin, D. Syafruddin, R. Suparman, Ajisuksmo et al. (2001) 'Menuju desentralisasi pengelolaan pendidikan dasar' [Towards decentralized management of basic education], in F. Jalal and D. Supriadi (eds) *Reformasi Pendidikan dalam Konteks Otonomi Daerah* [Education Reform in the Context of Regional Autonomy], Adicita, Yogyakarta.

Kramer, R.M. (1993) 'Cooperation and organization identification', in J.K. Murnigham (ed.) *Social Psychology in Organizations*, Prentice Hall, Englewood Cliffs, pp. 244–68.

Mackie, J. and A. MacIntyre (1994) 'Politics', in H. Hill (ed.) *Indonesia's New Order*, University of Hawai'i Press, Honolulu, pp. 1–53.

Malley, M. (1999) 'Regions: centralization and resistance', in D. Emmerson (ed.) *Indonesia beyond Suharto*, M.E. Sharp, Armonk, pp. 71–108.

March, J. (1994) *A Primer on Decision Making*, Free Press, New York.

Raihani (2007) 'Education reforms in Indonesia in the twenty-first century', *International Education Journal*, 8(1): 172–83.

Sadiman, A. and T. Pudjiastuti (2006) *Decentralized Basic Education: Toward a Better Teaching Performance and Learning Environment*, United States Agency for International Development, Jakarta.

Schwarz, A. (2000) *A Nation in Waiting: Indonesia's Search for Stability*, Westview Press, Boulder.

Shaeffer, S. (1990) *Educational Change in Indonesia: A Case Study of Three Innovations*, International Development Research Center, Ottawa.

Stewart, V. (2011) 'Singapore: a journey to the top, step by step', in M. Tucker (ed.) *Surpassing Shanghai: An Agenda for American Education Built on the World's Leading Systems*, Harvard Education Press, Cambridge, pp. 113–39.

Stewart, V. (2012) *A World-class Education: Learning from International Models of Excellence and Innovation*, ACSD, Alexandria.

Sumintono, B. (2009) 'School-based management policy and its practices at district level in post New Order Indonesia', *Journal of Indonesian Social Sciences and Humanities*, 2: 41–67.

Tucker, M.S. (ed.) (2011) *Surpassing Shanghai: An Agenda for American Education Built on the World's Leading Systems*, Harvard Education Press, Cambridge.

UNDP (United Nations Development Programme) (1994) *The Management and Delivery of the 1994 Junior Secondary Local Content Curriculum*, UNDP, Jakarta.

Utomo, E. (2005) 'Challenges of curriculum reform in the context of decentralization: the response of teachers to a competence-based curriculum (CBC) and its implementation in schools', unpublished doctoral dissertation, University of Pittsburgh, Pittsburgh.

Weston, S. (2008) *A Study of Junior Secondary Education in Indonesia: A Review of the Implementation of Nine Years Universal Basic Education*, United States Agency for International Development, Jakarta.

World Bank (1989) 'Indonesia: basic education study', Report No. 7841-IND, World Bank, Jakarta.

Young, M.S. (2011) 'A case of the global–local dialectic: decentralization and teacher training in Banten, Indonesia', unpublished doctoral dissertation, Florida State University, Tallahassee.

4 INTEGRATING ISLAMIC SCHOOLS INTO THE INDONESIAN NATIONAL EDUCATION SYSTEM: A CASE OF ARCHITECTURE OVER IMPLEMENTATION?

Robert Kingham and Jemma Parsons

4.1 INTRODUCTION

Indonesia's education system is the fourth largest in the world. Although data on the exact number of Islamic schools (*madrasah*) in the country differ, the Ministry of Religious Affairs claimed to manage about 45,000 in 2010. More than 90 per cent of these were private schools, many of them set up by local communities or major Islamic civil society foundations in the absence of state-sponsored alternatives. Although there are important exceptions, the majority of private *madrasah* have a lower income base, fewer resources and poorer facilities than the state-funded schools, and thus deliver a significantly lower standard of education. They are disproportionately represented in remote or disadvantaged areas and generally have higher proportions of poor students and girls than their state school equivalents. Private *madrasah*, funded primarily by their communities, deliver the mandatory nine years of basic education to around 6 million students: 3.5 million in 22,000 Islamic primary schools (*madrasah ibtidayah*) and 2.5 million in 14,000 Islamic junior secondary schools (*madrasah tsanawiyah*).

Two national ministries are responsible for education: the Ministry of Education and Culture, which has overall responsibility for the public schools; and the Ministry of Religious Affairs, which operates the faith-based schools. The two systems run parallel to each other; they both teach a core curriculum of general subjects, supplemented in the case of the Islamic schools by an additional 30 per cent or so of religious education subjects. This means in practice that few Islamic schools have the capacity to teach the full curriculum of general subjects, although some cope with the additional load by teaching religious subjects in afternoon sessions outside school hours.

The duration of schooling is the same for both the public and faith-based school systems; they offer six years of primary education, three years of junior secondary education and three years of senior secondary education. However, the graduation certificates issued by unaccredited *madrasah* are not recognized as a qualification for continuing education, and *madrasah* student participation in external national examinations is not automatic. To some extent, these deficiencies have been addressed by the establishment in 2007 of a national board (BAN-S/M) providing uniform standards of accreditation for all schools.

In principle there should be significant overlap between the two systems of education, given that the Ministry of Religious Affairs is responsible for delivering religious education in *all* schools, including public schools. In practice, however, this is rarely the case. The situation was complicated further by the decentralization of responsibility for public schools, but not *madrasah*, to the district level of government in 2001. Because the Ministry of Religious Affairs was not decentralized, there is no legal basis for interaction between it and the district governments that now have core responsibility for the funding and administration of education. This is particularly problematic for private *madrasah*, which have no right of access to support or funding from the governments of the districts in which they are situated because they are registered with the Ministry of Religious Affairs. It should also be noted that the district governments are supervised by the Ministry for Home Affairs, adding an additional layer to the bureaucratic complexity of education sector administration.

This chapter proceeds as follows. Section 4.2 discusses the current legal framework and funding mechanisms aimed at achieving an integrated national education system. Section 4.3 describes how the regulatory environment is impeding the development of such a system, despite advances in school registration and accreditation procedures. Section 4.4 describes the government funding arrangements for schools, and how they discriminate against privately run *madrasah* in particular. Section 4.5 examines challenges faced by the Ministry of Religious Affairs as it attempts to compile robust data on the number and state of its schools. The final section assesses the prospects for an integrated national education system that is able to deliver equality of access to resources for *madrasah*, and equality of access to quality education for all Indonesians.

The chapter focuses on primary and junior secondary schools, because they are the institutions responsible for delivering the compulsory nine years of basic education.

4.2   AN INTEGRATED NATIONAL EDUCATION SYSTEM

The emergence of an integrated national education system over the last decade has sought to address bureaucratic dysfunction and to protect the constitutional right of equal access to basic education. Law 20/2003 on the National Education System enshrines the concept of 'compulsory basic education' under one integrated national education system. It formally introduces the concept of legal equality of private *madrasah* and state schools as *satuan pendidikan,* or 'educational units' treated equally under the law. This critical step towards educational equality reflects both the Millennium Development Goal of achieving universal basic education by 2015, and the constitutional right to free basic education.

Law 20/2003 and the Grand Design for Basic Education acknowledge the legal equality of state schools and private *madrasah,* and grant all Indonesian citizens an equal right to quality basic education without discrimination. This means that private *madrasah* are now legally eligible to receive funding under the central government's Schools Operational Assistance (Bantuan Operasi Sekolah, BOS) scheme. BOS funding is based on enrolments. The Ministry of Religious Affairs predicts enrolments based on census information on the number of school-aged children in a district and previous enrolments, and on the enrolment figures submitted by *madrasah* to its district offices early in the school year.[1] Until 2010 the ministry tended to quote a figure of about 44,000 for the number of private *madrasah* and 4,000 for the number of state *madrasah,* together serving about 6 million school-aged children. The extension of BOS funding to the pre-school level, however, has led to an explosion of new, private Islamic pre-school facilities. Although these are deemed non-formal entities (and thus not accredited in the same way as formal schools), the Directorate General of Islamic Education in the Ministry of Religious Affairs now estimates the number of *madrasah* at 58,000 or more. The reliability of the ministry's data is questionable, however, as is discussed in greater detail below.

---

1   Particularly in densely populated areas where good schools are keenly sought after, parents are likely to enrol their children in a number of schools to increase their chances of getting into the one of their choice. In such cases the early enrolment figures may not be a reliable indicator of the actual school population.

The Grand Design for Basic Education is set out in a program of four five-year strategic development plans spanning 2007–25. The first five-year plan focused on teacher education.[2] The second (2010–14) addresses accreditation, aiming for all *madrasah* to be accredited by academic year 2014/15, with a minimum of 50 per cent of them to be accredited to rank B or better (Australia Indonesia Partnership 2010: 30).[3] This is an optimistic if not idealistic aim.

Particularly for the Ministry of Religious Affairs, working to a strategic plan, and being accountable for the results, is a new concept. It should be said, however, that the integration of private *madrasah* into a uniform national education system enjoys widespread popular support, particularly from parents concerned about the paucity of funding for private *madrasah*. Integration into the system has necessitated the development of a national accreditation body to ensure uniformity and to monitor quality control. This is the single most radical departure from former practice, and it is forging alliances at all levels.

The National Accreditation Board for Schools and Madrasah (Badan Akreditasi Nasional Sekolah/Madrasah, BAN-S/M) is an independent body established as a legal entity in 2005 and operational since 2007. It is housed within the Ministry of Education and Culture. BAN-S/M and the Directorate General of Islamic Education in the Ministry of Religious Affairs signed a memorandum of understanding in July 2012 that will increase the number of visits by assessors to the ministry's schools from 2013. The ministry has agreed to pay for the cost of those visits in the targeted provinces.

As a functional entity, BAN-S/M does not have routine structural funding and is basically a voluntary board with a small secretariat. Its principal functions are to develop the instruments and procedures to assess schools, to collate data and to issue accreditation certificates. The majority of its funding comes from the provinces, with provincial-level accreditation boards providing the assessors. It should be noted that the national and provincial-level accreditation boards sometimes differ in the interpretation of ratings by assessors. Also, the instrument initially developed to rate schools on the quality of their facilities proved to be inadequate; for example, it included the ratio of toilets to students, but did not allow assessors to comment on the sanitary condition or functionality of those toilets. The failings in the quality dimension of the instrument are currently being addressed by BAN-S/M, which plans to introduce a new instrument in 2013. This will necessitate a new round of assessor training, which is a provincial, not a national, responsibility.

2 The first plan began in 2005, before the ministries of education and religious affairs redrew the Grand Design to incorporate the *madrasah*.
3 Schools are ranked A to C where A is the highest level of accreditation.

4.3   EFFICIENCY AND EFFICACY OR OTHERWISE?

Despite the benefits from streamlining two parallel systems, the effort to establish an integrated national education system has increased, not reduced, bureaucratic complexity. The integration of *madrasah* into a national education system under the management of three separate ministries – the Ministry of Education and Culture, the Ministry of Religious Affairs and the Ministry of Home Affairs – has given rise to a number of core issues that tend to impede rather than facilitate effective implementation. Not the least of these has been the suggestion that the education and religious affairs ministries intend to restrict state funding, and eligibility to issue graduation certificates, to accredited schools; accompanied by proposed new and stringent regulations relating to school registration (*izin operasional*). There is no legal basis at present for restricting funding to accredited schools, but this could change as early as 2014 depending on the government's political will and its assessment of its position in a pre-election environment.

All schools must be registered at the district level before they can function: the state schools with the district education departments and the Islamic schools with the district offices of the Ministry of Religious Affairs. Only registered schools are eligible to receive BOS funding. This has provided a big incentive for registration – and therefore participation in the national education system – even though the BOS scheme is inadequate, covering on average less than 30 per cent of a school's costs.

District education departments and the district offices of the Ministry of Religious Affairs use separate systems of numbering to identify schools. The lack of a coordinated, national identification system creates the very real possibility of duplicate registration, where a school is registered, for example, both as a public junior secondary school with the district education department and as a *madrasah tsanawiyah* with the district office of the Ministry of Religious Affairs. Also, neither system contains a mechanism for deregistration once a school ceases to exist. There are numerous reports of 'ghost' schools – where the land once occupied by a registered, BOS-recipient school has been purchased and used for other purposes, but the school bank account continues to receive its regular BOS funding injections. As long as the monitoring of schools remains inadequate, such anomalies will continue to exist.

School registration is also the basis for the allocation of funds from the Ministry of Finance to the districts for education. To receive funding, districts must submit documentation to the finance ministry annually showing how their schools have performed against a set of minimum service standards. Each school measures its achievements against the standards by conducting a focus group workshop known as the School

Self-Evaluation. The government regulation relating to this provides for self-evaluation by *madrasah* as well, but they have never participated in this activity. In part this was because the schools registered with the Ministry of Religious Affairs were not eligible for district-level funding under the decentralization framework, so had no incentive to conduct self-evaluations. From 2013, however, the ministry's accreditation unit will introduce training in School Self-Evaluation procedures to establish a baseline for the quality of *madrasah* against the eight national education standards,[4] and to encourage a greater level of cooperation with district governments.[5]

Currently, the complexity of the regulatory environment is an impediment to the integration of the Islamic school subsector into the national education system. Recall, for instance, that the national education system is managed by three ministries: the centralized Ministry of Religious Affairs and the decentralized Ministry of Education and Culture and Ministry of Home Affairs. The district offices of the decentralized ministries are responsible to the district governments, which in turn are responsible to the Ministry of Home Affairs. As noted, the district governments assemble data to verify the achievements of schools against a set of minimum service standards, but this information is submitted to the Ministry of Finance, not to the 'line' education ministry, and the districts receive their funding allocations directly from the finance (not education) ministry. The Ministry of Education and Culture sets national education policy, which is then implemented by the provincial and district education departments. These offices are accountable, however, not to the education ministry but to the Ministry of Home Affairs.

The Ministry of Religious Affairs is one of six ministries that were not decentralized, and so is not subject to the country's decentralization laws. Its provincial and district-level offices are responsible to the national ministry. Managed and funded by the centre, these offices have no horizontal linkages with the local governments in whose areas they and the schools under their control are situated. As noted previously, the ministry runs a separate system of *madrasah* registration from its district education offices, with no synchronization of data between it and the Ministry of Education and Culture. District governments do not collect data on the *madrasah* situated within their jurisdictions, and do

---

4 The eight standards focus on 'curriculum, teaching and learning processes, learning outcomes, personnel, physical facilities, management, finance, and performance assessment processes' (Australia Indonesia Partnership 2010: 4).
5 This initiative is part of the Islamic School Accreditation component of Australia's Education Partnership with Indonesia. For more details, see Australia Indonesia Partnership (2010: 30).

not allocate funding to them in their budgets. The Ministry of Religious Affairs is funded entirely from the central government budget, with public *madrasah* receiving the majority of the funding, even though private *madrasah* comprise around 90 per cent of the Islamic school sector.

This inequitable funding arrangement potentially contravenes the constitutional right of Indonesians to a basic education paid for by the government.[6] Significantly, the Constitutional Court recently recognized the legal equality of private schools/*madrasah* to receive state funding for basic education. In September 2011, the court was asked to consider the constitutionality of article 55(4) of the National Education Law (Law 20/2003), which states that private schools 'may' (not 'must') receive government funding. In light of the government's obligation under article 31(2) of the Constitution, the court held that the word 'may' was unconstitutional so far as it purported to apply to basic education provided by private schools, including *madrasah*, and thus had no legal force.

The implications of this decision are far-reaching. Although elaboration is beyond the scope of this chapter, the primary consequence is that the government has no discretion about whether or not to wholly fund basic education, even where it is provided by private schools. As matters currently stand, however, the majority of private *madrasah* still do not have reliable access to public finances other than the BOS funding administered by the Ministry of Religious Affairs. In contrast, both state and private schools registered with the Ministry of Education and Culture are eligible to receive state funding, through the education departments of district governments.

4.4   DYSFUNCTIONAL INTEGRATION

As the preceding section has demonstrated, implementation of an integrated national education system remains a work in progress, particularly from the perspective of institutional integration and equality of access to quality basic education. This is evident in Figure 4.1, which shows the constituent parts of the national education financing system.

The diagram shows clearly how *madrasah* registered with the Ministry of Religious Affairs are financially marginalized; there are no institutional linkages between them and the schools of the Ministry of Education and Culture, or between them and the funding mechanisms administered by the provincial and district levels of government. In addition, the bureaucratic complexity of the funding structure illustrates the cumbersome and dysfunctional nature of administration in a supposedly 'integrated'

---

6   Consitution of the Republic of Indonesia (1945), article 31(2).

Figure 4.1   Institutional architecture of the national education financing system

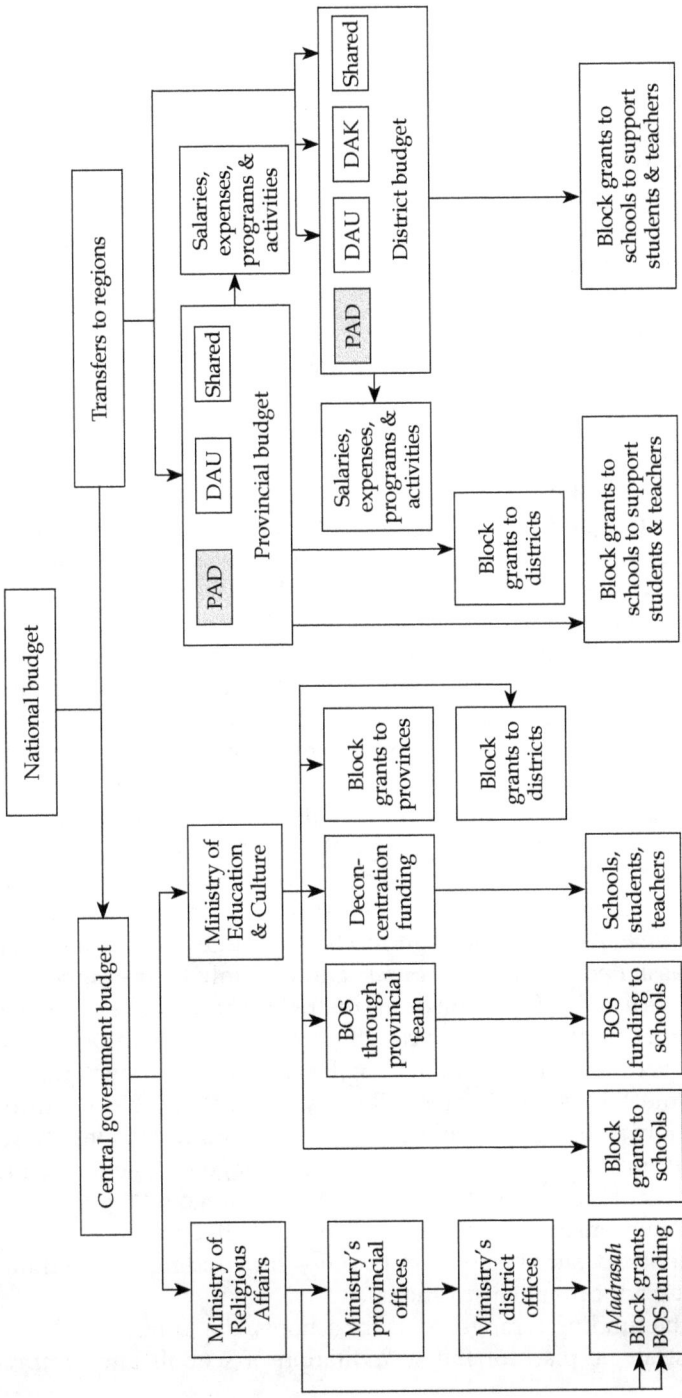

BOS = Bantuan Operasi Sekolah (Schools Operational Assistance); DAK = Dana Alokasi Khusus (Specific Purpose Fund); DAU = Dana Alokasi Umum (General Purpose Fund); PAD = Pendapatan Asli Daerah (locally derived revenue); 'Shared' = revenue (mainly from natural resources) shared between the centre and the regions.

Source: Adapted from USAID (2009: 38).

national education system. Certainly, the financial flows between the centre and the regions do not support claims of an integrated system.

The current system under which the Ministry of Religious Affairs is funded by the centre, and in turn disburses funds directly to the schools, is expected to change in 2013 when responsibility for infrastructure funding is handed to the ministry's provincial offices. In future this is likely to extend to other areas of planning and implementation as well. This anticipated devolution of administrative and financial responsibilities will significantly challenge the ministry's bureaucratic capacity. At least initially, it may impede rather than facilitate improved implementation of integrated education.

As Figure 4.1 shows, schools receive two types of funding: block grants and BOS. Which schools receive what type of funding depends on national education policy – and on data that, in the case of the Ministry of Religious Affairs, may well be unreliable. As noted earlier, the BOS division in the ministry estimates enrolment rates based on information that flows upward through the ministry's district and provincial offices. The system is renowned for its dysfunction, however. To take a concrete example, two *madrasah tsanawiyah* located 1 kilometre apart in South Jakarta submitted the required data for a 2012 BOS allocation on the same day to the same district office of the Ministry of Religious Affairs. In October 2012, ministry personnel noted that one of those schools had received its BOS allocation in April while the other had not yet received anything, and was unlikely to do so. No explanation for this discrepancy has been forthcoming. If such irregularities can occur in the nation's capital, it is likely they are rife in more remote districts in outlying islands.

The lack of administrative capacity in the Ministry of Religious Affairs can thus in itself act as a barrier to equality of access to resources for private *madrasah*, adding to the already disadvantaged status of private *madrasah*. Also, civil servant teachers recruited by the ministry are initially assigned to public *madrasah*, and can only be reassigned to private *madrasah* at the discretion of the district office should a suitable local regulation be in place (as is the case, for example, in Pasuruan).

As a conduit linking all subnational levels of government, the Ministry of Home Affairs could potentially play a significant role in improving the functioning of the national education system. It has already stated its support for regulation at the highest level of government – including the Ministry of Finance and the National Development Planning Agency (Badan Perencanaan Pembangunan Nasional, Bappenas) – for district governments to take some responsibility for funding the community, faith-based educational institutions.

Like the funding arrangements for schools, the Ministry of Religious Affairs' strategic plan for the accreditation of schools and *madrasah* is bewildering in its complexity, involving multiple levels of government, several directorates general and various other government bodies (Ministry of Religious Affairs 2011). Parliaments at all levels of government are also significant players. As elected bodies, they represent the aspirations of the community, as distinct from the executive and bureaucratic arms of government. A deficiency of the strategic plan is that there appears to be no obvious mechanism for cooperation and collaboration between the general schools and the *madrasah*. Also, the line ministries' reports tend to ignore the existence of the education boards and parliamentary education commissions that exist at all levels of government (see, for example, BAN-S/M 2009: Figure 1.2), even though they provide the very bridging mechanisms lacking in the line ministries.

4.5   DATA DISCREPANCIES: FURTHER EVIDENCE OF A LACK OF REAL INTEGRATION

Deficiencies with the data compiled by the Ministry of Religious Affairs can be seen by comparing the most recently available report on *madrasah* accreditation on the website of the Directorate General of Islamic Education, for academic year 2009/10, and the latest annual report issued by the accreditation board, BAN-S/M, dated December 2011. Both reports agree on the numbers of *madrasah ibtidayah* (22,239) and *madrasah tsanawiyah* (14,022) – making a total of 36,261 primary and junior secondary *madrasah* offering the basic nine years of education. The very fact that the numbers are the same is concerning, considering that the reports were issued 18 months (three school semesters) apart and were written at a time when the Australian Agency for International Development (AusAID) was helping to complete the construction of new *madrasah*. Also, although the source of the BAN-S/M data is clearly the Ministry of Religious Affairs, the ministry's information specifies that its figures include both public and private *madrasah*, whereas the BAN-S/M data do not differentiate (BAN-S/M 2011; Ministry of Religious Affairs 2012).

In theory, the Planning and Data Office in the Directorate General of Islamic Education should source its data from the ministry's Education Management Information System (EMIS), but according to officials no new data has been entered into it since 2006. The EMIS division claims that while it is true that the database has been off-line for some time, it is scheduled to go back online in 2013. *Madrasah* should then be able to access the EMIS site and input their data directly – as long as they are fortunate enough to have the computer literacy, computer availability and access to electricity to do so.

In the meantime, data on school registrations continue to be collected by the district offices of the Ministry of Religious Affairs. This information is then forwarded to the ministry's provincial offices, which submit it as part of their annual reports and budget submissions to the Planning and Data Office. As mentioned elsewhere in this chapter, the *madrasah* registration system itself is of dubious reliability owing to the infrequency of visits by school supervisors, and also because no system of deregistration is currently in place should a *madrasah* cease to operate.

To some extent, the introduction of the BOS scheme has increased the robustness of the ministry's data, through the requirement for schools to submit their enrolment figures in order to receive BOS funding. The Directorate General of Islamic Education projected in its budget priorities for 2012 that the BOS payments flowing to schools would fund a total of 3,152,564 *madrasah ibtidayah* students and 2,726,733 *madrasah tsanawiyah* students, that is, a total of 5,879,297 students enrolled in basic education in ministry-registered *madrasah*.[7] Interestingly, around 2.35 million of these students also received scholarship assistance of some kind from the Ministry of Religious Affairs in 2012. Whether this benefit was paid to schools or to the students themselves is unclear, however.

The most serious discrepancy between the ministry and BAN-S/M reports concerns the data on unaccredited *madrasah*. These numbers are important, because the ministry's strategic plan for 2010–14 sets the goal of having all *madrasah* providing the mandatory nine years of basic education (that is, all primary and junior secondary *madrasah*) accredited by the end of the 2014/15 school year. The ministry's report states that 4,292 primary schools (19.3 per cent of *madrasah ibtidayah*) and 3,365 junior secondary schools (24 per cent of *madrasah tsanawiyah*) were unaccredited in June 2010, making a total of 7,657 *madrasah* to be accredited by the end of 2014/15. The BAN-S/M report states, however, that 12,120 primary schools (54.5 per cent of *madrasah ibtidayah*) and 9,464 junior secondary schools (67.5 per cent of *madrasah tsanawiyah*) were unaccredited at the end of 2011, leaving a staggering total of 21,584 *madrasah* (59.5 per cent of all primary and junior secondary *madrasah*) to be accredited in order to achieve the goal in the five-year plan. Figures for 2012 are not yet available, but considering that the ministry's budget projections for 2013 cite an allocation of funds to BAN-S/M for 7,000 accreditation visits, the target is daunting.

How can such discrepancies occur? One possible explanation may be that the ministry bases its figures on data from a mix of accreditation systems – both its own system operating before the establishment of BAN-S/M as well as the current system operated by BAN-S/M. If this

---

7   See http://pendis.kemenag.go.id/index.php?a=artikel&id2=prioritas2012.

is so, then the discrepancies in the data may not be as astounding as they initially appear. Because BAN-S/M was established in 2007, its data include only the schools accredited by its assessors since then. Schools accredited by the ministry before the establishment of BAN-S/M would not require reaccreditation for five years. Thus, until 2011, a *madrasah* accredited by the ministry's accreditation body in 2006 would appear in the ministry's statistics as an accredited school, but in the BAN-S/M statistics as an unaccredited school. Although this explains much of the discrepancy, if the ministry has to drastically revise its figures in future years, when only BAN-S/M data will be valid, then the credibility of its reporting, and the basis upon which resources are allocated to the ministry and its schools, could be questioned.[8]

4.6 PROSPECTS FOR A FULLY INTEGRATED NATIONAL EDUCATION SYSTEM

Further challenges to the establishment of an integrated national education system loom in the lead-up to the third phase of the government's Grand Design for Basic Education (2015–19). These include the extension of compulsory schooling from nine to 12 years, which will involve significant investments in senior secondary schools. To help offset the costs, the government has proposed a ten-fold increase in BOS payments commencing in the 2013/14 school year. Some observers are concerned that the increased government support for independent *madrasah* may erode the schools' traditional community support base. This could be exacerbated by proposed changes to the primary school curriculum that would require schools to submit extensive documentation on their school-level curriculums as a prerequisite for accreditation, complicated by a lack of clarity on the guidelines for completing these documents. However, given that the changes would increase the emphasis on ethics and moral education (including religious studies) in the context of a thematic rather than subject-based approach, the new curriculum is more likely to reduce the subject load-related burden on Islamic schools, provide more work opportunities for religious teachers and allow the Ministry of Religious Affairs to participate more fully than it has in the past in integrated curriculum development.

Despite the government's attempts to create a robust regulatory environment for a single, integrated education system, there is limited

---

8 Of course, one could argue that the ministry should have been aware of this potential problem, considering that BAN-S/M was established well before the Ministry of Religious Affairs compiled its report.

awareness of this within the Ministry of Education and Culture, and even less at the subnational level. The socialization of regulations and of the concept of a single national education system should therefore be prioritized. The Ministry of Religious Affairs has taken the initiative thus far, but it needs the support of the Ministry of Education and Culture to extend awareness beyond the Islamic school subsector to the broader community.

An effective first step would be to rationalize the systems for identifying general schools and *madrasah*, as this would better support the sychronization of data. Having two national school/*madrasah* registration systems leads to confusion, creates the possibility of double registration and casts doubt on the reliability of data on the numbers and locations of schools.[9] Similarly, without a robust national data system that is standard across line ministries, the problems standing in the way of the development of an integrated national system will be perpetuated. In line with the memorandum of understanding signed by BAN-S/M and the Directorate General of Islamic Education in July 2012, the Ministry of Religious Affairs is in the initial stages of synchronizing its own and BAN-S/M's accreditation data in a suite of prioritized districts and provinces, with shared information at the district level feeding up through the provincial level to the centre. If successful, this will be extended to all districts and provinces. As BAN-S/M is located within the Ministry of Education and Culture, an ancillary benefit of the program is that it could facilitate greater cooperation between the two ministries.

Proposed changes to the decentralization architecture to expand the areas of authority of the provincial level of government may well assist in the move towards greater integration. The Ministry of Religious Affairs is already giving its provincial offices more funding and responsibilities in anticipation of such a move. It is not possible to predict, however, whether changes to the decentralization arrangements would give *madrasah* access to funding from district government budgets.

One of the biggest impediments to the integration of *madrasah* into the national education system is the prevailing generalization that they are uniformly substandard providers of education catering only to the poor and the overly religious. This notion is prevalent throughout the state education system, at all levels of government and among the community. More than anything else, this perception is responsible for the Ministry of Religious Affairs and the *madrasah* communities viewing themselves as the 'poor cousins' of the state system.

---

9 To complicate the situation further, different districts may use different systems of numbering for both general schools and *madrasah*, making data coordination at the provincial level extremely difficult.

The regulatory and policy environment has evolved significantly over the last decade in favour of far greater integration of state and Islamic schools. The Ministry of Education and Culture and the Ministry of Religious Affairs no longer work in silos, but are forced to jointly generate regulations and policies that apply equally to schools and *madrasah*. This is a positive milestone towards integration. Nonetheless, no structural mechanisms currently exist to encourage interministerial cooperation or to provide overarching authority and funding for the education system as a whole. Thus, comprehensive integration is still some way off. A more important question, of course, is whether policy and regulatory reforms of the type described above bring the country closer to the substantive goal of integration – that is, achieving equality of access to quality education for all Indonesian children, including equality of access to government resources for both state schools and private *madrasah*.

REFERENCES

Australia Indonesia Partnership (2010) 'Australia's education partnership with Indonesia: a contribution to the government of Indonesia's education sector support program', Australian Agency for International Development (AusAID), Canberra, October.

BAN-S/M (Badan Akreditasi Nasional Sekolah/Madrasah) (2009) *Kebijakan dan Pedoman Akreditasi Sekolah/Madrasah* [Policy and Guidelines for the Accreditation of Schools and Madrasah], BAN-S/M, Jakarta.

BAN-S/M (Badan Akreditasi Nasional Sekolah/Madrasah) (2011) Unpublished annual report delivered at a workshop in December 2011, BAN-S/M, Jakarta.

Ministry of Religious Affairs (2011) 'UPPAM: kerangka kerja strategis akreditasi madrasah' [Accreditation Program Implementation Unit: strategic plan guidelines on *madrasah* accreditation], available under Modul & Materials at www.akreditasi.madrasah.info.

Ministry of Religious Affairs (2012) 'Profil statistik pendidikan Islam: tahun pelajaran 2009/2010' [Profile of Islamic education statistics: academic year 2009/2010], Directorate General of Islamic Education, Ministry of Religious Affairs, Jakarta, available at http://pendis.kemenag.go.id/index.php?a=artikel&id2=profil0910.

USAID (United States Agency for International Development) (2009) 'Study of the legal framework for the Indonesian basic education sector', DBE 1 Special Report, second edition, prepared by RTI International for USAID/Indonesia.

5 EARLY CHILDHOOD EDUCATION AND DEVELOPMENT SERVICES IN INDONESIA

*Hafid Alatas, Sally Brinkman, Mae Chu Chang, Titie Hadiyati, Djoko Hartono, Amer Hasan, Marilou Hyson, Haeil Jung, Angela Kinnell, Menno Pradhan and Rosfita Roesli**

5.1 INTRODUCTION

Many of the factors that determine success in school stem from the period before children enter primary school. During this period the central nervous system and brain cells develop and neural pathways are established, laying the foundations for a child's future pathway through life (Irwin, Siddiqi and Hertzman 2007). Although children's later experiences can still change those pathways, developments in early childhood

* This chapter stems from a project to evaluate the impact of a government program to establish early childhood education and development services in 3,000 poor villages in Indonesia. The program was supported by a World Bank loan and a grant from the government of the Kingdom of the Netherlands. Details can be found at www.controlled-trials.com/ISRCTN76061874. Sally Brinkman, Angela Kinnell and Menno Pradhan gratefully acknowledge support from the AusAID Development Research Awards Scheme. Most of the findings reported in this chapter will appear in a book to be published by the World Bank in 2013. The findings, interpretations and conclusions expressed in this chapter are entirely those of the authors. They do not necessarily represent the views of the International Bank for Reconstruction and Development/World Bank and its affiliated organizations, or those of the Executive Directors of the World Bank or the governments they represent.

have long-lasting effects on health, behaviour and learning outcomes for years to come (Grantham-McGregor et al. 2007; Mustard 2007). Children whose early learning and development are promoted are likely to be far more engaged, productive and successful in later life (Heckman 2008).

The available statistics show big disparities in developmental outcomes for children in Indonesia both at an early age and in primary school, although there is a lack of data for children aged 0–6. Indonesia's maternal mortality rate fell from 340 to 220 deaths per 100,000 live births between 2000 and 2010, but remains far above the 2010 average of 83 for all developing countries in the East Asia and Pacific region. Similarly, the under-5 mortality rate fell from 54 to 35 deaths per 1,000 live births between 2000 and 2010, and the infant (under-1) mortality rate from 38 to 27, but both remain well above the 2010 regional averages of 24 and 20 respectively. Births attended by skilled health staff, immunization rates and rates of access to improved sanitation facilities are also below the averages for all developing countries in the East Asia and Pacific region. Moreover, an estimated 42 per cent of rural households have children whose growth is stunted, putting them at risk of long-term cognitive deficits, emotional and behavioural problems, and low school achievement.

Indonesia can pride itself on having primary school enrolment rates that are now close to 100 per cent for both boys and girls at all income levels. At higher levels of schooling, however, disparities emerge. Educational attainment profiles reveal that although almost all children from all segments of society start primary school, children from poorer households and those from rural areas are less likely to progress to higher levels of education. Only 55 per cent of children in rural areas make it to junior secondary school and less than a quarter to senior secondary school. In urban areas, in contrast, about 80 per cent of children proceed to junior secondary school and almost two-thirds enrol in senior secondary school. When the data are disaggregated further and we compare the richest and poorest quintiles in urban and rural areas, the differences are even starker (Figure 5.1).

The results of Indonesian students in standardized international tests have also been disappointing. Among the 65 countries participating in the 2009 Programme for International Student Assessment (PISA), which tests 15–16-year-old children who are still in school, Indonesia was ranked near the bottom in reading (57th), mathematics (63rd) and science (62nd) (OECD 2010). Disaggregating the data for Indonesia by wealth reveals that the subset of poorer students who have managed to stay in school until ages 15–16 perform worse than the subset of richer students (Figure 5.2).

There is a gap in knowledge about how children in Indonesia develop up to early primary school, and how services tailored for this age group

Figure 5.1   Share of 26–28-year-olds in poorest and richest 20 per cent of urban/rural households who have completed each year of schooling, 2010 (%)

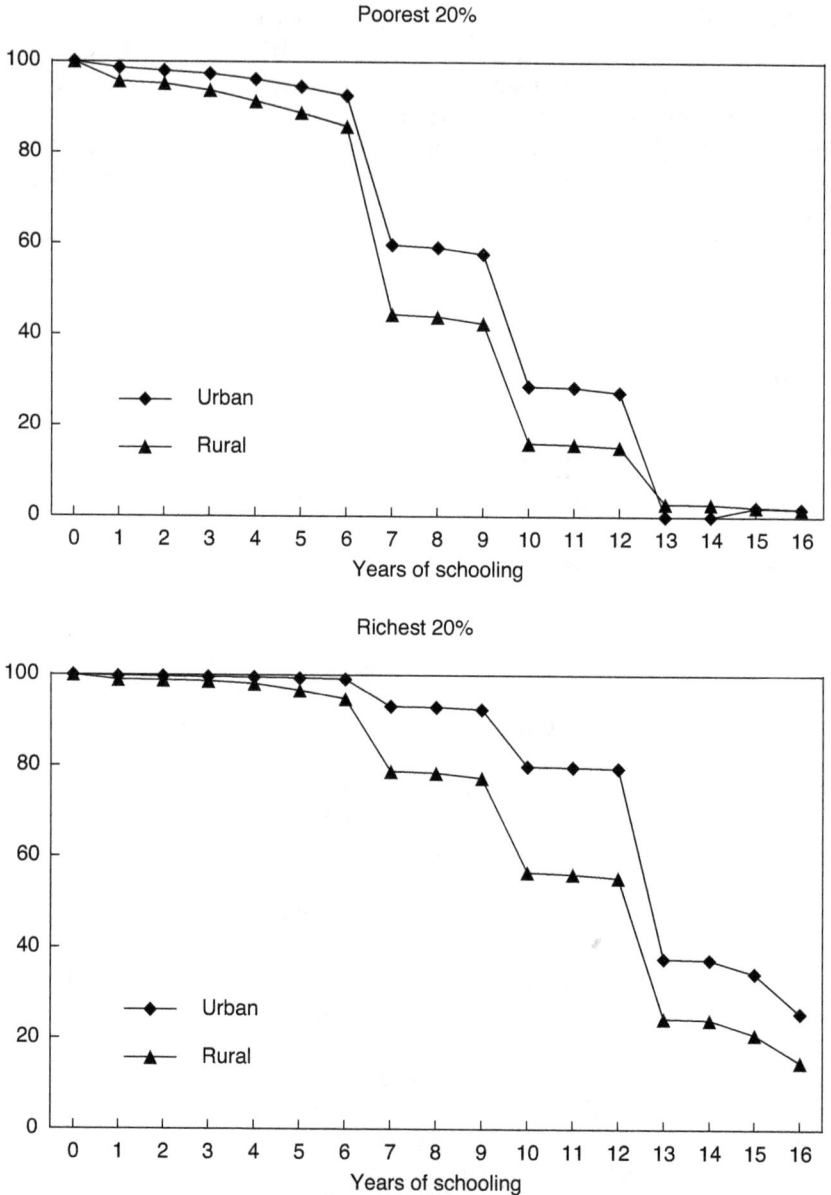

Poorest 20%

Richest 20%

Source: Authors' calculations using data from Susenas, 2010.

Figure 5.2   Performance in reading of children from poorest and richest
10 per cent of households, Programme for International Student
Assessment (PISA), 2003–09 (score)

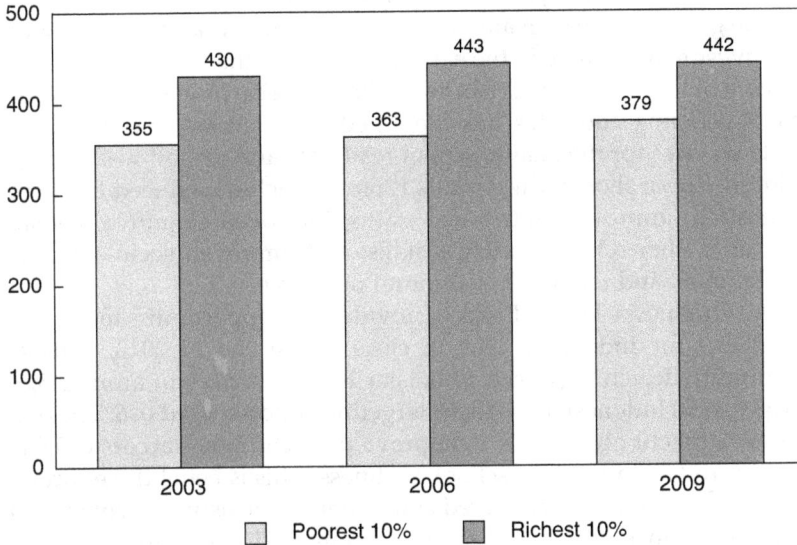

Source: Authors' calculations using data from PISA, 2003, 2006 and 2009.

affect child development. This chapter contributes to filling that gap. We
start by describing the types of early childhood education and development (ECED) services most commonly available in Indonesia and, based
on data from nationally representative household surveys, the extent of
access to those services. Next, we discuss findings from a dataset collected to evaluate the effects of the World Bank-supported Indonesia
ECED Project. Focusing on nine of the 50 districts participating in the
project, we assessed the development of around 3,000 children who were
1 year old at baseline, and 3,000 children who were 4 years old at baseline, using international tools adapted for the Indonesian context. The
dataset thus provides, for the first time, an internationally comparable
snapshot of the development of a large number of Indonesian children.

Our findings are both encouraging and worrying. We find that
although overall access to ECED services has been increasing, there are
large disparities in access between rich and poor children. Most services are provided by the private sector. In terms of child development,
we find that our sample of Indonesian children outperforms the Canadian reference population in the domain of communication and general
knowledge, but underperforms in the domains of physical health and

well-being, emotional maturity and, in particular, language and cognitive skills.

Exposure to ECED services can be a cost-effective way to change the developmental pathways of young children. Persuasive evidence exists that the greatest return on any investment in human capital comes when that investment is made in the early years, rather than waiting until children are older to intervene (Heckman 2006). Research in both developed and developing countries has identified many immediate benefits of ECED services for the health, school readiness and overall well-being of children. These short-term benefits typically include reduced frequency of stunting; improved nutritional status; improved cognitive development and other school-readiness skills; and improved socio-emotional development and reduced behavioural problems.[1]

The Indonesia ECED Project provided an opportunity to test this hypothesis for Indonesia. Due to close at the end of 2013, it uses a community-driven approach to bolster ECED services in around 3,000 villages in 50 Indonesian districts, targeting children aged 0–6. The overall development objective is to improve poor children's access to ECED services and enhance their school readiness. This is being done through a series of sequentially delivered components, consisting of community facilitation, block grants and teacher training. The purpose of community facilitation is to sensitize communities to the importance and benefits of ECED, and to teach them how to submit proposals to obtain and use project funds (provided as block grants). The villages receive block grants (of $9,000 over three years per centre) with which to set up and operate ECED services. Most villages have established two centres, and have used the funds either to upgrade an existing centre for pre-school-aged children or to establish a new one. The project also provides 200 hours of teacher training to two staff members per ECED centre.

The results presented in this chapter represent the very early effects of the Indonesia ECED Project, based on an evaluation conducted six to nine months after communities had received block grants. We found substantial enrolment impacts, indicating that the program had increased the probability of enrolment in a playgroup by 10–25 percentage points (see section 5.4 for details). We found no statistically significant effects on children's developmental outcomes in most domains, although all estimates were positively signed. However, for the most vulnerable groups of children, we did find significant positive effects in the communication and general knowledge, social competence, and language and cognitive

---

1   See, for example, various World Bank reports (Alderman and King 2006; Naudeau et al. 2010; Alderman 2011), Save the Children (2012) and the meta-analysis of data from 37 countries by Nores and Barnett (2010).

skills domains, and in executive function skills. These early signs of success give us hope that we will be able to find more substantial effects in the final round of the impact evaluation survey, planned for early 2013.

The chapter proceeds as follows. Section 5.2 provides an overview of ECED service provision in Indonesia, and of the government's ECED policies. Section 5.3 documents child development outcomes as observed through our surveys. It also discusses the sampling method, introduces the measures used to assess child development, describes how we determined the validity of those measures and presents the patterns we found. Section 5.4 highlights some of the early results of the impact evaluation of the Indonesia ECED Project, and section 5.5 brings together our conclusions to date.

5.2   ECED SERVICE PROVISION AND POLICIES IN INDONESIA

ECED services

The Ministry of Education and Culture, the Ministry of Religious Affairs, the Ministry of Home Affairs and the National Family Planning Coordination Agency (Badan Koordinasi Keluarga Berencana Nasional, BKKBN) all provide some form of ECED services. Between them, they offer at least eight different types of services emphasizing different aspects of children's development, and with different ways of involving families (Table 5.1). Integrated health service units (*posyandu*), for example, are available for families in the community to bring their young children to be weighed and measured, and for mothers to receive information about health, nutrition and child development. Staffed by volunteers from the community, they are usually opened once a month. In contrast, playgroups (KB) and kindergartens (TK) are more focused on education, with the former emphasizing learning through play and the latter often (but not always) adopting a more academic approach to learning. Both *posyandu* and toddler family groups (BKB) feature a high degree of family involvement. They are places where mothers and other caregivers can meet at least monthly to attend parenting classes. Playgroups and kindergartens may have parent volunteers or hold occasional parent–teacher meetings, but the core of their services is directed towards the children.

As seen in Table 5.1, Indonesia has historically considered these services as falling into two categories, the formal system and the non-formal system, until recently administered by different directorates in the Ministry of Education and Culture. Data from the Village Potential (Potensi Desa, Podes) surveys show that around 95 per cent of kindergartens in the formal sector are operated by the private sector, a figure that has hardly changed over the last decade.

Table 5.1   Types of ECED services by ministry

Type of service	Ministry of Education & Culture	Ministry of Religious Affairs	Ministry of Home Affairs with Ministry of Health staff	National Family Planning Coordination Agency
Formal	Kindergartens (*taman kanak-kanak*, TK)	Islamic kindergartens (*raudhotul atfal*, RA)		
Non-formal	Playgroups (*kelompok bermain*, KB)	Islamic kindergartens (*taman pendidikan quran*, TPQ)	Integrated health service units (*posyandu*)	Toddler family groups (*bina keluarga balita*, BKB)
	ECED posts (*pos perkembangan anak usia dini*, Pos PAUD)			
	Childcare centres (*taman penitipan anak*, TPA)			
	Other early childhood units (*satuan PAUD sejenis*, SPS)			

Source: Authors.

Although each type of ECED service is intended to cater to a specific age group (Figure 5.3), in practice these age groupings are not always adhered to. For example, children aged 4–6 would be expected to be in kindergarten (TK/RA), but because of local conditions, service availability and family preferences, some 4–5-year-olds may still be attending playgroup (KB) and some 6-year-olds may have already started the first grade of primary school.

Not all ECED services are equally intensive. Childcare centres (TPA) are generally open from 8 am to 4 pm to care for the children of full-time working parents. Kindergartens (TK), playgroups (KB) and ECED posts (Pos PAUD) typically operate from 8 am to 11 am, while Islamic kindergartens (TPQ) usually open from 2 pm to 4 pm. Thus, many children who have attended another ECED centre in the morning are able to attend an Islamic kindergarten in the afternoon. Most services are available daily (five to six times per week), although playgroups generally meet only three days a week. Toddler family groups (BKB) meet less frequently, with mothers typically attending one session a month.

Figure 5.3   Provision of ECED services by intended age group

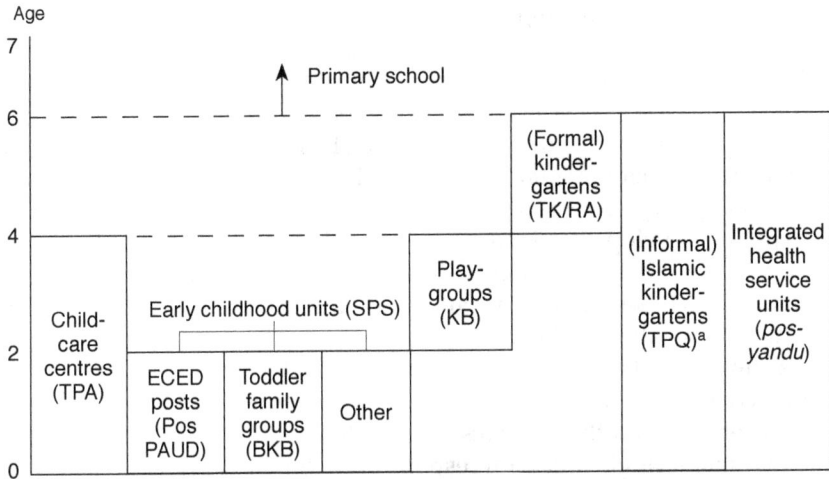

BKB = *bina keluarga balita*; KB = *kelompok bermain*; Pos PAUD = *pos perkembangan anak usia dini*; RA = *raudhotul atfal*; SPS = *satuan PAUD sejenis*; TK = *taman kanak-kanak*; TPA = *taman penitipan anak*; TPQ = *taman pendidikan quran*.
a   Also included in SPS.

Source: Authors.

The government has established national standards for ECED services, including a series of regulations on aspects such as class size. The regulations vary depending on whether the service is in the formal or non-formal category. In formal kindergartens, for instance, they stipulate that there should be one teacher for every 20 students (a teacher–child ratio of 1:20), whereas in non-formal institutions such as playgroups, the teacher–child ratio ranges from 1:4 for children aged 0–1 to 1:15 for 5-6-year-olds. In reality, however, the ratios may vary locally depending on the availability of teachers and the demand for services.

ECED policies

To improve the prospects of poor children, and influenced by the international evidence on the value of ECED, for at least a decade the Indonesian government has been implementing policies and programs that prioritize the early years of a child's life. The first critical step was taken in 2001, when a new directorate dedicated to early childhood was established within the Ministry of Education and Culture. Its early advocacy within and beyond the government influenced policy development, increased resources for community ECED services and created strategies to raise Indonesians' awareness about the importance of the first few years of life.[2]

The second critical step was taken when early childhood education was included in two key policy documents: Law 20/2003 on the National Education System, and the Ministry of Education and Culture's medium-term strategic plan (*rencana strategis*) for 2004–09.

Recognizing the need to consider ECED services holistically, across sectors and developmental domains, in 2008 the government issued an ambitious policy strategy and accompanying guidelines for the ECED sector. The development in 2009 of national standards for ECED by the Board of National Education Standards (Badan Standar Nasional Pendidikan, BSNP) situated early childhood education as the first tier in the country's education system.

A lingering barrier to coordinated ECED service provision was removed in 2010 when two directorates – one responsible for formal ECED services and the other responsible for non-formal services – were merged into a single unit with responsibility for all ECED activities.

Finally, the initiation of the first-ever ECED census in 2011 has begun to provide researchers and policy makers with essential data that will continue to inform ECED decision making in the future.

Access to ECED services

The National Socio-Economic Survey (Survei Sosio-Ekonomi Nasional, Susenas) collects data on enrolments in ECED services. The data show a steady increase in enrolments but continuing disparities between children from poorer and better-off households. In 2010, 68 per cent of children aged 4–6 from the richest 20 per cent of households were enrolled in some type of ECED service, compared with just 36 per cent for children from the poorest quintile (Figure 5.4).

5.3   ECED IN POOR AREAS OF RURAL INDONESIA

This section discusses the results of two surveys conducted to evaluate the initial impact of the Indonesia ECED Project. The broader project targets 738,000 children in around 3,000 poor villages in 50 Indonesian

---

2   The effectiveness of the directorate in attracting international support can be seen, for example, in the decision of the United Nations Children's Fund (UNICEF) to support the establishment of integrated health service clinics for mothers and children (*taman posyandu*) as part of its Smart Toddler (Balita Cerdas) program.

Figure 5.4   *Enrolments in ECED services of children from poorest and richest*
20 per cent of households, 2004–10 (%)

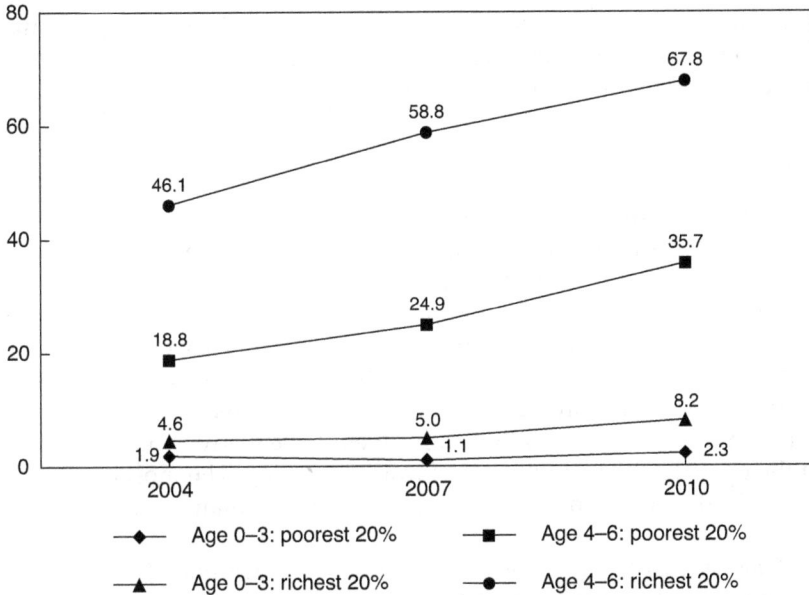

Source: Authors' calculations using data from Susenas, 2004, 2007 and 2010.

districts. We selected nine of these districts for the evaluation, namely Sarolangun in the province of Jambi; North Bengkulu (Bengkulu); East Lampung (Lampung); Majalengka (West Java); Ketapang (West Kalimantan); Kulon Progo (Yogyakarta); Central Lombok (West Nusa Tenggara); Sidenreng Rappang (South Sulawesi); and Rembang (Central Java). Within these nine districts, 217 villages were selected at random from all villages included in the project. In addition, we selected a control group of 93 villages with similar characteristics to project villages in the same districts, based on the recommendations of local administrators.

Within each village, 10 children aged 1 and another 10 aged 4 were randomly sampled between March and June 2009 to provide baseline results. Thus, in total, the sample consisted of about 3,000 children who were 1 year old at baseline, and 3,000 who were 4 years old at baseline. These children were next assessed in the midline survey that took place from July to August 2010. Thus, there was a gap of about 14 months between the baseline and midline surveys.

Because the main purpose of the evaluation was to assess the impact of the provision of additional ECED services in poorer districts, we did not attempt to make the households in our sample representative of the

Indonesian population as a whole. However, a comparison of households in the sample and those in the rural sample of the nationally representative Susenas household survey reveals that they have very similar characteristics, across all income quintiles (Figure 5.5). This suggests that the living conditions of children in the ECED sample are similar to those of children living in rural areas of Indonesia.

Domains of child development

Table 5.2 lists the six developmental domains on which we assessed children, and the seven instruments we used to do so. These domains are used worldwide to characterize aspects of child development and to define the outcomes that Indonesia and other countries aim for in providing ECED services. Each is important for children's overall well-being and school readiness, and each depends on the intersection of positive, or at times negative, influences. Progress in all domains is necessary for children to develop normally and for them to be ready to make the most of the opportunities provided by formal schooling. The most commonly recognized components of each developmental domain are as follows.

- *Physical well-being and motor development:* development of the brain and central nervous system; learning to stand, walk and run, and to use one's hands and fingers in a skilled way (Shonkoff and Phillips 2000; Mustard 2002; Gabbard 2008).
- *Social and emotional development:* learning to cooperate, to make friends and to be a friend (Dunn 2004; Zins et al. 2004); developing secure relationships; understanding other people's feelings; understanding and expressing one's own feelings (Raver 2002; Hyson 2004).
- *Language and cognitive development:* reasoning, thinking and problem solving (Goswami 2010).
- *Language skills:* beginning to connect letters, sounds and words; beginning to write (Neuman and Dickinson 2002); becoming interested in books, mathematics and numbers; developing a good memory.
- *Communication skills and general knowledge:* speaking, listening and understanding (Hoff and Shatz 2007); having an understanding of everyday places, people and events, and a basic knowledge of mathematics and science (NEGP 1995).
- *Growth and nutrition:* growth of the body.

To assess the development of children in these domains, we made use of the seven instruments listed in the first column of Table 5.2. In the remainder of this section we discuss these instruments in more detail, and the results we found.

Figure 5.5   *Characteristics of rural households and ECED sample households by income quintile (%)*

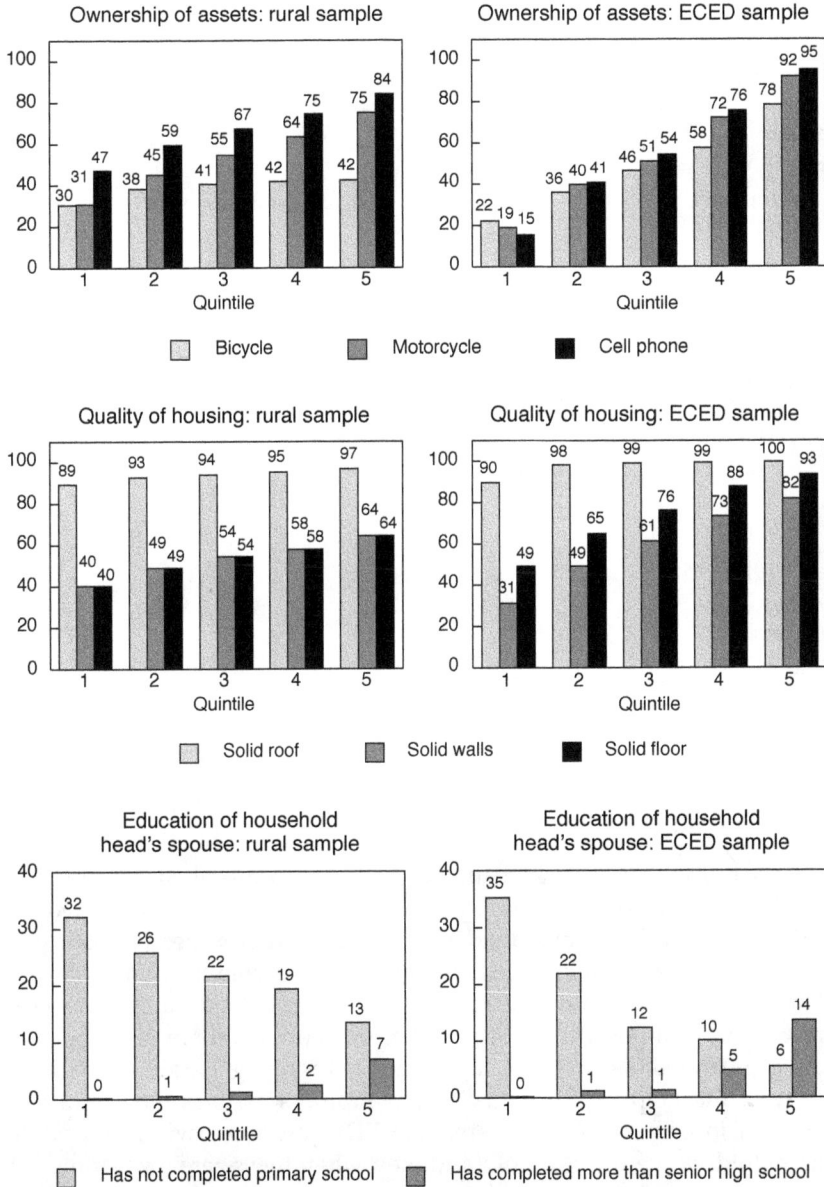

1 = poorest quintile; 5 = richest quintile.

Source: Rural sample: Susenas, 2010; ECED sample: baseline survey evaluating the impact of the Indonesia ECED Project, 2009.

Table 5.2   Child development instruments and the developmental domains to which they are related

Instrument	Physical	Social & emotional	Cogni-tive	Lan-guage	Commu-nication	Growth & nutrition
Height & weight measurements	✓					✓
Early Development Instrument (EDI)	✓	✓	✓	✓	✓	
Strengths & Difficulties Questionnaire (SDQ)		✓				
Dimensional Change Card Sort (DCCS) task			✓			
Child ability tasks, & mother-rated child skills	✓	✓	✓	✓		
Drawing tasks			✓			
Receptive & expressive language questions				✓	✓	

Source: Authors.

Early Development Instrument (EDI)

The Early Development Instrument (EDI) is a comprehensive measure of school readiness that is widely used internationally (Janus and Offord 2007). First developed by Canadian researchers, it provides a holistic picture of how well children are developing by the time they enter school. It assesses school readiness across five developmental domains: physical health and well-being; social competence; emotional maturity; language and cognitive skills; and communication skills and general knowledge.

With the help of the interviewers, mothers of the older cohort of children in our sample answered the EDI questions twice, first when their children were 4 years old and then when they were 5 years old.[3] A

---

3 The EDI is not suitable for use with very young children, so could not be used to assess the skills of the 1–2-year-olds in our sample.

Table 5.3   Mean scores of children aged 4–5 on Early Development Instrument (EDI), 2009–10 (%)[a]

Domain	Age 4	Age 5
Physical health & well-being	7.74 (1.11)	8.88 (1.02)
Social competence	7.71 (1.45)	8.31 (1.33)
Emotional maturity	6.57 (1.53)	6.97 (1.49)
Language & cognitive skills	3.14 (2.05)	5.71 (2.67)
Communication skills & general knowledge	9.58 (1.24)	9.66 (1.04)
No. of children	3,250–53	3,392–93

a   The maximum attainable score is 10. Standard deviations are in parentheses.
Source: Baseline and midline surveys evaluating the impact of the Indonesia ECED Project, 2009–10.

score, ranging from 1 to 10, was calculated for each EDI domain. Table 5.3 shows children's scores in each domain at age 4 (baseline, 2009) and at age 5 (midline, 2010). As expected, children have somewhat higher scores at age 5, as they would typically become more knowledgeable and skilled in most areas as they grow older, even without formal instruction.

The children in our sample score worst in the language and cognitive skills domain. The skills in this domain include the more formal elements of language development and skills such as being able to read a simple sentence or count to 20, having an interest in learning more about reading and maths, and aspects of cognitive problem solving. Although these skills are considered important elements of school readiness internationally, they are not a strength of the children in our sample, at least as reported by their caregivers.

On the other hand, the children score highly on everyday communication and general knowledge. These skills are more related to children's ability to use words to ask for what they need, in ways that others in the community would understand.

Compared with Canadian norms, a high proportion of children in the Indonesian sample are classified as 'developmentally vulnerable' on one or more domains of the EDI. Children are deemed vulnerable on a particular domain if they fall below the cut-off point for the lowest decile of the Canadian reference population on that domain (10 per cent of the

Table 5.4   Share of children aged 4–5 deemed developmentally vulnerable based on their Early Development Instrument (EDI) scores, 2009–10 (%)[a]

Domain	Age 4	Age 5
Physical health & well-being	26.3	5.6
Social competence	9.0	4.4
Emotional maturity	35.8	26.4
Language & cognitive skills	88.0	47.5
Communication skills & general knowledge	1.1	0.4
Vulnerable on one or more domains	93.2	60.9
No. of children	3,253	3,393

a   The definition of developmental vulnerability is based on Canadian norms; see text for an explanation.

Source: Baseline and midline surveys evaluating the impact of the Indonesia ECED Project, 2009–10.

Canadian children are therefore vulnerable by definition).[4] The proportion of children in each domain who scored low enough to be considered developmentally vulnerable is shown in Table 5.4.

The pattern of results shown in Table 5.4 is similar to that observed in Table 5.3. We see that, in each domain, the level of vulnerability has fallen and scores have increased by age 5. These improvements do not necessarily reflect the effect of policy-related interventions, but rather the fact that children naturally improve as they grow older. Nevertheless, based on both their scores and the proportions considered developmentally vulnerable, children appear to be doing especially poorly in two of the five domains: emotional maturity, and language and cognitive skills.

In the language and cognitive skills domain, even at age 5 almost half the sample scores below the cut-off point for developmental vulnerability, compared with about 10 per cent in both Canada and Australia. Children in other middle-income and developing countries, however, show a range of results on this domain, from 10 per cent through to 60 per cent (Janus et al. 2007; Brinkman 2009; CCCH and Telethon Institute 2009).

4   The measures used in Indonesia and Canada are not strictly comparable. The Canadian population is assessed on a version of the EDI that has 104 questions, whereas the Indonesian version has only 47 questions. Also, in Canada the EDI is completed by teachers, whereas in Indonesia caregivers provide answers to the questions.

Table 5.5   *Mean scores of children aged 4–5 on Strengths and Difficulties*
Questionnaire (SDQ), 2009–10[a]

Category	Age 4	Age 5
Emotional symptoms	3.70	3.55
	(2.04)	(2.02)
Conduct problems	3.48	3.41
	(1.90)	(1.98)
Hyperactivity/inattention	5.04	4.61
	(1.31)	(1.33)
Peer relationship problems	2.60	2.34
	(1.52)	(1.53)
Pro-social behaviour (reversed)	3.61	3.36
	(1.90)	(1.90)
Total score	**14.81**	**13.90**
	(4.52)	(4.55)
No. of children	3,243–53	3,372–93

a   The maximum score for each scale is 10. Standard deviations are in parentheses.
Source: Baseline and midline surveys evaluating the impact of the Indonesia ECED Project, 2009–10.

On the positive side, we see very low vulnerability (very few children scoring below the Canadian cut-off point) in the domains of communication skills and general knowledge, social competence and (at age 5) physical health and well-being. In other words, the children in our sample appear to be doing well in the domains of school readiness that emphasize aspects of verbal communication, interaction with peers and adults and (at age 5) physical health.

Strengths and Difficulties Questionnaire (SDQ)

To be considered ready for school, children need not only cognitive or academic skills, but also social and emotional skills (Raver 2002). Like the EDI and other, broader measures of development, the Strengths and Difficulties Questionnaire (SDQ) provides in-depth information on children's social and emotional development (Goodman 1997). The SDQ has been translated into 40 languages and is used in many countries.

For this measure, mothers were asked about both the behavioural and emotional problems and the pro-social assets of their children, first when the children were aged 4 and then again a year later. Table 5.5 shows the average SDQ scores of children as rated by mothers on each of the five scales. Typically, scores for the first four scales are coded such that a higher score represents more difficulties and therefore a worse outcome, while pro-social behaviour is coded such that a higher score represents fewer difficulties and therefore a more positive outcome.[5] For ease of readers' interpretation, however, in this case all scales have been coded with an identical metric, such that a higher score means more difficulties across all scales.

It is encouraging that on average the children in the sample score medium to low in every category (the maximum score on each scale being 10). The average scores are moderate to good, and certainly not high enough to cause concern, although individual children may still have significant problems in any area. The children's scores are some-what better at age 5 than at age 4; that is, their mothers said they had fewer difficulties with behaviour and emotions in 2010 than a year ear-lier. This is what one would expect as children mature, in part because of further development of their executive function skills.

Dimensional Change Card Sort (DCCS) task

The Dimensional Change Card Sort (DCCS) task uses a card-sorting game to assess the executive function skills of children aged 3–7 (Frye, Zelazo and Palfai 1995; Zelazo 2006). Children are shown a series of cards that usually display a picture of either a rabbit or a boat, although we used a cat and a motorcycle instead, for greater applicability in the Indonesian context. The images are either red or blue in colour, and some cards have a border while others do not.

In stage 1, children are asked to sort the cards by either the colour or the shape of the image. After successfully sorting the cards on this dimension, children are then asked to sort the cards on the other dimen-sion – that is, by shape if they first sorted by colour, and by colour if they first sorted by shape. In the more complex second stage of the game, cards with a border should be sorted by colour, and those without a bor-der should be sorted by shape. From extensive use of this measure in other countries, we know that 3-year-old children are usually unable to complete stage 1 of the task, but the majority of 4–5-year-olds can com-plete it successfully. International research finds that most 4-year-olds and about half of 5-year-old children are not successful at the more chal-lenging stage 2 (Zelazo 2006).

Table 5.6 shows that, at least for stage 1, the children in our sample are at roughly the same stage of development of executive function skills as children in other countries. They face more difficulty than the reference

---

5   See http://www.sdqinfo.com for more details on SDQ scoring.

Table 5.6 Performance of children aged 4–5 on Dimensional Change Card Sort (DCCS) task, 2009–10 (%)

Category	Age 4	Age 5
Sorting by colour & shape		
Failed to complete stage 1	34.82	11.95
Completed stage 1	49.14	66.48
Sorting by colour, shape & border: completed stage 2	16.04	21.57
No. of children	2,800	3,222

Source: Baseline and midline surveys evaluating the impact of the Indonesia ECED Project, 2009–10.

group, however, in completing the more challenging stage 2 at age 5. We observe an improvement in executive function between ages 4 and 5, evident in the higher percentage of 5-year-olds who can successfully complete stage 1 of the DCCS task.

Child ability tasks

In addition to asking mothers about various aspects of their children's development using the EDI and the SDQ, interviewers asked the children to demonstrate some skills directly. These skills covered much of the same developmental terrain as the EDI: physical skills (divided here into gross motor skills and fine motor skills), language skills, cognitive skills and socio-emotional skills. Interviewers tested children on a number of tasks within each category, awarding one point for each successfully completed task (Table 5.7).

The interviewer began by asking the child to perform the easiest in a group of tasks. For example, to test the gross motor skills of a 1-year-old, the interviewer first positioned the child on a table and observed whether the child could support him or herself with some assistance. For 4-year-olds, the test of gross motor skills began by assessing whether the child was able to walk upstairs using each foot alternately and without holding the handrail. The tasks were made progressively more difficult until the child reached the limit of his or her ability to perform the tasks. If the child would not perform the task for the interviewer, the mother was asked if the child could usually complete that task.

As is clear from the examples of gross motor skills, the tasks were very different for the 1–2-year-old cohort and the 4–5-year-old cohort; and not

Table 5.7   Mean scores of children aged 1–5 on child ability tasks, 2009–10[a]

Category	Cohort aged 1–2			Cohort aged 4–5		
	Maxi-mum possible score	Mean score		Maxi-mum possible score	Mean score	
		Age 1	Age 2		Age 4	Age 5
Gross motor skills	20	13.71 (4.59)	18.00 (1.56)	5	4.90 (0.41)	4.96 (0.22)
Fine motor skills	12	6.10 (2.32)	10.00 (1.50)	2	1.91 (0.30)	1.96 (0.20)
Language skills	5	2.95 (1.46)	4.75 (.52)	26[b]	13.49 (4.32)	21.05 (4.91)
Cognitive skills	8	4.43 (1.52)	7.00 (1.21)	–	–	–
Socio-emotional skills	2	1.63 (0.54)	1.45 (0.50)	–	–	–
No. of children		2,851– 3,107	2,539– 3,185		3,008– 239	3,382– 93

a   One point was awarded for each successfully completed task. Standard deviations are in parentheses.
b   In 2009, 4-year-olds were asked to name as many body parts as they could. The total score for language skills for 4-year-olds can therefore exceed 26 in the 2009 data.
Source: Baseline and midline surveys evaluating the impact of the Indonesia ECED Project, 2009–10.

all of the same categories of development were assessed. Between 2009 and 2010, both the younger and older children improved in most of the skill areas in which they were assessed.

Mothers' assessments of children's skills

Because the EDI and SDQ are not designed for use with very young children, for the 1–2-year-olds we also relied on mothers' assessments of their children's cognitive, socio-emotional, receptive language and gross motor skills. The questions covering cognitive skills included asking about the child's reaction to sour, bitter and salty foods, and his or her ability to intentionally make a sound with a toy such as a rattle. The questions about socio-emotional skills included asking about the child's ability to take turns and whether the child looked happy when carried by someone he or she knew. The receptive language questions asked

Table 5.8   *Mean scores of children aged 1–2 on child ability tasks as rated by mothers, 2009–10[a]*

Category	Maximum possible score	Mean score	
		Age 1	Age 2
Cognitive skills	6	5.48 (0.72)	5.95 (0.21)
Socio-emotional skills	6	4.45 (1.00)	4.85 (0.96)
Receptive language skills	5	4.54 (0.77)	4.80 (0.44)
Gross motor skills	3	2.53 (0.53)	2.94 (0.25)
No. of children[b]		73–3,079	454–3,175

a   One point was awarded for each skill that a child had acquired. Standard deviations are in parentheses.

b   Only a small number of children were assessed in some categories. For both cohorts, the lowest number of responses was for gross motor skills, possibly because interviewers and mothers deemed those questions redundant after watching the children demonstrate the same skills during the assessment of child ability tasks.

Source: Baseline and midline surveys evaluating the impact of the Indonesia ECED Project, 2009–10.

whether the child stopped crying when he or she heard soothing music or familiar voices, and about the child's ability to imitate sounds. The questions on gross motor skills covered whether the child was able to change from a sitting position to a crawling position, whether he or she could walk unassisted (with the occasional fall) and whether the child had well-coordinated body movements.

The descriptive statistics for mother-rated child skills show that the children in the younger cohort generally already possess most of these skills (Table 5.8). Although there is a small improvement in all skill sets as children grow older, it is striking how well all children are reported as doing – suggesting that mothers may be biased and may tend to over-report their children's abilities.

Drawing tasks

Another way of directly assessing the children's cognitive abilities was to invite them to draw two pictures: one of a human being and one of a house. Children were not told which parts of the person or house they should draw. Using a scoring system based on the Goodenough-

Table 5.9   Mean scores of children aged 4–5 on drawing tasks, 2009–10[a]

Category	Age 4	Age 5
Drawing of a person	5.17	10.70
	(5.57)	(6.12)
Drawing of a house	2.10	7.82
	(3.46)	(6.09)
No. of children	2,770–93	3,384–5

a   One point was awarded for each element included in a child's drawing. Standard deviations are in parentheses.

Source: Baseline and midline surveys evaluating the impact of the Indonesia ECED Project, 2009–10.

Harris Draw-a-Man Test (Goodenough 1954), we scored the children's drawings according to how many different body parts or house parts were included in each drawing. The more elaborate or complex a child's drawing was, the higher the score and the more advanced the child's conceptual thinking and ability to represent those concepts in a drawing were thought to be.

We originally asked both younger and older children to do the drawing task, but it quickly became clear that it was not suitable for 1–2-year-olds, some of whom could barely hold a pencil. We therefore report the results only for the older children (Table 5.9). At age 4, the children include relatively few elements in their drawings, especially in the case of the house. By age 5, the children typically include many more elements, suggesting advances in cognitive development. It is important to notice, however, that the standard deviations are very large, indicating a wide range in the ability of the children to accomplish this task.

Receptive and expressive language

Because the development of language and communication skills is so important in the early years, and such an important predictor of school readiness, we used a number of different measures to assess children's competence in this area, including parts of the EDI, mothers' reports of children's development and other tasks administered to children in their own homes.

We asked children in the younger cohort a series of questions to assess both their expressive language skills (ability to use words, say the names of things) and their receptive language skills (ability to understand what is said by others). To test their ability to use expressive language, the

Table 5.10   Share of children aged 1–2 correctly answering questions testing receptive and expressive language skills (%)

Category	Age 1	Age 2
Receptive language	37.01	85.33
Expressive language	39.73	100.00
No. of children	2,635–45	2,544–3,169

Source: Baseline and midline surveys evaluating the impact of the Indonesia ECED Project, 2009–10.

assessors showed the children a selection of items and asked them to name four of them. The items were a bunch of bananas, a chair, some goldfish, a spoon, a television, a chicken, a cat and a motorbike. To test their ability to use receptive language, the assessors named various body parts (such as a nose) and asked the children to point to those body parts on their own bodies. Each question was scored according to whether or not the child was able to answer correctly.

As seen in Table 5.10, at age 1 less than 40 per cent of the children are able to answer all receptive and expressive language questions correctly. As is the case with most other measures, children perform better at age 2 than at age 1: all 2-year-olds successfully answer the expressive language questions and around 85 per cent correctly answer the receptive language questions.

5.4   EARLY IMPACTS OF THE ECED PROJECT

In this section, we focus on the impact of the Indonesia ECED Project on enrolments and identify some broad trends evident from the midline survey conducted in 2010.

Enrolments

We begin by discussing the effect of the project on enrolments. If the program expanded access, we would expect this to have had a positive effect on the probability that a child enrols in an ECED centre.

We find that the program has had a clear positive effect on enrolments, with the impact varying by age. For the younger cohort, the provision of project services increases enrolments by 12 percentage points for children aged 1, and by 19 percentage points for children aged 2. For the older age group, the pattern is reversed: the provision of project services increases enrolments by 26 percentage points when children are aged 4, but by only 10 percentage points when children are aged 5. We believe this is because many children aged 5 have already started kindergarten (TK) or primary school.

The younger cohort of children

When we compare children in villages that had received project services for six months with children in villages that had not yet received those services, we find evidence of a negative effect of the intervention on socio-emotional skills (as assessed by child ability tasks) among the younger cohort of children (those aged 1 when we first observed them). There are reasons to be cautious when interpreting this finding: the measure of socio-emotional skills relies on only two questions, and the development of 1-year-olds is difficult to assess in field settings. Also, these results are not confirmed by mothers' ratings of their children's socio-emotional skills, which are assessed using six questions. The comparison also suggests a negative effect of the intervention on the gross motor skills of girls in the younger cohort.

When we compare children in villages that had received project services for 20 months with those that had received them for nine months, we again find some negative effects. At this point, most children in the younger cohort were 2 years old. Two-year-old children living in villages where project playgroup services were established earlier had lower scores on receptive language skills (as rated by their mothers) and gross motor skills (as assessed by child ability tasks) compared with those living in villages where ECED centres were established 11 months later.

In contrast, when we compare villages that had received project services for nine months with villages without such services at any two points in time, the effects are all positive, although most of the results are not statistically significant. This is not surprising given the short duration of exposure. We find none of the negative effects reported above, and, on the contrary, a positive effect on gross motor skills, particularly among children from poorer families.

The older cohort of children

For most child development measures, the average impacts for 4-year-olds are in the expected positive direction, although most are not statistically significant. We find that living in a project village has a positive effect on the scores of 4-year-olds in the social competence domain of the EDI. Although the differences seem small, they are significant both statistically and practically.

Figure 5.6   *Effect of Indonesia ECED Project participation on child*
development outcomes for 4-year-olds, 2009–10 (points)

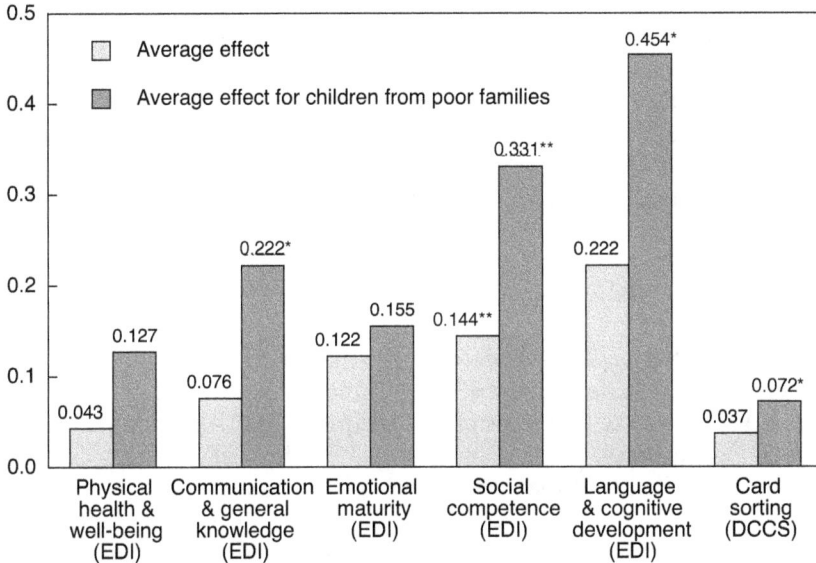

DCCS = Dimensional Change Card Sort (task). EDI = Early Development Instrument.
** = significant at 5 per cent; * = significant at 10 per cent.

Source: Authors' calculations using data from baseline and midline surveys evaluating the
impact of the Indonesia ECED Project, 2009–10.

Subgroup analysis

Among 4-year-olds, we find generally stronger positive effects for girls, for children from poorer families (those in the lower half of the asset index) and for children who were not enrolled in any services before the start of the project.

Figure 5.6 shows the average effect of project participation on the EDI scores of the older cohort, and of the poorest half of that cohort, across all domains. It shows clear positive effects of participation on the language and cognitive development of children from poorer families. This finding is important, because it is in the language and cognitive domain that the children in the sample were most behind at baseline. The effects are substantial: a 14 per cent improvement for poorer children, and a 10 per cent improvement for girls and for those not enrolled in any services before the project began.

The positive effects for poorer children and for girls are further confirmed by results from the DCCS task – a measure of executive function skills.

Parenting and nutrition outcomes

Parenting practices were assessed by interviewing mothers about practices that reflected different levels of warmth, consistency or hostility towards their children, resulting in a 'positive parenting' score. Children's nutrition was assessed by measuring height and weight and calculating whether the child was suffering from stunting or wasting. For both the younger and older cohorts, we did not find any evidence that the provision of ECED services had affected parenting practices or children's nutritional outcomes in the sample villages.

5.5   CONCLUSION

This chapter has presented internationally comparable statistics on child development for a large sample of children from poor villages in Indonesia. We find that although participation in ECED services has been increasing, income-related disparities are on the rise. In terms of child development, we find that most of the problems are in the domains of language and cognitive skills and emotional maturity. In other areas, particularly communication and general knowledge, Indonesian children are developing well.

Analysis of midline data from the Indonesia ECED Project indicates that the program has had a clear effect on enrolments for all children, but that improvements in child development are concentrated among children from poorer families and girls. This should not be too much of a surprise, as at this point the villages had received services for only six to nine months. We hope to find more substantial effects when we conduct the final round of impact evaluation, planned for early 2013.

REFERENCES

Alderman, H. (2011) *No Small Matter: The Impact of Poverty, Shocks, and Human Capital Investments in Early Childhood Development*, World Bank, Washington DC.

Alderman, H., and E. King (2006) *Investing in Early Childhood Development*, World Bank, Washington DC.

Brinkman, S. (2009) 'The impact and reach of the EDI around the world', conference presentation, The Early Development Imperative: A Pan-Canadian Conference on Population Level Measurement of Children's Development, 16–18 November, Winnipeg.

CCCH (Centre for Community Child Health) and Telethon Institute for Child Health Research (2009) *A Snapshot of Early Childhood Development in Australia: Australian Early Development Index (AEDI) National Report 2009*, Australian Government, Canberra.

Dunn, J. (2004) *Children's Friendships: The Beginnings of Intimacy*, Blackwell, Oxford.

Frye, D., P.D. Zelazo and T. Palfai (1995) 'Theory of mind and rule-based reasoning', *Cognitive Development*, 10: 483–527.

Gabbard, C. (2008) *Lifelong Motor Development*, fifth edition, Benjamin Cummings, San Francisco.

Goodenough, F.L. (1954) *Measurement of Intelligence by Drawings*, Harcourt, Brace and World, New York.

Goodman, R. (1997) 'The Strengths and Difficulties Questionnaire: a research note', *Journal of Child Psychology and Psychiatry*, 38(5): 581–6.

Goswami, U. (2010) *The Wiley–Blackwell Handbook of Childhood Cognitive Development*, second edition, Blackwell, Oxford.

Grantham-McGregor, S., Y.B. Cheung, S. Cueto, P. Glewwe, L. Richter and B. Strupp (2007) 'Developmental potential in the first 5 years for children in developing countries', *Lancet*, 369: 60–70.

Heckman, J. (2006) 'Skill formation and the economics of investing in disadvantaged children', *Science*, 312: 1,900–2.

Heckman, J. (2008) 'Schools, skills and synapses', *Economic Inquiry*, 46(3): 289–324.

Hoff, E., and M. Shatz (2007) *Blackwell Handbook of Language Development*, Blackwell, Oxford.

Hyson, M.C. (2004) *The Emotional Development of Young Children: Building an Emotion-centered Curriculum*, second edition, Teachers College Press, New York.

Irwin, L.G., A. Siddiqi and C. Hertzman (2007) 'Early child development: a powerful equalizer. Final report for the World Health Organization's Commission of the Social Determinants of Health', Human Early Learning Partnership, Vancouver.

Janus, M. and D. Offord (2007) 'Development and psychometric properties of the Early Development Instrument (EDI): a measure of children's school readiness', *Canadian Journal of Behavioural Science*, 39: 1–22.

Janus, M., S. Brinkman, E. Duku, C. Hertzman, R. Santos and M. Sayers (2007) *The Early Development Instrument: A Population-based Measure for Communities. A Handbook on Development, Properties and Use*, Offord Centre for Child Studies, Hamilton.

Mustard, J.F. (2002) 'Early child development and the brain: the base for health, learning and behaviour throughout life', in M.E. Young (ed.) *From Early Child Development to Human Development: Investing in Our Children's Future*, World Bank, Washington DC.

Mustard, J.F. (2007) 'Experience-based brain development: scientific underpinnings of the importance of early child development in a global world', in M.E. Young and L.M. Richardson (eds) *Early Child Development: From Measurement to Action*, World Bank, Washington DC.

Naudeau, S., N. Kataoka, A. Valerio, M.J. Neuman and L.K. Elder (2010) *Investing in Young Children: An Early Childhood Development Guide for Policy Dialogue and Project Preparation*, World Bank, Washington DC.

NEGP (National Education Goals Panel) (1995) *Reconsidering Children's Early Development and Learning: Toward Shared Beliefs and Vocabulary*, NEGP, Washington DC.

Neuman, S. and D. Dickinson (2002) *Handbook of Early Literacy Research*, Guilford Press, New York.

Nores, M. and W.S. Barnett (2010) 'Benefits of early childhood interventions across the world: (under) investing in the very young', *Economics of Education Review*, 29: 271–82.

OECD (Organisation for Economic Co-operation and Development) (2010) *PISA 2009 Results: What Students Know and Can Do: Student Performance in Reading, Mathematics and Science (Volume 1)*, Programme for International Student Assessment, OECD, Paris.

Raver, C.C. (2002) 'Emotions matter: making the case for the role of young children's emotional development for early school readiness', *Social Policy Report*, 16: 3–19.

Save the Children (2012), *Laying the Foundations: Early Childhood Care and Development*, Save the Children, London.

Shonkoff, J.P. and D.A. Phillips (2000) *From Neurons to Neighborhoods: The Science of Early Childhood Development*, National Academy Press, Washington DC .

Zelazo, P.D. (2006) 'The Dimensional Change Card Sort (DCCS): a method of assessing executive function in children', *Nature Protocols*, 1: 297–301.

Zins, J.E., R.P. Weissberg, M.C. Wang and H. Walberg (2004) *Building Academic Success on Social and Emotional Learning: What Does the Research Say?* Teachers College Press, New York.

6 WHERE DID ALL THE MONEY GO? FINANCING BASIC EDUCATION IN INDONESIA

*Samer Al-Samarrai and Pedro Cerdan-Infantes**

6.1 INTRODUCTION

Since emerging from the Asian financial crisis of 1997–98, Indonesia has embarked on a period of steady economic expansion and growing prosperity. Even by East Asian standards its post-crisis growth has been rapid, and Indonesia joined the ranks of middle-income countries in 2011. The benefits of growth have been shared widely across the population and poverty has declined significantly.

Economic growth coupled with prudent macroeconomic management has resulted in increasing revenues for the government, giving it the opportunity to invest more heavily in sectors vital to future development. Democratic decentralization began in parallel to multi-party elections at the national level in 1999. This has made locally elected governments responsible for providing basic public services to their electorates and shortened the lines of accountability between district populations and those responsible for local development.

These trends have had far-reaching consequences for the education sector. Education has been a key beneficiary of increased government spending. In 2009, a constitutional obligation for government to commit

---

* The findings, interpretations and conclusions expressed in this chapter are entirely those of the authors. They do not necessarily reflect the views of the World Bank, its Board of Executive Directors or the governments they represent.

a fifth of the total budget to education was first achieved, releasing an avalanche of new funding. Since 2001, decentralization of the education system has meant that local governments have played a more direct role in setting sectoral priorities and in managing and financing their education systems.

The purpose of this chapter is to assess the impact that these changes, mainly the increased investment in education and the decentralization of management, have had on education sector performance. We will show that the recent increases in education spending by government and households alike have been associated with significant improvements in access to education, particularly among the poorest and most disadvantaged. Advancements in the quality of education, however, have been far harder to achieve. We argue that this disappointing result has been driven partly by unsuccessful but expensive policies aimed at improving teacher quality, but also by significant public spending inefficiencies at the district level associated with shortcomings in intergovernmental transfer mechanisms and weaknesses in local governance. Maintaining the impressive advances in the education sector will require improvements in the quality of spending. Improving governance of the education system will be crucial to these efforts.

The chapter is structured as follows. Section 6.2 looks at the trends in public spending and section 6.3 at the impact of this spending on a range of education outcomes. Section 6.4 attempts to uncover why such a large increase in investment has not delivered the improvement in the overall level of skills that is vital for Indonesia's future economic development. The final section identifies some of the ways in which the pay-offs from future public investments in education could be improved.

6.2   TRENDS IN PUBLIC EDUCATION SPENDING

Few countries in the world have almost tripled public expenditure on education in real terms over a 10-year period, as Indonesia did between 2001 and 2010.[1] As a share of GDP, public spending on education increased from 2.4 per cent to 3.4 per cent over that period. As a share of the government budget, it doubled, from 11 per cent to 21 per cent. The largest increase occurred between 2008 and 2009, when the education budget increased by 17 per cent in real terms, the equivalent of an additional 6 per cent of the national budget (Figure 6.1).

---

1   The average real growth rate for the period, 21 per cent, has been surpassed by only two countries over a similar period, Mozambique and Tanzania (UNESCO 2011).

Figure 6.1   *Expenditure on education, Indonesia, 2001–10*

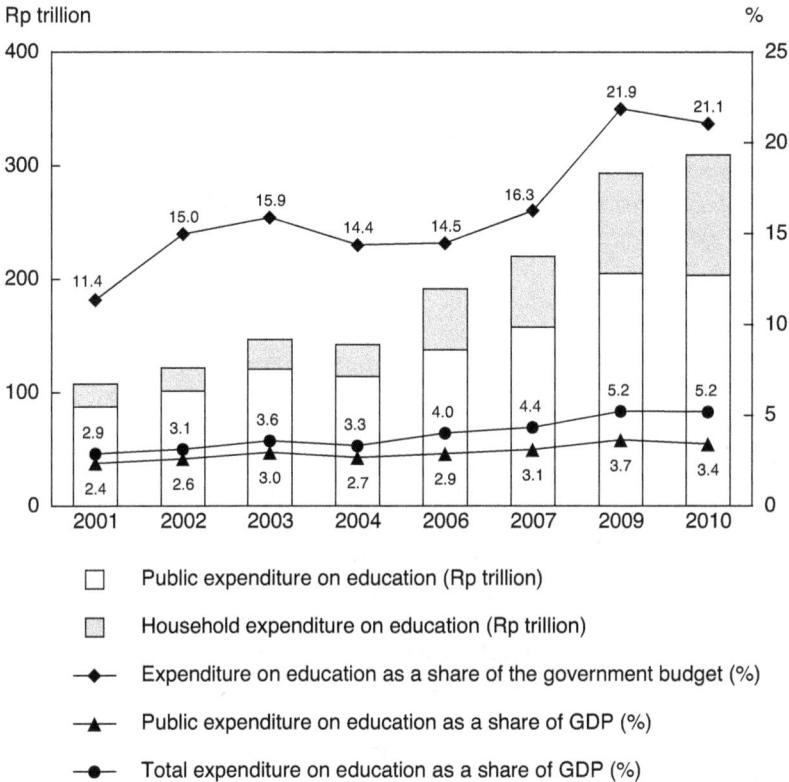

Rp trillion

%

- □ Public expenditure on education (Rp trillion)
- ▨ Household expenditure on education (Rp trillion)
- —◆— Expenditure on education as a share of the government budget (%)
- —▲— Public expenditure on education as a share of GDP (%)
- —●— Total expenditure on education as a share of GDP (%)

Source: World Bank estimates based on data from BPS, Ministry of Finance and regional government budgets.

What is particularly impressive is that this massive increase in public spending was driven by a constitutional amendment that mandated the allocation of 20 per cent of government expenditure to education (hereafter the '20 per cent rule'), signalling a commitment to education that is rare in the world.[2] The Constitution was amended in 2002 and spending rose to 20 per cent of the budget for the first time in 2009. The 20 per cent rule has led to a massive increase in resources for education, making it the largest government expenditure category after spending on energy subsidies (World Bank 2012a).

---

2 Only Brazil and several states in the United States have similar provisions in their constitutions.

Despite this fast increase in public spending, the Indonesian government still spends a smaller share of GDP on education than most other middle-income countries (Figure 6.2). The level of spending is also low compared with that of many other countries in East Asia and elsewhere. At 3.7 per cent of GDP, Indonesia spends less than Thailand, Vietnam or Malaysia, and half as much as high-income, high-performing countries such as Norway. Indonesia fares well when compared with lower-income countries in the region, spending a higher share of GDP on education than Lao, Cambodia or the Philippines. But relative to its wealth, Indonesia's spending is still low, especially when it comes to secondary education. As a share of GDP per capita, the country spends less per student than most developed countries and comparable Asian countries. It is at the lower end of the distribution shown in Figure 6.2 with respect to per capita spending on both primary and secondary education. In the case of primary education, it is positioned above the Philippines, and only slightly below Mexico and Malaysia, yet it lags behind not only the average for high-income countries but also the per capita spending of some other middle-income countries such as Vietnam and Thailand. The differences for secondary education are more pronounced; only the Philippines and Thailand spend less than Indonesia.

When private spending is included in the total resources devoted to education in Indonesia, the scale of the increase in resources is even more impressive (Figure 6.1). Total spending on education from public and private sources grew from about 3 per cent of GDP in 2001 to over 5 per cent of GDP in 2010. In fact, household spending on education grew faster than public spending, resulting in a larger share of households in total education spending despite the massive increase in public resources. Households went from directly contributing 20 per cent of the total resource envelope in 2001 to contributing over 30 per cent in 2010. The increase was largely due to an expansion in access to senior secondary and higher education, which are reliant on fees and other financial support from households.

With this increase in resources, one would expect huge improvements in education outcomes. It is well known, however, that increases in resources do not necessarily lead to better outcomes, especially when it comes to the quality of education (Patrinos 2012). Before examining trends in education outcomes, it is thus important to see where the resources have gone. Unfortunately, the complexity of education system management is matched by the difficulty of gathering reliable spending data. Districts' spending autonomy, coupled until recently with relatively rudimentary reporting mechanisms, meant that detailed district-level spending data were unavailable before 2008. More reliable data that have since become available allow, with some caveats, a detailed analysis of

Figure 6.2 *Public expenditure on education as a share of total government expenditure, GDP and GDP per capita, selected countries (%)*[a]

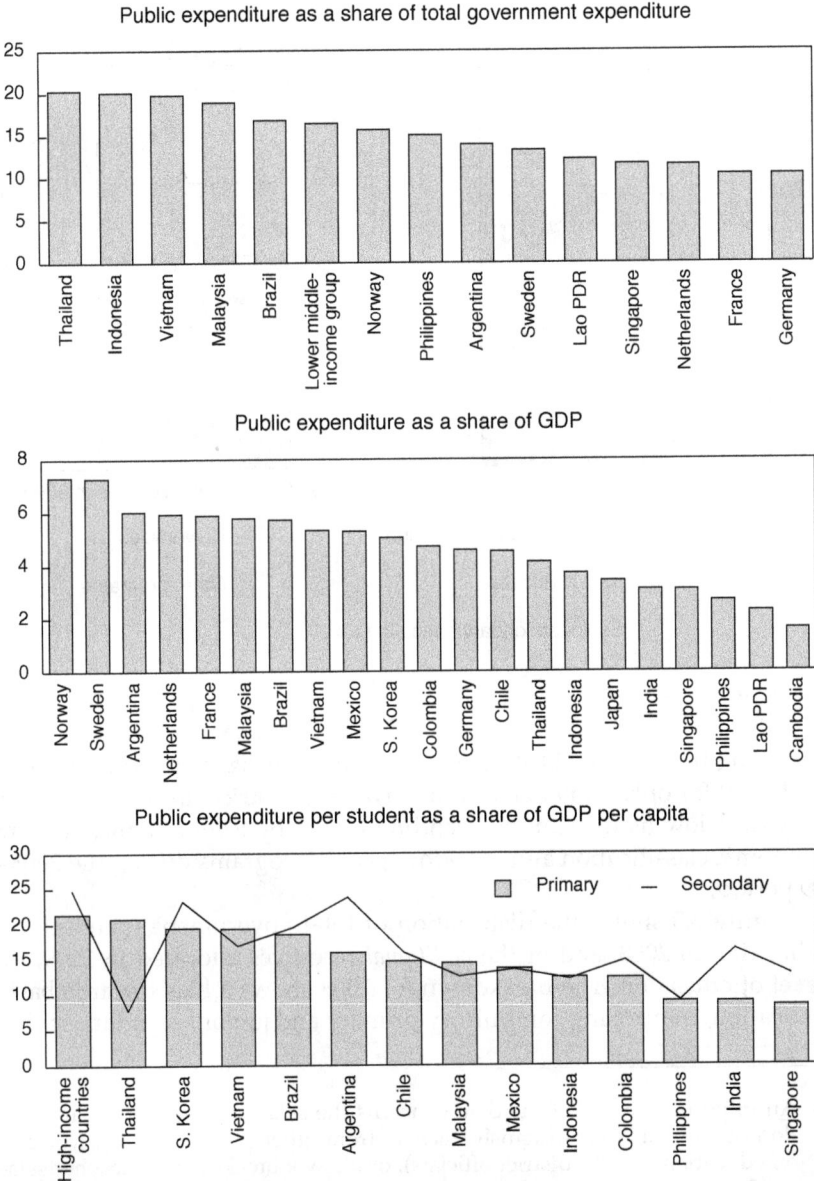

Public expenditure as a share of total government expenditure

Public expenditure as a share of GDP

Public expenditure per student as a share of GDP per capita

a   Data for Indonesia are for 2009. Data for other countries are for 2008 or the latest year available (not earlier than 2006).

Source: All countries except Indonesia: UNESCO Institute for Statistics; Indonesia: authors' calculations using Ministry of Finance central budget data and data from SIKD database.

Figure 6.3   Composition of government expenditure on education in 2008, and of additional resources in 2009, by level of education (%)

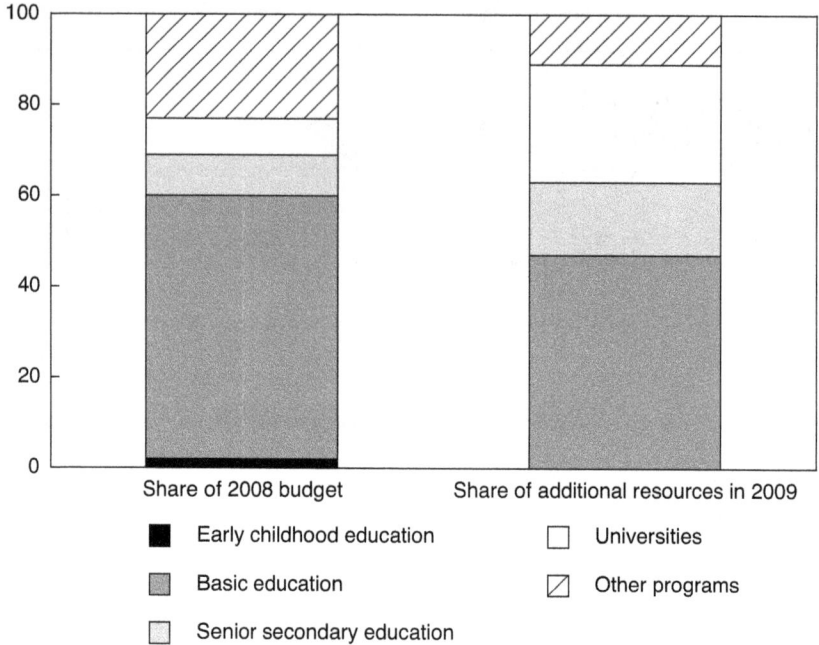

Source: Ministry of Finance.

spending trends from 2008.[3] These data cover realized spending in 2008 and 2009 for only 70 per cent of the over 500 districts in Indonesia, but they do allow us to examine spending trends by level of education, by economic classification and even for specific programs during the 2008–09 period.

Figure 6.3 shows the distribution of total government spending on education in 2008, and of the *additional* resources allocated in 2009, by level of education. The breakdown for 2008 shows a bias towards basic education, comprising compulsory primary and junior secondary school

---

3   An important caveat of the data concerns the salary classification. The data do not allow us to distinguish teachers from other public servants working on education (that is, district officials), or allow a breakdown of teacher salaries by level of education. In order to estimate spending by educational level, we assume that salaries are allocated across levels in the same way as teachers. We use the Ministry of Education and Culture's teacher database, based on a unique identity number for each teacher (*nomor unik pendidik dan tenaga kependidikan*, NUPTK), to calculate the share of teachers at each level.

Figure 6.4   *Share of education budget spent on non-basic education, selected countries (%)*[a]

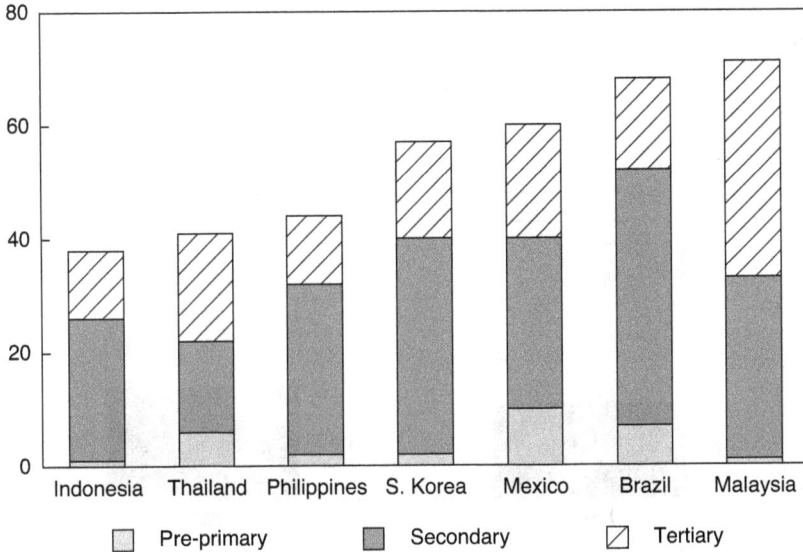

a   Data for Indonesia are for 2009. Data for other countries are for the latest year available after 2007.
Source: World Development Indicators.

education. In 2009, almost half the additional resources from the achievement of the 20 per cent rule still went to basic education, but senior secondary and, especially, higher education received disproportionately larger shares. Early childhood education, which received an extremely low share of resources in 2008, received an even lower share of the extra resources in 2009. As a result, senior secondary and higher education received somewhat higher shares of the total budget in 2009, whereas early childhood education received a smaller share overall.

It is clear from a cross-country comparison of spending on non-basic education that the composition of education spending in Indonesia will need to change (Figure 6.4). The share of the budget going to non-basic education will probably increase in the near future, in part through the natural expansion of enrolments in early childhood education and post-basic education. However, a conscious effort to increase spending on early childhood education may be needed in light of the extremely low level of public spending in this area, and the large returns to early childhood education shown in the literature, both in Indonesia and internationally (World Bank 2013a).

Figure 6.5   Share of total government budget spent on BOS grants program, universities, teacher certification, teacher salaries and other major programs, 2006–08 and 2009 (%)

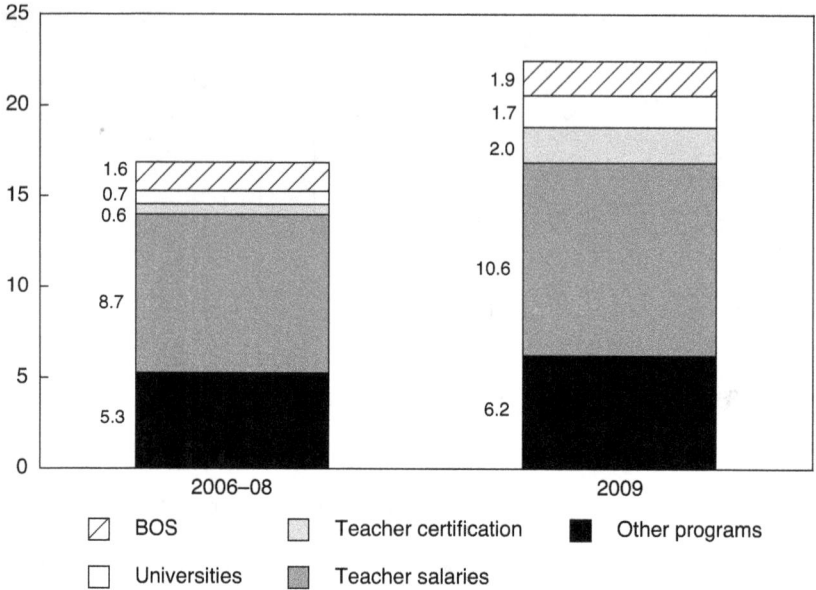

BOS = Bantuan Operasional Sekolah (Schools Operational Assistance).
Source: World Bank (2012b).

Where did the money go within each level of education? The allocation of additional funds differed significantly depending on the level of education. In higher education, the share going to salaries decreased, while the share going to capital and to goods and services increased sharply. In basic education and senior secondary education, on the other hand, most of the additional spending went to salaries and teacher certification. Taking the overall budget, about 60 per cent of the additional resources went to teacher salaries and the teacher certification program (Figure 6.5).[4] The teacher certification program almost doubled the pay of certified teachers through an allowance equivalent to a teacher's basic salary. The allowance absorbed more than 2 per cent of the state budget in 2009 even though only 30 per cent of teachers were certified. The rise in spending on teacher salaries was driven mostly by increases in the

---

4 Between 2006 and 2008 the education budget as a share of the total budget increased by five percentage points, of which 3.3 percentage points were allocated to teacher certification and teacher salaries (Figure 6.5).

total number of teachers, but the 'regularization' of contracts to give non-permanent teachers civil servant status also played a part. We explore the reasons for the explosion in teacher hiring and teacher certification, and the consequences, in section 6.4.

In the context of decentralization, where districts are responsible for teacher management (including paying salaries), these patterns of expenditure mean that district spending on salaries comes at the expense of other things. This is obvious when looking at district budgets; the share of spending on education going to staff remuneration increased from about half in 2001 to almost 80 per cent in 2009. Although the share of capital expenditure increased in the 2006–08 period, it fell back in 2009. Spending on salaries also crowds out direct support for schools, which are owned and managed by the districts. In 2010, about half of the public schools providing basic education reported not receiving any additional financial support from their district government. In light of the positive effects that this funding has on student performance, this is problematic (World Bank 2012b).

6.3   THE EFFECT OF INCREASED SPENDING ON EDUCATION OUTCOMES

The biggest pay-off from the increased spending on education in Indonesia has been an expansion in access to education, especially for the poor. The progress in access and equity has been especially rapid since 2006, with children from poor families enrolling earlier and staying longer in school. The share of 15-year-olds from the poorest consumption quintile enrolled in school increased from just over 60 per cent in 2006 to nearly 80 per cent in 2010 (Figure 6.6). The equity agenda is still incomplete, however: beyond the age of 15, the share from the poorest quintile enrolled in school drops dramatically, and by the ages associated with higher education, it falls to less than 2 per cent. The fall in the proportion of students from the richest quintile enrolled in higher education is equally alarming. Only 45 per cent of 19-year-olds from the richest quintile were enrolled in 2010, a share that, worryingly, has not changed since 2006.

The effect of the increased spending on the quality of education has been less dramatic. Indonesia's performance in international tests has been disappointing, with the country's students generally scoring near the bottom of international assessments of learning achievement. In the 2011 round of the Trends in International Mathematics and Science Study (TIMSS), for instance, Indonesian year 8 students performed significantly more poorly in maths than those from the other participating countries

Figure 6.6   Share of children enrolled in school by age and consumption quintile, 2006 and 2010 (%)

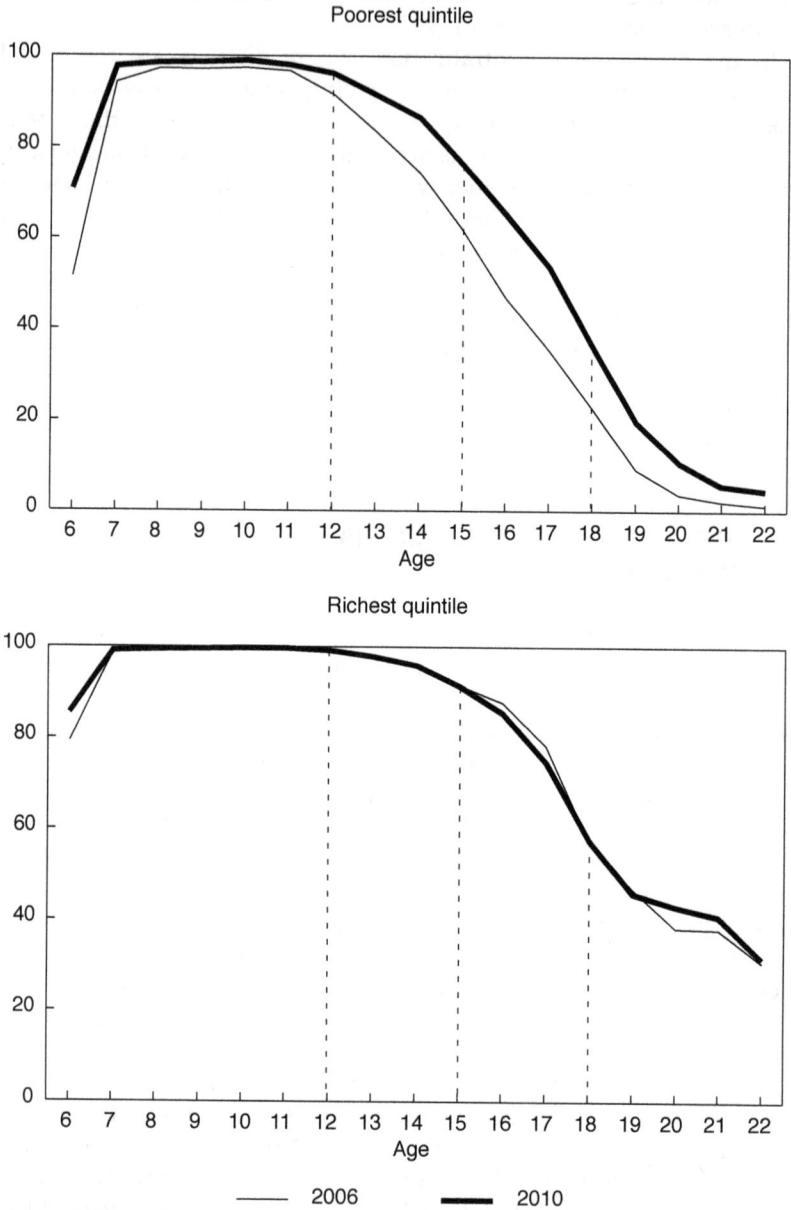

Poorest quintile

Richest quintile

—— 2006	▬▬ 2010

Source: Authors' calculations based on Susenas, 2006 and 2010.

in the region: Thailand, Malaysia and, of course, top-scoring South Korea and Singapore. In fact, only five of the 45 participating countries had lower scores than Indonesia (Mullis, Martin, Foy and Arora 2012). The results are almost identical for the TIMSS science assessment and for the reading and literacy tests in the Progress in International Reading Literacy Study (PIRLS) (Mullis, Martin, Foy and Drucker 2012).[5]

Not only are average scores low, but the share of Indonesian students performing at the highest levels is very small. In the 2011 TIMSS mathematics test, only 20 per cent of Indonesian students obtained at least an intermediate score, 3 per cent a high score and none an advanced score, according to the international benchmarks used (Mullis, Martin, Foy and Arora 2012). In contrast, almost 50 per cent of students in Thailand and Malaysia (which had similar average scores) were assessed as at least intermediate, 10 per cent as high and 1 per cent as advanced. Similarly, no Indonesian student performed at the highest level in mathematics or science in the 2009 Programme for International Student Assessment (PISA) (OECD 2010). Given recent evidence linking PISA scores and the percentage of top performers with GDP growth, this lack of advanced students is of serious concern (Hanushek and Woessmann 2007; Pritchett 2009; Pritchett and Viarengo 2009).

But perhaps the most worrying result is the lack of significant improvements in learning outcomes over the last decade, with the exception of reading. Figure 6.7 shows Indonesian students' PISA scores in 2003 and 2009 for mathematics and reading, broken down by socio-economic decile. The first point to note is that the change in the average score for mathematics between 2003 and 2009 was not statistically significant.[6] On the positive side, the average score for reading did improve significantly. These results are reassuringly similar to those for TIMSS and PIRLS, which indicated a lack of significant improvement in year 8 mathematics and science between 2007 and 2011, and a significant improvement in reading. Second, when the results are broken down by socio-economic decile, the inequality in access to a high-quality education becomes apparent. One sees a striking difference in performance between the richest and the poorest students in Indonesia, especially in mathematics. Poor students perform much worse than richer students, with no narrowing of the gap since 2003. The results in reading are more encouraging; not only did the average score improve, but the differences between socio-economic groups narrowed between 2003 and 2009.

---

5 In reading, only two countries had statistically significant results that were lower than Indonesia's.
6 We do not discuss the results for science, but they are similar to those for mathematics.

Figure 6.7   Indonesian students' PISA scores in mathematics and reading by socio-economic decile, 2003 and 2009

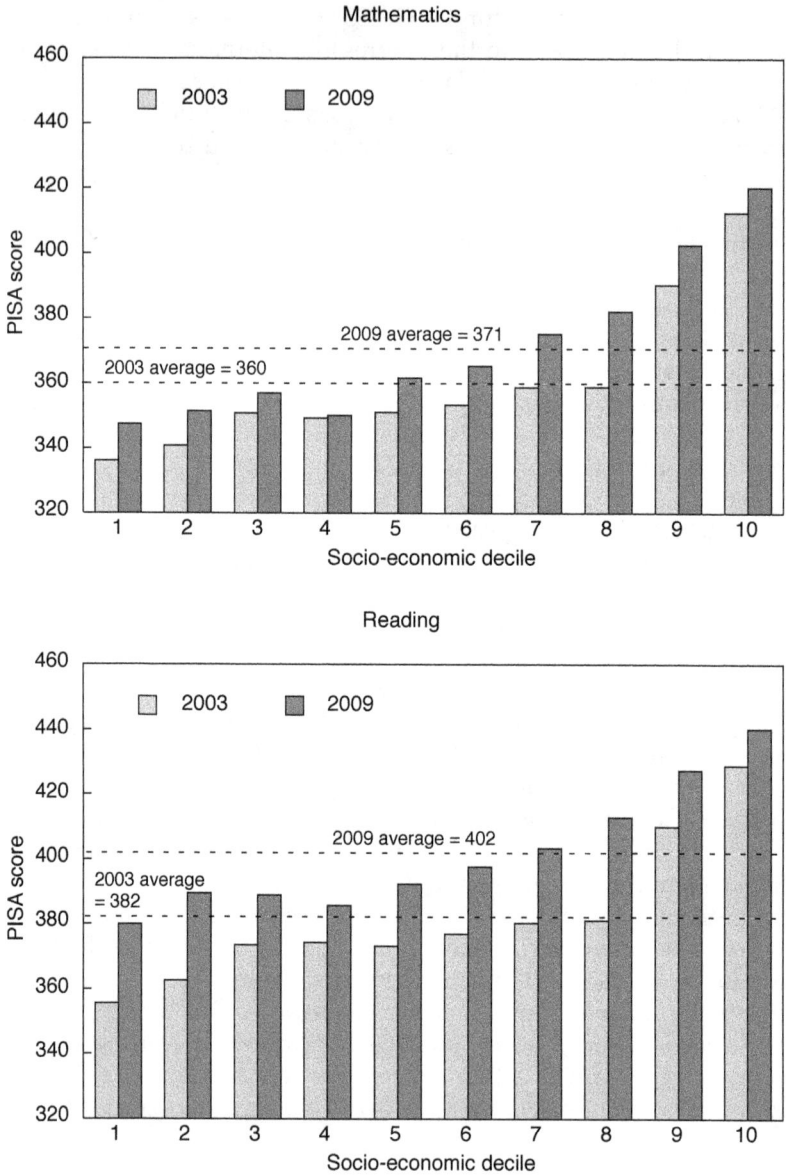

1 = poorest decile; 10 = richest decile. PISA = Programme for International Student Assessment.

Source: Author's calculations based on PISA, 2003 and 2009.

6.4 EXPLAINING THE LIMITED EFFECT OF INCREASED SPENDING ON BASIC EDUCATION OUTCOMES

The previous section has shown that the massive increase in resources from public and private sources has led to impressive improvements in access to education, especially for the poor. On the other hand, it is evident that the quality of education has not improved significantly, or at least not in proportion to the increase in resources. To what extent are these trends explained by the way resources are spent? In this section we explore the connection between the way money is spent, the governance of the education system and education outcomes. Since most additional resources went to teacher salaries and teacher certification, we start by examining the reasons for and consequences of this spending. We then discuss the problems with Indonesia's decentralized system of government, especially weaknesses in local governance.

Spending on teachers has increased with only limited effect on the quality of education

One thing is clear from the analysis of expenditure trends: teachers have collectively benefited from the recent increases in government education spending. About half of the Rp 67 trillion ($7 billion)[7] increase in real spending on education between 2006 and 2009 (in 2009 constant prices) went to expanding the number of teachers and paying them more through a number of allowances (World Bank 2012b).

Since decentralization reforms were introduced in the early 2000s, teacher hiring has continued to rise at a faster pace than increases in school enrolment. This has resulted in significant declines in student–teacher ratios in basic education (Figure 6.8), which are now well below those in comparable countries. In 2008, for example, the average student–teacher ratio in Indonesian primary schools was 18, compared with a ratio of 26 for lower middle-income countries. The current ratios are below international benchmarks associated with good education quality, and recent evidence for Indonesia shows that, at these levels, the relationship with learning outcomes is weak (Figure 6.9).[8] This implies that the increases in teacher numbers over the last decade have not really had the impact on learning that might have been expected had student–teacher ratios initially been much higher.

---

7   This chapter uses an exchange rate of Rp 9,600 per US dollar.
8   The weak relationship between student–teacher ratios and learning outcomes observed in Figure 6.9 is confirmed by regression analysis controlling for school characteristics, principal and teacher education and experience, and district fixed effects.

Figure 6.8   Student–teacher ratios in primary and junior secondary schools, 1995–2010[a]

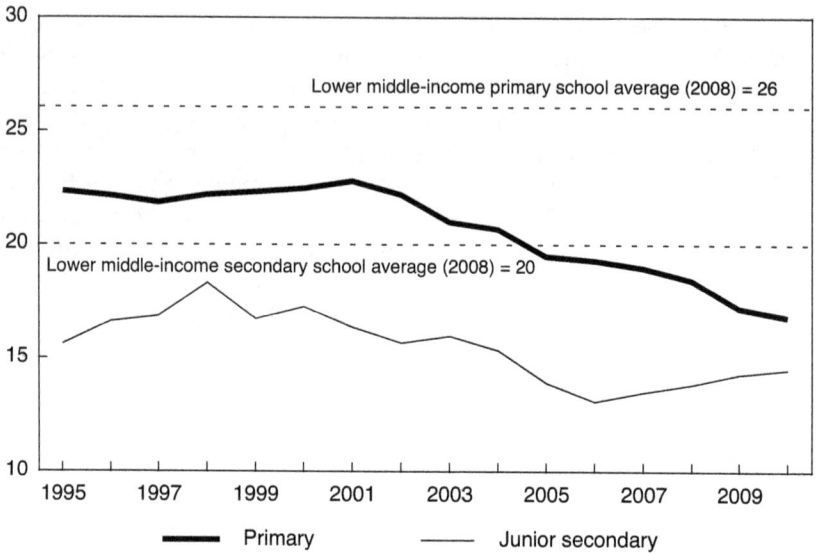

a   Data do not include Islamic schools.
Source: Ministry of Education and Culture teacher and enrolment data; UNESCO (2011).

Figure 6.9   Correlation between primary schools' student–teacher ratios and year 5 students' average mathematics scores, 2010

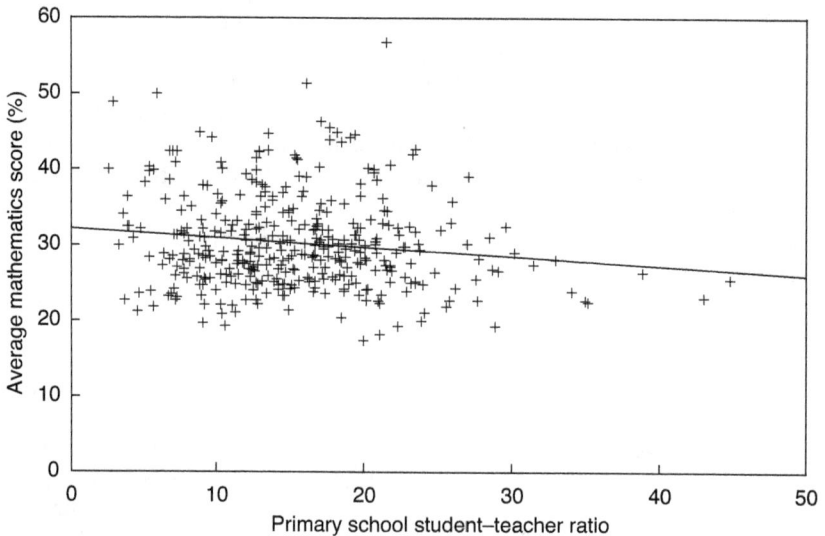

Source: World Bank (2012b, 2012e).

*Figure 6.10   Impact of teacher certification on teacher motivation/welfare,
teacher competency and student learning*

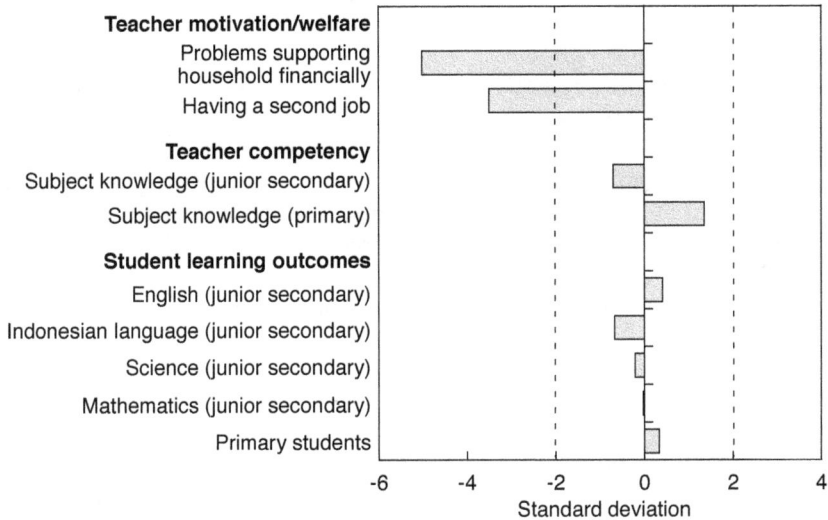

Source: De Ree et al. (2012).

Teacher certification has not produced the expected improvements in quality

As part of a broader set of reforms approved in 2005 to improve the quality of teaching, the government introduced a program to certify all teachers by 2015. The program was introduced in part to address a perception that the poor quality of the education system was related to low teacher motivation, which in turn was associated with low relative rates of pay. A professional allowance was introduced in exchange for teachers agreeing to be certified. Initially the certification process required teachers to hold at least a bachelor's degree and to undergo an assessment of their teaching competencies. Teachers who were successful in being certified received a professional allowance equivalent to their basic pay. By 2012, approximately 35 per cent of teachers had been certified, with the program absorbing about 9 per cent of the total education budget.

A rigorous evaluation of the impact of the program suggests that although certification has improved some measures related to teacher motivation, it has not improved student learning outcomes (De Ree et al. 2012). Figure 6.10 shows the effect of the program on a range of variables, measured in standard deviations. Certified teachers tend to be much more financially secure. They are less likely to report having a second job or to have trouble supporting their families. However, they do not score significantly better than uncertified teachers on a test of subject knowledge. Although the positive changes in teacher welfare recorded by the study may have improved teacher motivation, the study finds that certification has not improved student learning outcomes in either primary or junior secondary schools.

The disappointing early results of the certification program are largely the result of implementation issues (World Bank 2013b). Despite the law linking certification to competency, until recently teachers generally obtained certification through a 'portfolio' of past experience and training rather than a detailed assessment of their competencies. Moreover, pass rates for the competency testing that did take place were based more on filling certification quotas than on ensuring teacher quality.

Even though the certification program has had little impact on learning, it will continue to put significant pressure on the education budget. Medium-term budget projections show that total government spending is estimated to grow by approximately 3 per cent in real terms between 2012 and 2015 (World Bank 2012a). This suggests that the education budget will increase only marginally over the next few years if it is assumed that the share of government spending allocated to education remains constant at around 20 per cent. Based on these trends, paying and certifying all eligible primary and junior secondary school teachers would absorb approximately 41 per cent of the total education budget in 2015, compared with 32 per cent in 2012 (Figure 6.11). If non-salary spending on basic education is maintained at its 2012 level, this would imply that basic education would absorb almost two-thirds of the budget in 2015, compared with around 56 per cent in 2012. This increased spending would require cutbacks in spending on other levels of education. The remaining budget for other levels of education, after all civil service teachers had been certified, would be Rp 113 trillion ($11.8 billion) in 2015, compared with Rp 135 trillion ($14.1 billion) in 2012.

Government plans to give all contract teachers civil servant status and certify them would be financially unsustainable given current budget projections.[9] Approximately Rp 68 trillion ($5 billion) would be needed to carry out this plan.[10] The certification and conversion of employment status of all primary and junior secondary school teachers would imply that 89 per cent of the total education budget in 2015 would need to be

---

9   The current certification guidelines exclude school-hired, non-permanent contract teachers (*guru tidak tetap*, GTT), who make up about 30 per cent of the teaching force at the primary and secondary levels.

10 This includes the increased cost of the professional allowance associated with certification that school-hired, permanent contract teachers (*guru tetap yayasan*, GTY) would receive upon conversion.

Figure 6.11   *Impact of teacher certification program on the 2015 education budget (Rp trillion, in 2012 prices)*

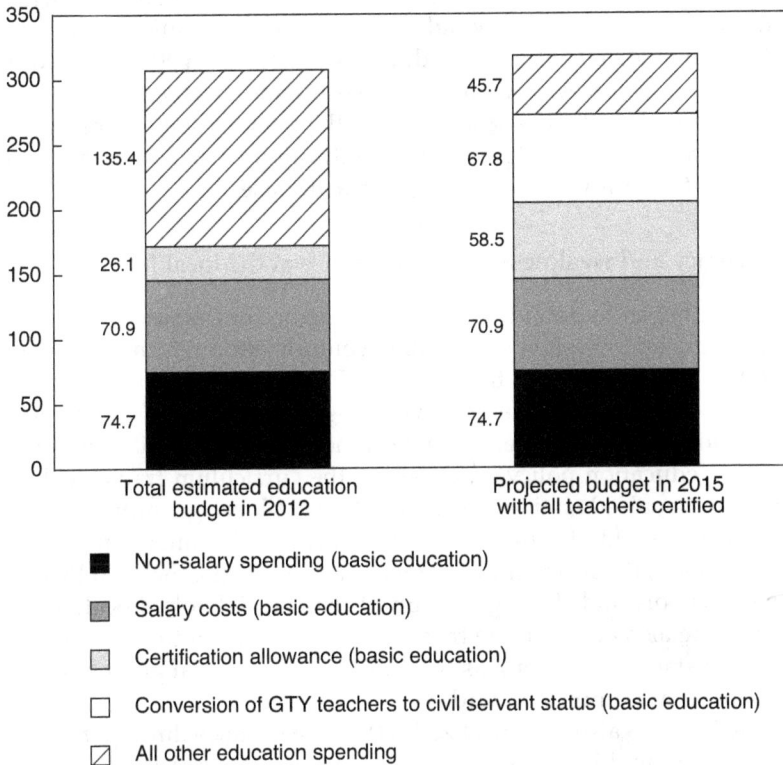

Non-salary spending (basic education)

Salary costs (basic education)

Certification allowance (basic education)

Conversion of GTY teachers to civil servant status (basic education)

All other education spending

GTY = *guru tetap yayasan* (school-hired teacher on permanent contract).

Source: Budget data and projections: World Bank (2012b, 2013b). Salaries: authors' calculation based on teacher numbers and salary grades from NUPTK (2010) and the 2012 civil service salary scale. Certification: authors' calculation of basic pay for all current civil servant teachers and a monthly Rp 1.5 million allowance for GTY teachers who are currently eligible to receive a certification allowance. Conversion: authors' calculation based on the assumption that GTY teachers would be distributed across the pay scale in a similar way to civil servant teachers; includes an increase in the professional allowance from Rp 1.5 million per month to an amount equivalent to the basic pay of all GTY teachers.

devoted to basic education (Figure 6.11). Given the commitments outside basic education, this level of spending is completely unsustainable.

Improving the use of teachers and raising student–teacher ratios holds out the prospect of lessening the budgetary impact of certification. Simple simulations demonstrate the significant savings that could be realized by increasing student–teacher ratios. If the ratio in basic education rose to 22 (the level in Indonesia in the early 2000s), the salary and certification cost would be Rp 102 trillion ($10.6 billion), or 21 per cent less than the cost estimated at the current ratio. If we compare this with the budget projections outlined earlier, we find that this increase in the student–teacher ratio would result in basic education absorbing a slightly smaller share of overall education resources in 2015. This would make more resources available for investments in access and quality. Clearly, raising student–teacher ratios to these levels would mean reducing the overall teaching force in basic education and adjusting staffing standards to improve the efficiency of teacher use.

Inefficiency and weaknesses in governance at the local level

Indonesia began to decentralize the governance of the primary and secondary education system as part of decentralization reforms that began in 2001. Law 20/2003 on the National Education System outlined the responsibilities of the different levels of government in the delivery of education services. The central government maintained its role in formulating education policy, establishing the curriculum framework and setting national education standards. District-level governments were given responsibility for the overall organization of primary and secondary education, the hiring and deployment of teachers, the establishment of new schools and the registration of existing schools. Local governments were also able to issue their own regulations outlining education provision standards as long as they adhered to national guidelines, particularly on minimum standards.[11]

Law 20/2003 also decentralized school governance through the introduction of school-based management (*manajemen berbasis sekolah*). Like broader decentralization reforms, school-based management was seen as a strategy to improve quality by bringing decision making closer to local communities and strengthening the accountability mechanisms between schools and the parents and children they served (AusAID Education Resource Facility 2011; Bruns, Filmer and Patrinos 2011). The law formally established district-level education boards and school committees designed to enhance community participation, improve transparency and strengthen accountability. The law was supported by the introduction, in 2005, of a detailed set of guidelines on how school-based management should be implemented. At the same time the central government introduced Schools Operational Assistance (Bantuan Operasional Sekolah, BOS), a nationwide grants program intended in part to support

---

11 Provincial governments were also mandated to support the implementation of primary and secondary education through, for example, the development of education staff.

the implementation of school-based management. Grants were provided on an equal per-student basis, with schools deciding how to make use of the funds to improve access and learning.

Decentralization shifted the bulk of decision making on education spending to local governments and schools, although the financing of basic education remained a shared responsibility. Of the total public spending on basic education in 2009, 60 per cent was provided by local governments and the rest by the central government. Increases in the overall budget for education, documented in the previous section, led to a 150 per cent increase in district education spending between 2001 and 2009. Moreover, a large part of central government financing went to financing the BOS school grants program, which accounted for Rp 24 trillion ($2.5 billion) of government education spending in 2012, or approximately 8 per cent of total spending on basic education.

The share of resources devoted to education differs greatly across districts, and is a good proxy for the priority given to education. In 2009, the average district allocated 31 per cent of its budget to the education sector, but 25 per cent of districts devoted less than 22 per cent to the sector and another 25 per cent devoted more than 38 per cent.[12] Across districts, about three-quarters of total education spending was allocated to salaries, including teacher certification.

Not only are there big differences in the share of resources devoted to education, but the ability of local governments to translate resources into improved outcomes also differs widely. Figure 6.12 plots local government spending on each student of primary or junior secondary age in 2009 against two measures of education outcomes: access to education as measured by the net enrolment rate in junior secondary schools, and student performance as measured by the performance of primary school students in the annual national examination.[13] It is clear that the overall relationship between education outcomes and levels of local government spending is weak.[14] Put another way, the graphs show that levels of spending are not a good predictor of education outcomes.

---

12 Authors' calculations based on data from the Ministry of Finance's Regional Financial Information System (Sistem Informasi Keuangan Daerah, SIKD).

13 Weaknesses in the ability of the national examination to measure education outcomes include the likelihood of widespread cheating. Nevertheless, the results provide an acceptable proxy of district learning outcomes to the extent that this cheating would be spread randomly across districts. Relationships similar to the ones described in the text exist between local government spending and other measures of education outcomes.

14 The R-squared for the plot of spending against access is 0.0003, and –0.002 for the plot of spending against examination results.

Figure 6.12   Correlation between average local government expenditure per primary or junior secondary student and education outcomes, 2009

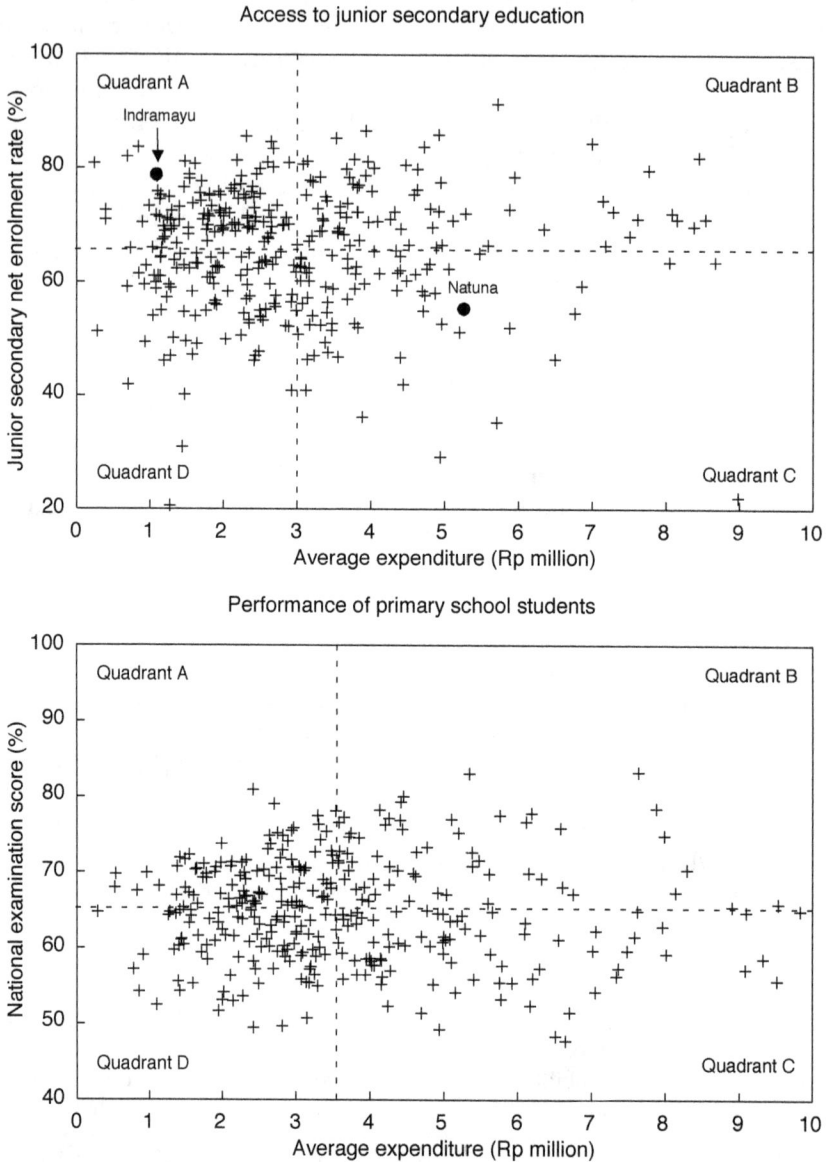

Quadrant A = above-average performance, below-average spending; quadrant B = above-average performance, above-average spending; quadrant C = below-average performance, above-average spending; quadrant D = below-average performance, below-average spending.

Source: Authors' calculations based on data from SIKD database and Susenas.

Some local governments appear to use their resources more effectively than others to deliver education services to their constituents. Districts in quadrant A of Figure 6.12 spend less than the average district on education but have better than average outcomes. For example, Indramayu in West Java spends about Rp 1.1 million per child of primary or secondary school age and has a junior secondary net enrolment rate of 79 per cent, 14 percentage points higher than the national average. Districts in quadrant C are relatively inefficient; they spend more than the average district but have outcomes well below the national average. For example, Natuna district in Riau Islands spends almost five times more per student than Indramayu but its junior secondary net enrolment rate is 24 percentage points lower.

The relationship between spending and education outcomes is complex and many factors affect it. Differences in outcomes are determined partly by the socio-economic status of the population, the geographical location of a school and the size of the school-aged population. For example, the less efficient districts in quadrant C have an average poverty rate of 19 per cent, compared with 16 per cent for the more efficient districts in quadrant A.[15] The more efficient districts also tend to have more children of school age than the less efficient districts in quadrant C.

The quality of local governance also contributes to the relatively weak relationship between spending and education outcomes, as a number of studies have shown. A 2009 survey of local education governance in 50 Indonesian districts found a strong positive relationship between measures of the quality of governance and education outcomes (World Bank 2010). It found, for example, a positive and statistically significant relationship between a district's enrolment rate and a composite measure of local governance quality. Another study explored the link between public spending, education outcomes and the level of corruption (Suryadarma 2011). It concluded that there was no statistically significant relationship between spending and enrolment rates in regions that rated high on a corruption perceptions index. However, where corruption was perceived to be low, spending did have a significant effect on enrolment rates. The study did not find a strong correlation between spending and national examination results regardless of perceptions of corruption.

The World Bank's (2010) survey of key areas of local governance in 50 districts provides a snapshot of the main weaknesses in local governments' management of education (Figure 6.13). The districts were spread across Indonesia and had slightly poorer education outcomes than the national average. The results show that a relatively large number of the sampled districts did well on measures of transparency and

---

15 The rates are based on BPS poverty lines for 2009.

Figure 6.13   Indicators of quality of local governance in 50 Indonesian
districts, 2009 (% of districts)[a]

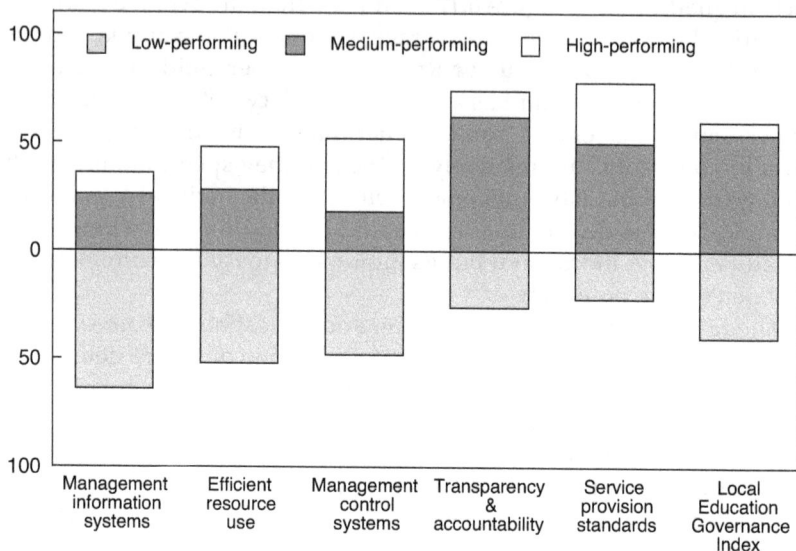

a   Management information systems refer to processes of data collection, management, secure storage, analysis and decision making that ensure that planning and budget allocations are determined on the basis of high-quality information. Management control systems refer to the existence of incentive systems and the governance of procurement and asset management.

Source: World Bank (2010).

accountability.[16] Many districts reported that the public had access to budget and monitoring sessions in the local parliament, that financial reports were widely publicized and that mechanisms existed to allow wide participation in local education decision making. The extent to which the information and opportunities for participation were meaningfully exploited is not clear, however.

The 50 sampled districts performed less well on measures of management information and control systems and the efficiency of resource use. In terms of management, incentive systems for teachers, principals and school supervisors were frequently absent. So too were mechanisms to ensure that local government planning took account of the deliberations of stakeholders.

16   We do not discuss the results for service provision standards (measuring current levels of education provision) because it is the indicator that the quality of governance is expected to influence.

Many of the sampled local governments were seen to be particularly weak in making reliable and timely information on the education system available. For example, none had databases that tracked student progress or students' test scores. This would seriously hamper the ability of local governments to plan and budget effectively, reflected in the survey's finding that about half of the sampled districts were rated as low performing in terms of the processes used to link education priorities to activities and resources. For example, districts often did not set priorities before the budget process began or include indicative budgets in their annual plans. Allocations were generally based, not on student need, but, for example, on the number of teachers or classrooms in a school. These weaknesses in planning and budgeting resulted in relatively low budget absorption rates and large differences between budgeted and realized spending.[17]

Weak local-level governance introduces additional incentives to hire more teachers than standards require. A symposium held by the Ministry of Education and Culture in 2011 concluded that the appointment of teachers was 'characterized by corruption, lack of transparency and primordial regionalism, and co-opted by the political interests of the ruling authorities' and that 'many teachers are not appointed in accordance with the requirements of the minimum standards of teacher competencies' (Ministry of Education and Culture 2012).

A number of studies have shown that it is common for Indonesians to make payments to obtain access to civil service positions. Based on interviews with 60 civil servants in two districts in West Nusa Tenggara, Kristiansen and Ramli (2006) found that payment for jobs was commonplace. The civil servants reported paying Rp 24 million on average in 2004 (Rp 50 million in 2012 prices) to obtain their positions – equivalent to about one year's basic pay for a primary or junior secondary teacher.[18] The authors also found that the amounts paid for posts had increased since decentralization was implemented in 2001. Payment for civil service positions is not always required, however. A 2005–06 study found that in seven of the eight districts surveyed, non-government respondents reported a need to pay for civil service positions, although the amount of the payment varied significantly. In the remaining district, Solok in West

---

17 The budget absorption rate is the proportion of the budget that is actually spent. It reflects the ability of districts to plan and spend effectively.

18 The study found that teachers as a subgroup of the civil service paid about the average price for their posts. The calculation of average teacher salary is based on data for 2010 from the NUPTK teacher database and on the 2012 civil service salary scale.

Sumatra, no payments were thought to be necessary to gain access to the civil service (von Luebke 2009).

For the individual, paying for a post provides access to a stable income and a number of non-monetary benefits that are generally not available outside the civil service. On the other side of the transaction, the payments not only benefit those allocating the posts, but are frequently part of revenue-generating schemes that support political activity at the local and national levels. Positions are also sometimes allocated as a reward for political support or as part of the pay-off for a broader local political settlement. The upshot of these recruitment practices is that a larger civil service often serves a number of personal and political objectives at the local level.

Such recruitment practices can have consequences for the quality of the national teaching force. Once in the civil service, teachers have the opportunity to recoup the payments made to obtain their jobs by, for example, charging informal fees at school or obtaining side payments from school suppliers (Rosser, Joshi and Edwin 2011). These practices can lead to the diversion of resources intended to improve access and quality. In addition, where payments are required for positions, it is rare for only the best qualified candidates to gain employment. This can have the effect of reducing the overall quality of the national teaching force.

Local-level incentives to hire more teachers are exacerbated by the intergovernmental transfer system. Since the introduction of decentralization in 2001, intergovernmental resource transfers have been determined in part by the size of a local government's payroll. Districts with larger numbers of civil servants receive more from the transfer system. It has been estimated that central government transfers cover approximately 75 per cent of the salary of an additional civil servant teacher. This in effect subsidizes the cost to a local government of additional teachers, creating an incentive for increased hiring.

At the school level, the introduction of school-based management and the roll-out of the BOS program have given schools a greater role in decision making. Evidence from Indonesia shows that improvements in school-based management can lead to better student performance. A study of primary schools found that schools with greater parental and school committee participation had better learning outcomes (Chen 2011). It showed that the effects of better school-based management worked through improved resource allocation decisions and higher teacher attendance rates. However, weaknesses in the implementation of school-based management had limited the effect of this reform on education quality.

Experience of implementing school-based management has been mixed. A study conducted in 2010 found that schools had significant autonomy in many areas but that community participation was still limited (World Bank 2012c). Over 80 per cent of the primary school principals surveyed indicated they were the final decision makers on issues such as the curriculum, school facility planning, and student admissions and promotion. Most school committees participated in planning and budgeting decisions, particularly with respect to the BOS program. However, qualitative evidence showed that the school committees were often only passive participants in school decision making. For example, the study found that the school principal and teachers would agree on the allocation of BOS funds, and only then communicate their decisions to the school committee chair and ask for his or her signature on the appropriate forms.

6.5   IMPLICATIONS FOR POLICY

Indonesia has made some remarkable gains in education over the past decade. Access to educational opportunities has increased rapidly, especially for the poorest households, and the government has continued to invest heavily in the sector. However, key reforms aimed at improving the quality of education have yet to register significant effects in improving student learning. In particular, the hiring of additional teachers and the teacher certification program have not had a big effect on quality but have absorbed a large share of the government's increased investment in education. While reforms to decentralize the management of the education system to local governments and schools themselves are still at an early stage, they too have not had a significant effect on the quality of education.

Changes must be made to the way the teacher certification program is being implemented if the quality of education is to improve. In 2012, in response to evidence of the limitations of the program, the Ministry of Education and Culture introduced competency testing into the certification process. The old portfolio method of certification was withdrawn and a competency test introduced to ascertain whether teachers were eligible for certification and the professional allowance. However, the need to fill certification quotas resulted in the pass rate being set at only 30 per cent. If the new competency test is to improve the quality of teaching, then it will need to be strengthened to bestow certification only on individuals who can demonstrate the required competencies associated with being an effective teacher.

The certification process could be improved further if it required teachers to be reassessed periodically. In the absence of recertification, a teacher's skills may become outdated, since certified teachers have no incentive to continue to upgrade their skills. Recertification could also help to address the weaknesses among the approximately 1 million teachers who have already been certified.

One way to improve education outcomes would be to address inefficiencies in teacher hiring and deployment. Because student–teacher ratios were already low in Indonesia, the increases in teacher hiring since decentralization are unlikely to have improved quality. Addressing the overhiring of teachers has the potential to release resources for other quality-improving investments and ensure the sustainability of the certification program. While the government has issued a decree setting out a new set of school staffing standards, these do not go far enough. In particular, they fail to address overstaffing issues in the large number of small schools spread across Indonesia (World Bank 2012d). Strategies to make better use of teachers in small schools need to be implemented nationwide. For example, multi-grade teaching has been used successfully in other countries to tackle staffing issues in small schools (Little 1995). In Indonesia, small pilot programs have demonstrated the applicability of this approach, but so far they have not been scaled up.

The unequal distribution of teachers is inefficient and reinforces other patterns of disadvantage. Estimates suggest that about 17 per cent of the primary and junior secondary teaching force would need to be moved to comply with existing staffing norms (World Bank 2012d). It is common for rural and remote schools to experience teacher shortages at the same time as urban schools have more teachers than national staffing standards dictate. Moreover, the more qualified and experienced teachers are frequently concentrated in wealthier urban areas. The government introduced a remote area allowance in 2005 to encourage teachers to work in remote areas and to improve their motivation. In 2012, about 53,000 teachers were in receipt of the allowance. This is a relatively small number compared to need, and the teachers receiving the allowance were often already working in remote areas. Despite the challenges, allowances of this kind have the potential to improve teacher distribution, and consideration should be given to expanding and strengthening such programs.

Changing the incentives associated with the intergovernmental transfer system could encourage local governments to spend their education resources more wisely. One option to improve spending efficiency would be to adjust the main transfer formula to remove the incentive for overstaffing. This would result in districts themselves taking on the bulk of the financial burden associated with hiring additional teachers, providing a strong motivation for them to rationalize their teacher salary spending. Existing incentive grants in the transfer system could also be deployed to improve spending efficiency. The Regional Incentive Fund

(Dana Insentif Daerah, DID), introduced in 2010 and developed further in 2011, is designed to reward districts that demonstrate improved educational performance. While the incentive is large for the districts receiving the grants, the program remains small; in 2011 total spending on the DID was just 1 per cent of the Rp 103 trillion (in constant 2009 prices) that local governments spent on education. Expanding programs of this kind could go some way towards strengthening the incentives associated with improved district education performance.

Strengthening the capacity of local governments to allocate their resources more efficiently could also improve education outcomes. As the previous section has highlighted, at present local government decisions on allocations are rarely determined according to student need. About 60 per cent of local governments use their own resources to provide additional funding directly to schools, and evidence suggests that this funding has had a positive effect on student learning (World Bank 2012e). Like the national BOS grants, most local grants are allocated to schools on a per student basis. While they are a step in the right direction, these local government programs represent only a small proportion of overall local government education spending, and funding has been unpredictable in recent years.

A pilot program in several districts to improve the formula for allocating local school grants by incorporating an equity-based component and performance incentives has had some success (World Bank 2012e). Allocating school grants on a per student basis fails to take account of the differences in operating costs schools face because of the populations they serve or their location. For example, schools in remote areas tend to have higher proportions of poor students than schools in wealthier areas. To supply a similar quality of education, they are likely to require more resources to provide, for instance, more teaching time or remedial coaching. The pilot program sought to introduce allocations that took account of school infrastructure, size and remoteness. In some districts, the formula also included rewards for improvements in a school's annual scores in the national examination.

Introducing more effective, formula-based mechanisms for the allocation of local grants is an important first step in improving the equity and efficiency of public spending. However, it needs to be recognized that these grants are only a small part of overall spending on education. To improve education spending further, the lessons learned from the pilot program about linking allocations to equity and school performance need to be applied more broadly.

Accountability mechanisms at the district and school levels should be strengthened further to improve the management of education and ensure better value for money. Law 20/2003 and the subsequent regulations set up a number of key accountability institutions at the district and school levels. It is essential to strengthen these institutions by ensuring broad stakeholder participation and greater transparency in the decision-making process. This chapter has shown that Indonesia's school-based management reforms have not delivered the results some other countries have achieved with this approach. In part this is due to the lack of real community participation in school affairs and the nature of social relations in many parts of Indonesia, which make the kind of accountability relationships envisaged under the reform difficult to achieve. But it is also due to the limited resources that schools currently control – and conversely, the large allocations they do *not* control in the form of civil service teacher salaries and other government programs.

Strengthened school-based management will be central to the success of other reform efforts, and ultimately in improving education outcomes. A comprehensive study by the World Bank (2012c) highlights three main areas where school-based management needs to be strengthened. Most importantly, the capacity of school-level stakeholders to implement school-based management needs to be improved. This encompasses a number of areas, but encouraging community participation and clarifying and increasing the authority of the school committee are central to improving implementation. Second, the study notes that the ability to translate improved management at the school level into better education outcomes relies on the professional capacity of teachers and the support structures surrounding the school. It highlights the need to strengthen and provide greater access to professional development opportunities, to equip teachers with the strategies necessary to improve and monitor education outcomes. Finally, the study emphasizes the need to develop the capacity of local governments to implement school-based management. If realized, these changes could deliver significant improvements in the quality of basic education.

Indonesia has taken a number of important steps to transform its education system to better meet its needs as an emerging and rapidly growing middle-income country. The reforms introduced have been far-ranging, and their effects are unlikely to fully work their way through the system for some time to come. The chapter has shown, however, that the reforms and the resulting increases in spending have had some unintended outcomes that threaten the effectiveness of the reform process. The government and the Ministry of Education and Culture have responded quickly to these implementation experiences. Addressing the challenges highlighted in this chapter and continuing this responsive policy making will be vital if future investments in education are to deliver the skills and knowledge so vital for Indonesia's continued economic and social development.

REFERENCES

AusAID Education Resource Facility (2011) 'School grants and school-based management', Current Issues in Education, AusAID, Canberra, July.

Bruns, B., D. Filmer and H.A. Patrinos (2011) 'Making schools work: new evidence on accountability reforms', World Bank, Washington DC.

Chen, D. (2011) 'School-based management, school decision-making and education outcomes in Indonesian primary schools', Policy Research Working Paper No. 5809, World Bank, Washington DC.

De Ree, J., K. Muralidharan, M. Pradhan and H. Rogers (2012) 'Double for what? The effects of unconditional teacher salary increases on performance', World Bank, Jakarta.

Hanushek, E. and L. Woessmann (2007) 'The role of education quality in economic growth', Policy Research Working Paper No. 4122, World Bank, Washington DC.

Kristiansen, S. and M. Ramli (2006) 'Buying an income: the market for civil service positions in Indonesia', *Contemporary Southeast Asia*, 28(2): 207–33.

Little, A. (1995) 'Multi-grade teaching: a review of research and practice', Education Research, Serial No. 12, Overseas Development Administration, London.

Ministry of Education and Culture (2012) 'Recruitment of teachers in the future', symposium organized by the Development Research Unit (Badan Penelitian Pembangunan, Balitbang), Ministry of Education and Culture, Jakarta, July.

Mullis, I.V.S., M.O. Martin, P. Foy and A. Arora (2012) *TIMSS 2011 International Results in Mathematics*, TIMSS & PIRLS International Study Center, Lynch School of Education, Boston College, Chestnut Hill.

Mullis, I.V.S., M.O. Martin, P. Foy and K.T. Drucker (2012) *PIRLS 2011 International Results in Reading*, TIMSS & PIRLS International Study Center, Lynch School of Education, Boston College, Chestnut Hill.

OECD (Organisation for Economic Co-operation and Development) (2010) *PISA 2009 Results: What Students Know and Can Do – Student Performance in Reading, Mathematics and Science (Volume 1)*, Programme for International Student Assessment, OECD, Paris.

Patrinos, H.A. (ed.) (2012) *Strengthening Education Quality in East Asia*, UNESCO and World Bank, Washington DC.

Pritchett, L. (2009) 'Long-term global challenges in education: are there feasible steps today?', background paper for Pardee Center Workshop: Shaping Tomorrow Today, 17 March.

Pritchett, L. and M. Viarengo (2009) 'Producing superstars for the economic Mundial: the Mexican predicament with quality of education', John F. Kennedy School of Government, Harvard University, Cambridge.

Rosser, A., A. Joshi and D. Edwin (2011) 'Power, politics, and political entrepreneurs: realising universal free basic education in Indonesia', IDS Working Paper No. 358, Institute of Development Studies, Brighton, March.

Suryadarma, D. (2011) 'How corruption diminishes the effectiveness of public spending on education in Indonesia', *Bulletin of Indonesian Economic Studies*, 48(1): 85–100.

UNESCO (United Nations Educational, Scientific and Cultural Organization) (2011) 'The hidden crisis: armed conflict and education', EFA Global Monitoring Report 2011, UNESCO, Paris.

von Luebke, C. (2009) 'The political economy of local governance: findings from an Indonesian field study', *Bulletin of Indonesian Economic Studies*, 45(2): 201–30.

World Bank (2010) 'Governance matters to education outcomes. The Indonesia Local Education Governance Index (ILEGI): a report card of 50 local governments', World Bank, Jakarta.

World Bank (2012a) 'Indonesia economic quarterly: maintaining resilience', World Bank, Jakarta.

World Bank (2012b) 'Spending more or spending better: improving education financing in Indonesia. Education public expenditure review', World Bank, Jakarta.

World Bank (2012c) 'School-based management in Indonesia', World Bank, Jakarta.

World Bank (2012d) 'Making better use of teachers: strengthening teacher management to improve the efficiency and equity of public spending', World Bank, Jakarta.

World Bank (2012e) 'The BOSDA improvement program: enhancing equity and performance through local school grants', World Bank, Jakarta.

World Bank (2013a) *Early Childhood Education and Development in Indonesia: Strong Foundations, Later Success*, World Bank, Jakarta.

World Bank (2013b) 'Teacher reform in Indonesia: the role of politics and evidence in policy making', World Bank, Jakarta.

7 AN ASSESSMENT OF POLICIES TO IMPROVE TEACHER QUALITY AND REDUCE TEACHER ABSENTEEISM

*Asep Suryahadi and Prio Sambodho**

7.1 INTRODUCTION

Since the early 1970s, Indonesia has been successful in expanding its education sector to serve the wider population. This is apparent in the pronounced improvement in the country's gross enrolment rates (GERs) – that is, in the number of students enrolled in school as a percentage of the relevant age group – shown in Figure 7.1. The GER for primary education rose significantly from 84 per cent in 1970 to over 100 per cent in 1980, and stood at 118 per cent in 2010.[1] The GER for secondary education increased from 17 per cent to 77 per cent between 1970 and 2010, and the rate for tertiary education from 3 per cent to 23 per cent.

The quantitative expansion of education has contributed greatly to Indonesia's development. A more educated workforce has made it possible for the country to shift the base of its economy from agriculture to industry and services. As Figure 7.2 shows, the contribution of agriculture to GDP fell from 45 per cent in 1971 to just 15 per cent in 2010, while the share of industry rose from 20 per cent to 36 per cent, and that of services from 35 per cent to 49 per cent. The shift from lower to higher-productivity sectors has resulted in sustained economic growth averaging 6.5 per cent per annum for four decades, interrupted only in

* We thank Novita Maizir, Joseph Marshan and Mayang Rizki for research assistance.
1 The GER can be greater than 100 per cent because of grade repetition and entry at atypical ages.

Figure 7.1   Gross enrolment rates by school level, 1970–2010 (%)

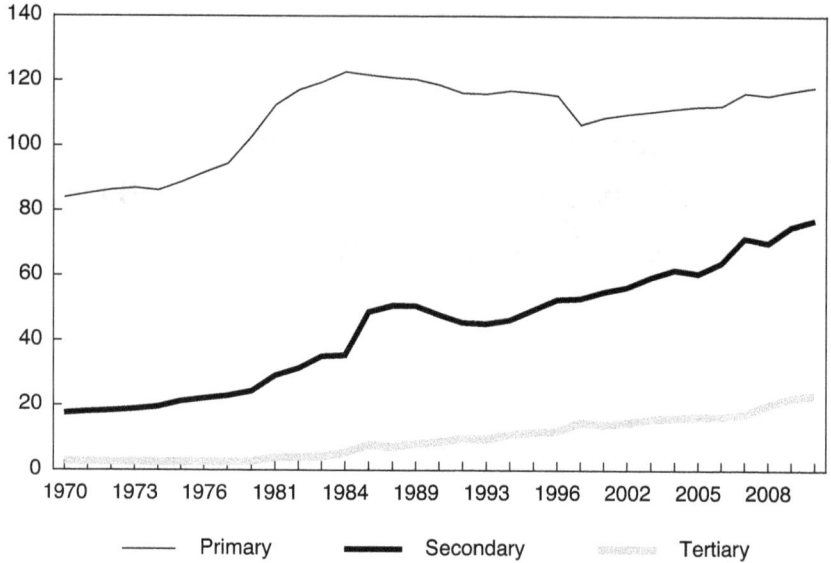

Source: World Bank country data (http://data.worldbank.org/country/indonesia).

Figure 7.2   GDP by sector, 1971–2010 (%)

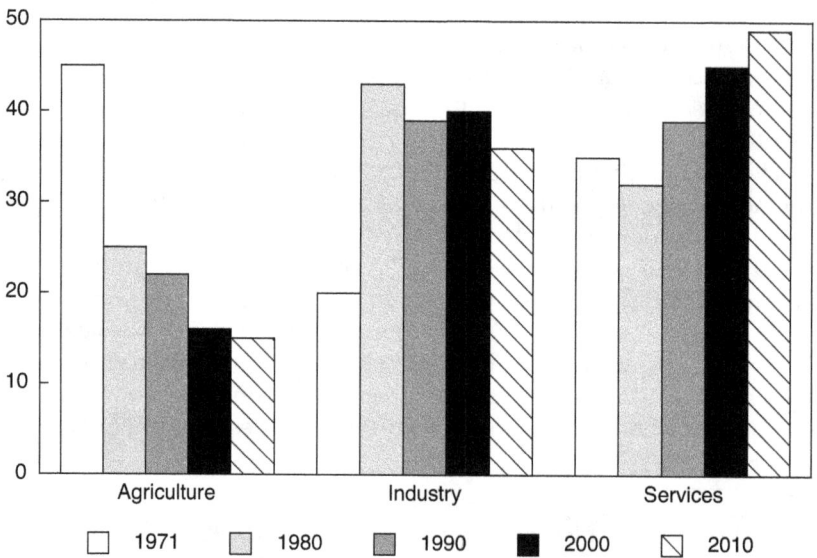

Source: Suryahadi, Hadiwidjaja and Sumarto (2012).

Table 7.1   The middle-income trap

Country	2010 GDP per capita (1990 PPP $)	Years in lower middle-income group until 2010	Years before falling into lower middle-income trap[a]	Average growth, 2000–10 (%)	Average annual GDP per capita growth to reach $7,250[b] (%)
Cambodia	2,529	6	22	8.2	4.9
India	3,407	9	19	6.1	4.1
Indonesia	4,790	25	3	3.9	14.8
Myanmar	3,301	7	21	9.0	3.8
Pakistan	2,344	6	22	2.6	5.3
Vietnam	3,262	9	19	6.1	4.3
Honduras	2,247	11	17	1.6	7.1
Mozambique	2,362	4	24	5.8	4.8

PPP = purchasing power parity.
a Calculated as 28 years minus the number of years the country had been in the lower middle-income group in 2010.
b Based on the country's income level in 2010, and calculated for the period from 2010 until the year in which the country would fall into the lower middle-income trap.
Source: Felipe (2012).

the late 1990s at the peak of the Asian financial crisis. Ultimately, this rapid economic growth has improved the general welfare of the population and reduced the incidence of poverty in its various dimensions.

With a per capita income of around $3,500 in 2011, Indonesia has achieved the status of a middle-income country. It now faces new and more complex challenges in its efforts to develop the economy and further improve the welfare of the population. The greatest challenge is to avoid the so-called middle-income trap – the situation where a country gets stuck in the middle-income range (of around $1,000–12,000) and is unable to increase its per capita income further to achieve high-income country status.

Based on GDP per capita and years in the same GDP bracket, Felipe (2012) calculated that 35 countries were caught in a middle-income trap in 2010. He further divided these countries into those in a lower middle-income trap (30 countries) and those in an upper middle-income trap (five countries). Felipe did not include Indonesia among the countries caught in a lower middle-income trap, although he projected that it was likely to join them by 2013 (Table 7.1). To avoid this fate and join the ranks of upper middle-income countries (those with GDP per capita of

$7,250 in 1990 PPP), he calculated that the Indonesian economy would need to grow by almost 15 per cent per annum for the three years from 2010 to 2013 – suggesting that there is practically no prospect of escape from the middle-income trap for Indonesia.[2]

7.2   THE QUANTITY AND QUALITY OF EDUCATION

To move into a higher income bracket, Indonesia needs to shift its economy to higher-value products. One of the key ingredients to achieve this is investment in education, to produce a qualified workforce that has the knowledge, skills and competencies to support the growth of innovation-based industries. This kind of investment has been credited as being one of the main factors in pushing South Korea, Finland and Ireland through the middle-income barrier and into the group of advanced economies (Foxley and Sossdorf 2011).

This implies that Indonesia urgently needs to improve the quality of education in order to be able to escape the middle-income trap as quickly as possible. As Arze del Granado et al. (2007) point out, the biggest challenge for the sector has shifted from increasing spending on education to improving the quality of education services, given that almost all Indonesian children now complete primary school, and most complete secondary school. Indeed, as the GERs in Figure 7.3 show, Indonesia's primary and secondary enrolment rates are already on a par with those of most developing countries in East Asia and the Pacific.

Indonesia still has a long way to go, however, to improve the quality of its education sector (Suryadarma 2011). The results of the Trends in International Mathematics and Science Study (TIMSS) show that more than half of Indonesian year 8 students are deficient in basic mathematics skills (Suryadarma and Sumarto 2011: 166). Indonesia's scores are well below the international average of 500, and consistently below those of neighbouring countries (Figure 7.4). The scores of Indonesian students on standardized international examinations are poor even after adjusting for socio-economic background, suggesting that deficiencies in the school system, rather than household conditions, are the principal contributor to Indonesia's poor performance (World Bank 2010: 2).

---

2   Felipe (2012) calculated that it had taken a median number of 28 years for nine countries that had entered the lower middle-income group after 1950 to graduate to the upper middle-income group. Since Indonesia had been a lower middle-income country for 25 years in 2010, it had only three more years to avoid the lower middle-income trap.

Figure 7.3 Gross enrolment rates in Indonesia and the developing countries of East Asia and the Pacific, 2000–10 (%)

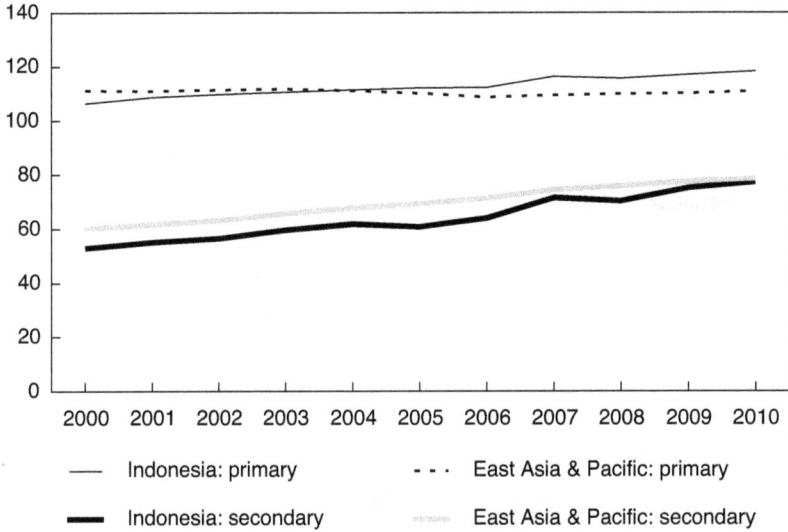

Source: World Bank country data (http://data.worldbank.org/country/indonesia).

Figure 7.4 Performance of year 8 students in TIMSS mathematics test, selected Southeast Asian countries, 1999–2011 (average score)

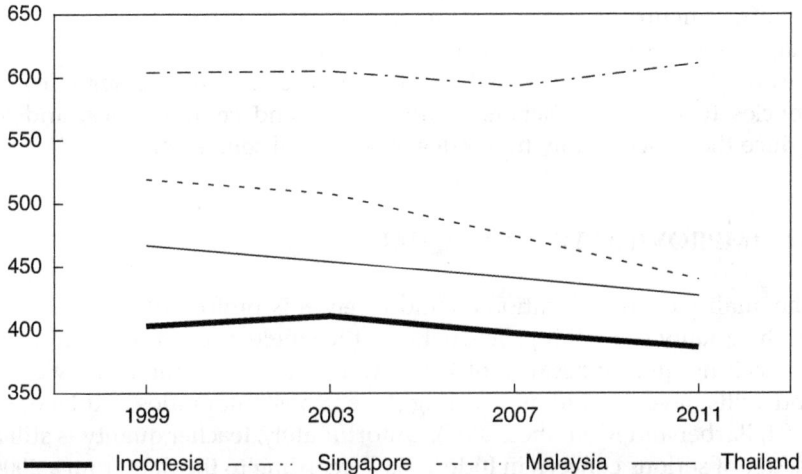

TIMSS = Trends in International Mathematics and Science Study.
Source: Suryadarma and Sumarto (2011); Mullis et al. (2012).

Figure 7.5   Educational attainment of teachers, 2006 (%)

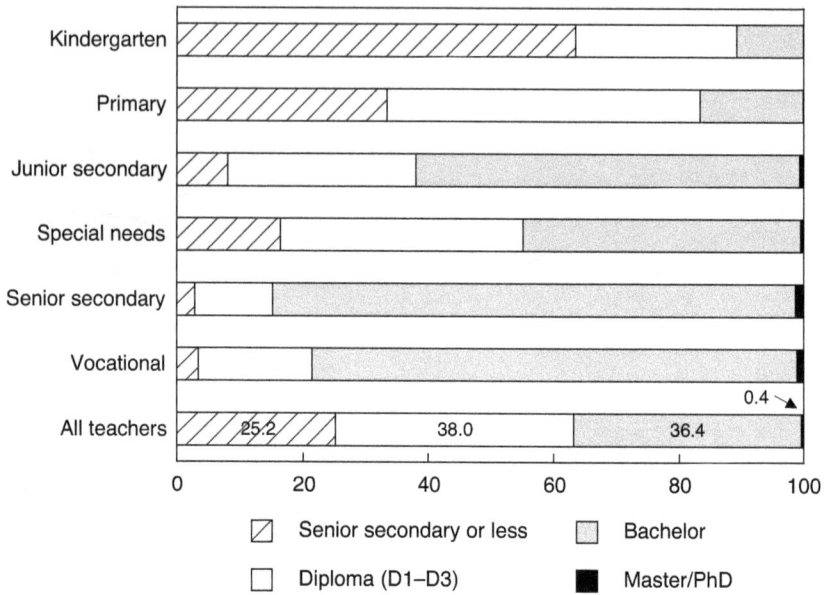

Source: Adapted from Jalal et al. (2009: 7).

A high-quality education system that encourages creativity and supports breakthroughs in science and technology depends on investments in infrastructure, curriculums, learning materials and teachers. This chapter focuses on teachers, who have a vital role to play in determining the quality of education (OECD 2004). In particular, this chapter assesses policies to improve teachers' qualifications and competencies, and to reduce the unacceptably high rates of teacher absenteeism.

7.3   IMPROVING TEACHER QUALITY

The quality of the education a child receives is profoundly determined by the quality of teaching. Teachers are the single most important factor in teaching quality because of the powerful influence their knowledge and skills have on student learning (Nye, Konstantopoulos and Hedges 2004; Barber and Mourshed 2007). Unfortunately, teacher quality is still a matter of serious concern in Indonesia. According to the data from a 2006 census of teachers presented in Figure 7.5, only 37 per cent of all teachers have the minimum qualification set by Law 14/2005 on Teachers and

Table 7.2   Comparison of teachers' salaries in selected Southeast Asian countries (PPP $)

Country	Year	Primary school teachers		Junior secondary teachers		Senior secondary teachers	
		Starting salary	Top salary	Starting salary	Top salary	Starting salary	Top salary
Indonesia	2004/05	2,733	3,941	2,913	4,281	3,373	4,756
Malaysia	2004	8,389	18,798	11,680	31,028	11,680	31,028
Philippines	2004/05	9,060	10,770	9,060	10,770	9,060	10,770
Thailand	2004/05	5,902	27,662	5,902	27,662	5,902	27,662

PPP = purchasing power parity.
Source: UNESCO and OECD (2005).

Lecturers – a four-year degree or higher – while 25 per cent have a secondary school education or less.

The poor quality of the Indonesian teaching body is associated with an oversupply of teachers, low teacher salaries (Table 7.2) and a weak national recruitment system that encourages districts and provinces to claim fictitious shortages of teachers (Jalal et al. 2009: 11). Arze del Granado et al. (2007: 19) point out that decentralization has provided a perverse incentive for districts to hire more teachers than they need because they do not have to pay for them; the central government covers teacher salaries through block grants from the General Purpose Fund (Dana Alokasi Umum, DAU). Another failing of the recruitment system is that it is regarded as a route to civil servant status, with its attendant privileges. This too contributes to an oversupply of teachers (Jalal et al. 2009: 11).

These problems are exacerbated by inadequate pre-service training and a weak performance assessment system for teachers. A study by Evans et al. (2009) finds that the content of pre-service education for teachers does not reflect the latest innovations and thinking, and that the standard of training provided is variable. Once they enter the profession, teachers discover that there is no clear career path for them, that opportunities for professional development are lacking and that the performance assessment system is not tied to financial rewards. There is also no effective way of managing or removing underperforming teachers. Clearly the current civil service-based appraisal system is inadequate to assess the performance of teachers.

Table 7.3   Average remuneration of tertiary graduates in the private and government sectors by age group, 2006 (Rp thousand per month)

Age group	Private sector	Government	Ratio: private to government
15–20 years	611.71	774.62	0.79
21–25 years	936.18	888.94	1.05
26–30 years	1,241.81	1,027.37	1.21
31–35 years	1,476.05	1,272.72	1.16
36–40 years	1,705.54	1,513.06	1.13
41–45 years	1,788.82	1,751.86	1.02
46–50 years	1,904.11	2,051.64	0.93
51–55 years	2,015.36	2,057.88	0.98
55–65 years	2,132.41	3,180.85	0.67
65+ years	2,132.54	–	–
Total	**1,543.44**	**1,642.46**	**0.94**

Source: National Labour Force Survey (Sakernas).

Teacher certification

The failure of past initiatives to strengthen teaching quality has been attributed to the piecemeal fashion in which they were implemented. To address this, in 2005 the government enacted Law 14/2005 on Teachers and Lecturers. Regarded as the most comprehensive strategy yet to improve teaching quality in Indonesia, it laid the foundation for a massive teacher certification program that attempts to set standards for teachers, upgrade their skills and ultimately improve the quality of education (Jalal et al. 2009: 24).

To improve the attractiveness of the teaching profession and provide a strong incentive for teachers to participate in the certification process, Law 14/2005 entitles certified teachers to a professional allowance that effectively doubles their base salaries, while those who are assigned to remote or disadvantaged areas receive an additional allowance that triples their salaries. This is a considerable incentive, considering that the private sector offers only a small pay premium for tertiary graduates. As Table 7.3 shows, in 2006, the year before the certification program started, the pay premium in the private over the public sector was just 21 per cent for 26–30-year-olds. This relatively low premium confirms Filmer and Lindauer's (2001) finding that the private sector pay premium for

Table 7.4   Forecast of costs associated with teacher certification, 2007–15
(Rp trillion, 2006 prices)

Year	Professional allowance	Assessment & certification	In-service upgrading	Total real cost
2007	158.74	360.90	1,323.30	1,842.94
2008	3,608.10	400.00	1,466.67	5,474.77
2009	8,649.72	693.00	2,541.00	11,883.72
2010	16,134.12	793.01	2,907.70	19,834.82
2011	24,698.61	793.00	2,907.68	28,399.29
2012	33,263.05	793.00	2,907.68	36,963.74
2013	41,827.49	516.11	1,892.40	44,236.01
2014	47,401.48	223.00	817.68	48,442.17
2015	49,809.92	223.00	817.68	50,850.61
Cumulative	**225,551.24**	**4,795.03**	**17,581.79**	**247,928.06**
%	91.0	1.9	7.1	100.0

Source: Jalal et al. (2009: 173, Table 7.5).

graduates in Indonesia is lower than commonly assumed, and in line with international practice.

The costs of certification, training and allowances imply considerable new investments in education. By the time the government completes the process of certifying all existing teachers, expected to be in 2015, the total cost of certification is estimated to reach around Rp 250 trillion in constant 2006 prices, with professional allowances making up more than 90 per cent of this (Table 7.4).[3] With a price tag as high as this, the government will need to be sure that the investment in teacher certification will ultimately improve the quality of teachers, and that this in turn will improve the quality of learning and raise the standard of education as a whole.

---

3 To provide some perspective on the magnitude of these costs, we can compare them to the cost of the emergency program of unconditional payments to poor and near-poor households known as Direct Cash Assistance (Bantuan Langsung Tunai, BLT). Between October 2005 and September 2006, the BLT program provided cash assistance of Rp 100,000 per month to more than 19 million households at a total cost of around Rp 20 trillion. This means that the funds allocated to the teacher certification program could be used to sustain the BLT program for 12.5 years.

Law 14/2005 mandates that teachers and lecturers develop four groups of competencies: pedagogical (teaching ability); personal (character and example); professional (training and education); and social (community participation). These are to be developed through a combination of teacher education and successful classroom performance. To be eligible for certification, a teacher must meet the minimum requirements, which include having at least a four-year diploma (D4) or bachelor (S1) degree, accumulating the required number of professional training credits and teaching a minimum of 24 hours per week.

The certification process was scheduled to begin in 2006 but was postponed so that the test instrument could be redesigned. Hence, the first batch of 200,000 teachers took the certification test in 2007. By 2015, only certified teachers should be teaching in the schools. The certification process operates through two institutional channels: the Ministry of Education and Culture, which handles the certification of teachers from regular schools, other than teachers of religion; and the Ministry of Religious Affairs, which handles the certification of teachers from Islamic schools (*madrasah*) as well as teachers of religion in state schools. Because of the failure to provide clear and complete information, however, the division of certification into two channels has created problems, including situations where teachers have been asked to undertake certification by both organizations or by the wrong organization (Hastuti et al. 2008).

Since being introduced, the certification mechanism has changed several times. The latest configuration, starting in 2012, provides three different ways in which teachers can obtain certification, depending on their qualifications: direct certification (Pemberian Sertifikat Pendidik secara Langsung); portfolio assessment (Penilaian Portofolio); and teacher retraining (Pendidikan dan Latihan Profesi Guru).

The direct certification channel is available to teachers who have a master's degree (S2) or doctorate (S3) and have civil service rank IVb, as well as all teachers who have civil service rank IVc.[4] Teachers certified through this channel are required to follow a document verification process. Those who are assessed as qualified would then be granted certification directly, while those who are not would have to enter the teacher retraining channel.

The portfolio assessment channel is for teachers who hold supervisory positions. Here, the certification process is based on the verification

4 Indonesia has four civil service levels, numbered I to IV, with IV being the highest. Each has four subdivisions, numbered (a) to (d), except for level IV, which has an additional subdivision (e). A newly appointed university graduate would be appointed to rank IIIa. The highest rank, IVe, would be equivalent to the rank of a full professor at a university.

and appraisal of documents that reflect a teacher's competencies. The areas covered are academic qualifications; education and training; teaching experience; lesson planning and presentation; appraisal by superiors and inspectors; academic achievements; professional development work; participation in scientific forums; experience in educational and social organizations; and relevant recognitions and awards (Hastuti et al. 2008: 23). Teachers who are not assessed as satisfactory must enter the teacher retraining channel.

During the first years of the teacher certification program, most teachers were assessed through the portfolio channel, with those who did not meet the minimum standard receiving just one week of remedial training. However, there were concerns that the process was being undermined by deception, with some teachers submitting false documentation to support their applications (Hastuti et al. 2008: 24).

Most teachers now have to follow the teacher retraining channel to achieve certification. Applicants first have to take a preliminary competency test. Those who pass then have to undertake 90 hours of retraining over 10 days in the form of lectures and workshops. They must then pass a final competency test to receive their certification.[5] Teachers who fail the test are allowed to retake it once.

Since the teacher certification program is relatively new, studies assessing its effectiveness in improving teaching quality are scant. Early evidence indicates, however, that it has not yet had a significant impact on students' performance. For example, Fahmi, Maulana and Yusuf (2011) found no evidence that teacher certification had improved student performance, based on a survey of certified and uncertified primary school teachers, and their students' results in national examinations. Similarly, De Ree et al. (2012) found that teacher certification had not improved learning outcomes in the 360 public primary and junior secondary schools they examined. They did find, however, that the doubling of teacher salaries had reduced the likelihood of teachers holding additional jobs, and of them having financial difficulties.

The higher salaries provide an incentive for teachers who do not meet the requirements for certification to upgrade their qualifications and teaching loads to meet the requirements (Hastuti et al. 2008). The impact of the program on teachers who have not yet undertaken certification is therefore potentially quite large.

---

5   The two-hour multiple choice test examines pedagogical competency (30 per cent of questions) and professional competency in relation to the teacher's particular teaching subject (70 per cent). One-quarter of the questions are 'easy', 50 per cent of 'medium difficulty' and 25 per cent 'difficult'. Each test package has to be validated by a panel of experts and a sample of representative teachers (Ministry of Education and Culture 2012).

While evidence for the effectiveness of certification in improving educational quality has yet to emerge, it does seem that the program has increased the attractiveness of the teaching profession. Studies by Evans et al. (2009) and the World Bank (2010) find that the new incentive structure is attracting more university graduates into teaching and creating a surge in enrolments in teacher education in universities.

Indeed, in the long run, one of the largest benefits of the teacher certification program may be its ability to draw a new pool of well-educated, high-quality people into the teaching profession – if the institutions responsible for educating the new body of teachers can be persuaded to lift their standards. According to Evans et al. (2009), teacher training institutions, which have the most comprehensive engagement in both pre-service and in-service teacher education and professional development, are still inadequately prepared to play a leading role in improving teacher quality.

Another challenge for the certification process is to improve teachers' scores on the competency tests. The 281,016 teachers who took the preliminary competency test in February 2012 received an average score of just 42 out of 100 (Akuntono 2012). Worryingly, teachers recorded their poorest results in the subjects of mathematics, physics and general science – that is, the subjects regarded as the most important for training a high-quality workforce fit for a modern economy. The fact that many teachers had difficulty using the online system for the competency test also shows that there is an urgent need to improve the technological literacy of teachers, if Indonesia is to keep up with the global technology-based economies.

Remote area allowance

In addition to a professional allowance for certified teachers that is equal a teacher's base pay, Law 14/2005 provides for an additional allowance, also equal to base pay, for certified teachers who teach in 'special areas'. Special areas are those that are considered remote, impoverished or conflict affected. The allowance is aimed at attracting teachers, especially better-qualified ones, to areas that have traditionally found it hard to obtain and retain good staff.

Teachers working in remote areas tend to have poorer qualifications than other teachers, and are less likely to be eligible for certification. To provide a more immediate incentive, in 2007 the government decided to introduce a new subsidy of Rp 1.3 million per month for uncertified teachers who had been teaching in a remote area for at least two years. The subsidy, which is currently given only to primary school teachers, had increased to Rp 1.5 million per month by 2012.

The process for selecting beneficiaries is as follows. The central government sets quotas for each province, and the provincial governments set quotas for the districts. The district governments then identify the schools whose teachers are to receive the subsidy, based on factors such as the school's distance from the district office, the availability of electricity in the village and so on. All teachers in the identified schools should receive the subsidy, as long as they have worked at the school for at least two years and have a minimum workload of 24 hours per week.

In their baseline survey of the remote area allowance, Toyamah et al. (2009: 9–11) found inconsistencies in the implementation of the program. The size of the allowance given to teachers differed between districts, and some teachers in eligible districts – or even in schools that had been designated as remote – knew nothing about the program. The authors found that, in general, only teachers who were actually receiving the allowance were aware of the program. In addition, some recipients did not know precisely how much they were supposed to receive, and many did not receive the full amount of the allowance.

Some of those surveyed complained that the procedure for determining recipients was unclear, resulting in incorrect targeting and undercoverage of the program. In practice, the majority of recipients did not receive their full entitlements, because many schools chose to distribute the allowance among all teachers in order to avoid jealousy. This has reduced the effectiveness of the program in achieving its objectives (Toyamah et al. 2009).

The remote area allowance is not intended to encourage teachers to move to a remote area, but rather to persuade those who are already in such an area to stay there. Because teachers in remote areas generally have lower qualifications and poorer teaching skills than those in urban areas, the subsidy is unlikely to significantly improve the quality of education in remote areas.[6]

Professional working groups

Currently there are two types of professional working groups for teachers, the Primary School Teachers Working Group (Kelompok Kerja Guru, KKG) and the Secondary School Subjects Teachers Working Group (Musyawarah Guru Mata Pelajaran, MGMP). Their purpose is to provide a forum for teachers within a cluster of schools to share information and improve their teaching skills. The government provides block grants for the groups through its Education Quality Assurance Institute (Lembaga

---

6 We thank the editors for pointing out this weakness in the remote area allowance program.

Penjamin Mutu Pendidikan, LPMP). The grants are mainly used for curriculum development, preparation of learning aids and teaching materials, classroom activity research, scientific writing and professional development.

Tedjawati (2010) found that KKG activities had helped primary school teachers to expand their knowledge of teaching materials, develop teaching plans, research classroom activities, improve their teaching techniques, better manage classes and provide feedback to students. Reducing the effectiveness of such activities, on the other hand, were a lack of support from university-based resource persons, holding activities outside working hours, teachers' failure to appreciate the importance of some KKG activities and a lack of supporting materials.

According to Evans et al. (2009: xii–xiii), the KKG and MGMP forums have not been effective in improving teachers' competence and skills in subject matter and pedagogy. Most suffer from poor management and oversight by local authorities, particularly school principals. The coverage of the groups is too limited and they do not disseminate practices or programs that have been found to work well. Like Tedjawati (2010), the authors identify a lack of support from experts, particularly in the tertiary education sector, as one of the gaps in improving the quality of teachers through the KKGs and MGMPs. Resistance to innovation is another constraint, especially among senior teachers. Though the forums have the potential to be a major force in reforming the teaching profession, at the moment many of them do little more than provide a venue for teachers to share lesson plans.

7.4   REDUCING TEACHER ABSENTEEISM

For learning among students to take place, teachers must be present in the classroom. Unfortunately, in Indonesia as in many other developing countries, teacher absenteeism is widespread. This is a major impediment not only to students' learning and development, but also to achieving national development objectives. Chaudhury et al. (2006) argue that excessive teacher absenteeism is consistent with the idea that teachers are extremely unlikely to be fired for being absent. They note, however, that teachers' decisions about whether to go to work are also influenced by the working conditions they face.

The magnitude of the problem and its impact

In its survey of teacher absence in six developing countries including Indonesia, the World Bank (2004) found that the average rate of teacher

Table 7.5   Rates of teacher absenteeism in Indonesia and Papua (%)

	2003	2008	Papua 2011
Total sample	**19.6**	**14.1**	**33.5**
School remoteness			
Non-remote schools	22.7	12.2	20.0
Remote schools	–	23.3	43.4
Employment status			
Civil servant teachers	18.8	12.5	32
Contract teachers	29.6	19.4	32
Position in school			
Principals	25.1	20.2	51
Classroom teachers	19.3	14.0	–

Source: 2003 and 2008: Toyamah et al. (2009); Papua 2011: UNCEN et al. (2012).

absenteeism in 2003 was around 19 per cent. This meant that on any single school day, one in every five teachers who were supposed to teach that day did not show up in the classroom.

In Indonesia, the latest nationally representative data available are for 2008. They indicate that around 14 per cent of teachers were absent from class on any given school day in that year (Table 7.5). This represented a decline from about 19 per cent in 2003, attributable to improved management by district authorities, better incentives for teachers and more regular supervision of schools (Toyamah et al. 2009). About 45 per cent of the teachers who were absent in 2008 were sick or on official leave; 28 per cent were working on teaching-related tasks; 12 per cent were working on tasks unrelated to teaching, had arrived late or had left early; and 14 per cent were absent for no clear reason (Toyamah et al. 2009: 23).

Teacher absence is a waste of the resources to educate children and adversely affects the quality of education. As Rogers and Vegas (2009) observe, if students end up doing 'busy work' or playing in the school-yard when they are supposed to be in the classroom, little learning is likely to take place. Moreover, if the poor quality of schooling discourages parents from making the sacrifices necessary to send their children to school, teacher absence can affect access to education and school completion rates. Equally importantly, high rates of teacher absence often signal deeper problems of accountability and governance that are themselves barriers to educational progress. More generally, Chaudhury et al. (2006) argue that teacher absenteeism reflects the larger problem of weak institutions for supplying public goods, which is a significant barrier to economic development in many countries.

Suryadarma et al. (2006) provide empirical evidence that teacher absence slows student learning in Indonesia. They find that an additional 10 percentage points in the average absence rate of teachers at a school is associated with a 0.09 standard deviation decrease in the maths scores of fourth graders, but has no effect on verbal test scores. This is consistent with findings for other developing countries such as Zambia (Das et al. 2007) and India (Duflo, Hanna and Ryan 2007). Moreover, absence tends to be more prevalent in schools serving disadvantaged children, such as schools in poor rural and remote areas. Hence, teacher absenteeism compounds the disadvantages already faced by students in poor communities.

The case of Papua

Although Papua has made significant progress in increasing access to education for its population, a number of problems remain, with teacher absenteeism being one of the most chronic. Among the other problems with basic education in Papua identified by Evans et al. (2009: 56) are that about 70 per cent of indigenous children live in remote rural communities where there are few if any teachers; that teaching conditions in rural and isolated areas are poor, with housing and food shortages, poor sanitation and a lack of clean water; that little administrative support (equipment, materials and books as well as teachers) is provided for interior, coastal, remote and isolated areas; and that students in remote and isolated areas must travel long distances to get to school, and may have to work to support their families.

The problem of teacher absenteeism in Papua has two distinct characteristics compared with other regions in Indonesia. First, the incidence is much higher than the national average. A recent study found that the rate of teacher absenteeism in the province in 2011 was at least 33.5 per cent (UNCEN et al. 2012: 10). In other words, one in three teachers who were scheduled to teach during the school day was absent from work. Second, the duration of teacher absence in Papua is much longer than is typically the case in other regions. While teachers in other parts of Indonesia tend to be absent for a few days, those in Papua can disappear for months. The average length of absence among a sample of absent teachers in Papua was 70 days, and around 15 per cent of the absent teachers had been absent for more than a year (UNCEN et al. 2012: 65).

As in other parts of the country, the incidence of teacher absenteeism in Papua is much higher in regions with difficult access. In highland districts, for example, almost one in two teachers is likely to be absent from class on any given day. The study by UNCEN et al. (2012: 12) found that male teachers tended to be absent more often than female teachers; non-diploma teachers more often than university graduates; and indigenous Papuan teachers more often than non-Papuan teachers. Teachers in schools that were monitored more frequently, however, had lower rates of absenteeism.

The remoteness of a region clearly influences the level of teacher absenteeism, not just in Papua but across the whole of Indonesia. Toyamah et al. (2009: x) find that, across Indonesia, teacher absenteeism tends to be lower in urban areas than in rural areas; and to be less of a problem in districts and cities located in more developed western Indonesia than in those located in less developed eastern and central Indonesia. They also find that male teachers are more likely to be absent than female teachers; that non-permanent teachers are more likely to be absent than permanent/civil servant teachers; and that teachers in schools located far from the district education office are more likely to be absent than those in schools located close to the district education office (p. 31).

Policies to reduce teacher absenteeism

The problem of teacher absenteeism is often viewed through the prism of teachers' welfare. Hence, policies to reduce teacher absenteeism mainly focus on efforts to improve welfare. The remote area allowance, for example, aims to reduce teacher absenteeism in remote and difficult to access areas, where the problem is worst. Various studies have shown the importance of effective supervision and monitoring in reducing teacher absenteeism. Policies to improve school supervision and monitoring by both education offices and school committees are therefore important to reduce rates of absenteeism.

Toyamah et al. (2009: x) found that local government policies were a significant factor in the decline in teacher absenteeism observed between 2003 and 2008 (Table 7.5). These included a competition to become the 'favourite' school in the city of Surakarta, the decision to place a supervisor in a multi-school complex in the city of Bandung and an increase in the work performance subsidy in the city of Pekanbaru. In the district of Sukabumi, a regulation requiring teachers working in remote areas to live near the schools in which they worked proved very effective in reducing teacher absenteeism. Other factors that had contributed to the reduction in teacher absenteeism were the physical presence of the school principal in the school; the availability of school facilities such as electricity and toilets; the availability of sufficient classrooms; regular inspections by school supervisors; and regular school committee meetings (Toyamah et al. 2009: 32).

In general, the introduction of a remote area allowance for teachers has not yet had an impact on rates of teachers' attendance in schools located in remote areas, perhaps because of the inconsistent implementation of the program (Toyamah et al. 2009: 46). Exceptions are found, however, in areas where the national policy is complemented by similar local government policies.

In Papua, teacher certification does not seem to affect rates of teacher absenteeism. However, the availability of government housing for teachers, and the quality of that housing, does appear to improve attendance rates (UNCEN et al. 2012: 129–30). Participation in professional working groups (such as a KKG) is positively correlated to attendance, with teachers who participate in professional organizations in their subdistricts almost twice as likely to turn up to class than those who do not (p. 126).

Effective implementation of the government's school-based management (*manajemen berbasis sekolah*) policy has also been found to have a positive effect on teacher attendance in schools in Papua (UNCEN et al. 2012: 13). In schools where principals, teachers, students, staff, parents and others were actively involved in decision making and the policy was judged to be working well, the average rate of teacher absenteeism was about 12 per cent – well below the rate of 27 per cent observed in schools with 'average' implementation of the policy. However, for school-based management to be effective, all its elements – transparency, school accountability to the local community, community monitoring of schools and community participation in school decision making – need to be implemented as a 'full package' (p. 14).

The Papua study identifies several other factors that tend to reduce teacher absenteeism (UNCEN et al. 2012: 14). First, good school infrastructure appears to be helpful in promoting teacher attendance; in schools with high-quality infrastructure, teacher absenteeism was only about 11 per cent. Second, teacher absenteeism is lower in schools where communities take an active role in the management and monitoring of schools. Third, incentive programs for teachers seem to improve attendance; a small number of schools had applied a mix of sanctions and incentives that, together with effective community participation, had led to very low rates of teacher absence from school. Fourth, schools led by an effective principal have been able to reduce teacher absenteeism and improve the quality of school management. In short, well-managed schools with effective leadership have much lower rates of teacher absenteeism.

7.5 CONCLUSION

The expansion of education has contributed significantly to Indonesia's entry into the ranks of middle-income countries. To avoid the middle-income trap, however, Indonesia needs a more highly trained workforce with the knowledge, skills and competencies to produce higher-value products. To achieve this, the government will need to make a more serious effort to improve the quality of education, by investing in infrastructure, curriculums, learning materials and especially teachers. Currently only 37 per cent of teachers have the minimum qualification required by Law 14/2005, and around 14 per cent of teachers are absent from class on any given school day.

To set minimum standards for teachers, upgrade their skills and ultimately improve the quality of education, the government has implemented a massive teacher certification program since 2006. Certification comes with a professional allowance that doubles teachers' base salaries, giving them a strong incentive to upgrade their qualifications and teaching loads to meet the requirements. There is evidence that the policy is attracting more university graduates into the teaching force, with a surge in enrolments in teacher education in universities. However, there is no evidence as yet that it has improved the performance of Indonesian students or reduced rates of teacher absenteeism. Teacher absenteeism remains an intractable problem, with the special allowance for teachers working in remote areas failing to lift attendance rates to acceptable levels.

Efforts to improve teacher quality should focus on the following areas. First, Indonesia needs to develop a system of professional development for teachers, ranging from improved quality of pre-service teacher education and the recruitment of highly qualified teachers based on competence, through to the provision of regular opportunities for in-service professional development. Second, the system for assessing teachers' performance needs to be overhauled. Such a system should be based on regular assessments of competencies, and linked to student performance. The performance assessment system for civil servants is not suitable for appraising the performance of teachers. Third, both the professional development and performance assessment systems need to be linked to salary and other incentives for teachers.

Efforts to further reduce rates of teacher absenteeism need to focus on the following areas. First, communities – especially school committees – should be encouraged to become more actively involved in monitoring teacher attendance. Second, schools should be given the flexibility to implement local and school-level initiatives to reduce teacher absenteeism, such as financial incentives or disincentives related to attendance. Third, to both increase the availability of teachers and reduce absenteeism in remote areas, the government should recruit teachers who come from those areas, or live near the schools in which they work.

REFERENCES

Akuntono, I. (2012) 'Rata-rata hasil uji kompetensi guru masih rendah' [The average score of teacher competency test results is still low], *Kompas. com*, 12 December.

Arze del Granado, F.J., W. Fengler, A. Ragatz and E. Yavuz (2007) 'Investing in Indonesia's education: allocation, equity, and efficiency of public expenditures', Policy Research Working Paper No. 4329, World Bank, Washington DC.

Barber, M. and M. Mourshed (2007) 'How the world's best-performing schools come out on top', McKinsey & Company, New York.

Chaudhury, N., J. Hammer, M. Kremer, K. Muralidharan and F.H. Rogers (2006) 'Missing in action: teacher and health worker absence in developing countries', *Journal of Economic Perspectives*, 20(1): 91–116.

Das, J., S. Dercon, J. Habyarimana and P. Krishnan (2007) 'Teacher shocks and student learning: evidence from Zambia', *Journal of Human Resources*, 42(4): 820–62.

De Ree, J., K. Muralidharan, M. Pradhan and H. Rogers (2012) 'Double for what? The effects of unconditional teacher salary increases on performance', World Bank, Jakarta.

Duflo, E., R. Hanna and S. Ryan (2007) 'Monitoring works: getting teachers to come to school', Massachusetts Institute of Technology, Cambridge.

Evans, D., S. Tate, R. Navarro and M. Nicolls (2009) 'Teacher education and professional development in Indonesia: a gap analysis', United States Agency for International Development, Jakarta.

Fahmi, M., A. Maulana and A.A. Yusuf (2011) 'Teacher certification in Indonesia: a confusion of means and ends', Working Paper in Economics and Development Studies, Center for Economics and Development Studies (CEDS), Padjadjaran University, Bandung.

Felipe, J. (2012) 'Tracking the middle-income trap: what is it, who is in it, and why? Part 1', ADB Economics Working Paper No. 306, Asian Development Bank, Manila.

Filmer, D. and D. Lindauer (2001) 'Does Indonesia have a "low pay" civil service?', *Bulletin of Indonesian Economic Studies*, 37(2): 189–205.

Foxley, A. and S. Sossdorf (2011) 'Making the transition: from middle-income to advanced economies', Carnegie Paper, Carnegie Endowment for International Peace, Washington DC.

Hastuti, B. Sulaksono, Akhmadi, M. Syukri, U. Sabainingrum and Ruhmaniyati (2008) 'Implementation of the teacher certification program: a case study of Jambi, West Java and West Kalimantan provinces', Research Report, SMERU Research Institute, Jakarta.

Jalal, F., M. Samani, M.C. Chang, R. Stevenson, A.B. Ragatz and S.D. Negara (2009) *Teacher Certification in Indonesia: A Strategy for Teacher Quality Improvement*, Ministry of National Education and World Bank, Jakarta.

Ministry of Education and Culture (2012) *Sertifikasi Guru dalam Jabatan Tahun 2012* [In-service Teacher Certification 2012], Badan Pengembangan Sumberdaya Manusia Pendidikan dan Penjaminan Mutu Pendidikan, Kementerian Pendidikan dan Kebudayaan, Jakarta.

Mullis, I.V.S., M.O. Martin, P. Foy and A. Arora (2012) *TIMSS 2011 International Results in Mathematics*, TIMSS & PIRLS International Study Center, Lynch School of Education, Boston College, Chestnut Hill.

Nye, B., S. Konstantopoulos and L.V. Hedges (2004) 'How large are teacher effects?', *Educational Evaluation and Policy Analysis*, 26: 237–57.

OECD (Organisation for Economic Co-operation and Development) (2004) 'The quality of the teaching workforce', Policy Brief, OECD Observer, February, OECD, Paris.

Rogers, F.H. and E. Vegas (2009) 'No more cutting class? Reducing teacher absence and providing incentives for performance', Policy Research Working Paper No. 4847, World Bank, Washington DC.

Suryadarma, D. (2011) 'The quality of education: international standing and attempts at improvement', in C. Manning and S. Sumarto (eds) *Employment, Living Standards and Poverty in Contemporary Indonesia*, Institute of Southeast Asian Studies, Singapore, pp. 161–82.

Suryadarma, D. and S. Sumarto (2011) 'Survey of recent developments', *Bulletin of Indonesian Economic Studies*, 47(2): 155–81.

Suryadarma, D., A. Suryahadi, S. Sumarto and F.H. Rogers (2006) 'Improving student performance in public primary schools in developing countries: evidence from Indonesia', *Education Economics*, 14(4): 401–29.

Suryahadi, A., G. Hadiwidjaja and S. Sumarto (2012) 'Economic growth and poverty reduction in Indonesia before and after the Asian financial crisis', *Bulletin of Indonesian Economic Studies*, 48(2): 209–27.

Tedjawati (2010) 'Pelaksanaan Kelompok Kerja Guru (KKG) bermutu: studi kasus KKG gugus Cisaat Gadis Kabupaten Sukabumi' [Implementation of Teacher Working Group (KKG) excellence: a case study of the Cisaat Gadis KKG cluster in Sukabumi district], Pusat Penelitian Kebijakan dan Inovasi Pendidikan, Badan Penelitian dan Pengembangan, Kementerian Pendidikan dan Kebudayaan, Jakarta.

Toyamah, N., B. Sulaksono, M. Rosfadhila, S. Devina, S. Arif, S.A. Hutagalung, E. Pakpahan and A. Yusrina (2009) 'Teacher absenteeism and remote area allowance baseline survey', Research Report, SMERU Research Institute, Jakarta.

UNCEN (Universitas Cendrawasih) et al. (2012) '"We like being taught": a study on teacher absenteeism in Papua and West Papua', UNCEN, UNIPA, SMERU, BPS and UNICEF, Jayapura.

UNESCO (*United Nations Educational, Scientific and Cultural Organization*) and OECD (Organisation for Economic Co-operation and Development) (2005) *Education Trends in Perspective: Analysis of the World Education Indicators*, UNESCO and OECD, Paris.

World Bank (2004) *World Development Report 2004*, World Bank, Washington DC.

World Bank (2010) 'Transforming Indonesia's teaching force. Volume II: From pre-service training to retirement: producing and maintaining a high-quality, efficient, and motivated workforce', Report No. 53732-ID, World Bank, Jakarta.

8 INDONESIAN UNIVERSITIES: RAPID GROWTH, MAJOR CHALLENGES

*Hal Hill and Thee Kian Wie**

8.1 INTRODUCTION

As befits its size and rising income, Indonesia now has one of the largest and fastest-growing tertiary education systems in the world. In 2010, about 5.2 million students were enrolled in some sort of institute of higher education, including universities, academies, polytechnics and advanced schools (*sekolah tinggi*), with almost three times as many enrolled in private as in public institutions. These students were enrolled in about 3,600 institutions administered mainly by the Ministry of Education and Culture and the Ministry of Religious Affairs. The focus of this chapter is on the country's approximately 550 universities, which attract most of the public funding, and which are seen as the major vehicle for lifting the standard of knowhow and intellectual discourse, and for providing high-level policy advice to government.

We commence by making five broad generalizations about these institutions. First, Indonesian universities are essentially a creation of the second half of the twentieth century, with most of the growth occurring in the last quarter of that century. For all practical purposes, Indonesia barely possessed a tertiary education sector in the colonial era; during the first two decades of independence the growth of the sector was constrained by other nation-building priorities, including the necessity to

* This chapter draws in part on research work sponsored by the Australian Agency for International Development (AusAID). We thank the agency and various staff members, while emphasizing that the views expressed here are solely our own. We also thank the editors of this book and participants at the 2012 Indonesia Update Conference for helpful comments and suggestions.

expand primary and secondary education, and by the country's indifferent economic performance.

Second, as a result of this history, the country has been an educational laggard, consistently ranking behind the Asian giants, China and India, and behind its middle-income ASEAN neighbours. Educational disadvantage typically takes decades to overcome, even with very high levels of expenditure and commitment, neither of which Indonesia has in abundant proportions.

A third feature is that the sector began to grow very rapidly from the 1980s, driven by several factors. One was the large cohort beginning to graduate from the country's primary and secondary schools as a result of the commitment to universal education at these levels. Another was that the country was by then about to graduate into the ranks of lower middle-income developing countries, crossing a threshold where the demand for higher education would become highly income-elastic, and the labour market more 'credentialed' in the sense of requiring more formal professional qualifications, and demanding a more skilled workforce. Moreover, the private tertiary education sector began to grow quickly, and was by then operating in a somewhat less restrictive regulatory regime.

Fourth, and not surprisingly, there are huge variations in quality. A handful of 'elite' universities, mostly public, aspire to join the ranks of internationally recognized institutions; some already have pockets of international excellence. There is also a growing group of mid-tier universities, mainly in the private sector, that deliver good-quality, market-attuned undergraduate education. But as would be expected for a system still in its infancy, the great majority of the country's universities could not yet be described as institutions that function in the traditional sense of offering a high-quality research and teaching environment.

The fifth feature is that much of the philosophical domain governing higher education policy remains a matter of contention, as it does in many university systems in the developing world. Government policy continues to be dominated by a strongly interventionist approach. The initial cautious steps towards a less centralized regime, in which universities have the autonomy to operate according to prescribed objectives, have been strongly resisted in some quarters. Many senior officials within the Ministry of Education and Culture continue to believe that public universities should be run along civil service lines, under the direction of the ministry's Directorate General of Higher Education.[1] There is also a tension between official egalitarian objectives, and the fact that the

---

1 It also needs to be remembered that, unlike primary and secondary education, tertiary education was not decentralized under the 2001 regional autonomy program.

government is able to finance only about one-quarter of the country's expenditure on tertiary education. In reality, public expenditure priorities in higher education do not accord closely with equity objectives.

The funding shortfall has to be met by private resources, but there is a reluctance within some quarters of the Ministry of Education and Culture to redefine its objectives and modus operandi in order to play an enabling role in fostering efficiency, equity and quality objectives, rather than a 'central planning' role of directly running universities. The ministry's embrace of the worldwide trend towards internationalization of higher education has also been hesitant, with the result that Indonesian universities are rather isolated from the regional and global mainstreams. It is perhaps not an exaggeration to state that practically all Indonesian families with the requisite financial resources aspire to send their children abroad for tertiary education. One political implication of this preference is, arguably, that the country's political and business elites do not yet have as strong a commitment to the development of high-quality tertiary education as has been the case in the Asian NIEs and China.

The purpose of this chapter is to survey these and related issues in two parts. In section 8.2, we review the development of Indonesian universities in recent times, against the backdrop of official objectives, comparable regional developments and what may be considered international best practice. In section 8.3, we focus on some of the key tertiary education policy issues and debates under the second Yudhoyono administration. We then sum up our main arguments in section 8.4.

8.2   INDONESIAN UNIVERSITIES: OVERVIEW AND CONTEXT[2]

An overview

Indonesia's status as an educational latecomer is revealed in the widely used Barro–Lee schooling attainment data. In 1960, 68 per cent of the population aged 15 years or over had no or incomplete primary education, while the average years of schooling for this section of the population was 1.6. The comparable figures for Indonesia's low to middle-income ASEAN neighbours were: Malaysia, 49.7 per cent and 2.0 years; the Philippines, 25.6 per cent and 4.2 years; and Thailand, 36.9 per cent and 4.3 years. The low figures for Indonesia reflected colonial neglect. In 1939, for example, only 1,380 Indonesian students graduated from the elite Dutch secondary schools, compared with 1,261 European and 572 'other Asian' (mostly ethnic Chinese) students. Booth (1989) estimates that just 2,000 university

---

2   This section draws heavily on, and updates, Hill and Thee (2012).

Table 8.1   Higher education enrolments in Indonesia, 2005–10 (thousand)

	2005	2006	2007	2008	2009	2010
Total	**3,868.4**	**4,285.7**	**4,375.5**	**4,501.5**	**4,657.5**	**5,226.5**
Gross enrolment rate (GER) (%)	18.3	20.2	20.7	21.3	22.0	24.7 (26.3)[a]
Type of institution						
Public	805.5	824.7	978.7	966.0	1,011.7	1,030.4
Private	2,243.8	2,567.9	2,392.4	2,410.3	2,451.5	2,886.6
Special	48.5	51.3	47.3	47.3	66.5	93.0
Religious-based	508.5	518.9	506.2	556.8	503.4	571.3
Open University	262.1	322.9	450.9	521.3	624.4	645.1

a   The figure refers to the revised estimate for 2010 based on the population census.

Source: Unpublished data from the Directorate General of Higher Education, Ministry of Education and Culture, July 2011.

students were enrolled in 1945 at the time of independence. Educational disadvantage of this magnitude takes generations to overcome.

Since 1970 educational enrolments have risen rapidly, initially at the primary level, then at the secondary level and more recently at the tertiary level. In 1975 about 260,000 students were enrolled in tertiary education, a little over half of them in public institutions. Since then, more than 1 million students have been added every decade, the numbers rising to 1.52 million in 1985, 2.68 million in 1995 and 3.87 million in 2005. The increase since 2005 has been faster still, with more than 1.3 million students added over the period 2005–10, to the current figure of over 5 million (Table 8.1). Correspondingly, the gross enrolment rate (GER) – that is, students enrolled as a percentage of the group aged 19–23 years – has also been rising quickly, from 18.3 per cent in 2005 to 26.3 per cent in 2010.

Table 8.1 also classifies tertiary enrolments by type of institution. In order of size, these are private institutions, by far the largest with over half of total enrolments; public institutions; the rapidly growing Open University; religious-based institutions (administered by the Ministry of Religious Affairs); and a small group of special institutions, mainly administered by government ministries and agencies.

Indonesia's tertiary GER is comparable to that of China and around the average for developing countries in East Asia and the Pacific. But it is well below that of its higher-income ASEAN neighbours, Malaysia and Thailand, and only about one-third the OECD average (World Bank

Figure 8.1   *Public expenditure on tertiary education in East Asia (% of GDP)*[a]

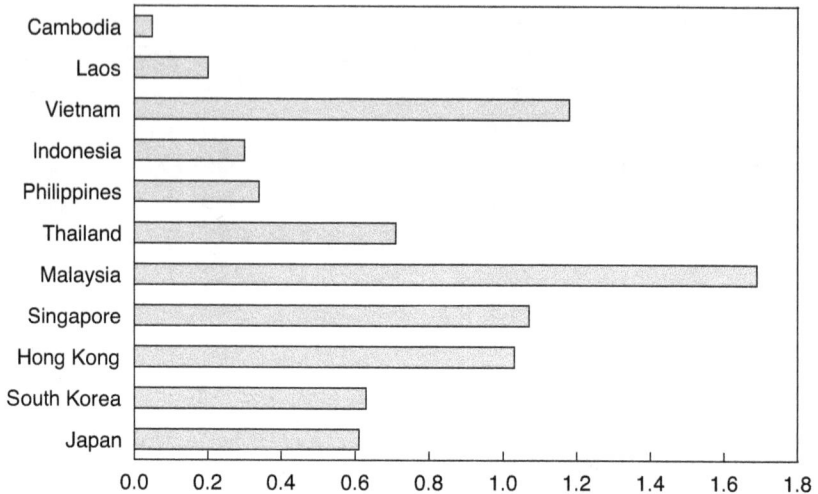

a   The World Bank (2012) reports the Indonesian figure as 1.2 per cent, but this is actually the percentage for public plus private expenditure. The correct figure for Indonesia has been substituted.

Source: World Bank (2012: 113).

2012). Indonesia also lags behind its higher-income neighbours in its public expenditure on higher education (Figure 8.1). As a percentage of GDP, Indonesia spends 0.3 per cent – about the same as the Philippines but only half the figures for South Korea and Japan (both well known for their very large private expenditures), less than half the Thai figure and under one-third the percentages for Singapore and Vietnam. Since the 2002 constitutional amendment requiring the government to allocate at least 20 per cent of its budget to education, overall expenditure on all levels of education has risen rapidly. There is arguably a case on both efficiency and equity grounds for concentrating this expenditure on the primary and secondary levels, as Indonesia has in fact been doing.

These developments need to be viewed against the backdrop of a worldwide trend for universities to increase their global reach and to emphasize quality in teaching and research. In this context, it may be useful to briefly highlight some of the key features that are considered to constitute international best practice in the management of universities.[3] We will assess their relevance to the Indonesian case below.

3   See Salmi (2009) for a very useful survey. See also Hill and Thee (2012) for a brief discussion of universities in selected East Asian countries.

Table 8.2   Higher education institutions in Indonesia by type, 2009/10 (no.)

	Ministry of Education & Culture			Ministry of Religious Affairs		
	Public	Private	Total	Public	Private	Total
University	48	412	460	6	87	93
Institute	6	47	53	14	26	40
Advanced school (*sekolah tinggi*)	2	1,314	1,316	32	409	441
Academy	0	1,015	1,015	0	0	0
Polytechnic	27	140	167	0	0	0
Total	**83**	**2,928**	**3,011**	**52**	**522**	**574**

Source: Unpublished data from the Directorate General of Higher Education, Ministry of Education and Culture, July 2011.

At least four features deserve emphasis. First, leading universities are internationally connected institutions, with many aiming for international populations of at least 30 per cent for faculty and 20 per cent for students as useful rules of thumb. This in turn requires high levels of cross-country mobility, with minimal regulatory barriers. Second, the universities need to be well resourced. The United States, for example, spends more than double the proportion of GDP (public plus private) on higher education as compared with the EU25 – about 3.3 per cent versus 1.3 per cent. A third factor is high-quality university governance. This typically involves autonomy from government and freedom from political pressure, incentives for performance and a collegial yet competitive spirit (Aghion et al. 2010). A fourth key attribute is the importance of arm's-length, independent review processes for all aspects of university operations, including appointments, promotions, academic output and general resource allocation.[4]

The current situation

The 5.2 million students in Indonesian higher education are enrolled in about 3,600 institutions (Table 8.2). There are three tiers of universities in the public sector: the elite public universities, numbering five to

---

4   Indeed, the president of a leading American university has observed that: 'The bedrock of university quality in the United States is peer review' (quoted in Salmi 2009: 59).

seven depending on one's definition; another 47–49 public universities of mixed but generally low quality; and some other institutions, also of variable quality, administered by the Ministry of Religious Affairs and other government departments (such as foreign affairs and finance). In practice, however, the system is dominated by the private sector. Almost three-quarters of all students are enrolled in the private sector, and these institutions account for most of the recent growth. Moreover, the state universities are de facto increasingly 'privatized' in terms of their funding. Indonesia has about 410 private universities and an additional 2,900 private polytechnics, academies and *sekolah tinggi*. The quality of these institutions is even more variable than in the public sector.

Although state universities constitute just 4 per cent of Indonesia's higher education institutions, they account for almost 30 per cent of enrolments, and they set the standard for academic quality and performance (Buchori and Malik 2004). Most Indonesian academics with foreign PhDs are products of the elite state universities, and state and foreign scholarships at the PhD level go disproportionately to these universities, which also have the highest proportions of graduate students. Until the early 2000s, the state universities were run along civil service lines. Resources were provided by the central government, permanent staff were required to be civil servants, and major decisions about resource allocation, fees and staffing were determined at the centre. It is only in the past decade that there have been gradual moves towards increased autonomy and greater flexibility, focused mainly on the elite group. Direct grants from the Directorate General of Higher Education now typically account for between a third and a half of state university revenues, with the leading state universities at the lower end of this range owing to their much greater financial strength.

Private universities are a relatively recent phenomenon, although some of the larger ones began to emerge in the early 1960s. Typically they were established by either a major business conglomerate or a religious order; for example, Universitas Pelita Harapan in Tangerang was established by the Lippo Group, the various campuses of Muhammadiyah University by the Islamic organization of that name, and Sanata Dharma University in Yogyakarta by the Jesuits. The number of private institutions began to grow very rapidly in the 1980s, in response to rising incomes, limited state fiscal capacity, increased commercial demand for graduates and general economic deregulation. Their status was regularized by a 1999 presidential decree on higher education, PP 60/1999.

The private higher education institutions receive very little public money, typically amounting to less than 5 per cent of their revenue. They vary widely in quality, ranging from several large, relatively well-endowed private universities closely integrated with the labour market, to small *sekolah tinggi* with very rudimentary facilities. The ethnic Chinese community is disproportionately represented among the better private universities owing to the semi-formal policy of affirmative action in favour of indigenous Indonesian (*pribumi*) students at the state universities. The quality of the Islamic universities is also highly variable, with a few strong institutions, such as Universitas Islam Negeri (UIN) Syarif Hidayatullah in Jakarta, alongside many of low quality.

As the World Bank (2012) observes, the bulk of financing for higher education comes from private sources, principally student fees and levies. This applies obviously to the private institutions, but increasingly also to the state universities. In addition, low-cost social science and business courses increasingly dominate course offerings in Indonesia's tertiary institutions. Among student enrolments by faculty, the World Bank (2012) concludes that Indonesia has one of the highest concentrations in these two fields (second only to Cambodia), and one of the lowest in engineering and science. There is some specialization between public and private universities, with the latter more likely to offer low-cost courses in high demand, such as IT, finance, accountancy and management. State universities are usually expected to offer a full range of courses, including less lucrative ones such as agriculture, public health and mathematics, and there is an expectation that they will undertake research.

Financial arrangements for Indonesian higher education institutions are complex. Of the Directorate General of Higher Education's 2009 budget of Rp 18.5 trillion, about 85 per cent went to tertiary institutions: 69 per cent to 75 non-autonomous state institutions, 11 per cent to the seven autonomous public universities and 6 per cent to private institutions (World Bank 2010). There are evidently no uniform funding formulas for standardized courses; nor do the directorate's allocations reward efficient course delivery. The directorate's recurrent allocations are generally incremental and based on those of the previous year. Capital budgets are on a 'needs' basis and appear to be negotiated case by case.

Although increasing numbers of Indonesian citizens are studying abroad, the Indonesian university system is rather isolated internationally. This in part reflects the country's latecomer status and the relatively poor English-language proficiency of most Indonesian students. But the government's policies reinforce this isolation. Visa regulations frustrate the movement of faculty and students. For example, Indonesia attracted 5,366 international students in 2007, predominantly from Malaysia and East Timor, whereas Malaysia had about 48,000 international students in that year.[5] Indonesia is also missing out on the growing trend for students

---

5 The number of foreign students studying in Malaysia has risen quickly since then. See Chapter 10 by Khong Kim Hoong for more details.

to study abroad for a semester or year. Although Indonesian universities are developing various international twinning and other arrangements, the country's investment laws discourage a more substantial foreign university presence, of the type now expanding rapidly in several ASEAN countries, especially Malaysia and Singapore (Magiera 2011).

Performance indicators

As would be expected, there are very large differences in tertiary enrolments across regions and socio-economic groups. According to the 2011 Susenas, 55 per cent of tertiary students come from the top income quintile, 24 per cent from the fourth quintile and only 2.6 per cent from the bottom quintile. It is clear that the poor are seriously under-represented in Indonesian universities, in the sense that only 3 per cent of students from families in the bottom quintile make it to university.

Educational disadvantage is of course deep-rooted, commencing with low-quality education and high dropout rates at the primary and secondary levels. Equity-oriented programs are also very limited. The World Bank (2012) estimates that financial aid to students enrolled in tertiary education covers only 3 per cent of total costs, even though the government's official objective is for students to pay 33 per cent at most of those costs. Moreover, although in principle 20 per cent of students from the poorest quintile are eligible for scholarships, in practice very few receive them – in part because they fail to meet the merit-based eligibility requirements, in turn arising from the fact that most students in this group do not successfully complete secondary schooling to a high standard. In fact, the World Bank (2012: 107–9) concluded that Indonesia was the only country among five sampled[6] where the completion gap between the poorest and richest quintiles had been widening in recent years. We return to the issue of equity and access in the next section.

There are also very large regional differences in tertiary education participation rates, with GERs ranging from about 75 per cent in Jakarta and Yogyakarta down to 10 per cent or less in the provinces of Bangka-Belitung Islands, West Sulawesi, Riau Islands, Banten, East and West Kalimantan, and West Papua.[7] The regional concentration is even more pronounced when one considers that the elite institutions are all located in Java – in the cities of Jakarta, Bandung, Bogor, Surabaya and Yogyakarta. Educational disparities by socio-economic status and region are far greater than those by gender.

---

6 The other countries were Cambodia, Mongolia, Thailand and Vietnam.
7 These GERs overstate the regional differences to the extent that many students move to the major cities of Java for their tertiary education.

Indonesian universities are built on relatively weak educational foundations, as reflected in the low scores of secondary school students in standardized international tests. They have also struggled to attract and retain high-performing academic staff, because of the country's latecomer status, the rapid growth of the sector and the unattractive incentives regime for staff (on which see below). In consequence, Indonesian universities are not highly ranked in the now widely used international comparisons. For example, in the 2012 Times Higher Education Supplement rankings, no Indonesian university was listed among the top 400, even though in some earlier rankings a small number had made it into the list. But perhaps this is an unrealistic comparison, as only three Southeast Asian universities – the National University of Singapore (ranked 40), Singapore's Nanyang Technological University (169) and Thailand's Mahidol University (in the range 351–400) – were included.[8]

In a comparative survey of academic qualifications in nine East Asian economies, the World Bank (2012: Table 3.3) found that just 7 per cent of Indonesian academic staff had a PhD in 2007 (with the figure in public universities about double that in private universities), while 40 per cent had a master's degree. The Indonesian figure for PhDs was the lowest in the sample, lower even than the proportions for Cambodia, Mongolia and Vietnam.[9] Over the period 2000–05 Indonesia produced about 524 scholarly publications of international quality, compared with Thailand's 2,059.

University governance and incentive systems

We comment here on various aspects of the internal administration of Indonesian universities, and their systems of governance and incentives. It is important to emphasize that these are general observations about what is a highly heterogeneous and rapidly evolving system.

First, the academic salary structure in state universities is generally complex, obscure and poorly geared towards incentives. Actual incomes often bear little relationship to official salaries, since most academics earn a significant proportion of their income – often as much as three-quarters – off-campus.[10] This applies particularly to the better-known academics

---

8   It is worth observing that only three African universities and three from South America made it into the top 400, while China had 10 and India one.

9   See Guggenheim (2012) for a range of instructive comparative indicators.

10   Detailed studies of academic remuneration practices and structures are lacking, but the following are indicative. In a study of staff at three top state universities (the University of Indonesia, the Bandung Institute of Technology and the Bogor Agricultural Institute), Clark and Oey-Gardiner (1991) found that academics typically devoted only 30 per cent of their time to official

from leading universities with ample external consulting and teaching opportunities. Salary structures are complicated, with many components, not many of which are performance related. There is also little opportunity for serious academic research. This is effectively precluded if academics pursue the option of heavy teaching as a means of salary supplementation, either at their own institution or (very often) at an outside private institution. It is also very difficult to sustain serious research if academics follow the consultancy route to salary supplementation. Moreover, there is an incentive for academics to quickly assume an administrative post, both for the control it provides over resources and because it offers a more secure path to a reasonable income, or because they just don't have the necessary academic inclination.

Attempts are being made, however, to gradually shift the incentive system towards a stronger emphasis on research and teaching. For example, most of the elite public universities offer some sort of special lecturer (*dosen inti*) scheme, whereby academics receive higher salaries in return for greater research output. These schemes are still in their infancy, so it is too early to evaluate their impact.

A second problem is that academic promotion is largely based on seniority, and is governed by an extremely complex academic credit (KUM) system developed by the Directorate General of Higher Education. Consistent with the civil service culture of state university administration, recommendations for promotion at the middle and senior academic levels have to be approved by the directorate. The essential resources that academics at leading universities in OECD countries take for granted are rarely available in Indonesia. Foreign journal subscriptions are inadequate (particularly since the Asian financial crisis), even at the top universities, effectively cutting academics off from the international mainstream. There are, moreover, few incentives or opportunities for international intellectual engagement, such as conference participation. Sabbaticals are rarely available. A well-established 'seminar culture' is nonexistent in most Indonesian universities.

Third, there is very little interinstitutional academic mobility, owing to regulatory restrictions, compounded by a sort of institutional 'tribal culture'. University staff are typically recruited at junior levels, very often after having graduated from the same institution, and they remain

---

university duties. More recently, in a survey of remuneration practices in Indonesian research institutions, Suryadarma, Pomeroy and Tanuwidjaja (2011) found that about three-quarters of researchers' incomes came from supplementary or non-core activities such as research projects, consulting and additional teaching (often in another institution). See also Guggenheim (2012).

in the institution for life. Here too the private universities display more flexibility than their state counterparts.

A fourth factor is that virtually no peer review work is undertaken, both for academic output and for competitive grant assessments. In fact, very few genuinely competitive grant facilities are available for Indonesian academic research, and there is very little recourse to outsiders in the evaluation processes.

8.3 MAJOR POLICY ISSUES

So much for the backdrop. In this section we focus on some of the key contemporary policy issues and debates in Indonesian higher education. We address three in particular: course accreditation and the incentives for academic quality; the challenge of equity; and the question of university autonomy. All have been matters of public debate in recent years, and they remain largely unresolved. They highlight the lack of clarity in the government's higher education objectives, and its ambivalence towards the sector. There is no better illustration of this than the fact that the government's revised education law, approved by parliament in July 2012, may well be challenged in the Constitutional Court, and could possibly be rendered unconstitutional. As a result, the country's educational institutions will continue to operate in a legal vacuum and an environment of great uncertainty.

Accreditation and incentives for academic quality

We have argued above that the incentives for academic quality in teaching and research are weak, especially in the public universities. These problems arise from low salaries, the lack of connection between performance and reward, the absence of peer review procedures, problems with internal university governance, and deficiencies in the general academic support environment. The result is that, while many Indonesian academics return well trained from graduate study abroad, they struggle to maintain their teaching and research interests at an international standard. Many drop out of academic life altogether, and turn to more financially rewarding careers. This in turn adversely affects the quality of the next generation of graduates. It also reinforces the country's continuing low international academic ranking, and its unhealthy dependence on foreign consultants for policy advice. The problem is likely to become more serious over time as, with the increased globalization of the international academic labour market, the country's best international graduate students elect to remain abroad in pursuit of academic careers.

With a few exceptions, there is as yet no serious and concerted attempt to lift academic quality, comparable to that under way in China and some Southeast Asian nations, particularly Singapore and Malaysia. For example, the various *dosen inti* schemes do not yet appear to have had any discernible impact on academic performance. Procedures in the public universities are as cumbersome as ever; if anything the Ministry of Education and Culture is attempting to recentralize decision-making authority, as we demonstrate below.

Academic publishing remains tenuous in Indonesia despite the large number of journals. According to the Centre for Scientific Documentation and Information at the Indonesian Institute of Sciences, in May 2011 more than 7,000 scientific journals were published in Indonesia. Of these, around 4,000 were regularly sent to the centre, while some 5,100 were said to be accessible through their websites. Few if any of these journals were refereed and accredited, however.[11]

The challenge of maintaining academic journals of quality is illustrated by the experience of one of the country's oldest social science journals, *Economics and Finance of Indonesia*. Formerly known as *Ekonomi dan Keuangan Indonesia*, it was established in 1948 by Dutch and Indonesian economists. The main economics journal in Indonesia, over the years it has published seminal papers by local and international academics. Its publication was discontinued for a period in the 1960s, but it has been published more or less continuously since the late 1960s, with one of the authors of this chapter serving as its co-editor since 2004. Despite its long and venerable history, however, it has not yet obtained the essential prerequisite for international academic recognition – entry in the Social Science Citation Index – and it is not available online. As a result, its international circulation is rather limited, thus restricting submissions from outside the country. It has also struggled to maintain the rigorous peer review system that is the sine qua non of a respected academic journal. *Economics and Finance of Indonesia* is certainly one of the country's leading academic journals, so its experience indicates that Indonesian academic publishing is still in the very early stages of development.

Indonesia is also in the very early stages of developing effective accreditation procedures. In 1994, a law was enacted to establish the National Accreditation Agency for Universities (Badan Akreditasi Nasional Perguruan Tinggi, BAN-PT). BAN-PT is responsible for the accreditation of

---

11 The number of journals might have proliferated further still if the Directorate General of Higher Education had succeeded in its attempt in early 2012 to require all university graduates to publish the results of their research before graduation. The proposal was dropped in the face of widespread protests that the scheme would be unworkable.

all universities and institutes of higher education in Indonesia, including state, private and religious institutions, the academies operated by government ministries and agencies, as well as the Open University for long-distance education. The mission of its board of 13 members, mostly professors at state universities, is to advise the minister on the quality of these various institutions and their programs.

In practice, however, the agency has had difficulty carrying out its mission. It is estimated that in 2012 there were around 6,000 programs at state and private institutions that had not been accredited owing to a shortage of qualified assessors (*Kompas*, 19 May 2012). This has created a major problem for these institutions, because the Directorate General of Higher Education has stated that institutions that have programs that have not been accredited by BAN-PT may not issue diplomas to their graduating students (*Kompas*, 28 August 2012). It seems unlikely that the problem will be addressed quickly, since the available academic resources are insufficient to tackle the backlog.

How then might the accreditation issue be addressed? There is in principle a case for a high-quality, well-resourced, arm's-length accreditation process to provide an independent assessment of course quality for prospective students. The question is whether it is feasible for the government to establish credible institutional mechanisms to regulate quality in the private sector – and, for that matter, public universities. For such a system to be effective, there would need to be a group of high-quality, well-paid, independent evaluators, arguably including some foreign academics, given that the Indonesian academic community is still quite a small one. There is certainly a strong preference within the bureaucracy for control by the centre, even as the system is becoming increasingly market driven and de facto 'privatized'. However, as we have seen, the Ministry of Education and Culture is not able to undertake this task credibly and efficiently, and is unlikely to be able to do so in the near future. The danger of requiring full accreditation is that it will simply impose another layer of bureaucratic complexity on tertiary institutions, and with it the opportunity for corruption, especially for small and remote institutions that do not possess political–bureaucratic connections in Jakarta.[12]

The inevitable reality is that, for at least the next decade, the market will be the effective arbiter of quality. Parents and students will vote with their feet in selecting institutions and courses. This means in practice that students with good secondary school grades and/or wealthy parents will apply for the elite public and private universities. At this level the

---

12 Another serious problem afflicting Indonesian higher education concerns plagiarism, which is reportedly widespread (*Kompas*, 6 June 2012).

'market' works quite effectively, in the sense that course offerings, education quality and job prospects upon graduation are well defined. At the other end of the spectrum are the hundreds of small private institutions offering a limited range of low-cost and low-quality courses, such as IT and commerce, where graduation offers uncertain employment prospects, with or without accreditation. If Indonesia ever faces an 'Arab Spring' of discontented young graduates unable to secure employment that matches their aspirations, then these institutions could well be the source.

It might in principle be possible to co-opt professional societies to assist with the process of course accreditation. Such societies understand the requirements of the market place, and they could play a role in strengthening the generally weak links between tertiary institutions and the private sector. But although this is a useful aspirational objective, in practice it is unlikely to be a viable option, except perhaps in a few specialist fields such as law, medicine and accounting. In general, Indonesia's professional societies are not well developed. It is unlikely that even long-established bodies such as the Association of Indonesian Physicians (Ikatan Dokter Indonesia, IDI) could be entrusted with this function; IDI is a large, unwieldy organization without much interest in adopting a proactive stance towards course accreditation. Also, as in other countries, the objective of the professional societies is as much about protecting members' interests as about promoting broader educational development objectives.[13]

The challenge of equity

As we saw above, Indonesia's university student body is drawn disproportionately from higher-income families, especially when it comes to the elite public and private sector institutions. This inevitably reflects the fact that it is generally only the children of better-off families who can obtain a high-quality secondary education with good grades. The inequities of tertiary education therefore have to be addressed at their source, with the main focus being the primary and secondary levels. The government's major educational initiatives have been directed at the primary and secondary levels, a priority that is appropriate on both equity and efficiency grounds. Nevertheless, there is some scope for greater emphasis on equity in access to and the provision of tertiary education.

---

13 In this regard, as with managing the internationalization of higher education, Indonesia has much to learn from the recent Malaysian experience, where the accreditation and quality control system reportedly works well. For more details, see Chapter 11 by Khong Kim Hoong.

In 2010, the government initiated the Beasiswa Pendidikan untuk Mahasiswa Miskin (Bidik Misi) program, loosely translated as the 'targeted mission' program. It provides eligible students with free tuition and a monthly living allowance of Rp 600,000 (about $60). Under the program, institutions receiving government funding are required to admit at least 20 per cent of their students from the poorer groups of society, the so-called *golongan miskin*. Now in its third year, the program is estimated to cover a total of about 50,000 students, in both public and private institutions, under both the Ministry of Education and Culture and the Ministry of Religious Affairs. In February 2012 the minister announced that the program would be expanded further, to 40,000 students per year.

The program has achieved some success, at least to the extent that most of the students admitted through it have scored satisfactorily on the admissions exam, through the Preliminary Achievement Index (Indeks Prestasi Sementara, IPS). Some 1 per cent achieved a perfect score of 4.0, more than 20 per cent achieved a score of 3.5–4.0, while only 4 per cent recorded a score of less than 2.0.

Inevitably, however, there have been problems. The dropout rate is disappointingly high, because the students struggle to meet the required academic standards, and for financial reasons. It is estimated that about 70 per cent of students admitted under the program have either dropped out altogether or suspended their studies (*Kompas*, 28 February 2012). The universities have also struggled to meet their admission targets, because they have had difficulty identifying students eligible to receive scholarships under the program. For instance, Padjadjaran University, a leading public university in Bandung, recently stated that it was able to identify only 480 qualified students out of its target of 900. The university surveyed the houses of Bidik Misi applicants to ascertain whether they really did come from poor households (*Kompas*, 30 August 2012), and used utility bills to verify their socio-economic status. Procedures of this type are time consuming, inefficient and open to abuse.

Bidik Misi is an unfunded obligation imposed on universities, in the sense that the government is not providing matching funds as an incentive for universities to admit and nurture these students. Originally funding was to be directed to the program from the savings accruing from a proposed reduction in fuel subsidies. However, when the parliament rejected this package in early 2012, the government was not able to offer alternative funding. The universities have responded by seeking to package and 'rearrange' their admissions in order to be seen to be meeting their targets. The Bidik Misi provisions are also vague and open to interpretation, especially as concerns who qualifies for the program.

If the government is serious about facilitating access to tertiary education for the poor, a preferable approach would be a national scheme of merit-based, fully portable scholarships, with explicit means test provisions targeted at low-income families. The government could also encourage greater private philanthropy for the provision of scholarships, by inculcating a stronger sense of social responsibility among the country's leading business conglomerates. Currently such private philanthropy is meagre.

In the past the government has experimented with student loan schemes, operating through the major banks. These schemes have been discontinued owing to very high default rates, with government guarantees evidently creating moral hazard problems. Another option might be the 'Australian model' of a higher education contribution scheme (HECS), under which the government in effect provides loans to students that are repayable as a tax surcharge once the recipients' incomes exceed some threshold level, such as median wages in the formal sector.[14] Such schemes are being widely adopted, including in developing countries such as Thailand; a scheme of this type is also under consideration in Malaysia.

The HECS model relieves the government of funding obligations while preserving equity objectives, since students repay the loans only if they graduate and their incomes exceed the threshold. However, the scheme works only if there is an efficient and clean taxation office, or some other facility such as a national pension scheme. Although Indonesia is not yet at this stage in its institutional development, a HECS-type option should certainly be an aspirational objective for future education planners.

University autonomy

For several years the Ministry of Education and Culture was moving cautiously towards a more decentralized system of management and regulation of the public universities, starting with the elite institutions. In 2010 the Constitutional Court declared the relevant regulations unconstitutional; they were considered 'too liberal' in the sense of being excessively reliant on both markets and the private provision of education. This was a major setback for these much needed reforms. In the meantime, senior personnel changes within the Ministry of Education and Culture have also signalled a reversal of the trend towards greater university autonomy. Thus the regulatory environment in which tertiary institutions operate is becoming increasingly obscure and complex.

Parliament responded to the Constitutional Court's decision by drafting a revised education bill. The draft law presented to the parliament in

---

14 For details, see Chapter 10 by Bruce Chapman and Daniel Suryadarma.

April 2012 attracted a lot of criticism from both public and private universities, directed mainly at the provisions regulating the organization of universities, curriculums, and the hiring and firing of academic staff (*Kompas*, 14 July 2012). For instance, the draft provided that the minister could regulate the statutes of universities, whereas tertiary institutions argued that the proper task of the minister was to facilitate and guarantee their autonomy. Another controversial provision that ran counter to the objective of autonomy stipulated that the minister – rather than the universities – should approve study programs. Moreover, the draft stated that the government would regulate the appointment of academic staff and prescribe financial incentives. This provision attracted widespread criticism, including concerns that it might jeopardize academic freedom, a much cherished feature of Indonesian academic life since the fall of Suharto.

For these and other reasons, most sectors of Indonesia's higher education industry, both private and public, expressed their opposition to the draft law. The Association of Private Universities explicitly rejected it, and the country's most respected daily newspaper editorialized against it (*Kompas*, 30 May 2012). Two of the nation's leading education academics also voiced their opposition to the draft law. One was a former Director General of Higher Education, Professor Satrio Soemantri Brojonegoro (2012); the other was a former rector of the prestigious Gadjah Mada University, Professor Sofian Effendi, who addressed his concerns both to senior staff of the Ministry of Education and Culture and to the parliament. Nevertheless, parliament approved the law on 13 July 2012. Responding to the criticisms, the minister, himself a former rector (of the 10 November Institute of Technology in Surabaya), acknowledged the concerns, and argued that the law had sought to respond to them. He also said that the various criticisms could be accommodated in subsequent regulations.

Two general conclusions may be drawn from these events. The first is the enduring propensity of Indonesian policy makers, both bureaucrats and parliamentarians, to regulate and supervise all kinds of activities, including, in this case, academic affairs. Obviously the management of tertiary institutions should be in the hands of academic institutions and their boards of trustees, operating in a general environment where the rules of the game are clearly established by the government. The irony is that the government is unable to provide this enabling environment, as illustrated by its failures with respect to accreditation and equity of access. The new law also illustrates a general trend in Indonesia towards greater regulation of economic and social activity, seen also in, for example, trade policy, labour markets and cultural policy.

The second conclusion is that this is unfinished business. The new law will almost certainly prove to be unworkable. Tertiary institutions will find ways of circumventing its more onerous and impractical provisions, either by ignoring them altogether or by coming up with more workable informal arrangements. An appeal to the Constitutional Court to reject the law cannot be discounted, resulting in a further period of policy uncertainty at the very time that the country's tertiary institutions need to be nurtured through an era of rapid growth and upgrading.

8.4 CONCLUSIONS

Several key themes emerge from this analysis. Indonesia's higher education sector, including its universities, is growing rapidly and is one of the largest in the world. This growth reflects the country's strong economic growth, the growing appetite for tertiary educational qualifications and the supply-side response coming mainly from the private sector. Inevitably there will be growing pains in a system that is underfunded, that is built on relatively weak educational foundations and that is somewhat cut off from the regional and international mainstreams owing to language, regulatory and incentive barriers. For Indonesian universities to take their rightful place in the regional and global arenas, with respect not only to size but also to quality and impact, there will need to be substantial reforms in funding, regulatory arrangements, academic and institutional quality, and access.

Indonesia's spending on higher education, from both public and private sources, is barely adequate to keep pace with the rapid growth in enrolments, let alone to lift quality and make any substantial progress towards improving participation by the poor. In spite of the official rhetoric emphasizing the importance of higher education, expenditure patterns are still the best indicator of revealed preferences and priorities. Regrettably, in 2012 the Indonesian government allocated about 13 times more funding to fuel, electricity and other subsidies than to higher education (respectively about 4 per cent and 0.3 per cent of GDP). Not only is the government's funding of higher education paltry, but its policies continue to hamper the development of a strong and viable private sector.

Funding is of course only part of the problem. Academic cultures will need to change – to provide greater incentives for excellence in teaching and research, to open up recruitment processes and facilitate greater staff and student mobility, to encourage stronger peer review mechanisms, to establish the notion of contestability in resource allocation and to foster engagement with the regional and international educational mainstreams. Access needs to be broadened to students from lower socio-economic classes through the provision of merit-based scholar-ships and, at some future time, income-contingent student loans. These changes will take time, and they will require a fundamental change in the mind-set of politicians and senior education officials.

REFERENCES

Aghion, P., M. Dewatripont, C. Hoxby, A. Mas-Colell and A. Sapir (2010) 'The governance and performance of universities: evidence from Europe and the US', *Economic Policy*, 25(61): 7–59.

Booth, A. (1989) 'The state and economic development: the Ethical and New Order periods compared', in R.J. May and W.J. O'Malley (eds) *Observing Change in Asia: Essays in Honor of J.A.C. Mackie*, Crawford House Press, Bathurst, pp. 111–26.

Brojonegoro, S.S. (2012) 'Kriteria pemimpin amanah' [Criteria for the leadership mission], *Kompas*, 31 August.

Buchori, M. and A. Malik (2004) 'The evolution of higher education in Indonesia', in P.G. Altbach and T. Umakoshi (eds) *Asian Universities: Historical Perspectives and Contemporary Challenges*, Johns Hopkins University Press, Baltimore, pp. 249–78.

Clark, D.H. and M. Oey-Gardiner (1991) 'How Indonesian lecturers have adjusted to civil service compensation', *Bulletin of Indonesian Economic Studies*, 27(3): 129–41.

Guggenheim, S. (2012) 'Indonesia's quiet springtime: knowledge, policy and reform', in A. Reid (ed.) *Indonesia Rising: The Repositioning of Asia's Third Giant*, Institute of Southeast Asian Studies, Singapore, pp. 141–69.

Hill, H. and Thee K.W. (2012) 'Indonesian universities in transition: catching up and opening up', *Bulletin of Indonesian Economic Studies*, 48(2): 229–51.

Magiera, S. (2011) 'Indonesia's negative list: an evaluation for selected services', *Bulletin of Indonesian Economic Studies*, 47(2): 195–219.

Salmi, J. (2009) *The Challenge of Establishing World-class Universities*, World Bank, Washington DC.

Suryadarma, D., J. Pomeroy and S. Tanuwidjaja (2011) 'Economic factors underpinning constraints in Indonesia's knowledge sector', unpublished paper prepared for the AusAID Knowledge Sector Project, Jakarta.

World Bank (2010) 'Indonesia: higher education financing', Policy Brief, Jakarta, October.

World Bank (2012) *Putting Higher Education to Work: Skills and Research for Growth in Asia*, World Bank, Washington DC.

9 BEATING THE ODDS: LOCALLY RELEVANT ALTERNATIVES TO WORLD-CLASS UNIVERSITIES

*Rivandra Royono and Diastika Rahwidiati**

9.1 INTRODUCTION

The aspiration for world-class university status

Ask the managers of any university in Indonesia about their vision for their institution and an almost automatic response would be 'to become a world-class university'. This sentiment is shared by the Indonesian government and the public, who seem to believe that it is high time for the country to have its own world-class universities. What that aspiration entails, however, does not seem to be well understood.

While there have been several attempts to define what a world-class university is (see, for example, Niland 2000; Altbach 2004), this chapter will refer to the framework put forward by Salmi (2009) because of its simplicity and its general acceptance by international scholars.[1] He made the case that:

---

* The authors would like to thank Sherria Puteri Ayuandini, Department of Anthropology, Washington University, St Louis, for providing assistance during the interview process, for lending an anthropological lens to the study and for helping the authors to devise a framework for the analysis.

1 The dominant preconception of world-class universities is that they should prioritize their research performance. The two most widely recognized rankings of universities, the World University Rankings published by the Times Higher Education Supplement and the Academic Rankings of World Universities published by Shanghai Jiao Tong University, both put a heavy emphasis on research output and scientific publications as part of their selection criteria (Levin, Jeong and Ou 2006).

... the superior results of these institutions (highly sought graduates, leading edge research, and technology transfer) can essentially be attributed to ... (a) a high concentration of talent (faculty and students), (b) abundant resources to offer a rich learning environment and to conduct advanced research, and (c) favorable governance features that encourage strategic vision, innovation, and flexibility, and that enable institutions to make decisions and to manage resources without being encumbered by bureaucracy (Salmi 2009: 6–7).

Indonesia's 3,600 tertiary education institutions (TEIs) vary considerably in size, structure and quality. The 140 or so public institutions cater for about a third of the country's entire tertiary education student body. Of the 3,400 or more private institutions, most located in Java, only a few can be considered on a par with the top public institutions. None of Indonesia's TEIs, however, have a high international standing. The country's leading university, the University of Indonesia, ranked only 201st in the 2009 Times Higher Education World University Rankings.[2] On the research front, the Scopus database of peer-reviewed literature records only 51 Indonesian universities producing scientific publications. The top 15 universities on that list produce more than 85 per cent of Indonesia's total scientific publications.

Indonesian TEIs face severe resource constraints. Although a group of seven elite universities have been given greater autonomy to raise their own funds and manage their own affairs over the past decade, the average per student spending of these flagship research universities is just one-sixth that of, for example, the Australian National University in Canberra.[3] Indonesia's small and regional TEIs are even less well resourced. This situation prevents these institutions from recruiting the most talented academics and from conducting internationally recognized research.

It is obvious that the overwhelming majority of Indonesia's TEIs are not, and are unlikely ever to become, world-class universities. This should not be a problem in and of itself. The literature on tertiary education development emphasizes the need for a diversified system that can

---

2 Gadjah Mada University was ranked second at 250 and the Bandung Institute of Technology third at 351. Since the indicators were revised in 2010 to put more emphasis on research output, no Indonesian university has made it into the top 400.

3 The seven autonomous universities are Gadjah Mada University (Universitas Gajah Mada), the University of Indonesia (Universitas Indonesia), Bandung Institute of Technology (Institut Teknologi Bandung), Bogor Agricultural University (Institut Pertanian Bogor), the University of North Sumatra (Universitas Sumatera Utara), Indonesia University of Education (Universitas Pendidikan Indonesia) and Airlangga University. The first four were given autonomy status in 2000. The last three gained autonomy in 2003, 2004 and 2006 respectively.

accommodate the varied learning and training needs of the population (Salmi 2009). And while a strong argument can be made that Indonesia needs to develop several globally recognized research universities, the value and importance of such institutions should not be overdramatized.

The problem lies in the apparent ambition of too many Indonesian institutions to become world-class universities. Not only is such an aspiration unfeasible in most cases, but it may disadvantage a population that needs and expects a variety of different services from the tertiary education sector. This misplaced ambition is arguably caused by both a failure to acknowledge the need for 'non-world-class' universities and the lack of a framework to guide and encourage TEIs to take an alternative path.

An alternative to the world-class university framework

Responding to the concerns described above, this chapter sets out to explore possible alternative frameworks for describing and benchmarking the quality of Indonesian TEIs that are not and are unlikely to become world-class universities, at least according to the prevailing definition. The study focuses on three main groups of questions. First, how do Indonesia's non-world-class universities – most of them small or regional institutions – stack up against world-class universities?[4] Second, how do these institutions operate? How do they manage their talent and resources? And third, what kinds of outcomes do they produce, and what is their role in Indonesia's development?

Although this chapter does not purport to offer definitive answers to these questions, we hope it will provide a platform for long-overdue discussion of the role of small TEIs and their contribution to Indonesia's development; a working framework to benchmark and improve the quality of these institutions; and some ideas on how best to support them.

The chapter progresses as follows. Section 9.2 describes the method of the study and points out some limitations. Section 9.3 explores some of the arguments in the literature for universities to aim for diversity and local relevance rather than world-class status. Section 9.4 describes how the three sample TEIs selected for this study stack up in a world-class university framework. As section 9.5 shows, high-quality small TEIs

---

4 Not all of Indonesia's regional TEIs are small. Indonesia has at least one public TEI in every province, some with student populations of over 10,000. However, these large regional institutions face the same constraints as their smaller counterparts, namely a lack of resources, talent and governance. In the study described in this chapter, we include one large regional TEI in our sample to provide a more complete picture of the challenges faced by Indonesia's non-world-class universities.

have a unique set of strengths not found in the world-class universities. These strengths help us to construct a preliminary framework for non-world-class universities, depicted in the concluding section.

9.2   STUDY METHOD AND LIMITATIONS

Method

This study relies on the framework offered by Salmi (2009) for a world-class university. Of the three factors he identifies as contributing to the superior performance of these institutions – talent, resources and governance – we felt that the level of resources was the easiest to use as an initial criterion for selecting sample institutions for our study. Using population size as a proxy for economic strength, we decided to examine universities that were located outside Indonesia's 10 largest cities, yet with populations large enough to support a thriving tertiary education institution. We wanted universities with relatively low tuition fees[5] and low per student spending,[6] and located in areas with relatively high poverty incidence, on the assumption that TEIs with these characteristics would have higher proportions of students from the lower end of the wealth distribution. Finally, we wanted to examine a mix of public and private institutions that represented a spectrum of organizational development, from small, newly established universities to larger, more established institutions.

Although they differ in size, structure, mission and organizational culture, the three TEIs chosen as case studies for this study – the Fahmina Institute of Islamic Studies, Wiraraja University and Nusa Cendana University – share the above characteristics. Another trait they have in common is a reputation for progressive management. By looking at how these institutions operate and what they produce, we were able to gather enough information to construct a preliminary, alternative framework for high-quality small TEIs. The three universities are described briefly in Box 9.1.

---

5   We define a 'low' fee as a mean tuition fee per student per semester in a regular undergraduate program equal to or less than Rp 3 million. We set the bar in comparison with the tuition fees per semester charged by the University of Indonesia (Rp 5–7 million), the Bandung Institute of Technology (Rp 4 million) and Paramadina University (Rp 8–8.4 million).

6   The World Bank (2010) estimates average per student spending on tertiary education in Indonesia at slightly above $1,500 per annum, which is one of the lowest among middle-income countries. The three institutions included in this study all have per student spending below that average.

BOX 9.1   A BRIEF LOOK AT THE SELECTED TEIs

The Fahmina Institute of Islamic Studies (Institut Studi Islam Fahmina) is a private institution located in Cirebon, West Java. Established only in 2009, this fledgling institution has 59 lecturers and researchers and a student population of 221. It operates rather like a liberal arts college, with an emphasis on progressive interpretation of the Islamic scriptures to promote pluralism, gender equality and human rights.

Wiraraja University is a small private university located in the district of Sumenep on Madura Island, East Java. Sumenep is significantly less developed than other parts of Java, and even some areas outside Java. Wiraraja is a medium-sized university founded in 1986. It has a faculty of 130, less than half working full-time, and around 2,700 students. The university is not known for its research output, but its graduates appear to be in demand from local businesses and the public sector.

Nusa Cendana University is a public university located in Kupang, the capital of one of the poorest provinces in Indonesia, East Nusa Tenggara. Founded in 1962, this relatively mature university serves a student population of around 15,000. It has been making a conscious effort to increase its research output but has been hampered by a lack of resources and research capacity.

We carried out structured interviews and focus group discussions with three groups at each institution: managers, staff and students. We gathered information from a total of 23 managers (including two university presidents), 32 lecturers and researchers, and 28 students. The interviews and discussions, conducted separately with each group, focused on how the TEIs operated and how they defined success. We tailored the questions and points of discussion to each group. For instance, university managers were asked to explain their strategies to recruit and retain staff, while lecturers and researchers were asked to recount their reasons for choosing to work at a particular institution.

Limitations

The study has a number of limitations. First, it is a preliminary study, intended to provoke discussion on complementary measures of quality for a diverse range of TEIs. The small sample size means that the results cannot automatically be generalized, and may not apply to other TEIs.

Second, the general unavailability of publicly accessible tracking data on the family incomes of students in Indonesian TEIs meant that we had to rely solely on the universities themselves for information on the proportion of students coming from poor families.

Finally, owing to time and resource limitations, we were not able to consult a broader cross-section of stakeholders in the regions where our sample TEIs were located to confirm their claims of relevance to their local communities. Our findings on relevance are therefore very preliminary, and are included only to inform thinking about alternative expectations for locally relevant universities.

9.3 THE CASE FOR MORE DIVERSIFIED UNIVERSITIES

When we look at the vision and mission statements of Indonesia's most prominent universities, we find that achieving 'global recognition' for excellence seems to be the dominant agenda. The three Indonesian institutions included in the 2009 Times Higher Education World University Rankings – the University of Indonesia, Gadjah Mada University and the Bandung Institute of Technology – all aim for international recognition of excellence (ITB 2011; UGM n.d.; UI n.d.). Several large, respected private universities, most of them located in the major cities, also aspire to world-class university status (Binus University 2011; Universitas Surabaya 2012; Gunadarma University n.d.).

The pervasiveness of the ambition for global competitiveness and world-class university status even extends to a wide range of TEIs situated outside the major cities, well away from the economic power hubs. Mulawarman University in Samarinda, for example, aspires to become an 'international-standard university'; Manado State University wants to produce graduates that are 'globally competitive'; and Nusa Cendana University hopes to become a 'globally oriented university'.[7] There seem to be as many perceptions, definitions and permutations of a 'world-class university' as there are universities that want to become one. There are also common threads, however; most of the above universities mention some variation of 'research excellence', 'globally competitive graduates' and 'good governance'.

While recognizing that world-class research universities have an important role to play as a subset of a tertiary education system, Salmi (2009) questions whether a country would not be better off investing in the development of the most locally relevant tertiary education system suited to its own needs, rather than aspiring to some 'world-class' standard. One of the criticisms of the global rankings of universities is that

---

7 Personal communication, Prof. Frans Umbu Datta, Rector of Nusa Cendana University, 13 August 2012.

they are 'look-alike competitions', with large American research universities the model to be emulated (Lang 2005). Indeed, China's quest for
world-class universities has been labelled 'imitative rather than creative'
(Mohrman 2005, quoted in Ngok 2008: 557). Lang (2005) asks whether, in
the long run, this push towards conformity and 'isomorphism' may create disincentives for change, innovation and the creation of new knowledge, ultimately leading to less institutional diversity and less accessible
tertiary education systems as a whole.

Clarke, Thomas and Wallace (n.d.) outline several potential benefits of
systemic diversity in a tertiary education system, including ensuring that
the diverse needs of different segments of the population are met; providing a basis for healthy competition that encourages innovation and
adaptation to change; encouraging more effective use of scarce resources;
and building the capacity to come up with solutions to problems that
arise within the institution's own operating environment.

While some tertiary education systems have diversified almost
organically in response to economic and perceived labour market needs
(Teichler 2004), others have been designed specifically to do just that. An
example of this is the 1960 California Master Plan for Higher Education,
which established a three-tiered public higher education system with
clearly differentiated functions, but a clear system of linkages (Altbach
2011). Although the plan is not without its critics, the system's differen-
tiation of functions does take into account and play to the core strengths
of each institutional type.

Small universities have obvious resource constraints. Nevertheless,
based on a study of small universities in Canada, Daniel and Belanger
(1989) argued that many of them produced high-quality academic work;
indeed, small universities and liberal arts colleges in America led the
larger universities in producing eminent scientists and business leaders. In Canada, the proportion of faculty members of small universities
who were awarded research grants in humanities and social science
was roughly the same as that in the larger universities. The authors suggested that it was the greater interaction between faculty members, and
between faculty members and students, in the smaller universities that
helped them produce high-quality work despite the resource constraints.
Moreover, the tightness of resources meant that these small institutions
had a smaller margin of error in their operations, forcing management
to think carefully about the best use of resources and to ensure that they
had the means to meet their goals.

Daniel and Belanger (1989) also emphasized the need for smaller and
regional universities to be attuned to the needs of the geographic and
professional communities they served. This meant that they needed to
be more flexible in defining their institutional missions. The authors sug-

gested that such universities should concentrate on research activities, partnerships and technological innovations that were relevant to their immediate communities. In terms of student recruitment, they should focus less on setting high academic standards of entry and more on educating all qualified applicants. They should focus on adding value, for which the performance indicator should be the extent to which the skills of the students were developed during their time at the university.

9.4   INDONESIA'S SMALL OR REGIONAL UNIVERSITIES: A REALITY CHECK

How small Indonesian TEIs stack up in a world-class university framework

Like officials at other public institutions, the managers we spoke to at Nusa Cendana University cited an aspiration to make the university 'world-class'. Top management at Wiraraja University and the Fahmina Institute said they were more focused on providing the best possible service for their students, while still believing that achieving world-class status should be a natural long-term goal. Such statements probably reflect a general view across the tertiary education sector. An objective consideration of conditions at small TEIs, however, suggests that the probability of attaining such an aspiration is low.

Lack of talent

One of the most important aspects of a world-class university – if not *the* most important aspect – is that it should host some of the brightest minds in the world. This concentration of talent then becomes the driving force behind the university's ability to produce top-quality research, technological innovations and highly sought-after graduates. Indonesia's leading universities have historically recruited the country's brightest secondary school graduates, whereas small regional TEIs recruit mainly from the areas in which they are situated. The majority of Nusa Cendana University's students are secondary school graduates of East Nusa Tenggara, academically one of the poorest-performing provinces in Indonesia. The academic profiles of Wiraraja and Fahmina are similar to that of Nusa Cendana.

Small TEIs face a huge challenge in competing with the top research universities to recruit lecturers and researchers. They simply do not have the resources to provide remuneration packages that would attract academics with a national, let alone international, reputation. University of Indonesia faculty members can receive as much as Rp 30 million per

Table 9.1   Expenditure per student by selected tertiary education institutions ($)

Institution	Expenditure per student
Seven autonomous universities	5,000
Nusa Cendana University	1,200
Wiraraja University	330
Fahmina Institute of Islamic Studies	160

Source: Seven autonomous universities: World Bank (2010); Nusa Cendana University, Wiraraja University and Fahmina Institute: interviews.

month, making them some of the most highly paid academics in Indonesia. Lecturers at Nusa Cendana University, in contrast, receive around Rp 6 million per month. Wiraraja and Fahmina pay their academics on an hourly basis; their lecturers receive up to Rp 25,000 per teaching hour, or about Rp 2 million per month. Clearly, small TEIs cannot hope to have access to the same pool of high-calibre individuals that institutions such as the Bandung Institute of Technology and the University of Indonesia can draw from.

This does not mean, however, that the small TEIs are not attracting good researchers and lecturers. It is true that they do not produce many international publications. In 2011, of 51 Indonesian TEIs recorded by Scopus as having produced international publications, the University of Indonesia came first with 2,150 publications, and Nusa Cendana University 41st with only 14. The Fahmina Institute and Wiraraja University were not even on the list. However, as discussed later, some small TEIs have shown that they are fully capable of attracting the best individuals to meet their specific goals, which may be different from those of a research university.

Limited resources

A world-class university requires massive resources to conduct high-level research and attract the best researchers and lecturers. A comparison of per student expenditure by Indonesia's seven autonomous research universities and the three small institutions investigated in this study reveals the wide gulf in available resources. Table 9.1 shows that per student spending by small TEIs can be as little as 3 per cent the expenditure of the top universities.

World-class universities receive their funding from the government, research contracts, endowment returns and student fees (Salmi 2009).

A careful look at each of these funding sources reveals the tremendous challenges faced by the small TEIs.

Public funding. In developed countries, public funding is the principal source of financing for public universities (Salmi 2009). In Indonesia, small public TEIs receive significantly less public funding than large institutions, while private TEIs receive negligible public funding (World Bank 2010). Among our sample universities, the central government covers about half of Nusa Cendana University's $25 million annual budget, contributing approximately $600 per student.[8] This is less than Botswana's public spending per student on basic education. Fahmina and Wiraraja, meanwhile, derive less than 2 per cent of their budgets from public funding.

It is unlikely that public funding for higher education will increase significantly in the near future, especially as the government still needs to improve the quality of basic education. As the economy grows, however, there should be more scope for increased public funding of the tertiary education sector. Better funding channels, such as competitive grants, have the potential to make more resources available to the best performing institutions, but this reform will take time (World Bank 2010).

Research contracts. World-class universities consistently win research contracts from the public and private sectors. In Indonesia, however, university financial regulations and government procurement laws that restrict the ability of non-profit organizations to provide contracted services to the government are significant disincentives for universities to enter into research contracts with government or the private sector. Currently, both the central government and local governments can only procure services from for-profit organizations. Since the commissioning of policy research is considered the procurement of a service, and because TEIs are by law non-profit organizations, government cannot commission research directly from these institutions. In some cases, government institutions and TEIs circumvent this barrier by dealing through an intermediary, or through the commercial arm of a TEI established specifically for this purpose. Such measures would increase the transaction cost of commissioning research.

The top research universities would probably be the main beneficiaries from any reforms to this system. Indeed, the seven autonomous research universities, which are exempt from many of the provisions imposed on other public TEIs, are already partnering with the private sector and providing evidence to inform public policy. Small regional TEIs could also play a bigger role in providing policy research to local governments. However, they would be unlikely to generate much revenue from

---

8 $1 is approximately Rp 10,000.

this activity, especially if they have decided to emphasize teaching over research. Wiraraja University, for instance, receives about $15,000–18,000 per year, or approximately 2 per cent of its total budget, from competitive research grants administered by the Directorate General of Higher Education. Its research projects are geared towards equipping students with scientific, analytical and communication skills. While staff and students feel the benefits of the research grants, this source of funding does not contribute significantly to the university's total budget.

Endowment funds. Endowment funds are a major contributor to world-class university funding. Harvard University has amassed an endowment fund that is now larger than Kuwait's entire foreign exchange reserves. The leading British and American universities have benefited over the centuries from accommodative financial and taxation systems that encourage philanthropic contributions to educational institutions. In Indonesia, although philanthropy is widespread, it is mainly directed at religious, not academic, causes. Moreover, the Indonesian financial system does not accommodate the establishment of endowment funds by public universities. At present, any revenue generated by a public TEI is considered state revenue and must be transferred to the state treasury, with no guarantee that it will be returned in ensuing years.

Several of the seven autonomous universities have started to establish endowment funds, now that they no longer have to surrender the yields to the government. The University of Indonesia and the Bandung Institute of Technology were the first to do this, and others have followed suit. These universities usually rely on their alumni, many of whom are successful businesspeople, professionals and high-ranking government officials, to contribute to these funds. Chiefly through this strategy, the Bandung Institute of Technology had amassed around $9 million by 2012, a sum that is likely to grow further. Airlangga University plans to set up an endowment fund in 2013.

Nusa Cendana University does not have an endowment fund, no doubt for the reasons mentioned above. Private TEIs have more room to set up endowment funds because they own the revenues they generate. However, unlike the top public universities, most of them do not have pools of rich alumni to draw on. The Fahmina Institute and Wiraraja University receive only several hundred dollars per year from their alumni, most of which is used to help the poorest students pay their tuition fees.

Tuition fees. Student tuition fees are the major source of income for the Fahmina Institute and Wiraraja University, comprising more than 95 per cent of their total budgets. Tuition fees are also an important source of funding for Nusa Cendana University, making up around one-quarter of its total budget. Nusa Cendana uses the revenue to fund non-salary operational expenditure, including utilities and maintenance. Since many of their students come from poor or disadvantaged families, these small TEIs cannot afford to set their fees too high. The tuition fees of the three sample TEIs range from around $90 to $120 per semester. The lowest tuition fee at the University of Indonesia is about $500 per semester, and indicative fees for 2012 at the Australian National University show that its students are expected to contribute around $5,600–9,400 per year.

With their high proportions of poor students, these small TEIs cannot expect to significantly increase their financial resources by raising tuition fees. The flip side of this situation, however, is that they have a strong interest in retaining their students. As we explore further below, this can be considered a positive aspect of the role of small TEIs in providing tertiary education for the masses.

How small or regional TEIs operate

Although the institutions in our sample may not have what it takes to become world-class universities, our study indicates that what may at first seem to be a weakness can potentially be a strength. In particular, if a small TEI can identify a suitable role in the provision of tertiary education and perform it well, it may be able to operate effectively under a different framework from that of a world-class university.

Attracting faculty and retaining students

The small TEIs may lack the ability to provide attractive remuneration packages, but they can find other ways to lure good lecturers and researchers. Most notably, they provide opportunities for academic staff to upgrade their qualifications, to work in an intellectually stimulating environment and to contribute to the development of the local community.

First, the better-quality small TEIs devote significant resources to staff training and to programs to allow academics to upgrade their qualifications. This is a strong incentive for some of the most capable individuals in a region to work at those institutions. Second, in many cases, capable individuals are drawn to a small TEI because it provides a stimulating intellectual environment where they can meet 'kindred spirits' and debate ideas. Finally, many small TEIs make it their mission to contribute to the regions in which they are located. Individuals who are committed to the same ideal may be drawn to these institutions for this reason. The specific ways in which the three sample TEIs attract good academic staff are described in Box 9.2.

The extent of academic 'inbreeding' – academics gaining positions at the institutions from which they have graduated – tends to be far less at

---

BOX 9.2   HOW THE SELECTED TEIs ATTRACT TALENT

Nusa Cendana University has historically been proactive in tapping the resources of the government and international agencies to upgrade the academic qualifications of its faculty. It is one of the major recipients of the scholarship program conducted by the Australian Agency for International Development (AusAID) and sends staff members to study at Australian universities almost every year.

Wiraraja University has been sending its lecturers to training programs every year since 2006. The university managers proactively seek scholarship opportunities for staff, and even provide subsidies for lecturers who wish to further their studies.

By providing such opportunities, not only do Nusa Cendana and Wiraraja continually improve the capacity of their existing staff, but they also attract capable individuals to come and work at their institutions. Both report high retention rates among staff who have received scholarships to pursue higher academic qualifications. They attribute the high levels of staff satisfaction to the shared ideals of developing the region and contributing to the local society.

The Fahmina Institute of Islamic Studies prides itself on a culture of open discussion and debate. Progressive Islamic scholars who might find it difficult to air their opinions in public are able to find a 'safe haven' at Fahmina. The prevalence of individuals who value unrestrained critical thinking and the clash of ideas creates a highly interactive and student-centred learning environment for the institute's students.

---

small TEIs than at some of the leading public universities. For instance, only about 10 per cent of Wiraraja's teaching staff are its own graduates, whereas virtually all faculty at the Bandung Institute of Technology in 2009 had received their bachelor's degrees from the institute (ITB 2009: 22). Despite having the privilege of selection, the top universities seem to prefer to perpetuate a 'tribal culture' in which they hire their own alumni, who gravitate towards their own institutions for reasons of affinity and pragmatism (Hill and Thee 2012: 248; see also Chapter 8 of this volume, p. 171).

Small TEIs such as the Fahmina Institute and Wiraraja do not have the privilege of selection. Moreover, some teaching universities, such as Wiraraja, actively encourage their graduates to work in the private sector and not to teach at a TEI. While this may appear to be a constraint on recruitment, it has in fact led to a higher degree of diversity among faculty staff at small TEIs.

A 2007 survey of European universities found an inverse correlation between academic inbreeding and research performance (Aghion et al. 2008, cited in Salmi 2009: 21). In other words, having a faculty with diverse backgrounds can potentially be a strength for small institutions. Lecturers at Wiraraja University say that they are able to learn from and build on each other's experiences studying at different institutions to improve their teaching skills and the ways in which they support their students. Researchers at the Fahmina Institute claim that exposure to the 'foreign' ideas of their peers has enriched their own views on Islam (see also Box 9.2).

In general, small TEIs do not attract secondary school graduates with the best academic performance. However, as demonstrated by America's Posse scholarship program for youth from disadvantaged backgrounds, scoring well in standardized tests is not the main factor contributing to successful completion of higher education and later success in life. The Posse Foundation (2012) noted that it was the students with leadership qualities such as resilience, self-reliance and creativity that usually fared best. Such individuals are not on the radar of Indonesia's top universities, but it is exactly this type of student that is catered to by the small TEIs.

Because they rely on tuition fees for the bulk of their budgets, small TEIs also have a higher stake than the top universities in retaining their students. The Fahmina Institute and Wiraraja University have come up with various creative tuition instalment schemes and are very lenient towards late payments. At Wiraraja, lecturers try to detect signs of financial stress among students, in order to provide support. It is not uncommon for the lecturers to visit the homes of students who have missed classes to find out what the university can do to help them continue their studies. They are also very active in seeking out scholarship opportunities for their students. Institutionalized efforts such as these to retain disadvantaged students are far less visible at the top universities.

Although financial constraints remain a barrier for disadvantaged students studying at any university, those studying at small TEIs may face significantly fewer non-financial barriers. For instance, whereas students from Sumenep studying at the Bandung Institute of Technology are likely to find it difficult to adapt to the social environment of Bandung, a big modern city at the other end of Java, those studying at Wiraraja University are likely to feel quite at home. The academic gap between disadvantaged students from poor areas and their better-educated counterparts from the big cities is another source of difficulty for poor regional students. Faculty at the top universities generally do not have the time or the capacity to accommodate the specific academic needs of such students. But in small TEIs where the majority of students are from poor backgrounds – the Fahmina Institute, for instance, claims that all of its students are poor – academics are likely to be more sensitive to the issue of disadvantage. Although the prevalence of poor students undoubtedly poses a challenge for small TEIs, it also puts them in a better position to ensure that their students successfully complete their studies. Unlike their counterparts at the University of Indonesia, lecturers at Nusa Cendana, Fahmina and Wiraraja specifically tailor their approaches to support students who need more academic support.

Attracting resources and using them effectively

Despite having fewer resources than the world-class universities, small TEIs can be very creative both in finding alternative funding sources and in managing the available resources effectively. Although tuition fees remain the main source of revenue, especially for private institutions, high-quality small TEIs may be able to gain access to research grants and donations; set up business units; and receive financial support from local governments.

All three sample TEIs seem to rely heavily on their networks either to obtain research grants and contracts or to attract donations. Nusa Cendana University has been able to obtain grants from the local government for research on dry-land farming, which is very relevant to the region. The Fahmina Institute uses the network of its sister research institute to obtain grants from the local government and international donors to conduct research. Wiraraja University has a relatively strong alumni network that provides scholarships for its poorest students on a regular basis.

Setting up business units also seems to be a viable option for small TEIs hoping to diversify their sources of revenue. This, however, requires additional resources to manage the business. The Fahmina Institute has addressed this issue by getting its more entrepreneurial students to manage its catfish farms; the students can then use the income to pay their tuition fees. If managed well, business units can provide additional revenue for small TEIs and at the same time increase retention rates among students from disadvantaged backgrounds.

This study finds that although small private TEIs are unlikely to receive financial support from the central government, they are in a better position to tap local government funding. Unlike the big public universities, small private TEIs cater almost exclusively to local students. As a result, local governments are more inclined to provide financial support, knowing that most of the money will be used for the benefit of the local people. On the other hand, funding from local governments is small, irregular and very dependent on the local political landscape. Wiraraja University, for instance, can receive from as little as Rp 65 million to as much as Rp 250 million per year from the Sumenep district government.

Relying on local government spending also poses a tricky dilemma for small institutions, because the more students from outside the district that a TEI admits, the less willing the local government will be to make a contribution. Hence, there may be a trade-off for small TEIs between gaining more national recognition and receiving funding from the local government.

Notwithstanding their innovative approaches to generating revenue, small TEIs still face considerable resource constraints. The high-quality institutions therefore make a conscious effort to maximize the utility of available resources. Wiraraja University has set up a system to ensure that resources such as laboratories and classrooms are shared across different study programs, even in different faculties. Schedules show that the university's laboratories and classrooms are in almost constant use throughout a typical week. Wiraraja has also established partnerships with other universities, including East Java's flagship research university, Airlangga, that allow its students to use their facilities. Nusa Cendana University is larger than Wiraraja and Fahmina, but it too relies on resource sharing. At Nusa Cendana, it is compulsory for each faculty to make its facilities available to every researcher, lecturer and student. At the Fahmina Institute, a lack of classrooms simply means that learning takes place in the cafeteria, the library or the mosque.

Leadership and strategic planning

Although autonomy and competition are crucial for the establishment of world-class universities, these two characteristics alone are not sufficient to propel an institution into the top ranks. As Salmi (2009: 28) notes, other key governance features are also required, most notably:

> ... inspiring and persistent leaders; a strong strategic vision of where the institution is going; a philosophy of success and excellence; and a culture of constant reflection, organizational learning, and change.

In the sample TEIs, the presence of these features to some extent seems to offset the lack of supportive regulatory environments characterizing these institutions.

All three TEIs have strong leadership and a clear strategic vision. These seem to be key factors contributing to their ability to function despite the considerable constraints. Regardless of their stated aspirations to become world-class universities, interviews with the leadership indicate that they in fact have very different visions. Wiraraja University, for instance, focuses heavily on imparting employable skills to its students. Its main mission is to produce graduates who can successfully find employment or create jobs in the local economy. The main mission of the

Fahmina Institute is to induce social transformation, by actively using its research output and courses to popularize a progressive interpretation of Islam and influence local policy making. Nusa Cendana University envisions its graduates becoming public and private sector leaders in East Nusa Tenggara province. The university conducts research that is geared towards locally relevant technologies, such as those related to dry-land farming. This stands in contrast to the research conducted in Indonesia's top research universities, which put more emphasis on international publications and globally recognized technological innovations.

As noted earlier, private TEIs such as Wiraraja University and the Fahmina Institute have more autonomy over their finances than public institutions such as Nusa Cendana. Although this comes with the trade-off of less government support, it also means that Wiraraja and Fahmina can be more creative and flexible in using their resources to reach their goals. Since 2008, Wiraraja has been encouraging its students to become more entrepreneurial – to look beyond the comfort of the civil service and find ways to contribute to the local economy by working in the private sector. Despite its limited resources, the university provides seed money for its business students to start up businesses as part of the learning process, and assists them to continue their enterprises after they have graduated.

Strong leadership and a clear strategic vision can also affect the incentive structure within an institution. Academics in public TEIs are part of the civil service, where length of service tends to be more highly valued than performance (Hill and Thee 2012). But although Nusa Cendana is a public university, it has introduced a merit-based system of career progression for lecturers and researchers that prioritizes academic performance. It is no longer uncommon to see a young lecturer or researcher holding a high-level position at Nusa Cendana University, although this is not the rule at most public TEIs.

Improvements in the enabling environment are nevertheless necessary. Greater autonomy would allow Nusa Cendana University to become even more innovative, and more competition would likely make all three sample TEIs lift the quality of their service. Yet, a clear vision and strong leadership do seem to have enabled these TEIs to identify a suitable role and play to their strengths to fulfil that role. This leads to the final dimension in the proposed framework of a well-functioning small TEI – becoming locally relevant.

Becoming locally relevant

A world-class university has its eye set on becoming 'globally recognized'. In contrast, high-quality small TEIs strive to become *locally relevant.* The three sample TEIs in our study are very attuned to the needs of their local economies and communities. Being relatively small and in close proximity to their areas of service allows them to make their output locally relevant.

Wiraraja University has identified a need for the Sumenep economy to grow by having a stronger private sector and more skilled workers. It has therefore decided to focus more on teaching local secondary school graduates, to give them the skills the local economy needs. It has established strong links with local industries to inform the content of its study programs.

For the Fahmina Institute, becoming locally relevant is about making the Cirebon community more open-minded and ready to embrace diversity, and empowering it to become more involved in policy-making processes. Its research is accordingly geared towards informing local policy makers and educating the local community. Students are strongly encouraged to write opinion pieces for local newspapers and publish blogs.

Nusa Cendana University is a major supplier of skills to both the private and public sectors in East Nusa Teggara. Seventy per cent of its graduates are employed by the provincial or district governments, and virtually all of the province's district heads have studied at the university. Given that about 80 per cent of teachers in the province are graduates of the university, Nusa Cendana is focusing on improving the quality of its teacher training college. It has also established very strong links with local industries. To support the local economy, Nusa Cendana has identified three study programs as its 'core business': dry-land farming, tourism and fisheries. Its technological innovations are also intended to be locally relevant – the university's research and innovation in dry-land farming has been of great practical assistance to the province's farmers. The university's researchers have even taken it on themselves to introduce these locally relevant technological innovations to small nearby islands, despite the difficulty of getting to them by boat.

9.5 WORLD-CLASS VERSUS LOCALLY RELEVANT: WHAT DO SMALL TEIs PRODUCE?

While Indonesia's small TEIs do not have the resources or the capacity to become top research universities, they may not need to. With their own unique set of strengths, these institutions should play a different role from that of the research universities. They cater to local students; they recruit individuals who are motivated to develop the region; and they are in a better position to establish strong links with local government.

High-quality small TEIs realize this and hence work hard to become *locally relevant*. Below, we describe the four major outcomes high-quality, locally relevant TEIs can be expected to produce, and what they do to deliver those outcomes.

Supply skills to the local economy

Some small TEIs may opt to focus less on research and more on teaching. Being geographically close to local businesses and industries, they are in a good position to establish links with key players in the local economy. This allows them to tailor the skills they impart to their students to actual demand in the local job market. The stronger the links between a small TEI and the local economy, the more relevant the skills it can supply.

Small private TEIs have a particularly strong incentive to ensure the relevance of the skills they impart to students. Because they rely heavily on tuition fees, they need to keep attracting students. To do this, they have to build and maintain a reputation for producing graduates who are wanted by local businesses and industries, or who are capable of starting up new enterprises.

Induce social transformation

As an institution of learning, a small TEI can play a major role in driving social transformation. As noted previously, most students at small regional TEIs come from the local community. These institutions therefore have the opportunity to help young people from the surrounding region to think critically, challenge conventional wisdom and promote change. These new ideas can permeate through the community, thus inducing social transformation.

The Fahmina Institute's stated mission is to induce social transformation through its students, graduates and researchers. It was established by a thinktank in Cirebon dedicated to spreading a progressive interpretation of the Islamic scriptures – one that promotes pluralism, gender equality and human rights. The principal motivation for establishing the Fahmina Institute was both to house the thinktank's researchers and to disseminate its ideas to Cirebon youth.

Influence local policy making

Small TEIs may be strategically placed to inform local policy-making processes. In many small districts and provinces, the local TEIs are the most viable institutions to rely on for supplying evidence and ideas to policy makers. For a small institution to play this role, it needs to have a relatively strong research capacity, and a strategy to influence local policy makers.

Of the three sample TEIs, Nusa Cendana University and the Fahmina Institute are visibly playing this role. Nusa Cendana relies on international scholarships, mainly from Australia, to continually develop its researchers' capacity. It then uses its network, generally alumni occupying high positions in the provincial and district governments, to inform and influence policy-making processes. The central government is also aware of Nusa Cendana University's policy-making capacity, and often consults its researchers on policy-related matters. Adopting a different strategy, the Fahmina Institute draws talent from its sister institution, and forms partnerships with several European universities, to conduct quality research. The Fahmina Institute's strategy is to adopt a more grassroots approach to policy making, mobilizing the community to get involved in this process.

Produce locally relevant technological innovations

A relatively research-intensive small university can produce technological innovations that have direct application at the local level. This requires not only technical skills but also the ability to identify what the local community really needs. Resources may need to be devoted both to the actual research and to the dissemination of the technology. Since this requires relatively large resources, it is conceivable that, in the Indonesian context, the public TEIs are in a better position than the private ones to play this role.

9.6   IN PLACE OF A SWEEPING CONCLUSION

This chapter has made the case that although Indonesia needs world-class research universities, that aspiration is not realistic for many of its TEIs. The Indonesian community also requires a different breed of TEI, and many small ones can fill that role. While the findings presented in this chapter should be interpreted cautiously, an alternative framework can be proposed for the establishment of high-quality small TEIs. This framework is visualized in Figure 9.1.

Small TEIs may be able to attract talented staff by offering them the opportunity to upgrade their qualifications and to take part in a shared ideal. Resource constraints can be overcome by adopting innovative revenue-generating schemes and by making effective use of what is available. Strong leadership and a clear strategic vision can go a long way towards overcoming a less than favourable environment. At heart, a

Figure 9.1   Proposed alternative framework for high-quality small TEIs

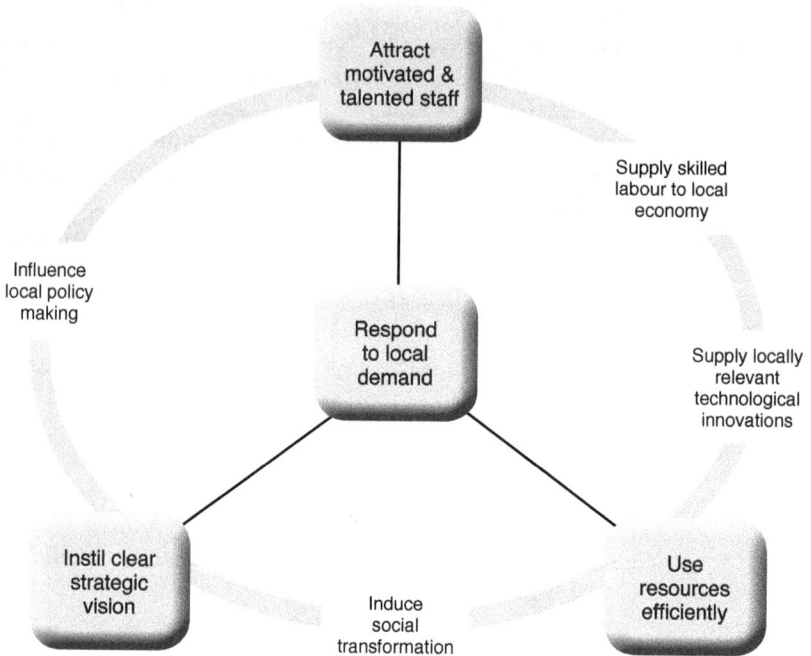

Source: Authors.

high-quality TEI needs to establish itself as an institution that responds to local needs – it has to be relevant to the local economy and the local community. By doing this, small TEIs can hope to supply skills to the local economy, induce social transformation, influence local policy-making processes and provide the local community with relevant technological innovations. This is the role of small regional TEIs, and it supplements that of world-class universities.

It is difficult to draw general conclusions from such a small sample of TEIs; the framework we have proposed for high-quality small TEIs must therefore be considered preliminary. It would be interesting to test this framework on a larger sample of small regional TEIs to evaluate its efficacy. The views of a wider group of stakeholders, for instance local industries, could be included to verify the claims of a TEI to be locally relevant. A more practical endeavour would be to explore whether the proposed framework could be translated into a quality assurance system for regional or small TEIs, accompanied by government support to encourage the development of a diversified tertiary education system. These are matters that will have to be addressed in future studies.

REFERENCES

Aghion, P., M. Dewatripont, C. Hoxby, A. Mas-Colell and A. Sapir (2008) 'Higher aspirations: an agenda for reforming European universities', Bruegel Blueprint 5, Bruegel, Brussels.

Altbach, P.G. (2004) 'The costs and benefits of world-class universities', *Academe*, 90(1): 20–23.

Altbach, P.G. (2011) 'The past, present, and future of the research university', in P.G. Altbach and J. Salmi (eds) *The Road to Academic Excellence: The Making of World-class Research Universities*, International Bank for Reconstruction and Development/World Bank, Washington DC, pp. 11–32.

Belanger, C.H. (1989) 'University entrepreneurship and competition: the case of the small universities', *Canadian Journal of Higher Education*, 19(2): 13–22.

Binus University (2011) 'Vision & mission', Binus University, Jakarta, available at http://binus.ac.id/vision-mission/.

Clarke, J., P. Thomas and I. Wallace (n.d.) 'How should diversity in the higher education system be encouraged?', position paper developed for the Business/ Higher Education Round Table Summit Task Force, available at http://www. bhert.com/publications/discussion-papers/How-Should-Diversity.pdf.

Daniel, J.S. and C.H. Belanger (1989) 'Academic vitality and informed opportunism: a prescription for smaller universities', *Higher Education in Europe*, 14(3): 34–40.

Gunadarma University (n.d.) *UG, PTS terbaik di Indonesia* [UG, best private tertiary education institution in Indonesia], Gunadarma University, Depok, available at http://www.gunadarma.ac.id/id/page/ug-pts-terbaik-di-indonesia.html.

Hill, H. and Thee K.W. (2012) 'Indonesian universities in transition: catching up and opening up', *Bulletin of Indonesian Economic Studies*, 48(2): 229–51.

ITB (Institut Teknologi Bandung) (2009) 'Data dan informasi ITB 2009' [Data and information, ITB 2009], ITB, Bandung.

ITB (Institut Teknologi Bandung) (2011) 'Informasi umum Institut Teknologi Bandung' [Information about the Bandung Institute of Technology], ITB, Bandung, available at http://www.itb.ac.id/about-itb/.

Lang, D.W. (2005) '"World class" or the curse of comparison?', *Canadian Journal of Higher Education*, 35(3): 27–55.

Levin, H.M., D.W. Jeong and D. Ou (2006) 'What is a world class university?', paper prepared for the Conference of the Comparative and International Education Society, Honolulu, 16 March, available at http://www.tc.columbia. edu/centers/coce/pdf_files/c12.pdf.

Mohrman, K. (2005) 'World-class universities and Chinese higher education reform', *International Higher Education*, 39(Spring): 22–3.

Ngok, K. (2008) 'Massification, bureaucratization and questing for "world-class" status: higher education in China since the mid-1990s', *International Journal of Educational Management*, 22(6): 547–64.

Niland, J. (2000) 'The challenge of building world class universities in the Asian region', *On Line Opinion*, 3 February, available at http://www.onlineopinion. com.au/view.asp?article=997.

Posse Foundation (2012) 'Fulfilling the promise: the impact of Posse after 20 years. 2012 alumni report', Posse Foundation, New York, available at http:// www.possefoundation.org/m/alum-report-web.pdf.

Salmi, J. (2009) *The Challenge of Establishing World-class Universities*, International Bank for Reconstruction and Development/World Bank, Washington DC.

Teichler, U. (2004) 'Changing structures of the higher education systems: the increasing complexity of underlying forces', Centre for Research on Higher Education and Work, University of Kassel, Kassel.

UGM (Universitas Gajah Mada) (n.d.) 'Visi & misi Universitas Gadjah Mada' [Vision & mission of Gadjah Mada University], UGM, Yogyakarta, available at http://www.ugm.ac.id/content.php?page=0&display=1.

UI (Universitas Indonesia) (n.d.) 'Visi & misi' [Vision & mission], UI, Jakarta, available at http://www.ui.ac.id/id/profile/page/visi-misi.

Universitas Surabaya (Ubaya) (2012) 'Ubaya menuju world-class university' [Ubaya heading towards a world-class university], Universitas Surabaya, Surabaya, available at http://www.ubaya.ac.id/ubaya/news_detail/958/Ubaya%20Menuju%20World%20Class%20University.html.

World Bank (2010) 'Indonesia: higher education financing', Policy Brief, World Bank, Jakarta.

10 FINANCING HIGHER EDUCATION: THE VIABILITY OF A COMMERCIAL STUDENT LOAN SCHEME IN INDONESIA

Bruce Chapman and Daniel Suryadarma

10.1 INTRODUCTION AND BACKGROUND

Several contemporary Asian economies, including China, Vietnam and Indonesia, have two major things in common: unusually rapid economic growth, and significant expansions of their higher education enrolment and graduation rates. The association between economic growth and growth in higher education is both easy to understand and multi-faceted: as GDP per capita increases, so too does the demand for higher education, with this growth in the skill base of the labour force itself facilitating the economic growth that has helped generate the higher demand for university places. The processes are clearly endogenous.

Many of these economies share another and darker characteristic, which is that they have poorly developed financing systems for higher education. This is an emerging issue for policy because it implies that, even quite soon, the impressive economic growth of the transitional Asian economies could face important constraints with respect to the required expansions in higher education. The most pessimistic of these assessments would allude to the possibility of a country being caught in a 'middle-income trap', through the incapacity of its education system to meet the ever-increasing demand for a better-educated labour force.

As far as Indonesia is concerned, it would seem obvious that in order to meet the rising demand for higher education while enhancing quality with limited resources, greater cost sharing with students through increases in tuition fees is unavoidable. It is well known that the only equitable and efficient way to collect significant contributions from students is through the use of a student loan system (Friedman 1955; Chapman 2006), but it is also apparent that Indonesian higher education lacks a well-designed and universal financing mechanism. This chapter explores the implications of the adoption in Indonesia of student loan reforms.

Our approach is to ask, if Indonesia adopted the type of student loan system that is most often used around the world, would this provide a solid foundation to help prevent the growth rates of university enrolments and graduations from stalling? This type of higher education financing system involves government-backed loans provided by banks. It is known as a 'mortgage-type' arrangement because loan repayments are made on the basis of pre-determined amounts over a given time period. This is the type of scheme currently used to help finance higher education in many countries, including the United States, Canada, the Philippines and Thailand. It would be a natural initial reform for a government intent on requiring students to make greater tuition payments.

Our focus is on reporting of the so-called 'repayment burden', the proportion of graduate income per period that needs to be allocated to repay this type of loan. As is explained below, the repayment burden is critical to an understanding of the effects of mortgage-type student loan systems, because the higher the proportion of a graduate's income that needs to be allocated to the repayment of a loan, the lower will be that person's disposable income. Lower disposable incomes have two adverse and related consequences for graduates: a lower level of consumption, and a higher probability of default on the student loan. There is arguably no more important aspect of the feasibility of a student loan system than the associated repayment burden.

To find out what the introduction of this kind of financing system could mean for Indonesia, we design a hypothetical, but plausible, loan scheme, and simulate the repayment burden for graduates. Following Chapman et al. (2010), Chapman and Lounkaew (2011), Chapman and Sinning (2011) and Chapman and Liu (forthcoming), we simulate the repayment burden for graduates in different parts of the earnings distribution using the unconditional quantile regression (UQR) approach that has formed the methodological basis of analyses of student loan schemes in Thailand, the United States, Germany and Vietnam.

The critical finding is that the repayment burden for a mortgage-type loan system would be extremely high for a minority of Indonesian graduates, and would pose financial difficulties for the majority of borrowers. The prospects for default, and the adverse consequences for both students and the government, are implicit and clear. Thus, our exercises have important policy implications for the reform of higher education in Indonesia, and contribute to the literature on the design of student loan schemes for low-income developing countries in transition.

This chapter is organized in five sections. Section 10.2 examines the concept of repayment burdens. Section 10.3 describes the hypothetical loan scheme, including the repayment amounts required. Section 10.4 describes the earnings data and presents unconditional quantile age–earnings estimates for both Java and Sumatra and for male and female graduates. Section 10.5 presents the repayment burdens for different groups and discusses the calculations. We conclude with a summary, and note the use in some countries of a different approach to student financing – income-contingent collection – that avoids a high repayment burden. It is difficult to know if an income-contingent loan scheme could be administered effectively in Indonesia, but it seems clear that there is a strong case for finding out.

10.2   THE CONCEPT OF THE REPAYMENT BURDEN[1]

Defined simply, a loan repayment burden is the proportion of income required to service a loan. Therefore, the repayment burden in period t is:

$$Repayment\ burden_t = \frac{Loan\ repayment_t}{Earnings_t} \tag{10.1}$$

From this formula, it is clear that a repayment burden will increase with higher loan levels or with lower earnings. It is also evident from other analyses that as the repayment burden increases, the probability of default also increases. In the case of loans in the United States, borrowers with low incomes are the most likely to default (Dynarski 1994; Gross et al. 2009).

It is useful to ask what level of repayment burden is *too* much. Woodhall (1987) states that loan repayments should not exceed 10 per cent of income. Salmi (2003) suggests that no repayment schedule can be sustainable if the burden exceeds 18 per cent of income. Finally, Baum and Schwartz (2006) argue that students should not be forced to allocate more than 8 per cent of their incomes to servicing student loans. Perhaps we could consider 18 per cent as the critical threshold for a repayment burden, above which a loan has a very high default risk. We admit, however, that the repayment burden becomes less of a concern in situations where graduates are earning high absolute incomes.

---

1   This discussion follows Chapman and Liu (forthcoming).

We now examine the repayment burden in a number of countries. In Vietnam, graduates in the bottom 25 per cent of the earnings distribution face a repayment burden of between 20 and 85 per cent of their incomes (Chapman and Liu forthcoming). The same study shows that even graduates in the top 25 per cent of the earnings distribution have to spend 14–17 per cent of their incomes in the first 10 years to pay off the debt. In Thailand, where student loans enjoy a relatively large public subsidy, the repayment burden ranges from 5 per cent to 30 per cent (Chapman et al. 2010). Finally, even in developed countries, graduates face high repayment burdens, ranging from 50 per cent for lawyers in the United States to 70 per cent for East German women (Chapman and Sinning 2011).

As noted, although no higher education loan scheme currently exists in Indonesia, it is still important to show whether a typical mortgage-type loan would be feasible for the country. In the analysis that follows, we design a hypothetical higher education loan scheme for Indonesia and calculate the repayment burden.

10.3   A HYPOTHETICAL STUDENT LOAN SCHEME FOR INDONESIA

The hypothetical student loan used in this chapter is a mortgage-type loan. It has the following features. First, the loan covers both education costs (tuition and other associated costs) and living expenses (assumed to be the same as the education costs) for four years. Second, the loan repayment period starts after the student graduates from university, with a one-year grace period. In this chapter, we assume that individuals enrol in university at age 18 and graduate at age 21. Therefore, the repayment period starts when the individual is 23 years old. Third, the loan must be fully repaid within 10 years.

According to the 2006 National Socio-Economic Survey (Survei Sosio-Ekonomi Nasional, Susenas), the average total annual cost of attending university in Indonesia is Rp 3.8 million. Combined with living expenses, the total loan taken out by a student to complete a four-year university degree would be Rp 30.4 million. We assume that the loan carries a nominal interest rate of 8 per cent, and that the annual inflation rate is 5 per cent. The real interest rate of 3 per cent and the 10-year repayment period are similar to those used in the United States and Canada.

Based on the design described above, Figure 10.1 shows the repayment stream for our hypothetical student loan. In nominal terms, the annual repayment is around Rp 4.4 million, with the real value of the repayment declining to about Rp 3 million by the tenth year.

Figure 10.1   Repayment schedule for a hypothetical loan of Rp 30.4 million

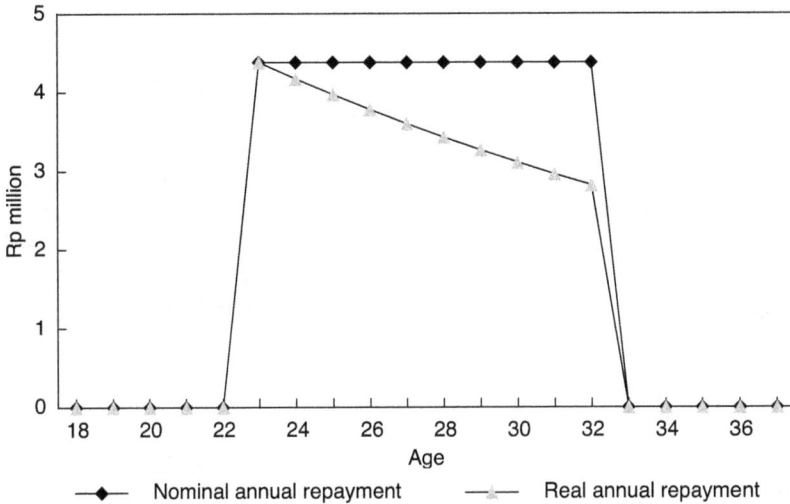

10.4   AGE–EARNINGS PROFILES OF UNIVERSITY GRADUATES IN INDONESIA

Data

The dataset we use to estimate the earnings of university graduates is the 2006 National Labour Force Survey (Survei Angkatan Kerja Nasional, Sakernas). We restrict the sample to those living in Java and Sumatra, given that the Sakernas shows that 81 per cent of university graduates live on these two islands. We also restrict the sample to individuals below 40 years of age. This is relevant, as the student loan scheme is designed to have a repayment period of 10 years, beginning at age 23. Finally, we estimate the profiles only of graduates who are currently employed as wage workers. We exclude self-employed graduates because the Sakernas does not collect data on the earnings of the self-employed,[2] and we do not consider graduates who are currently not working.

Model and methodology

The model we use to estimate the age–earnings profile is the following:

$$\ln Y_i = \alpha + \beta PE_i + \gamma PE^2_i + \varepsilon_i \tag{10.2}$$

---

2 The Sakernas shows that only about 14 per cent of university graduates are self-employed.

where $\ln Y_i$ is the monthly earnings of worker i, and PE_i is the potential experience of the individual, calculated as current age minus 22.[3] We estimate the earnings of university graduates using the UQR methodology. The method allows us to estimate the age–earnings profiles of individuals in different parts of the distribution. As mentioned in Chapman and Liu (forthcoming), this methodology is chosen over ordinary least squares (OLS), the workhorse of econometrics, for the critical reason that it provides a disaggregated picture of the earnings distribution. This is important, because the repayment burden must be higher for individuals who earn less. In contrast, the OLS method estimates only the mean earnings distribution and would not be able to capture the differing repayment burdens faced by workers in different parts of the earnings distribution.

Earnings function estimation results

We estimate the age–earnings profiles for the 25th, 50th (median) and 75th percentiles of the earnings distribution (Q25, Q50 and Q75 respectively), with separate estimations carried out by gender and by location (Java and Sumatra). Java represents the relatively more affluent areas of Indonesia, and Sumatra the less affluent areas.

The profiles are shown in Figure 10.2; the estimation results are in Table A10.1 in the appendix. Comparing Java and Sumatra, we find that graduates in Java, especially those in Q25 and Q50, earn more than those in Sumatra at every age. For both islands, there does not appear to be a concave age–earnings profile for workers in these quantiles. In contrast, graduates in Q75 in both islands start out earning very similar wages at the age of 22. They then follow different trajectories, with the graduates in Java having a concave age–earnings profile and those in Sumatra experiencing a convex profile. By the age of 40, however, graduates in Q75 in Sumatra appear to have caught up to those in Java.

The patterns for males and females are somewhat different. In general, males in all three parts of the earnings distribution have higher incomes than females. Although males and females in Q75 have fairly similar earning levels and trajectories, females in Q25 and Q50 consistently earn much lower wages than males in the corresponding quantiles. In addition, we see no evidence of a concave age–earnings profile for male or female workers in Q25 and Q50.

---

3 The figure of 22 is the sum of the 16 years required to graduate with a four-year university education, including 12 years of primary and secondary education, and the age at which an individual is first enrolled in school, assumed to be six years old. So 22 = 16 + 6.

Figure 10.2   Age–earnings profiles by area and gender

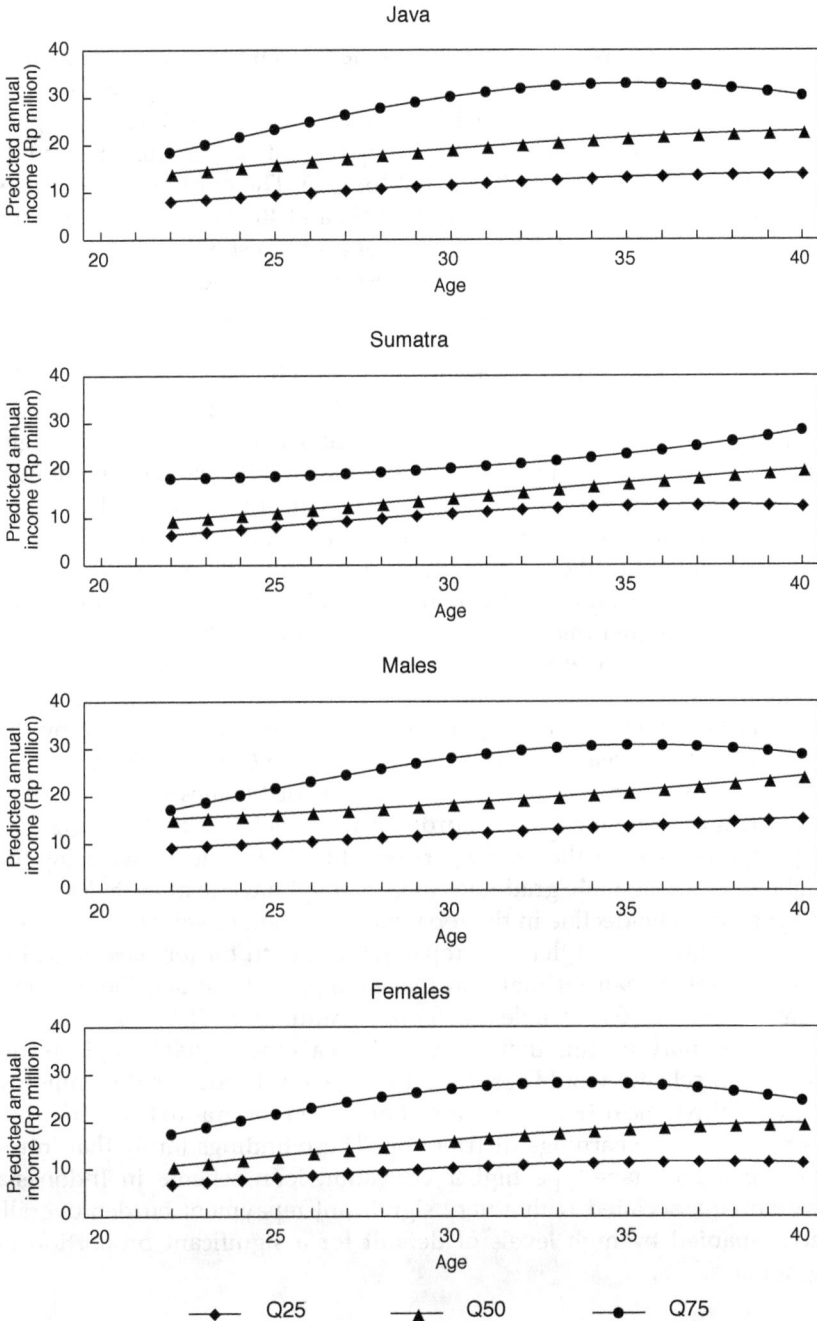

10.5   REPAYMENT BURDEN FOR THE HYPOTHETICAL LOAN SCHEME

After estimating both the repayment schedule and the earnings profiles by age, we now calculate the repayment burden for the hypothetical student loan scheme (Figure 10.3). For graduates working in Java, the repayment burden during the first year of repayment ranges from around 20 per cent for Q75 to about 50 per cent for Q25. The burden then declines as income increases, to 15 per cent for Q75 and 40 per cent for Q25 in the final year of repayment. Using the 18 per cent threshold, we find that the loan would have a very high default risk for graduates in Q25 and Q50, and also for graduates in Q75 except in the last few years of the repayment schedule.

The pattern is similar for graduates in Q75 living in Sumatra. Unlike in Java, however, the repayment burden for Q75 graduates in Sumatra remains more or less the same at around 20 per cent of income throughout the life of the loan. For those in Q25, meanwhile, the repayment burden exceeds 60 per cent in the first year, with those in Q50 having to spend more than 40 per cent of their incomes in the first year to service the debt. Although the repayment burden eventually declines to 40 per cent and 30 per cent respectively for Q25 and Q50 graduates, it remains significantly higher than the 18 per cent default threshold.

Comparing male with female graduates, we find that the patterns for individuals in Q75 are very similar. For both groups, the repayment burden starts at a little over 20 per cent and declines only slightly by the end of the tenth year. For graduates in Q25 and Q50, however, we find that the repayment burden is much higher for females than for males. The most extreme repayment burden is for female graduates in Q25. At age 23, they have to allocate 60 per cent of their incomes to servicing the debt. In contrast, male graduates in Q25 'only' have to allocate less than 50 per cent. The decline in the repayment burden, however, is faster for females. Having said that, the repayment burden for females in Q25 is always higher than for males in the same part of the distribution. The same pattern holds for male and female graduates in Q50.

In summary, we find that our hypothetical (and arguably typical) student loan scheme would result in a repayment burden that commonly exceeds the critical 18 per cent threshold, even for graduates in the 75th percentile of the earnings distribution. These findings imply that introducing a mortgage-type higher education loan scheme in Indonesia would be associated with a very significant repayment burden overall, accompanied by high levels of default for a significant proportion of graduates.

Figure 10.3   Loan repayment burden for the hypothetical loan scheme

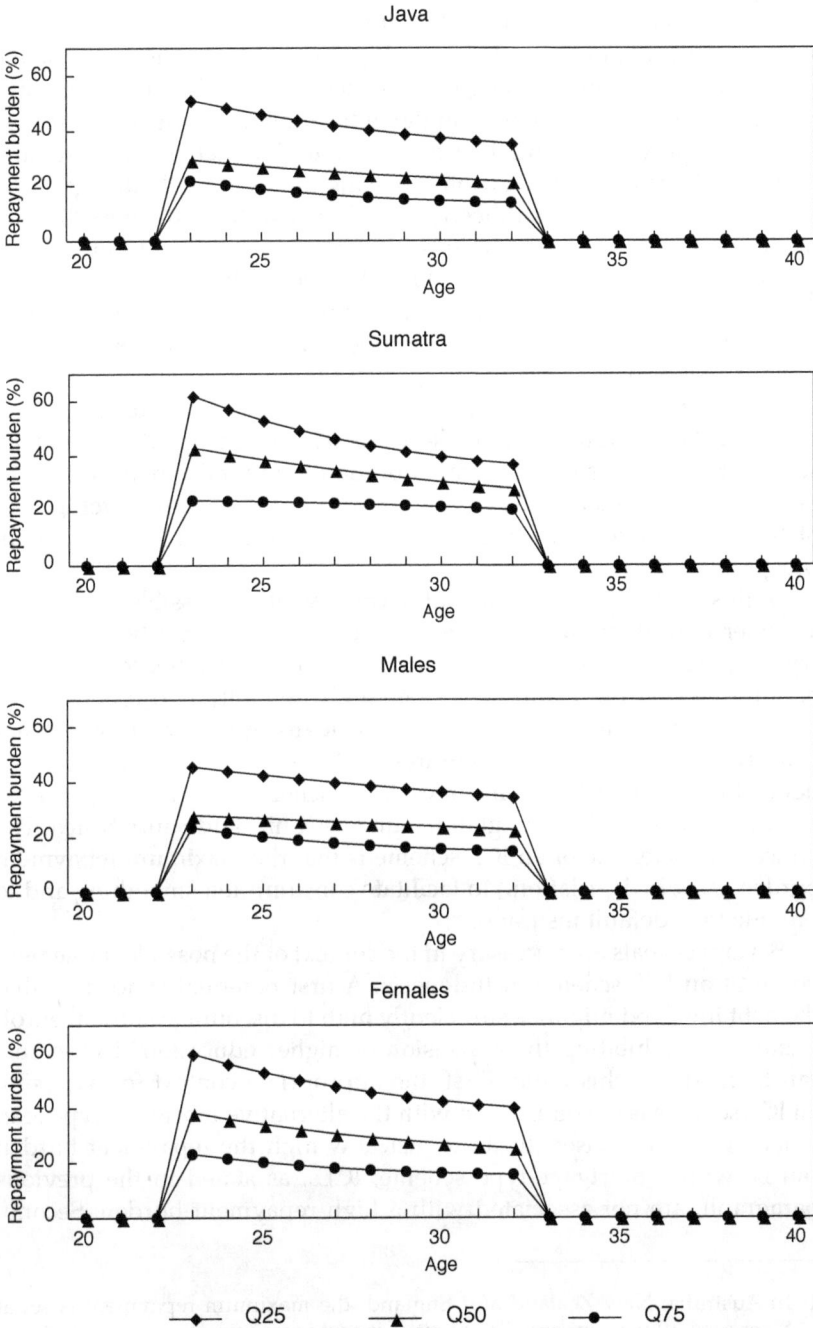

Java

Sumatra

Males

Females

Q25   Q50   Q75

10.6 CONCLUSION

Using the 2006 Sakernas and a hypothetical yet plausible student loan scheme for Indonesia, we have explored empirically the issue of the likely repayment burden in light of the clear need in the future for a different and expanded system of higher education financing for this country. Importantly, the calculations have been undertaken in different parts of the graduate earnings distribution using the UQR methodology.

In line with previous studies, our results show that estimates of repayment burdens at the mean hide the variations in different parts of the graduate earnings distribution. Our calculations illustrate quite clearly that there would be a heavy repayment burden for graduates with low and very low incomes, particularly those living in poor areas of Indonesia, and that the burden would persist for a number of years into the repayment period even if students borrowed money only to cover their tuition costs. It would seem to follow that a better-designed student loan scheme that reduces the repayment burden to minimize both consumption hardship and loan default risk is critical for the future development of higher education, and thus to Indonesia's future economic growth prospects.

In this context it may be useful to canvass other possible designs for a higher education student loan scheme that would not be associated with a potentially very costly repayment burden. Discussion needs to be informed by the reality that there are essentially two types of student financing schemes: mortgage-type loans and income-contingent loans (ICLs). An ICL scheme requires students to commit to repay debts depending on their future incomes. Such schemes currently operate in Australia, New Zealand, England, Hungary, Chile and South Korea. The critical characteristic of an ICL scheme is that the maximum repayment burden is set by legislation,[4] to facilitate consumption smoothing and to provide loan default insurance.

Several caveats are necessary in the context of the possible implementation of an ICL scheme in Indonesia. A first potential concern is that the debt involved might be sufficiently high to discourage student enrolments, thus inhibiting the expansion of higher education. Two points can be made on this issue. First, the appropriate context for assessing an ICL scheme is in comparison with the alternative mortgage-type loan schemes. Our exercises illustrate just how high the repayment burden can be with a mortgage-type scheme; ICLs, as stated in the previous paragraph, are not associated with a high repayment burden. Second,

---

4 In Australia, New Zealand and England, the maximum repayment is set at 8 per cent, 10 per cent and 9 per cent of income respectively.

other countries' experience illustrates compellingly that even students from poor backgrounds have not changed their enrolment behaviour in response to either the introduction or the expansion of ICLs, although this evidence is so far limited to high-income countries such as Australia (Chapman 2006).

The most important issue with respect to the possible introduction of an ICL scheme in Indonesia is that loans of this type require accurate identification of a borrower's lifetime income and consequently usually rely on the country's personal income tax system to collect debts. However, Indonesia's tax system collects very little revenue from personal income tax. According to Lestyowati (2011), Indonesia has only 18.1 million registered individual taxpayers, with a compliance rate of 62 per cent.[5] Thus, while the successful institution of an ICL scheme would avoid the adverse potential consequences of a high repayment burden for student borrowers in Indonesia, such a policy debate would need to start in the area of governance reform to strengthen the capacity of the income tax system to collect repayments.[6] The case for a beginning to this debate is highly persuasive.

REFERENCES

Baum, S. and S. Schwartz (2006) *How Much Debt Is Too Much? Defining Benchmarks for Manageable Student Debt*, College Board, New York.

Chapman, B. (ed.) (2006) *Government Managing Risk: Income Contingent Loans for Social and Economic Progress*, Routledge, London.

Chapman, B. and A. Liu (forthcoming) 'Repayment burdens of student loans for Vietnamese higher education', *Economics of Education Review*.

Chapman, B. and K. Lounkaew (2011) 'The effects of different loan schemes for higher education tuition: an analysis of rates of return and tuition revenue in Thailand', *Higher Education in Europe*, 34(2): 211–26.

Chapman, B. and M. Sinning (2011) 'Student loan reforms for German higher education: financing tuition fees', IZA Discussion Paper No. 5532, February.

Chapman, B., K. Lounkaew, P. Polsiri, R. Sarachitti and T. Sitthipongpanich (2010) 'Thailand's student loans fund: interest rate subsidies and repayment burdens', *Economics of Education Review*, 29(5): 685–94.

Dynarski, M. (1994) 'Who defaults on student loans? Findings from the National Postsecondary Student Aid Study', *Economics of Education Review*, 13(1): 55–68.

Friedman, M. (1955) *Capitalism and Freedom*, University of Chicago Press, Chicago.

Gross, J.P.K., O. Cekic, D. Hossler and N. Hillman (2009) 'What matters in student loan default: a review of the research literature', *Journal of Student Financial Aid*, 39(1): 19–29.

5 This implies that only 11 million registered individual taxpayers submit income tax statements.

6 A full discussion of these issues is in Chapman (2006).

Lestyowati, J. (2011) *Meningkatkan Rasio Kepatuhan Pajak* [Improving taxation compliance rates], Ministry of Finance, Jakarta.

Salmi, J. (2003) 'Student loans in an international perspective: the World Bank experience', Working Paper No. 27295, World Bank, Washington DC.

Woodhall, M. (1987) 'Establishing student loans in developing countries: some guidelines', Education and Training Series Discussion Paper EDT No. 85, World Bank, Washington DC.

Table A10.1   *Age–earnings profiles, ordinary least squares (OLS) and unconditional quantile regression (UQR) estimations*

	OLS	UQR		
		Q25	Q50	Q75
Java				
Potential experience	0.074***	0.058*	0.048***	0.089***
	(0.020)	(0.032)	(0.017)	(0.024)
Potential experience squared	−0.002**	−0.002	−0.001	−0.003***
	(0.001)	(0.002)	(0.001)	(0.001)
Constant	16.238***	15.906***	16.463***	16.730***
	(0.082)	(0.125)	(0.079)	(0.090)
No. of observations	1,020	1,020	1,020	1,020
R-squared	0.038	0.019	0.031	0.022
Sumatra				
Potential experience	0.063**	0.090**	0.057**	0.005
	(0.027)	(0.044)	(0.024)	(0.034)
Potential experience squared	−0.001	−0.003	−0.001	0.001
	(0.001)	(0.002)	(0.001)	(0.002)
Constant	16.062***	15.684***	16.080***	16.723***
	(0.117)	(0.221)	(0.104)	(0.106)
No. of observations	455	455	455	455
R-squared	0.061	0.040	0.089	0.028
Males				
Potential experience	0.062**	0.036	0.022	0.087**
	(0.025)	(0.033)	(0.028)	(0.035)
Potential experience squared	−0.002	−0.000	0.000	−0.003*
	(0.001)	(0.001)	(0.001)	(0.002)
Constant	16.302***	16.042***	16.542***	16.661***
	(0.115)	(0.177)	(0.125)	(0.132)
No. of observations	817	817	817	817
R-squared	0.027	0.017	0.033	0.017
Females				
Potential experience	0.058***	0.069*	0.066**	0.082***
	(0.022)	(0.037)	(0.027)	(0.026)
Potential experience squared	−0.002	−0.002	−0.002	−0.004**
	(0.001)	(0.002)	(0.001)	(0.001)
Constant	16.162***	15.743***	16.190***	16.678***
	(0.083)	(0.145)	(0.099)	(0.087)
No. of observations	658	658	658	658
R-squared	0.038	0.023	0.049	0.019

*** = $p<0.01$; ** = $p<0.05$; * = $p<0.1$. Standard errors, in parentheses, are robust to heteroskedasticity.

11 THE TRANSFORMATION AND INTERNATIONALIZATION OF HIGHER EDUCATION: THE MALAYSIAN EXPERIENCE

Khong Kim Hoong

11.1 INTRODUCTION

There is no doubt that very significant changes have taken place in the higher education landscape in Malaysia over the past 30 years. Where only government-established institutions were once allowed, a myriad of private institutions now offers a wide range of diplomas and degrees up to the doctoral level. Some of these institutions confer their own degrees, while others offer academic qualifications from foreign universities. At present, as many students are pursuing higher education in private institutions as in public institutions. An elitist system has been discarded with the rapid democratization of the tertiary education sector. Higher education has also been transformed from a Malaysian-based system into an open international system. The liberal policies that have been put in place have helped bring about this revolution in higher education.

This chapter will focus on the changing face of higher education in Malaysia – the growth of the private sector together with the infusion of foreign university programs and the development of Malaysia as an international hub for higher education.[1] Twinning arrangements with foreign universities and the franchising of entire degrees to Malaysian colleges are discussed in section 11.2. Section 11.3 describes the changing

---

1 For another recent study on the internationalization of Malaysian higher education, see Tham (2013).

attitude of the government towards private higher education, the upgrading of private colleges into degree-conferring institutions and the policy to allow foreign universities to establish branch campuses in Malaysia. It also looks at the policy to make Malaysia a hub for international education through the recruitment of foreign students. To increase the attractiveness of their programs to foreign students in particular, some private institutions now offer dual or joint degrees in association with reputable foreign universities.

The chapter also highlights some of the challenges accompanying the transformation and internationalization of higher education. It describes the regulatory environment for the private higher education sector (section 11.4), and the steps that have been taken to ensure quality (section 11.5). It then assesses the success of the strategy to make Malaysia a hub for international education, in the context of both inflows and outflows of students (section 11.6).

How does the Malaysian experience compare with that of neighbouring countries? Singapore has developed a thriving private higher education sector, quite similar in scope to that of Malaysia, working with some of the same foreign universities. But in Indonesia, where national pride in domestic institutions influences policy making, the private higher education sector is less internationalized, and likely to remain so.

11.2 TWINNING PARTNERSHIPS

The context

The origin of twinning partnerships has to be viewed in the context of Malaysia's political and economic development. Until 1969, the country had only one university, with four more established over the next decade. All were highly elitist institutions, in the sense that they admitted only small numbers of students. They also catered only to students from government schools that used English or Malay as the medium of instruction. Thus, large numbers of other students who had been taught in Chinese could not gain entry to university. For students who were educated in Chinese schools, the alternative was Nanyang University, a private university established by the Chinese community in 1955 in Singapore. A few lucky students from wealthy families could, of course, continue their tertiary education abroad.

The government felt that higher education was its prerogative and responsibility. In any case, it wanted to ensure that it retained control over the sector, given what it considered to be the negative influence of Nanyang, which it viewed as a hot-bed of anti-government political activism. The demand for a similar institution in Malaysia – to be called Merdeka [Independence] University – reinforced the determination of the government to keep control over the establishment of universities. In 1973, amendments to the Universities and University Colleges Act 1971 (Act 30) stipulated in no uncertain terms that the establishment of all universities had to be approved by the Yang di Pertuan Agong (the King) – in effect, the government. The law stated that only universities established by the government would be empowered to confer academic degrees and made it clear that the provision and organization of higher education would remain the prerogative of the government.

Even in the 1970s, the five government-established universities could not satisfy the demand for higher education. Modernization and development had changed the aspirations of Malaysians, who now viewed higher education as the key to a desirable job and a good career. This increased the pressure from all sections of the population for access to a university-level education. But there were simply not enough places to meet demand, which far outstripped supply. At the time, only about 5 per cent of the eligible age group could hope to gain entry to university.

Access to tertiary education became even more contentious with the implementation of the New Economic Policy in 1970. The government had identified dissatisfaction among Malays as the main cause of the 1969 race riots. One of the major instruments it used to rectify the situation was to give Malays special opportunities for higher education, by introducing fixed quotas for admission to university based on ethnicity. Chinese and Indian students were allocated only about 35 per cent of the places, where previously they had constituted about 70 per cent of the student population. The result was that many who had achieved better academic results than some Malay students were denied admission to university. This pushed education once more to the forefront of Malaysian political debate. The government was unwilling to back away from its policy of affirmative action in favour of the Malays. Its solution was to adopt a more laissez-faire policy towards higher education in which the private sector would be allowed to play a role.

In the 1970s, private education in Malaysia was confined to the primary and secondary levels, except for a few institutions offering post-secondary education to prepare students for entry to Australian and British universities. Although the government was not prepared to countenance the Chinese community's proposal to establish the private Merdeka University, it was willing to consider arrangements with foreign universities whose degrees were already recognized by Malaysia. It was in this context that the government relented in the 1980s to allow the establishment of private colleges that would offer the degree programs of foreign universities.

Twinning structures

The new twinning arrangements allowed local Malaysian colleges to conduct the first year – and later also the second year – of the partner universities' degree programs within Malaysia. Students then had to complete the remaining years of study abroad. In local education terminology, these arrangements are referred to as 1+2 (one year in Malaysia followed by two years of study abroad) and 2+1 (two years in Malaysia followed by one year abroad).

Initially, it was the less well-known tertiary institutions in Australia and the United Kingdom that were the most active in establishing twinning arrangements in Malaysia. Some already had distance learning programs in their own countries. This made it quite easy for them to offer their programs internationally, as they could send their existing study materials to the partners in Malaysia. The Malaysian colleges then provided lectures and tutorial support based on the materials provided. Because students completed their degrees abroad, these arrangements complied with the stipulation that only institutions set up with the approval of the Agong could confer degrees within Malaysia.

The degrees offered under twinning arrangements were identical in program structure, course requirements, syllabus and subject content to those in the home campuses of the foreign universities. Depending on the specific arrangements, academic quality could vary, although the foreign partners generally aimed for a similar quality to that in the home campus. The revenue split also varied – and still varies – from college to college. Some foreign universities charge a fixed amount while others take a percentage of the tuition fees.

Initially, the twinning arrangements between Malaysian private colleges and foreign universities raised some eyebrows. Public university academics were doubtful about the quality of the programs as well as the method of delivery. The lecturers who taught at private institutions were considered underqualified, often lacking advanced degrees or research experience. There were doubts, too, about the 'money-making' ethos of institutions set up for purely commercial purposes. This was evident in the poor facilities of many of the private colleges, which lacked libraries, classrooms and recreation areas.

These deficiencies notwithstanding, the twinning programs benefited several parties. For students who would not have had the chance to enter a public university, the programs provided a great opportunity to obtain a higher education. Though the fees charged by the private colleges were significantly higher than those of the public universities – RM 5,000 as opposed to RM 500 per year in the late 1980s – this did not prove to be much of a deterrence. Students could make substantial cost savings by studying in Malaysia for the first one or two years of their degrees –

sometimes saving as much as A$20,000–30,000 on an Australian degree program, depending on the university and its location. The overseas programs enriched university life by exposing students to other cultures and global academic trends. And with a foreign degree based on English as the medium of instruction, graduates found they could get jobs more easily in the expanding international commercial sector.

Both the private colleges and the foreign universities that provided the service, of course, benefited financially. But the government also benefited because it did not have to use its own resources to get trained labour. The country made substantial savings in foreign exchange because students no longer needed to study overseas for the entirety of their degrees. The twinning arrangements also solved a thorny political problem. By providing an alternative channel for university education, they spared the government the pressure it would have faced from a large section of the population, mainly Chinese, that had been 'discriminated' against in access to university education.

The twinning partnerships took deeper root in 1998 when the Malaysian government took the bold step of allowing private colleges to offer entire foreign degrees in Malaysia. This became known as the 3 + 0 policy, that is, all three years of study in Malaysia and none abroad. The precipitating factor may have been the recession accompanying the Asian financial crisis, which led to a severe devaluation of the ringgit and the collapse of the local stock market. With many Malaysians experiencing severe hardship, students on twinning programs often did not have the resources to complete their studies abroad. The government permitted 11 colleges to offer the entire degrees of their foreign partners in Malaysia. This gave further impetus to private higher education and reinforced the presence of foreign universities in Malaysia.

It should be noted that, by this time, private higher education was no longer the small-scale affair it had been in the 1980s. The growth of the private colleges and their potential commercial viability had not gone unnoticed by large companies, which hoped to share in the profitability of this new 'growth industry'. In the early 1990s, publicly listed companies, many of them involved in property development, began to buy into existing colleges or submitted plans for new ones in the housing areas they were developing.

The 'invasion' of the publicly listed companies greatly increased the resources available to the private colleges, transforming their position in the eyes of the public. They were no longer viewed as inferior to the public universities, but rather as a viable alternative to them for getting a good education. With their enhanced resources and better-qualified staff, the private colleges began to attract a fair share of students with excellent results.

The improved status and financial position of the private colleges allowed them to do things they had not been able to do in the past. They were able to develop courses and programs independently, without having to rely entirely on their foreign partners. This capability extended to the development of diploma and advanced diploma programs. Equally important was the transfer of control over examinations. Malaysian lecturers began to set examination papers and to mark them in cooperation with the foreign lecturers. The relationship between the private colleges and foreign universities gradually changed to become more one of equal partners. The local institutions were allowed to offer the second year of their partners' degree programs (the 2 + 1 arrangement described earlier), and their diplomas became acceptable to universities in many parts of the world. The types of programs offered by the private colleges also changed. Rather than being confined to the social sciences and business, they began to offer degrees in areas such as engineering and medicine. Not only professional bodies but also universities in the United Kingdom, Canada, Australia and even the United States recognized these degrees, improving their acceptability to Malaysian students.

Enrolments at the Malaysian private institutions of higher education have grown phenomenally to reach 451,947 in 2011 (Ministry of Higher Education 2012: 52). The numbers are comparable to those in the 20 public universities, which together enrolled 508,256 students in the same year (Ministry of Higher Education 2012: 3). Details of students enrolled in higher education by level of study are given in Table 11.1.

11.3 PRIVATE UNIVERSITIES, BRANCH CAMPUSES AND DUAL DEGREES

Three government-linked companies – Telekom Malaysia (telecommunications), Tenaga Nasional (electricity) and Petronas (oil and gas) – established the country's first private universities in 1996, 1997 and 1997 respectively, after being encouraged by the government to found institutions that specialized in their business areas. It was perhaps with this in mind that the government passed legislation in 1996 permitting the establishment of private universities at the invitation of the Minister of Education (Act 555, section 21).

While these universities were set up without much fanfare, they had a significant impact on the higher education landscape. This was the first time that the government had allowed private universities to be set up in Malaysia. Because the three were founded by giant, financially strong companies, their facilities were equivalent to those in the public universities and they were able to hire academic staff on competitive terms

Table 11.1 Students enrolled in higher education in Malaysia by type of institution and level of study, 2011

Type of institution (no.)	PhD	Master	Post-graduate diploma	Bachelor	Advanced diploma	Diploma	Certificate	Professional	Other	Total
Public										
Universities (20)	22,594	53,267	1,924	299,179	0	105,736	22,061a	2,018	1,477	508,256
Tunku Abdul Rahman College (1)	0	0	0	0	6,606	14,836	880	0	1,314	23,636
Polytechnics (30)	0	0	0	0	162	84,514	4,167	0	241	89,084
Community colleges (70)	0	0	0	0	0	0	25,125b	0	0	25,125
Total	22,594	53,267	1,924	299,179	6,768	205,082	52,682	2,018	3,032	646,546
Private										
Universities (36)	5,758	12,389	5,123	133,838	1,338	27,581	9,464	1,802	14,880	212,173
Branch campuses (4)	188	713	0	5,902	0	688	616	0	616	8,723
University colleges (15)	4	449	456	15,532	12	21,622	1,395	0	2,570	42,040
Colleges (310)	0	766	50	24,793	1,531	121,306	12,353	1,490	26,722	189,011
Total	5,950	14,317	5,629	180,065	2,881	171,197	23,828	3,292	44,788	451,947
Total (public + private)	**28,544**	**67,584**	**7,553**	**479,244**	**9,649**	**376,279**	**76,510**	**5,310**	**47,820**	**1,098,493**
Private as % of total	20.8	21.2	74.5	37.6	29.9	61.8	31.1	62.0	93.7	41.1

a Comprises matriculation certificates.
b Figure includes 18,806 modular certificates.
Source: Public: Ministry of Higher Education (2012: 4-19); private: Ministry of Higher Education (2012: 53-61, 71-103).

and conditions. They pioneered the way for other private universities, including institutions offering medical qualifications. It would have been difficult to imagine 30 years earlier that Malaysia would one day offer private medical degrees.

In 2005, the government implemented another bold move – to upgrade some of the existing private colleges into university colleges. Private colleges that offered degree programs from foreign universities were now empowered to confer their own degrees, not only at bachelor level, but also up to the doctoral level. By 2011 Malaysia had 51 degree-conferring private universities and university colleges (Ministry of Higher Education 2012: 48), with a total enrolment of 254,213 students (Table 11.1).

The decision to allow the establishment of private universities and university colleges was part of a strategy to make Malaysia a centre of excellence to attract foreign students. The country had always been an important consumer of foreign education, and thousands of students still depart annually to study at universities overseas.[2] While this has contributed significantly to the country's human resources, it has placed considerable pressure on its foreign exchange reserves. The establishment of private universities and university colleges should help to address this problem: it will encourage more Malaysians to pursue higher education within the country, thus reducing the outflow of foreign exchange, while attracting more international students to the country, thus increasing foreign exchange earnings. Malaysia's exports of education services are still relatively small compared with those of Australia, the United Kingdom and the United States,[3] but the government anticpates that the country will catch up with the leading countries soon.

Another prong in the government's strategy to make Malaysia an international education hub was the policy to allow reputable foreign universities to establish branch campuses in the country. This was done in the expectation that these internationally well-known, longer-established universities would be able to attract more foreign students to come to Malaysia to pursue their higher education. In 2011 there were four branch campuses – three Australian and one British (Ministry of Higher Education 2012: 48). Two more have since been set up. While these branch campuses do not offer the full gamut of degrees available in the home campuses of the foreign universities, the programs they do

---

2 In 2011, 89,686 Malaysians were studying abroad. Of these, 27,003 were sponsored by the government or other organizations and 62,683 were self-supporting (see Table 11.3 below).

3 Malaysia has 2 per cent of the world's international students. By comparison, the United States has 21.2 per cent, Australia 7.5 per cent, France 9 per cent and Germany 9.4 per cent (Ministry of Higher Education 2011c: 7).

offer are identical to those in the home campuses. The branch campuses are supported financially by local partners, but unlike the twinning programs, they are run autonomously by the home universities. While the presence of a chief executive and some staff from the home university is a clear indication of branch status, these branch campuses also recruit local Malaysians to be part of the academic team.

Though the branch campuses normally charge higher fees than the local colleges offering foreign degrees, they have been quite successful in attracting both Malaysian and foreign students. The well-established names of the foreign partners and the affordable fees have certainly helped in this area. In 2011, 8,723 students were registered for study at the branch campuses of foreign universities. (Table 11.1). Of these, 1,893 (22 per cent) were foreign students (Ministry of Higher Education 2012: 63). It should be noted that this represented a significant drop from the previous year's total enrolment of 17,010 students and 3,730 foreign students, perhaps indicating greater confidence in Malaysia's private universities, which have been upgraded over the past three years.

Another interesting development in the higher education sector has been the introduction of dual (or double) degrees and joint degrees. Students who complete the requirements for a degree whose academic quality has been moderated by a foreign university may be able to get a dual degree – one from the local university and one from the foreign institution. In this way, the local institutions hope to increase the acceptability of their degree programs, especially among foreign students. This arrangement helps to allay concerns among students – especially foreign students – that a degree from a relatively unknown Malaysian private university may not have wide acceptability.

This practice is not encouraged by the Ministry of Higher Education, which prefers Malaysian universities to develop joint degrees with foreign partners as equals. Under this arrangement, students would receive a single degree conferred by both universities. So far, only one joint degree at the undergraduate level is being offered in Malaysia, between HELP University and Flinders University for a degree in psychological science.

The government relaxed its foreign ownership laws in 2010 to allow foreign education providers to take partial stakes in Malaysian institutions. It is expected that by 2015, the policy on foreign ownership will be liberalized further to allow foreign entities to have 100 per cent ownership of institutions of higher education. In 2010, the Laureate group from the United States took control of INTI University and its sister colleges. While this is in line with the government's liberalization policy and allows INTI to use the worldwide links of its parent company to market its products worldwide, it is still too early to assess the impact and benefits of this development.

11.4   THE REGULATORY ENVIRONMENT

Until the 1970s, legislation on higher education focused mainly on the public institutions. With the proliferation of private institutions in the 1980s and 1990s, the government saw the need for some form of regulation. This took two forms. First, the Ministry of Education revamped the department responsible for monitoring and regulating the private education sector. Second, the government passed new laws to ensure that it retained tight control of private education. These would be essential to the success of its strategy to make Malaysia a hub for international higher education.

Until the mid-1990s, the department responsible for private education within the Ministry of Education was small in terms of numbers, and was not given much prominence. The people appointed to positions in the department were part of the routine rotation of school teachers, the senior ones invariably close to retirement age. Most did not have higher qualifications beyond a basic degree.

Given the magnitude of the tasks facing it and its far greater responsibilities, the department is now given greater prominence. After all, it handles nearly as many private students as the department responsible for the public sector. Not only has the department grown substantially in size, but it appoints highly qualified personnel, sometimes seconded from the universities, to fill its positions. It will probably continue to grow in importance, considering that the government has stated that it will not establish any more new public universities but expects the private institutions to cater to the increasing demand for higher education. Reflecting the growth and increasing importance of higher education, a separate Ministry of Higher Education was established in 2004 to take charge of the development of both the public and private sectors.

In 1996, the government passed major legislation to regulate and control private higher education: the Private Higher Educational Institutions Act 1996 (Act 555) and the National Accreditation Board Act 1996 (Act 556). Act 555 gives the minister or his agents absolute power over the private educational institutions, ranging from establishment and registration to the courses of study that can be offered and advertised (section 38). Act 556 established the National Accreditation Board (Lembaga Akreditasi Negara, LAN), which had responsibility for the approval of programs and quality assurance. In 2007 it merged with the Quality Assurance Division of the ministry, which had responsibility for the public institutions, to form the Malaysian Qualifications Agency (MQA). The new agency has the power to ensure that all institutions of higher education comply with the standards laid out in the MQA's Malaysian Qualifications Framework.

The establishment of the accreditation agency gave the government control and monitoring powers over the private educational institutions. This was important, because the government wanted to ensure that a reasonable quality of programs was maintained, possibly benchmarked against the local public universities. For this reason, initially only academics from public universities were used as assessors for approvals and accreditations. While there were grumblings among the private institutions about the additional layer of bureaucracy imposed on them, the agency has worked well, and MQA accreditation is now seen by the public to be an important indicator of educational quality. The agency also plays a watchdog role; any acts of 'wrongdoing' on the part of the private institutions are reported to the agency for redress.

While the government has loosened the restrictions on higher education, thus allowing the private sector to move and expand very quickly, it has also put in place laws, regulations and structures to ensure that it maintains tight control. Perhaps this was inevitable given the expanding role of the private sector, and the fact that private higher education has become a very lucrative business. The Ministry of Higher Education (2011c: 7) estimates that foreign students generate about RM 4 billion in revenue annually for the country.

11.5   QUALITY ISSUES

The issue of quality in higher education is always a matter of concern, but especially when institutions are run for profit by private providers. It is sometimes assumed that the shareholders of these private companies would demand a good return, but this is not necessarily the case; many of them believe that education is a good cause, and as long as they do not lose money on their initial contributions, they are happy to let their investments remain with the institutions.

Malaysia's private institutions are subjected to many layers of quality control, both internal and external. First, within the private colleges and universities, academics are now well qualified to ensure quality. Many of them have postgraduate degrees, in marked contrast to the situation 20 years ago. Highly qualified academics are aware that the private institutions can offer them good salaries, rewarding academic careers and an environment comparable to that in the public universities. The government's policy of retiring academics at age 55 has also helped, with senior academics from public universities finding that they can extend their working lives and contribute positively in the private sector. The increase in standards is evident in the criteria imposed on private university colleges wishing to become universities; the Ministry of Higher

Education requires around 25 per cent of academic staff in private universities to hold doctoral qualifications.

Second, although there is no reason to believe that academics in public universities would have a monopoly on the sense of responsibility to ensure quality, having a demanding fee-paying clientele certainly keeps the academics in the private institutions on their toes. Lecturers who arrive late, end classes early, cancel classes or deliver unsatisfactory lectures are reported and held accountable. Students who pay a much higher price for their education have a low level of tolerance for incompetence.

The other layer of quality control is external. First, the programs of foreign universities offered by private institutions are subjected to quality audits by the partner universities as well as the external examiners of the foreign universities. The process involves moderation of examination papers, checks of students' answer sheets and joint board meetings to review results.

The programs offered in Malaysia by foreign universities are also scrutinized by government authorities in the home countries, such as the Quality Assurance Association for Higher Education (QAA) in the United Kingdom or the Australian Universities Quality Agency (AUQA) in Australia. Although the primary attention of these agencies would be on the operations of each university in totality, they do increasingly look at the international programs as part of their audits. The professional associations in the foreign countries also monitor the quality of the degrees touching on their competencies. Thus, Australia's body for certified practising accountants, CPA Australia, has an indirect say in the accounting degrees offered by Australian universities in Malaysia, as does the Association of Chartered Certified Accountants (ACCA) in relation to the British accounting degrees. The Law Society in the United Kingdom also sets out rules and regulations to ensure quality in the twinning programs between British universities and Malaysian private colleges, since eventually these law degrees would be recognized for legal practice in the United Kingdom.

Finally, within Malaysia itself, the MQA has strict rules covering both the academic and non-academic aspects of the degree programs offered by Malaysian private universities and colleges. On the academic side, this includes the duration of the program, credit requirements, the nature of the courses, course content, teaching hours for each subject, the nature of the evaluation, learning outcomes and the qualifications of teaching staff. The agency also audits the administrative rules and regulations for programs, including record maintenance, and subjects physical facilities, such as classrooms, laboratories, IT infrastructure, library and books, to scrutiny.

In short, Malaysia takes quality assurance seriously; in fact, the government imposes more checks and balances on the private education sector than it does on the public universities. The international benchmarking used for the twinning and 3 + 0 programs has also been useful in ensuring that the quality of the programs offered in Malaysia matches that in respected institutions around the world.

The issue of academic quality is not a public versus private divide, but has many dimensions. It is of course closely related to the spread of mass education. As noted earlier, Malaysia had only one university until 1969, catering to an elite group of students whose academic results ranked in the top 5 per cent of those who had sat for the pre-university entrance examination. These students naturally performed well in a university that had the financial resources to employ highly qualified staff and to provide good infrastructure. In the 1970s, the government responded to the increasing demand for higher education by expanding the number of public universities, then, in the 1980s, by permitting the entry of private colleges. With much larger numbers of students now entering the higher education sector, rather than just the top echelon, it was inevitable that both the physical and human resources of the private institutions would be stretched, inevitably leading to a lower quality of education.

Most private institutions do not get any government funding, but have to depend on the fees paid by students. They therefore adopt an open door policy – as long as the students have the minimum entry qualifications required by the partner universities, they will be admitted. As a result, the students in private institutions are a very mixed group, ranging from those who have scraped through the pre-university examination to those who have gained the best possible results. Given such diversity, teaching has to be pitched at the middle ground, invariably affecting overall quality. The top public universities, which accept only the cream of the students, do not face this problem, and can afford to cater to this elite group at a very high level.

The rapid expansion of higher education to cater to a broader section of the population has always affected quality. In countries such as the United States, where private higher education has existed for hundreds of years, a clear distinction between private universities has emerged on the basis of quality. The highly reputable universities are very selective, accepting only the top students. Students who do not achieve very good results would not even think of applying to these institutions. In Malaysia, a clear-cut pecking order between private universities has not yet emerged. Until that happens, private institutions will have to continue to cope with the problem of a varying quality of students within the same classroom.

Figure 11.1 *Enrolments of foreign students in public and private higher education institutions (thousand), and annual growth in enrolments (%), 2001–11*

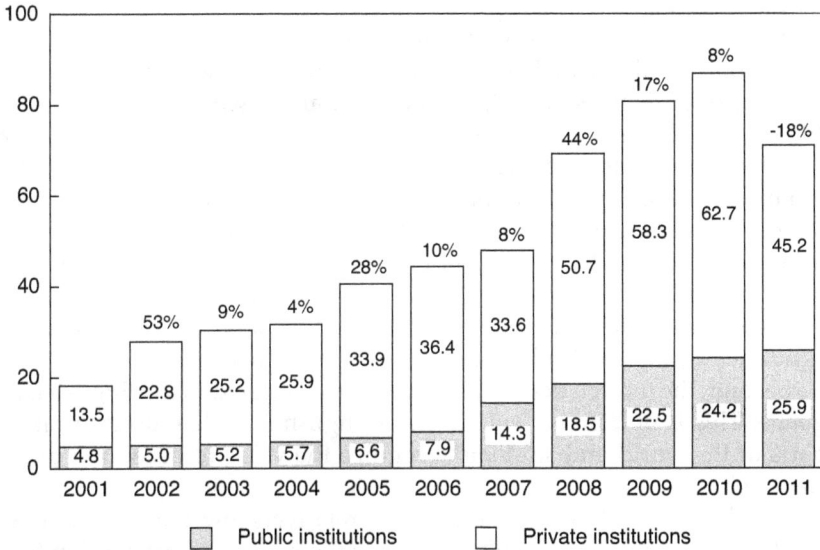

| | Public institutions | | Private institutions |

Source: 2001–10: Ministry of Higher Education (2011b: 8); 2011: Ministry of Higher Education (2012: 22, 63).

11.6 INTERNATIONAL STUDENTS

Until recently, the gap between imports and exports of educational services was very wide, in the sense that far more Malaysians studied overseas than foreign students studied in Malaysia. In the 1970s and 1980s, the government sent thousands of students abroad each year, partly to build up the country's human resources and partly to meet the requirement of the New Economic Policy to give more Malay students the benefit of a higher education abroad.

Except for a few carrying out research at the public universities, hardly any foreign students were studying in Malaysia in 1990. A decade later, a breakthrough had been made. In 2001, Malaysia had 18,242 international students, rising to a peak of 86,919 students in 2010 (Figure 11.1). The number then dropped sharply to 71,101 in 2011, owing to bureaucratic delays in student visa approvals and to policy changes in China that allowed Chinese students to pursue foreign degrees within their own country. Under the Internationalization Policy for Higher Education, the government aims to accelerate the flow of international students to 200,000 by 2020 (Ministry of Higher Education 2011a: 7). Malaysia currently ranks eleventh in the world in education service exports, with 2 per cent of the international student population (Ministry of Higher Education 2011c: 7).

Malaysia has several factors in its favour as it attempts to become an international hub for higher education. First, its public and private universities offer degrees at all levels across many disciplines. In addition, 19 private colleges offer 89 Australian degree programs, another 30 offer 88 British programs, and a few offer the degree programs of two American universities.[4] Not many countries can boast such a wide and diverse range of academic programs. While these foreign universities are by no means the most highly ranked in the world, they are reputable institutions that are well regarded in their own countries and internationally. Moreover, their programs are all accredited by both countries' quality assurance agencies as well as their respective professional bodies.

Second, the foreign degree programs are all offered in the English language. This is of definite benefit, since English is widely used in many parts of the world and students recognize the value of becoming proficient in it.

Third, the cost of living in Malaysia is relatively low. Foreign students can live on around RM 15,000 per year while paying annual tuition fees of about RM 20,000 for an Australian or British university degree. The total annual cost of RM 35,000 (roughly $11,000) is about one-third what they could expect to pay in Australia or the United Kingdom.[5]

Fourth, Malaysia is an attractive destination for Muslim students from the Middle East, who have had difficulty obtaining visas for study in the United States and the United Kingdom since September 2001.

Finally, Malaysia offers a multi-ethnic cultural and linguistic environment for foreign students. The society is open, cosmopolitan and generally receptive to foreigners. Life in Malaysia is relatively comfortable for international students.

Details on the countries of origin of foreign students studying in Malaysia are shown in Table 11.2. It shows that Iran, Indonesia, China, Yemen and Iraq were the main sources of international students in the public system in 2011, while China, Indonesia, Nigeria, Iran and Yemen were the main sources in the private sector. An interesting dimension to the statistics is that more foreign students are enrolled in private than in public institutions – 45,246 in 2011, compared with 25,263 enrolled in the public universities (Table 11.2; Figure 11.1).

---

4 Compiled from the Malaysian Qualifications Agency Register, available at http://www.mohe.gov.my/web_statistik/.
5 See http://www.studymalaysia.com/education/art_msia.php?id=affordable.

Table 11.2   Countries of origin of foreign students enrolled in higher education in Malaysia by sector and gender, 2011 (no.)

No.	Country of origin	Public institutions			Country of origin	Private institutions		
		Male	Female	Total		Male	Female	Total
1	Iran	3,490	2,458	5,948	China	2,665	2,607	5,272
2	Indonesia	2,377	1,386	3,763	Indonesia	2,670	2,136	4,806
3	China	1,130	992	2,122	Nigeria	3,848	836	4,684
4	Yemen	1,493	346	1,839	Iran	2,628	1,312	3,940
5	Iraq	1,038	291	1,329	Yemen	1,403	310	1,713
6	Nigeria	830	228	948	Bangladesh	1,474	228	1,702
7	Libya	593	263	856	UK	408	1,122	1,530
8	Thailand	328	389	717	Sudan	1,223	237	1,460
9	Somalia	582	107	689	Pakistan	1,092	254	1,346
10	Sudan	468	163	631	Botswana	532	438	970
11	Bangladesh	486	135	621	Maldives	471	393	864
12	Singapore	178	373	551	Saudi Arabia	709	138	847
13	Jordan	480	55	535	Kazakhstan	422	407	829
14	Pakistan	408	55	535	India	569	224	793
15	India	332	162	495	Sri Lanka	497	237	734
16	Palestine	383	50	433	South Korea	334	307	641
17	Brunei	85	87	172	Tanzania	329	213	542
18	Algeria	136	33	169	Somalia	439	87	526
19	Oman	134	21	155	Zimbabwe	289	221	510
20	Other	1,813	981	2,797	Other	7,708	3,829	11,537
	Total	**16,764**	**8,499**	**25,263**		**29,710**	**15,536**	**45,246**

Source: Public: Ministry of Higher Education (2012: 25–6); private: Ministry of Higher Education (2012: 66–7).

The reasons are many. First, apart from the desirability of being able to offer English as the medium of instruction, the private universities and colleges have been promoting themselves internationally for many years, and are still more aggressive in marketing themselves through exhibitions, trade visits and agents. Second, unlike the public universities, the private institutions do not place limits on admissions to popular programs such as the business-related disciplines. Third, the public universities impose quotas on foreign students to limit their numbers.

This is logical given that the government provides the budgets of the public universities, and would therefore have to subsidize the cost of those students.

Despite the rapid growth in the number of tertiary education institutions within Malaysia since the 1970s, Malaysians continue to study abroad in significant numbers. Between 2010 and 2011 alone, the number studying overseas rose by 16 per cent, from 77,623 to 89,686 students (Ministry of Higher Education 2012: 114–15). The country still has a very liberal policy towards Malaysians venturing abroad for higher education, with no restrictions on the remittance of funds for study in a foreign country. It does seem, however, that the foreign exchange benefits from enticing foreign students to Malaysia are being cancelled out by the number of Malaysians leaving the country to study abroad, since the numbers in each direction are broadly equivalent.

As shown in Table 11.3, Australia takes the lion's share of Malaysian students, accepting 23,245 in 2011, or almost 26 per cent of the total. It is followed by the United Kingdom (13,982 students), Egypt (10,758) and Taiwan (7,556). Only around 30 per cent of these students are sponsored, receiving financial scholarships from the government, public agencies or private companies. The rest are more likely to be dependent on their families for financial assistance.

11.7   CONCLUSION

What lessons can be derived from Malaysia's experience in transforming and internationalizing its higher education sector? In many respects, the country can relate a success story. The higher education base has expanded rapidly; and the share of the eligible age group that is able to gain a tertiary education has grown from 5 per cent in the 1970s to 40 per cent currently (Table 11.1). Access to higher education is no longer a political issue decided on ethnic grounds, although the cost of education is still of some concern. Malaysia provides a cosmopolitan environment for higher education in which students can aspire to gain a degree from a British, Australian, American, Indian or (soon) Chinese university. From almost none in the 1970s, Malaysia now receives over 70,000 foreign students from over 100 countries. While the internationalization of higher education in its present form grew out of domestic exigencies, the 'Malaysian model' is now used quite widely in other parts of the world. Malaysian institutions were among the pioneers of twinning programs, and foreign universities now use the '1+2', '2+1' and '3+0' terminology to negotiate similar arrangements with partners elsewhere in the world.

Table 11.3 Main destinations of Malaysian students studying abroad, and whether sponsored or self-supporting, 2011 (no.)

No.	Destination country	Total number of students studying abroad	Sponsored	Self-sponsored
1	Australia	23,245	4,184	19,061
2	Canada	696	536	158
3	China	2,252	192	2,506
4	Czech Republic	365	359	6
5	Egypt	10,758	5,163	5,595
6	France	516	505	11
7	Germany	654	648	6
8	India	2,604	2,000	604
9	Indonesia	5,914	2,214	3,700
10	Japan	1,689	1,641	48
11	Jordan	1,438	521	917
12	South Korea	338	338	0
13	Morocco	113	85	28
14	New Zealand	2,270	1,279	991
15	Pakistan	109	13	96
16	Poland	142	140	2
17	Romania	120	0	120
18	Russian Federation	2,946	417	2,529
19	Saudi Arabia	165	0	165
20	Singapore	4,010	10	4,000
21	Syria	127	0	127
22	Taiwan	7,556	0	7,556
23	United Kingdom	13,982	4,754	9,228
24	United States	6,600	1,819	4,781
25	Yemen	570	0	570
26	Other[a]	507	183	324
	Total	**89,686**	**27,003**	**62,683**

a   Countries with fewer than 100 Malaysian students.
Source: Ministry of Higher Education (2012: 115–16).

Although the private sector took the initiative in establishing partnerships with foreign universities, the government also played a significant role. The policy of liberalization provided a good environment for private institutions to flourish. When the strategy of making Malaysia a hub for higher education was adopted, the government made important moves to facilitate the growth of the private institutions, ranging from playing an intermediary role with the Immigration Department to encouraging the upgrading of colleges to become universities. The ministry has just established a one-stop centre to expedite the visa applications of foreign students, perhaps inspired by the one-stop centres that were so successful in bringing foreign investment into Malaysia in the past. At the same time, the government is trying to improve the international status of the public universities by boosting their capacity for research. Initially it is focusing on five public universities, including Universiti Sains Malaysia (USM), which has been given 'apex' status because it is considered to have the greatest potential to become a world-class university. By focusing resources on these universities, the government hopes to build them into centres of international research excellence, attracting top scholars and graduate students from around the globe.

In considering whether the Malaysian experience in expanding and internationalizing private higher education would be relevant for Indonesia, a few issues come to mind. Would the Indonesian government be willing to accept a role for foreign universities and their programs? Would it welcome English as the medium of instruction in those private institutions? Are foreign universities themselves ready to expand into Indonesia?

Although foreign universities may be willing to consider offering their programs in Indonesia, they would probably proceed cautiously and at a slower pace than in Malaysia. Whereas Malaysians have long been comfortable with the idea of studying in English, Indonesians generally take a more nationalistic approach to education. The Indonesian government is therefore unlikely to welcome the use of English in its private colleges and universities in the same way as Malaysia has, or to allow foreign universities to play such a big role.

REFERENCES

Ministry of Higher Education, Malaysia (2011a) *Higher Education Malaysia: Internationalization Policy 2011*, Ministry of Higher Education, Putrajaya.

Ministry of Higher Education, Malaysia (2011b) 'Indikator pengajian tinggi 2009–2010' [Higher education statistics 2009–2010], Ministry of Higher Education, Putrajaya, available at http://www.mohe.gov.my/web_statistik/.

Ministry of Higher Education, Malaysia (2011c) 'Way forward for higher education. Malaysia: the preferred destination for higher education', Ministry of
Higher Education, Putrajaya.

Ministry of Higher Education, Malaysia (2012) *Malaysia Higher Education Statistics 2011*, Ministry of Higher Education, Putrajaya, available at http://www.
mohe.gov.my/web_statistik/perangkaan2011.htm.

Tham S.Y. (ed.) (2013) *Internationalizing Higher Education in Malaysia: Understanding, Practices and Challenges*, Institute of Southeast Asian Studies, Singapore.

12 ROLE OF THE EDUCATION AND TRAINING SECTOR IN ADDRESSING SKILL MISMATCH IN INDONESIA

*Emanuela di Gropello**

12.1 INTRODUCTION

In Indonesia, the past two decades have been a time of great progress but also massive transformations and abrupt setbacks. A period of fast economic progress between 1990 and 1997 was characterized by high GDP growth (averaging 7 per cent per annum) and profound changes in the structure of employment. At a pace not seen even in other Asian countries, poor rural workers left the farms to find work in the industrial and service sectors. By 1997, almost half of all working adults were employed in the formal sector, and in just a few years the share of agriculture in total employment had shrunk by 14 percentage points, mostly to the benefit of the services sector, whose share grew by over nine percentage points. This trend came to a brutal stop when the Asian financial crisis hit Indonesia in 1997, causing a massive contraction in economic activity (real GDP fell by 13 per cent in one year), an escalation of poverty and a movement back to the farms. Between 1997 and 1999, the share of agriculture in employment again grew, at a rate of 1.3 percentage points yearly. Although the share has decreased as the economy has rebounded, the World Development Indicators database shows that 38 per cent of employment in 2010 was still in agriculture.[1]

---

* This chapter is based on the overview in Gropello, Kruse and Tandon (2011: 1–39).
1 See http://data.worldbank.org/data-catalog/world-development-indicators.

The recovery in economic growth in the post-crisis period has not translated into as much employment growth as previously. Although there are many reasons for the Indonesian phenomenon of jobless growth, decomposition of the factors behind the slowdown in formal-sector employment growth point to a sharp decline in the employment elasticity of growth in the services sector. In other words, there are now fewer jobs created for the same amount of growth in the economy. While 'high' wages have been blamed for undermining job creation, workers' skills are an important part of the equation. It appears that the skill profile of the Indonesian workforce has not evolved in line with the demands of the labour market. The problem may therefore be a lack of skills for employability. High youth unemployment, while also related to other factors, may be another indication of this challenge.

As the Indonesian economy returns to higher growth rates, identifying and addressing potential skill mismatches will be crucial not only to boost job creation in the formal sector, but also to support higher productivity, competitiveness and growth. Skills have a key role to play in driving the growth and competitiveness of both the services sector and the manufacturing sector (which has remained quite low in value added), and more generally in enhancing the long-term ability of the country to innovate and to adapt and assimilate new technologies. In spite of a significant increase in levels of educational attainment, preliminary evidence, including global competitiveness rankings and education quality indicators, suggests that this has not translated into higher productivity and competitiveness. Although other factors need to be in place for competitiveness to grow – including a comprehensive national innovation framework, which is still clearly underdeveloped in Indonesia – a lack of skills to create the conditions for greater productivity and competitiveness is clearly evident in the country.

In this context, this chapter reviews the main trends in the demand for skills in Indonesia (section 12.2). It seeks to document the existence of a possible skill mismatch between employer demand and available supply (section 12.3), and the ways in which the education and training sector contributes to this mismatch (section 12.4). Finally, it proposes measures to improve the responsiveness of the education and training sector to the needs of the labour market and the economy as a whole (section 12.5). The chapter makes use of a comprehensive survey of employers and employees to identify trends in the demand for skills, the drivers of demand, the gaps in skills, and the main strengths and weaknesses of the education and training sector (see Box 12.1 for details).

The chapter pays particular attention to the functional skills that workers must possess to be employable and to support firms' competitiveness and productivity, and to the role of the education and training

BOX 12.1   THE INDONESIA EMPLOYER/EMPLOYEE SURVEY
OF SKILLS/LABOUR DEMAND AND JOB VACANCIES

The Indonesia Employer/Employee Survey of Skills/Labour Demand
and Job Vacancies was conceived as a collaborative project between
World Bank researchers and a team of researchers at the Institute for Economic and Social Research, Faculty of Economics, University of Indonesia (LPEM-FEUI). In 2008, the survey team interviewed managers and
200 employees of 473 medium and large firms (those with more than 20
employees) in the manufacturing and service sectors. The purpose of
the survey was to ascertain the magnitude and nature of the demand for
skills at the employer and employee levels and what was driving that
demand; to identify any developing skill mismatches and their drivers;
and to assess firms' strategies to develop workers' skills.

The survey took place in the five provinces where economic development is concentrated: Riau Islands, DKI Jakarta, West Java, East Java and
Banten. Within those five provinces, it focused on representative samples
of manufacturing and service firms. The focus on services is new, as all
previous surveys have focused solely on manufacturing. It therefore represents a significant contribution to understanding of the skills demanded
(and provided) in a sector that has traditionally been skill intensive and
that has consistently demanded increasingly higher levels of skills.

Table 12.1 shows the main characteristics of firms in the employer
module of the survey, stratified according to key variables to ensure

Table 12.1   Main characteristics of firms in the employer module of the
survey

Sample size & coverage	Stratification variables	Distribution by economic activity
No. of medium & large firms (20+ employees)	Manufacturing Employment size Propensity to export Propensity to import Foreign/domestic ownership Skill intensity	Manufacturing: 57% Construction: 3% Wholesale & retail trade: 10% Hotels & restaurants: 7% Transport, storage & communication: 4%
Manufacturing: 273 Services: 200 Total: 473		
Distribution Riau Islands: 15% DKI Jakarta: 18% West Java: 35% East Java: 24% Banten: 8%	Services Employment size Propensity to import Propensity to export Skill intensity	Financial services: 4% Real estate, rental & business services: 5% Health & social assistance: 4% Other services: 6%

Source: Indonesia Employer/Employee Survey of Skills/Labour Demand and Job
Vacancies, 2008.

proportional representation. All the results in the chapter are derived from the weighted sample. The employee module was less comprehensive, but the 200 interviewed employees were randomly sampled across firms. The quality of both surveys was judged to be satisfactory.

The survey team obtained responses from 473 firms out of an initial sample of 500 firms, taking care to maintain representativeness. The refusal rate was low and non-respondents were systematically replaced by equivalent firms taken from the larger pool of firms. Interviews were conducted in person after sending the questionnaires in advance. Most questions were well answered, usually by both the human resources manager and the firm manager, with relatively few missing data. In any event, the chapter presents only the most robust findings, leaving aside questions that were either not well answered or had too many missing data. Significant time was taken to double-check all figures.

system in providing those skills. Skills can be broadly disaggregated into three main categories. The first is the academic skills associated with subject areas, such as mathematics, literacy and English, and generally measured through standardized scores. The second is generic (or life) skills. This broader set of skills, transferable across jobs, usually includes thinking skills (critical and creative thinking, problem solving), behavioural skills (communication, organization, teamwork, leadership) and computer skills. The third category is technical skills. These are the skills associated with a profession. They are generally a mix of the specific knowledge and skills to perform a job.

While the chapter focuses on education and training, it is important to acknowledge that skills are produced in many different ways – through pre-employment education and training (formal and informal), on-the-job training (formal and informal), work and life experience, and learning from peers at school and at work. Skill acquisition is fundamentally a cumulative and dynamic process starting at birth with parental education and continuing through schooling, formal training and life experience. Although a person's skills can grow over time, they can also decay if the possibilities for lifelong learning are not well developed. A section of the population can miss out on acquiring skills if vulnerable young people are not given alternative, 'second-chance' pathways to develop their skills.

Mapping skills with skill providers, and with the other mechanisms to acquire skills, is not an easy task. A broad correspondence is attempted in Box 12.2. The relevance of the different sources will depend very much on personal trajectories, but also on the design, strengths and weaknesses of the education and training system, which is the focus of this chapter.

**BOX 12.2   THE THREE MAIN SKILL SETS
AND HOW THEY ARE ACQUIRED**

Academic skills are acquired mainly in formal (and informal) educational institutions.

Generic (or life) skills are acquired through:
- early childhood parental education;
- education and training institutions, through curriculums and peda-gogical approaches that enhance such learning;
- on-the-job training, including non-formal learning from co-workers and supervisors; and
- work experience and learning-by-doing.

Technical skills are acquired through:
- upper secondary and tertiary education and training institutions, through curriculums that enhance such learning;
- on-the-job training (including non-formal learning from co-workers and supervisors); and
- work experience and learning-by-doing.

The complexity of the skill acquisition process, with its inter-related objectives of producing a skilled labour force, continuing to update workers' skills over time and helping unskilled youth and adults to gain skills, necessarily leads us to consider skill development systems rather than isolated providers. What type of skill development system should be in place? This is not an easy question to answer because there is no magic bullet and several options and arrangements are possible. But a benchmark can nonetheless be useful. Typically a comprehensive skill development system would include the following:

- Sufficient high-quality and relevant school-based formal education and training opportunities to provide basic academic and generic skills at the primary level; more advanced academic and generic skills, and some technical skills, at the secondary level; and higher-order academic, generic and technical skills at the tertiary level.
- Quality non-formal education and training to provide academic, generic and technical skills to out-of-school groups; to complement formal education with additional generic and technical skills; and to provide opportunities to update academic and technical skills over time.
- Sufficient firm training to complement formal and non-formal educa-tion and training with additional (job-relevant) technical and generic

Figure 12.1   *Employers' perceptions of the importance of education, knowledge and experience among managerial/professional and skilled workers: share rating variable as 'very important' (%)*

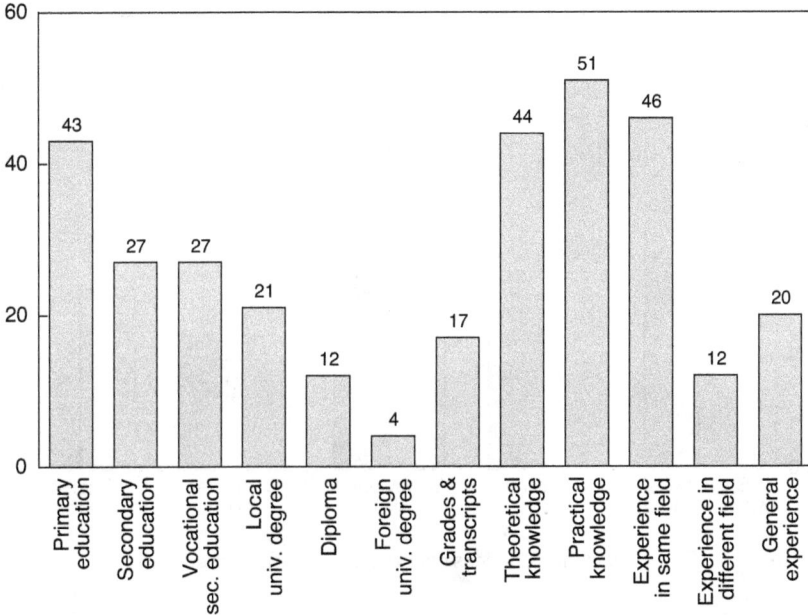

Source: Indonesia Employer/Employee Survey of Skills/Labour Demand and Job Vacancies 2008, Employer Module.

skills; and to provide opportunities to keep technical and generic skills up to date.

These different elements in turn need to be linked and integrated through a well-functioning national qualification framework that includes, among other things, effective skill certification procedures.

12.2   DEMAND FOR SKILLS IN INDONESIA

What skills are most in demand? Today's job market in Indonesia appears to place a premium on theoretical and practical knowledge of the job. The survey results suggest that theoretical and practical knowledge, acquired through schooling and experience, is very important to develop the technical skills of managerial/professional workers and skilled production workers (Figure 12.1). Employers clearly consider on-the-job experience to be a particularly valuable source of job-specific skills.

Figure 12.2   Employers' perceptions of the importance of core subject-based and generic skills among managerial/professional and skilled workers: share rating variable as 'very important' (%)

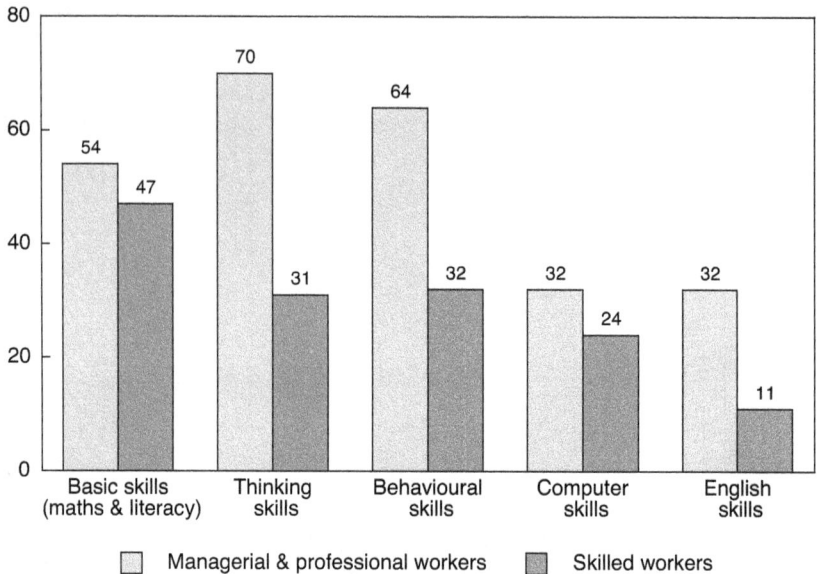

Source: Indonesia Employer/Employee Survey of Skills/Labour Demand and Job Vacancies 2008, Employer Module.

Employers also rate core subject-based skills such as basic mathematics and literacy very highly, reflecting the finding that primary education remains the building block of worker quality across the board. But they also consider generic skills such as thinking and behavioural skills to be very important for the Indonesian workforce. Thinking and behavioural skills are considered particularly important for managers and professionals, and basic academic skills for skilled production workers (Figure 12.2). Among behavioural skills, communication skills and the ability to work independently are particularly highly valued by firms (Figure 12.3). Employees' perceptions are generally aligned with those of their employers. They stress the importance of communication skills and creative thinking (Figure 12.4).

Where are skills in most demand? Demand is higher in the services sector than in manufacturing. Service firms appear to put greater emphasis on job-specific skills, regardless of whether these are acquired in the classroom or on the job (Figure 12.5). The relative ranking of skills is similar across sectors, although theoretical knowledge appears to be somewhat more important in the services sector. Behavioural skills are also

Figure 12.3   Employers' perceptions of the importance of behavioural skills among managerial/professional and skilled workers: share rating variable as 'very important' (%)

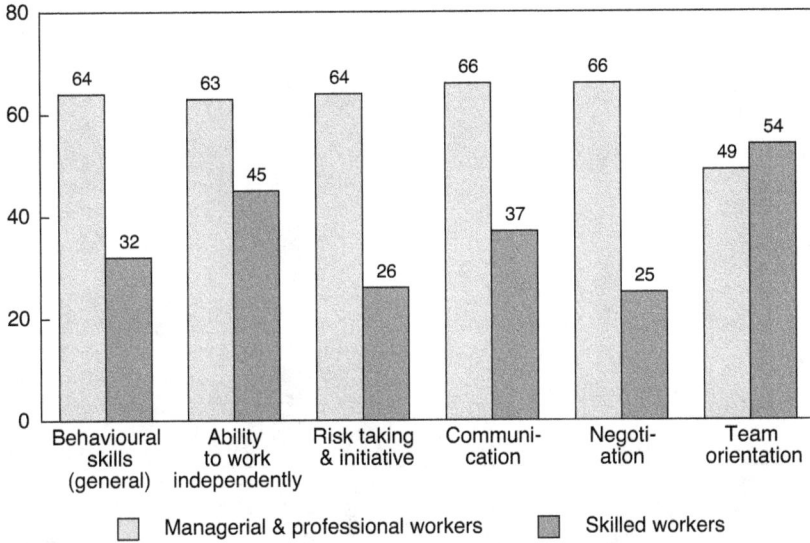

Source: Indonesia Employer/Employee Survey of Skills/Labour Demand and Job Vacancies 2008, Employer Module.

Figure 12.4   Employees' perceptions of the importance of on-the-job skills (%)

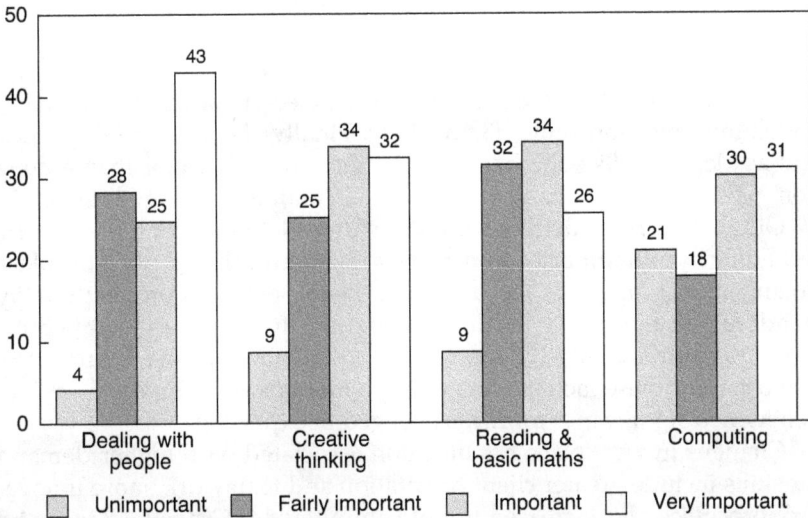

Source: Indonesia Employer/Employee Survey of Skills/Labour Demand and Job Vacancies 2008, Employee Module.

244   *Emanuela di Gropello*

*Figure 12.5   Employers' perceptions of the importance of education,
            knowledge and experience by sector: share rating variable as
            'very important' (%)*

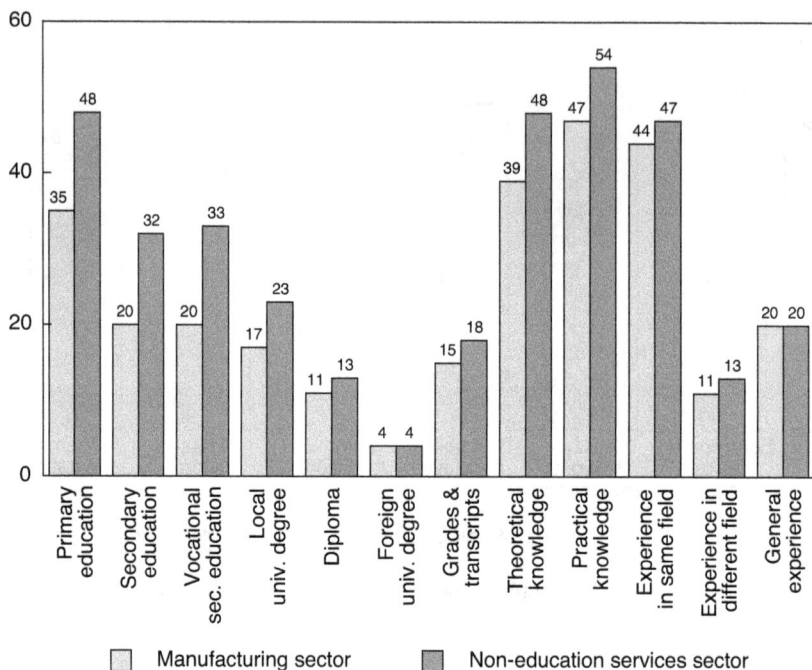

Source: Indonesia Employer/Employee Survey of Skills/Labour Demand and Job Vacancies 2008, Employer Module.

given particular pre-eminence in the services sector, especially leadership and communication skills (Figure 12.6). Finally, demand for all generic and academic skills is higher in the export-oriented sector than among non-exporting firms (Gropello, Kruse and Tandon 2011: Figure O.5).

Other drivers of demand for skills are related to competitiveness, technology (both imported and home grown) and changes in workplace organization. Employers also underline the role of higher product-quality standards (as a proxy for product innovation) and of a more competitive business environment (di Gropello, Kruse and Tandon 2011: Figure O.6). Almost all of these factors – including home-grown technology – are of heightened significance for firms engaged in exporting.

Changes in workplace organization associated with higher demand for skills include greater client orientation and teamwork, more innovatory processes and increased use of computers (di Gropello, Kruse and Tandon 2011: Figure O.7). There is an obvious correspondence between

Figure 12.6   *Employers' perceptions of the importance of behavioural skills among managerial/professional and skilled workers, by sector: share rating variable as 'very important' (%)*

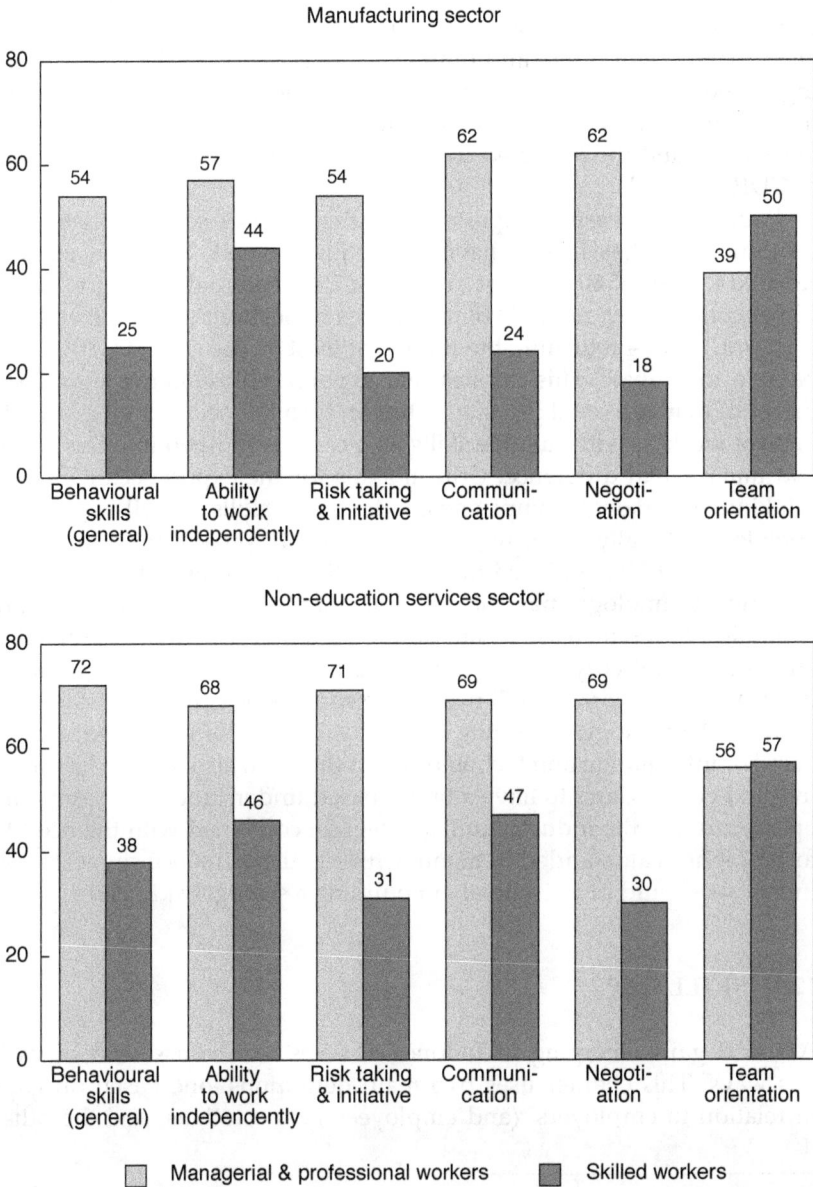

Manufacturing sector

Non-education services sector

☐ Managerial & professional workers   ■ Skilled workers

Source: Indonesia Employer/Employee Survey of Skills/Labour Demand and Job Vacancies 2008, Employer Module.

greater client orientation and the need for better communication skills; and more generally between changes in workplace organization and the demand for skills in the services sector.

Will demand for skills continue to grow? Virtually all employers expect their skill requirements to continue to increase over the next 10 years (di Gropello, Kruse and Tandon 2011: Figure O.8). Other data pointing in the same direction are the changes in long-run sectoral employment shares, which have seen a gradual but steady increase in the share of services, and the projected changes in exports and imports as a share of GDP.

First, the increasing importance of the services sector will require continued emphasis on behavioural skills. Second, although exports reached a peak of 60 per cent of GDP in 2000 before declining to about 20 per cent in 2009, recent IMF projections indicate an upward trend – at least until 2014 – returning the ratio to at least 30 per cent of GDP (comparable to China).[2] This implies that exports will remain a significant driver of demand for skills, suggesting in turn the need for an adequate mass of workers with suitable skills who can be absorbed into this sector and make a real difference. Critical skills for the export sector include thinking, negotiating, computing and language skills as well as practical knowledge. Finally, according to the latest IMF projections, imports as a share of GDP have picked up since 2009. This implies that the role of imported technology may increase and that technology may therefore maintain or even increase its importance as a driver of demand for skills (although admittedly more evidence would be needed on this point). If this is the case, workers will need to be equipped with the critical skills to adapt technology, including creativity, critical thinking and a command of information and technology. But they will also need to be proactive and curious, and to have a broad-based understanding of company operations and the industry milieu. Overall, combined with the need to foster higher value-added in manufacturing, this evidence suggests that Indonesia should invest actively in building a stronger skill base.

12.3   SKILL GAPS

Are skill gaps emerging in Indonesia? Gaps can be assessed in various ways. This chapter uses two main definitions, one based on gaps in relation to employers' (and employees') expectations, and the other

---

2   The IMF projections in this section are from the International Financial Statistics database, 2009. They are based on IMF Article IV Medium-term Expenditure Framework data.

Figure 12.7   Employers' perceptions of the difficulty of filling vacancies by sector: share rating variable as 'rather' or 'very' difficult (%)

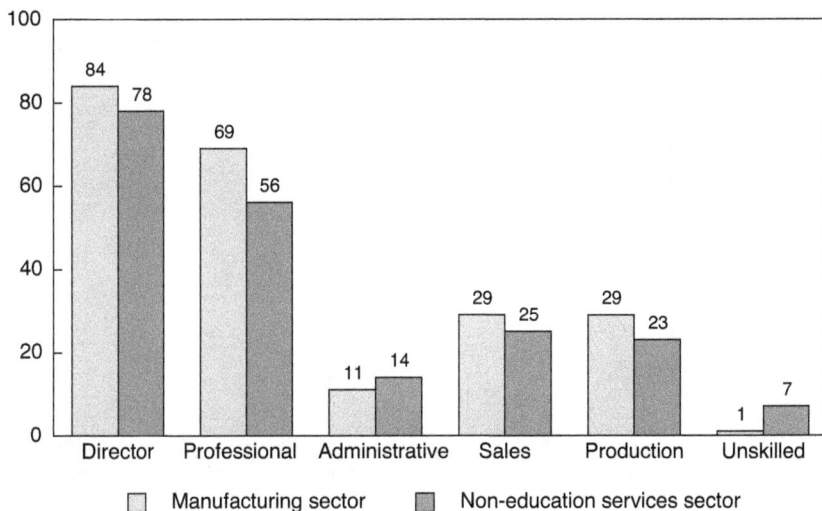

Source: Indonesia Employer/Employee Survey of Skills/Labour Demand and Job Vacancies 2008, Employer Module.

based on gaps in relation to an international average or an average in higher-income countries. The first definition is based on a demand-side approach and is often the only way to measure gaps in higher-level skills. The second definition is based on a supply-side approach, namely standardized international testing. Such testing is conducted only up to the lower secondary level, and therefore assesses more basic skills – mainly, though not solely, academic skills.

While skills do not yet appear to be among the most important constraints facing the economy, the situation is different for larger, more export-oriented manufacturing firms. While unskilled positions are logically – almost by definition – easy to fill, about 80 per cent of manufacturing and service firms say they have difficulty finding the right person to serve as a director, and around 60 per cent have trouble filling professional positions. The manufacturing sector generally finds it harder to fill vacancies than the services sector, although both sectors face serious difficulties (Figure 12.7). Similarly, exporters have more trouble than non-exporters in finding skilled staff, though both report difficulties (Figure 12.8).

For both managerial/professional and skilled workers, the widest gaps are for English and computer skills, followed by thinking and behavioural skills (Figure 12.9). The gaps in thinking and behavioural

Figure 12.8 Employers' perceptions of the difficulty of filling vacancies by export orientation: share rating variable as 'rather' or 'very' difficult (%)

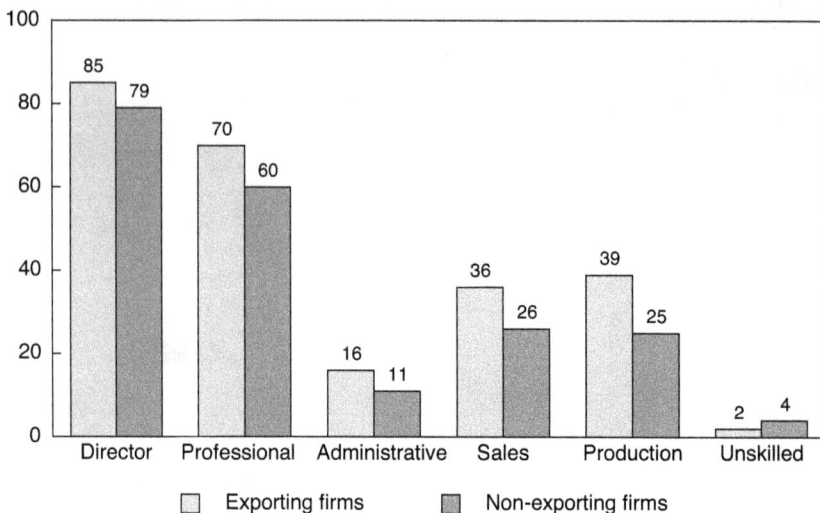

Source: Indonesia Employer/Employee Survey of Skills/Labour Demand and Job Vacancies 2008, Employer Module.

Figure 12.9 Employers' perceptions of gaps in core subject-based and generic skills among managerial/professional and skilled workers (%)

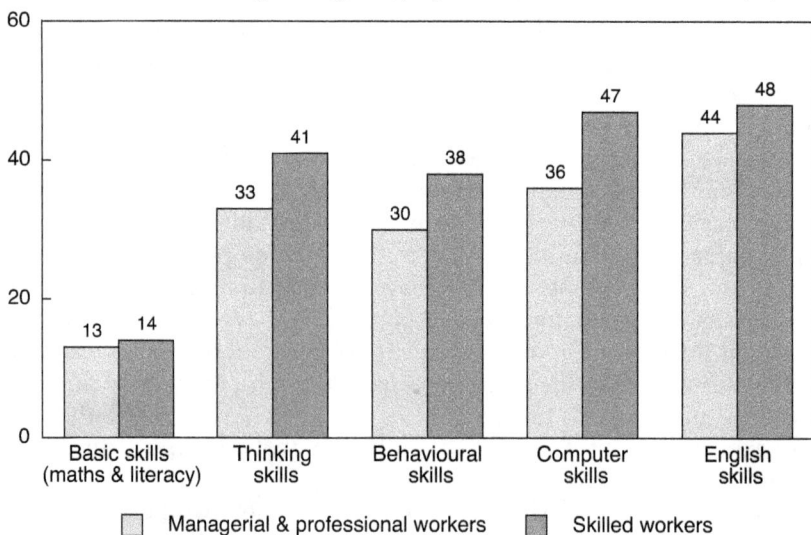

Source: Indonesia Employer/Employee Survey of Skills/Labour Demand and Job Vacancies 2008, Employer Module.

skills are particularly critical given their overall level of importance for employers (Figure 12.2). Gaps in computer and English skills are likely to be felt more in export and technologically oriented sectors and subsectors. Within behavioural skills, the areas of particular weakness are leadership, team orientation and the ability to work independently.

The strongest gaps in job-specific skills are confirmed to be theoretical and practical knowledge of the job, in accordance with employers' perceptions of the importance of job-specific skills (Figure 12.5). Interestingly, as well as being a product of schooling, these gaps are related to a large extent to a lack of experience in the same field.

Workers' perceptions of the need for skills differ according to age group. This may be attributable to differences in occupation (including level of responsibility) as well as being indicative of more profound generational shifts.[3] For instance, younger workers perceive a greater need for teamwork and adaptability, and, conversely, less of a need for leadership and independent thinking (di Gropello, Kruse and Tandon 2011: Figure O.12). Young people also value creativity, computer skills and technical skills. While younger workers may not consider English to be a particularly relevant skill, like older workers and employers they identify it as the skill most lacking in the workforce (di Gropello, Kruse and Tandon 2011: Figure O.12). Other important skills lacking in the workforce, according to young workers, are leadership, problem solving, creativity, computer skills and some technical skills. Of these, creativity, computer skills and technical skills are the most critical given the current need for skills.

Unemployment is very high among younger Indonesians – almost 25 per cent compared with 5 per cent for the overall population – and is particularly high for secondary school graduates (approaching 40 per cent).[4] Apart from slow employment growth, the causes are likely to include insufficient skills owing to a lack of previous experience (which, as we have seen, is a very important source of skills) and the poor quality and lack of relevance of schooling.[5] Young people who do obtain employment tend to be placed in unskilled occupations that do not make use of their relatively higher levels of educational attainment. A majority of young workers experience a 'somewhat' low sense of preparedness for their jobs or for professional life in general (di Gropello, Kruse and

---

3 Comparisons between generations are made difficult by the possibility of selection bias ('survival of the fittest') or of skill decay among older cohorts – two somewhat counteracting effects – and as such need to be taken with care.

4 These figures are based on the 2011 National Socio-Economic Survey (Survei Sosio-Ekonomi Nasional, Susenas).

5 These results are derived from regression analysis that controls for family wealth.

Tandon 2011: Figure O.13), with about 40 per cent agreeing strongly that additional skills would improve their performance. It is not surprising that older workers feel more prepared owing to their much longer exposure to the job market, but the fact that a sizeable 40 per cent consider themselves to be only 'somewhat' prepared for their jobs probably points to an element of skill decay that may not be sufficiently addressed in the Indonesian context.

Finally, standardized testing reveals significant room for improvement in Indonesians' basic academic skills.[6] While neither employers nor employees highlight significant gaps in subject-based skills such as literacy and numeracy, standardized international assessments do. The difference may in part be because testing captures students' academic skills only at the lower secondary level, and their skills may improve subsequently. It may also be because testing provides a more accurate picture of academic strengths and weaknesses, which are typically difficult to measure in the workplace.

What are the main reasons for these skill gaps? Most of the empirical evidence confirms the existence of problems with the relevance and quality of education and training. Other factors, such as a lack of diversification of recruitment practices, poor certification processes, high job turnover and low starting wages, can also explain the difficulties in matching skills to needs in the manufacturing and service sectors. Despite sustained demand for skills in the services sector, there is no major shortage of secondary and tertiary graduates in that sector (with the possible exception of specific subsectors); moreover, there is only limited evidence of shortages in the manufacturing sector (di Gropello, Kruse and Tandon 2011: Figure O.16).

The ways in which firms assess applicants' skills reveal a less than perfect alignment between schooling and job-relevant skills (di Gropello, Kruse and Tandon 2011: Figure O.17). Interviews and probation periods are the most popular methods of assessing candidates' skills, ahead of formal educational qualifications such as diplomas. This finding points to a possibly important constraint in job matching: a lack of adequate skill certification. High job turnover, particularly in manufacturing, can also be a proxy for lack of experience in the same field. Finally, low starting wages can be an indication of wage compression, and therefore of demand-side constraints, as will be illustrated further below.

As we have seen, the quantity (as opposed to the quality) of education and training is not the main cause of skill shortages, although it does play a role in the manufacturing sector. This suggests the need for

---

6   See Chapters 2, 5, 6 and 7 of this book for a discussion of Indonesian students' results as measured by standardized international testing.

suppliers to increase the relevance of secondary and tertiary education to the needs of the manufacturing sector (as indicated also by the high pay premiums for education in that sector), without compromising its relevance to the services sector.

Demand for educated workers remains strong in Indonesia, driven by the services sector. However, signs of longer-term wage compression and 'overqualification' among workers, together with high unemployment rates, are pointing to constraints in the ability of the economy to absorb educated workers. This could cause the numbers of secondary and tertiary graduates to shrink. In other words, while the demand for skills is growing and will continue to grow, it will not necessarily translate into a larger pool of better-educated workers. As a consequence, employers may find in the future that they cannot get the skill sets they need. If they cannot get those skills through other means (for example, by training up less well-educated workers), they will need to be ready to pay a premium for the additional skills brought by secondary and tertiary graduates. Indeed, the high unemployment rates among secondary and tertiary graduates may well be driven in part by the low wages paid to them.

Further economic development and improvements in the quality of graduates may help to increase demand for secondary and tertiary graduates; the existing push to develop the services sector may also help to increase demand for education. The current situation is particularly problematic for tertiary graduates, who are still in short supply in Indonesia compared with other Asian countries, but are more likely than their Asian counterparts to be unemployed or to be considered overqualified for the job.

Demand for high-quality education and training remains strong among Indonesian manufacturing and service firms. Gaps in the quality of education and training are visible in employers' assessments of the quality of their graduates. Almost one-third of secondary school graduates are considered very poor or below average, and most of the rest just fair (Figure 12.10). While tertiary graduates fare somewhat better, the majority are considered only fair, with a very small proportion assessed as being very good (Figure 12.11).

12.4 GAPS IN THE QUALITY AND RELEVANCE OF EDUCATION AND TRAINING

To explore the quality and relevance of education and training in more depth, this section provides an overview of the characteristics of the education and training sector in Indonesia, focusing particularly on secondary and tertiary education. It also touches on the sector's capacity

Figure 12.10   Employers' perceptions of the quality of secondary graduates
hired within the 12 months preceding the survey (%)

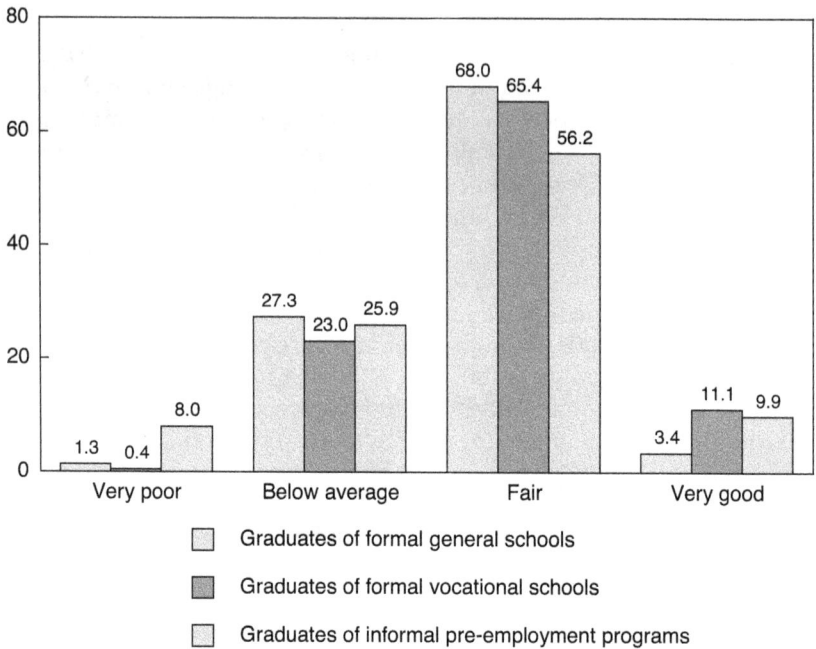

Source: Indonesia Employer/Employee Survey of Skills/Labour Demand and Job Vacancies 2008, Employer Module.

to provide skill development opportunities for the unskilled ('second-chance' programs), and discusses on-the-job training. It emphasizes three core aspects of skill production: the general ability of a system to produce a skilled labour force; its ability to ensure that the skills of workers are updated over time; and its ability to help unskilled adults (both young and older) to acquire skills. These three inter-related dimensions comprise a skill development system. The section focuses first on formal secondary and tertiary education, before discussing non-formal education and training and on-the-job training.

Formal secondary and tertiary education to produce a skilled labour force

Analysis of the education provided by secondary schools suggests that formal vocational secondary schools (Sekolah Menengah Kejuruan, SMK) and general secondary schools (Sekolah Menengah Atas, SMA) each have specific advantages and shortcomings, and that both systems urgently

*Figure 12.11   Employers' perceptions of the quality of tertiary graduates
hired within the 12 months preceding the survey (%)*

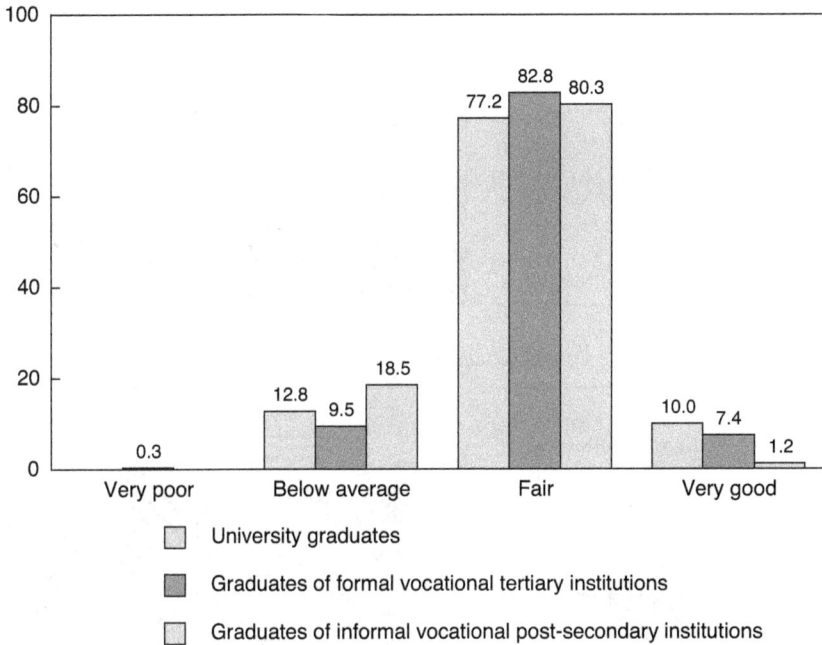

Source: Indonesia Employer/Employee Survey of Skills/Labour Demand and Job Vacancies 2008, Employer Module.

need to be improved. According to employers, the general secondary schools produce fairly rounded and flexible graduates who clearly satisfy an important section of the labour market (Figure 12.12), and therefore have more options to move between jobs. According to employees, however, the general schools fail to provide specific skills and contacts with the productive world (Figure 12.13), making it more difficult for their graduates (especially fresh graduates) to find jobs. The vocational secondary schools, on the other hand, offer the advantages of links with industry and a curriculum that is tailored to specific labour market needs (Figure 12.12), which may increase the employability of their graduates (particularly fresh graduates). But according to employees, the vocational schools suffer from inadequate coverage of the general curriculum and poor quality teaching (Figure 12.14). This could depress the earnings of graduates (particularly over the medium to longer terms, and possibly in the services sector) and restrict their ability to find employment in jobs that match their qualifications. At the same time, it appears that the curriculum of the vocational schools may not yet be specific enough, or their

Figure 12.12   Employers' perceptions of main strengths of secondary options (%)

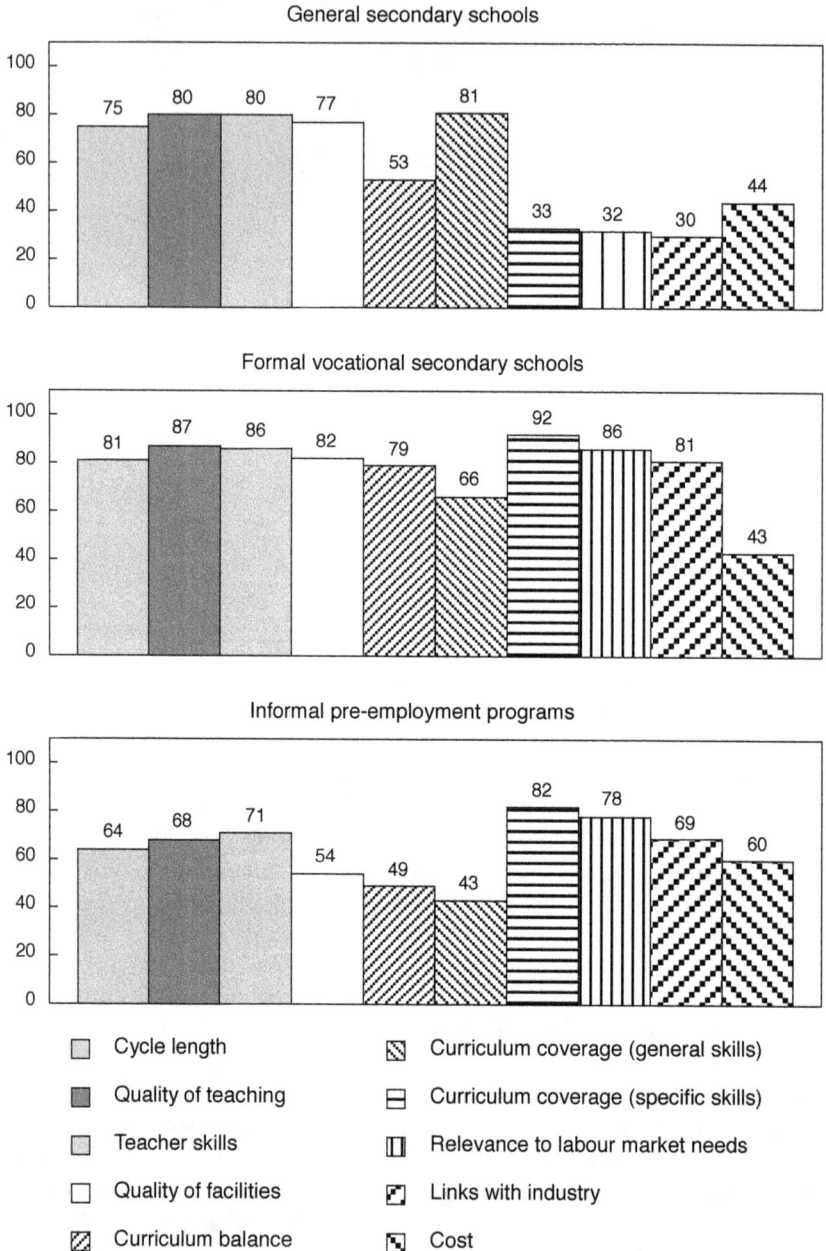

General secondary schools

Formal vocational secondary schools

Informal pre-employment programs

Cycle length
Quality of teaching
Teacher skills
Quality of facilities
Curriculum balance
Curriculum coverage (general skills)
Curriculum coverage (specific skills)
Relevance to labour market needs
Links with industry
Cost

Source: Indonesia Employer/Employee Survey of Skills/Labour Demand and Job Vacancies 2008, Employer Module.

Figure 12.13   Employees' perceptions of main weaknessses of general secondary schools (%)

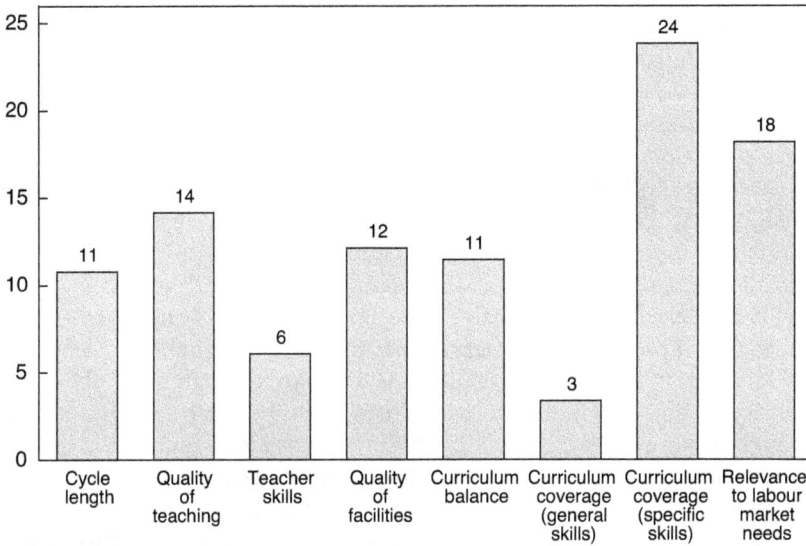

Source: Indonesia Employer/Employee Survey of Skills/Labour Demand and Job Vacancies 2008, Employee Module.

Figure 12.14   Employees' perceptions of main weaknessses of vocational secondary schools (%)

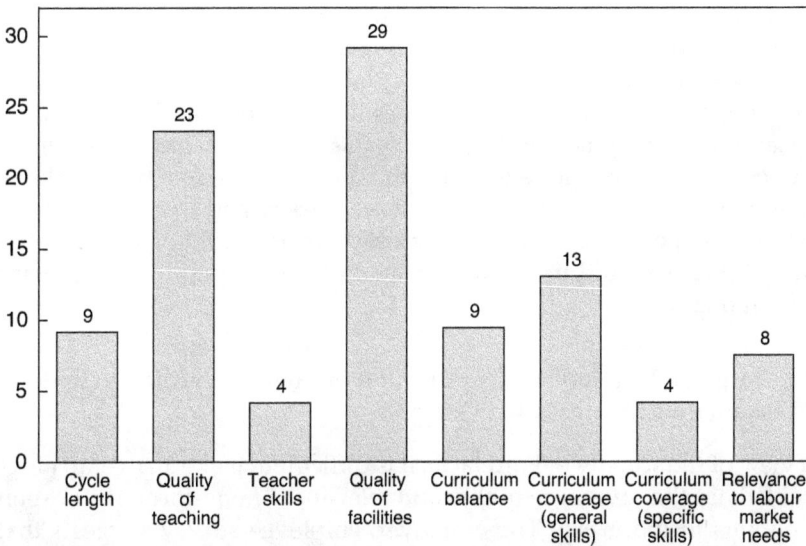

Source: Indonesia Employer/Employee Survey of Skills/Labour Demand and Job Vacancies 2008, Employee Module.

links with industry strong enough, to allow them to fulfil their potential to meet the needs of the manufacturing sector.

The cost effectiveness of the vocational secondary schools can be questioned given the mixed results of their graduates. Recent evidence shows declining returns and increasing unemployment rates among vocational graduates, even though it costs Rp 6.8 million per year to educate a public vocational secondary school student, but only Rp 5.3 million to educate a public general secondary school student (World Bank 2010).

Although Indonesia's tertiary education institutions are generally considered to be of better quality than its secondary institutions, they still have a long way to go to produce high-quality graduates who can provide the skills needed by the manufacturing and service sectors. This is the case for both vocational tertiary institutions and universities. Although employers are generally happy with the quality of teaching and facilities in both sets of institutions, they are less sanguine about the capacity of the universities to form links with industry and to adapt to labour market needs (Figure 12.15). Employees also identify the lack of opportunities to acquire specific skills as a weakness of both sets of institutions (Figures 12.16 and 12.17). The lack of links with industry is likely to be particularly serious for manufacturing firms, given the difficulties they encounter in filling professional positions. Judging from the fact that Indonesia lags on all innovation indicators, universities do not yet have the capacity to support innovation through applied research and technology transfer, or to produce graduates who can help firms innovate.

Employers rate vocational tertiary institutions higher than universities on the strength of their links with industry (Figure 12.15), but employees consider them to be weaker on nearly every aspect covered by the survey (Figure 12.17). In general, graduates with diplomas perform more poorly than university graduates in the labour market (according to standard employment indicators), suggesting that the vocational institutions urgently need to re-examine the role and design of their diploma programs to improve curriculum balance, variety and flexibility. Finally, it is worth noting that the weaknesses identified for vocational tertiary institutions and universities are amplified among private tertiary institutions.

Non-formal education and training and on-the-job training to update skills and give the unskilled skills

In view of the scarcity of hard facts, it is difficult to make an overall judgment about the coverage, quality and relevance of non-formal education programs in Indonesia. The employer/employee survey suggests that non-formal programs are generally of lower quality than the formal programs, but that – like the formal vocational options – they tend to be

Figure 12.15 Employers' perceptions of main strengths of tertiary options (%)

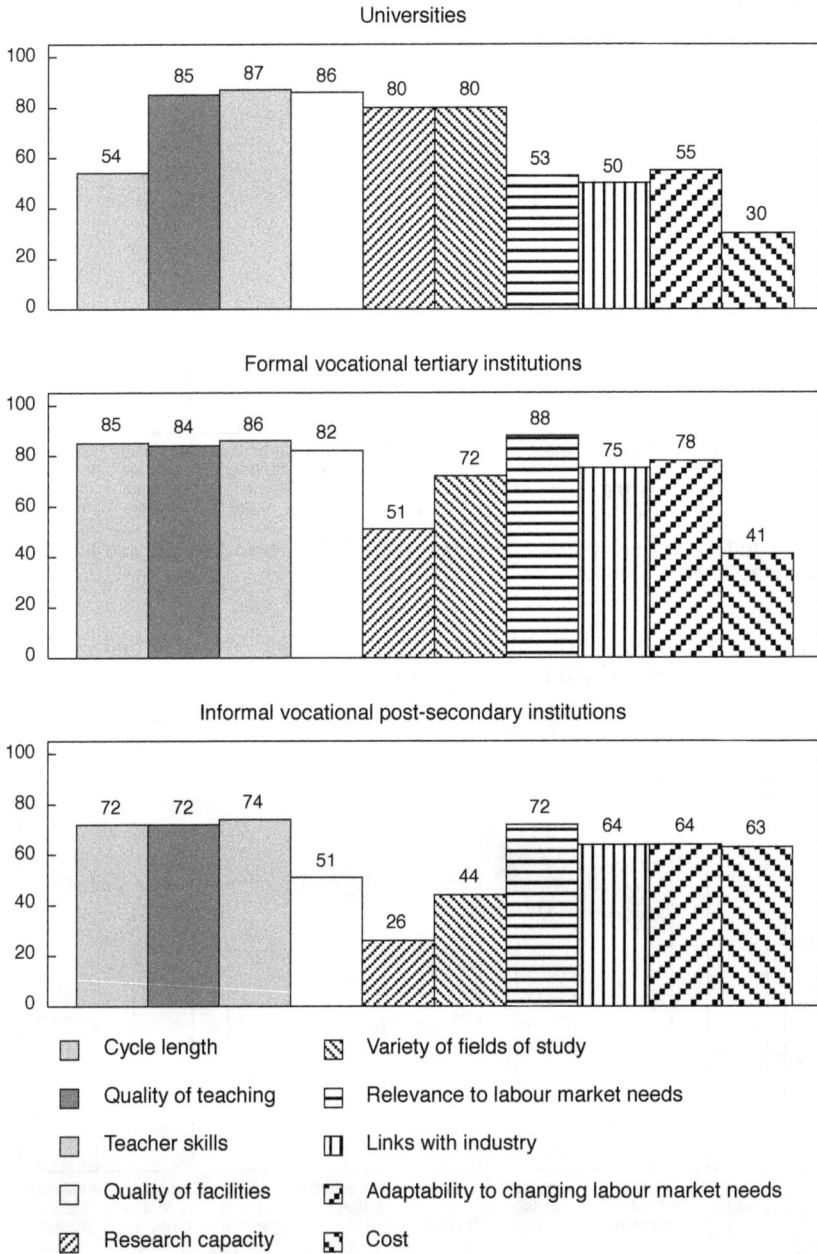

Universities

Formal vocational tertiary institutions

Informal vocational post-secondary institutions

▢ Cycle length	▨ Variety of fields of study
▨ Quality of teaching	▤ Relevance to labour market needs
▢ Teacher skills	▥ Links with industry
▢ Quality of facilities	▨ Adaptability to changing labour market needs
▨ Research capacity	▨ Cost

Source: Indonesia Employer/Employee Survey of Skills/Labour Demand and Job Vacancies 2008, Employer Module.

Figure 12.16   Employees' perceptions of main weaknessses of universities (%)

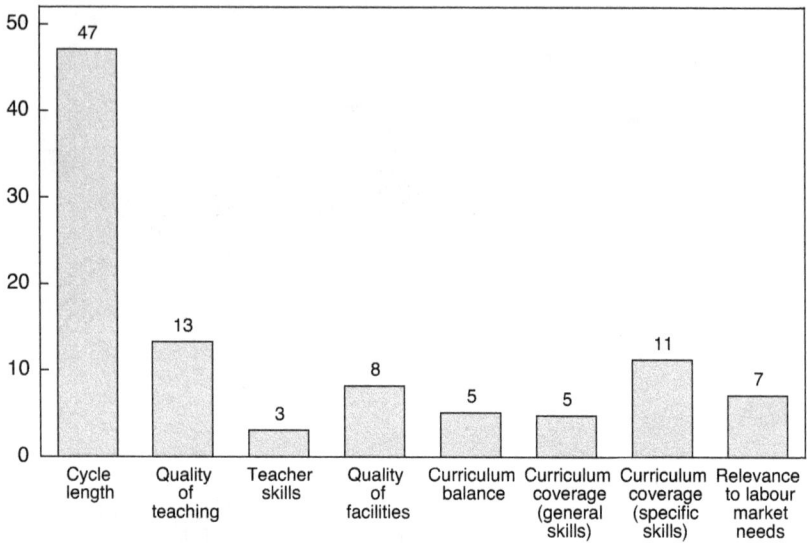

Source: Indonesia Employer/Employee Survey of Skills/Labour Demand and Job Vacancies 2008, Employee Module.

Figure 12.17   Employees' perceptions of main weaknessses of formal vocational tertiary institutions (%)

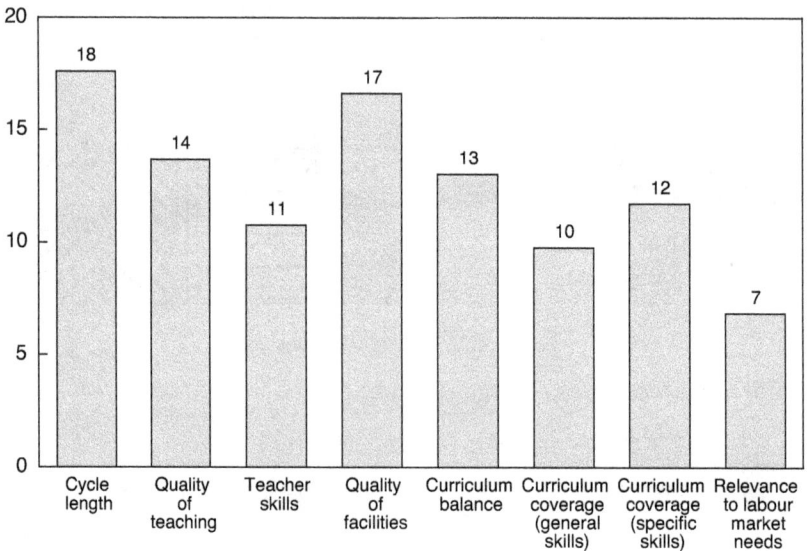

Source: Indonesia Employer/Employee Survey of Skills/Labour Demand and Job Vacancies 2008, Employee Module.

Figure 12.18   Employees' perceptions of main weaknessses of informal vocational post-secondary institutions (%)

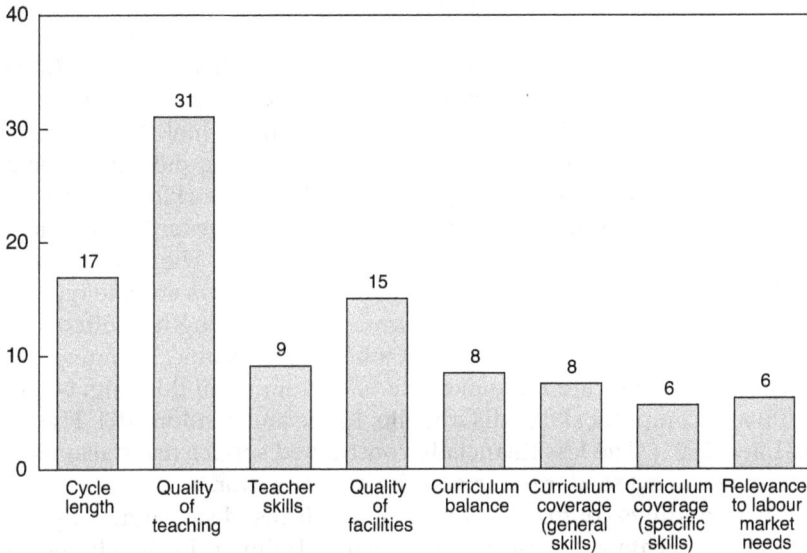

Source: Indonesia Employer/Employee Survey of Skills/Labour Demand and Job Vacancies 2008, Employee Module.

reasonably responsive to labour market needs (Figures 12.12, 12.15 and 12.18). The initial results of informal vocational programs such as the Para Professional Course (Kursus Para Profesi, KPP) and the Education for Youth Employment (EYE) scheme support these findings, though the results need to be evaluated more thoroughly.

The KPP program provides training and education to disadvantaged youth. Under this government-initiated scheme, private providers are given incentives to provide training in skills that are in demand from employers. The government's EYE scheme focuses on out-of-school young people aged 16–24 who are undereducated, poor and unemployed. It supplements an education equivalency package that gives participants a formal junior secondary qualification with training in life skills, vocational training and assistance to find employment. The program has had some success in placing youth in jobs through its links with industry and business: 82 per cent of participants were employed after receiving three to four months training, and employee retention rates remained above 80 per cent after three years.[7]

7 These results should be treated with care because they do not control for the possibility of selection bias.

The Ministry of Manpower and Transmigration has also developed a skill-based competency and qualification framework that creates bridges between the informal and formal sectors and lays the ground for lifelong learning. It would be useful for the ministry to re-examine the role of its extensive network of vocational training centres (Balai Latihan Kerja, BLK), the main public providers of non-formal vocational training and job placement services, in light of the increasing focus on lifelong learning.

Firms themselves are more interested in providing short-term remedial training than in developing the skills of their workforces over the longer term. The formal training programs of firms nevertheless constitute an important source of practical on-the-job skills. The areas of training tend to reflect the skill gaps identified by employers and the types of skills that will help them build on a firm's relative strengths. Both manufacturing and service firms focus on job-specific technical training, but service sector firms are more likely to offer training in thinking, behavioural and computer skills (di Gropello, Kruse and Tandon 2011: Figures O.31 and O.32). The less financially constrained service firms also make greater use of external training and the private sector.

These findings confirm the rationality of firms' decision making, but they also indicate a short-term approach to training. In the absence of significant financial incentives to train workers, firms focus most of their efforts on upgrading the skills of young workers and skilled production workers (di Gropello, Kruse and Tandon 2011: Figure O.33), while relying mainly on informal training and learning-by-doing for professionals and managers. This approach is not conducive to addressing the need for lifelong learning. There is also a sense that manufacturing and exporting firms may not provide enough training, and certainly not to a level that would allow their professional and managerial staff to become more competitive and innovative. Improving the skills of professional and managerial staff would require more investment in generic skills and higher-level industry knowledge.

12.5   MAIN PRIORITIES AND POLICY IMPLICATIONS

Several policy implications can be derived from these main findings. This section summarizes those critical to building an effective skill development system in Indonesia.

Overall priorities

Indonesia should prioritize five areas to improve the general skills of the population. First, the country needs to improve its skill measurement capacity, to get a better understanding of what skills are needed and what skills are lacking. The current gaps in knowledge could be filled by, for example, undertaking more employer/employee skill surveys (which could simply be integrated into existing firm surveys), making more and better use of firm and tracer surveys, and participating in programs to assess adults' literacy, numeracy and other skills, such as the Programme for the International Assessment of Adult Competencies promoted by the OECD.

Second, Indonesia urgently needs to address the unsatisfactory quality and lack of relevance of formal education. More than quantity, quality and relevance are the critical issues for the formal education and training sector. Changes are needed at all levels to improve the quality of teaching and to strengthen links with firms. It is particularly important to improve the quality and relevance of secondary education so that young workers get the skills the labour market needs, thereby improving their employment prospects.

Third, the country needs to set up multiple pathways for skill development. As well as improving the quality and relevance of formal education, Indonesia needs to continue to build a skill development system that creates opportunities for employees to acquire complementary skills, for workers to update their skills over time, and for out-of-school or vulnerable youth and adults to gain relevant skills. Although the development of a national qualification framework that articulates competency goals is a promising step, more work needs to be done to strengthen regulatory bodies and institutional accreditation, skill standardization and skill certification procedures. The constraints to building a multi-purpose system need to be fully understood, and appropriate action taken to address those constraints. For instance, the institutional and funding incentives for lifelong learning should be strengthened, including encouraging firms to provide training that will meet the country's longer-term needs. At the same time, it is important to assess more fully and rigorously the outcomes of the existing non-formal education and training institutions and programs, to tap their potential as providers of relevant skills to vulnerable youth and adults, and as providers of complementary skills and skill development over time.

Fourth, the country needs to develop an integrated approach to tackle skill development for youth. Although they have higher levels of educational attainment than older age groups, young Indonesians tend to be deficient in practical skills and therefore experience difficulty in the labour market. An integrated approach would include improving the quality and relevance of formal education (particularly secondary education); developing and improving non-formal 'second-chance' programs; building more bridges between educational institutions and the labour market through school-to-work transition programs that provide labour market information, employment placement opportunities and complementary life and technical skills; and focusing firms' youth training programs on complementary job-specific skills.

Fifth, Indonesia should tackle labour market constraints that affect the skill-matching process. A study of labour market constraints should be undertaken to complement the analysis of skill supply and demand. Such research would provide a broader view of skill-matching constraints and ensure that inefficiencies were minimized. For instance, even if skill supply were greatly improved, a lack of diversification of recruitment practices could still constrain the skill-matching process in Indonesia. Labour market segmentation issues should also be examined closely.

Priorities for secondary education

Improving the quality and relevance of secondary education should be Indonesia's top priority, especially as most students do not proceed beyond this level. The government should start by improving quality and relevance within each track – general and vocational – including ensuring a better allocation of technical and vocational graduates between the manufacturing and service sectors. The evidence presented in this chapter does not support the intention of the Ministry of Education and Culture to increase the ratio of students enrolled in vocational secondary schools to those enrolled in general secondary schools to 70:30 by 2015.

First and most importantly, both the general and vocational tracks need to improve the balance of their curriculums. This implies the need for more specific and practical knowledge to be included in the general secondary track, and for vocational institutions to strengthen their provision of core academic skills.

Second, the general and vocational schools need to strengthen their teaching of both academic and generic skills, given the gaps identified in maths, literacy and English (among academic skills) and thinking and behavioural skills (among generic skills). While employers tend to be more concerned about specific skills than core academic skills, and therefore identify fewer weaknesses among employees in this area, employees are aware that the coverage of general skills in the curriculum is deficient in vocational schools, and that the quality of teaching could be improved in both tracks. To enhance proficiency in core subjects while introducing generic skills, schools will need to modify their curriculums and make pedagogical changes. Vocational schools will need to ensure a good balance between teachers with academic backgrounds and those with practitioner backgrounds.

Third, the vocational schools need to improve the design and implementation of the specific skills component of the curriculum. Indonesia already has at least one example of vocational secondary schools that appear to have been very successful in meeting industry needs: the Chemical Analyst Vocational Schools (Sekolah Menengah Analisis Kimia, SMAK) (di Gropello, Kruse and Tandon 2011: 179). Learning from this example and German experience with vocational education, Indonesia should be able to design a more demand-driven curriculum for vocational secondary schools that includes more systematic industry input (including financial input), sufficient practitioners on staff, and stronger consultation mechanisms with industry and other relevant ministries and bodies. At the same time, support should continue for the Dual Education System (Pendidikan Sistem Ganda, PSG) methodology, which combines education and training in schools with internships in firms, sometimes leading to dual skill certification. Now being applied more widely, this approach would be particularly suitable for aligning the technology and industry component of the curriculum with industry demand for skills. This part of the curriculum is by nature more difficult to design and implement well than the business and management component, probably explaining why there are fewer technical and vocational graduates in manufacturing. In the Indonesian context, where firms and vocational secondary schools tend to be small, the government may need to step up its support to make such a model work. This would necessarily mean selective rather than broad-based support, with consequences for enrolment targets. A policy of consolidating private vocational secondary schools would help to ease the financial burden on the government.

Fourth, general schools need to place more emphasis on specific skills and improving links with industry. Rather than adding very specific technical subjects, the schools should concentrate on improving their ability to teach applied subjects such as business, economics, computing and English. Teachers would be asked to give students the skills to communicate more effectively, and students would be required to undertake short internships in relevant economic sectors. These changes would make graduates of general secondary schools more appealing to the services sector, which currently prefers to take vocational graduates. But a stronger emphasis in the general curriculum on science, mathematics, and information and communication technology, together with an increased emphasis on developing analytical and creative thinking, could well serve the needs of the manufacturing sector as well.

Finally, researchers should carry out tracer studies following secondary school graduates to learn lessons about the relevance of their education. Such studies could be based on regular interviews with both graduates and their employers, to identify the most desirable skills for particular industries, which fields of education are in increased or decreased demand, and how secondary education institutions can benefit from this information and incorporate it into their curriculums.

Priorities for tertiary education

There are also strong grounds for improving tertiary education. First, like secondary schools, tertiary institutions need to improve the balance of their curriculums. Universities must strengthen their provision of practical knowledge and their capacity to adapt to labour market needs, and vocational tertiary institutions must make sure they provide a solid set of core academic skills.

Second, the government needs to provide incentives to improve university–industry links. Universities should be encouraged to form links with industries to improve the relevance of their curriculums (particularly critical in the case of manufacturing), and of their training and research. While geater flexibility of university management would help, the government may also need to play a role by improving the legal framework and providing other incentives for collaboration. Such incentives might include establishing technology-licensing organizations within universities to promote collaboration with industry and to facilitate industrial technology transfer.

Third, researchers should carry out tracer studies following tertiary graduates to learn lessons about the relevance of their education. Like the tracer studies on secondary school graduates, these could be based on regular interviews with graduates and employees, to identify the skills and fields of education that are most in demand. This type of information is essential for tertiary institutions to make their curriculums more relevant to the needs of industry.

Fourth, it is time to rethink the role of diploma programs, because they are not fulfilling their function of providing valuable higher-level vocational skills. What type of education should the vocational tertiary institutions provide? How should they achieve this? It would be worth doing research focusing specifically on diploma programs and the institutions that provide them.

Fifth, tertiary institutions need to step up their provision of skills for innovation. Universities are particularly well positioned to address the general lack of international exposure and knowledge among firm employees (presumably linked to language barriers), and to enhance creative thinking by exposing students to different teaching methodologies.

Finally, the quality of private tertiary institutions should be monitored more closely. Although they have to obtain accreditation like other tertiary institutions, the private institutions generally provide a poorer quality of education than the public institutions. Remedial action should be taken to reduce the number of underperforming private institutions, including closing failing or non-performing institutions where necessary. This – together with regular publication and dissemination of outcomes and accreditation results – would signal a commitment to quality in the tertiary sector, guide and influence the behaviour of the private tertiary institutions, and give students the information they need to choose the institutions that provide the best education.

Priorities for non-formal education and training

Non-formal institutions and programs have huge potential in Indonesia, given the difficulties faced by young and unskilled workers and the growing need for lifelong learning. Examples include the informal vocational training centres (BLK) and the KPP and EYE programs discussed above.

To improve the quality of non-formal education, the first priority is to collect better data and to undertake systematic monitoring and evaluation of the sector. To improve the quality of data, surveys of individual programs and participants, and tracer studies following graduates, should be conducted regularly. Ongoing programs should be monitored and evaluated comprehensively and rigorously, especially when the incentives for providers and users of training services are changed.

The second priority is to set up successful school-to-work transition programs, learning from international experience. Indonesia already has a number of programs with good potential, but it could still learn a great deal from successful examples elsewhere.

The third priority is to improve the quality of school-based informal vocational training. As well as ensuring that such programs are responsive to demand, schools need to address weaknesses in teaching quality, the quality of facilities, instructors' qualifications and curriculum coverage. Revitalizing the BLKs should clearly continue to be a priority. It may also be useful to re-examine their role in light of the increasing focus on lifelong learning.

Finally, the government needs to do further work to improve its skill competency and qualification framework, in order to support the development of the non-formal vocational sector and promote lifelong learning. This effort should include developing a competency-based curriculum; improving skill certification procedures, including procedures for dual certification by schools and professional associations; encouraging industry participation; ensuring a consistent quality of vocational training; and strengthening the framework for lifelong learning.

REFERENCES

di Gropello, E., A. Kruse and P. Tandon (2011) *Skills for the Labor Market in Indonesia: Trends in Demand, Gaps, and Supply*, World Bank, Washington DC.

World Bank (2010) 'Indonesia jobs report: towards better jobs and security for all', World Bank, Jakarta.

INDEX

A

access and equity, 10, 133, 153
  ECED services, 90
  financing system, 50, 81, 117
  gender, 4
  poverty, 4, 10, 24–5, 34, 90, 117, 133, 168, 174–6
  schools, 3, 4, 12, 24, 34n, 81, 117
  tertiary sector, 168, 174–6
  underfunding of *madrasah*, 12, 73–4, 81
agriculture, 3, 9, 139, 236
Airlangga University, 190, 195
Algeria, 231
ASEAN, 161, 162
Asian financial crisis, 27–8, 109, 141, 170, 220, 236
Association of Indonesian Physicians (IDI), 174
Association of Private Universities, 177
AusAID, 77, 192
Australia, 10, 17, 96, 192, 199, 218, 219, 220, 221, 232, 233
  Australian National University, 181, 191
  degree programs in Malaysia, 230
  Flinders University, 224
  HECS scheme, 176, 212, 213
Australian National University, 181, 191
Australian Universities Quality Agency (AUQA), 227

B

Bandung Institute of Technology, 181n, 183n, 185, 188, 190, 192, 193
Bangladesh, 47, 231
BAN-PT
  see National Accreditation Agency for Universities
BAN-S/M
  see National Accreditation Board for Schools and Madrasah
Bappenas
  see National Development Planning Agency
Bidik Misi program, 175
BKKBN
  see National Family Planning Coordination Agency
BLK
  see vocational training, informal centres
BLT
  see Direct Cash Assistance
Board of National Education Standards (BSNP), 90
BOS
  see Schools Operational Assistance scheme; government expenditure/ funding, BOS grants program; financial resources, Schools Operational Assistance scheme
Botswana, 189, 231
Brazil, 115
Brunei, 231
BSNP
  see Board of National Education Standards

C

California Master Plan for Higher
    Education, 186
Cambodia, 47, 112, 141, 163, 167, 169
Canada, 10, 64, 65, 85, 96, 186, 204,
    221, 233
Chemical Analyst Vocational Schools
    (SMAK), 263
childcare centres
    see early childhood sector,
    childcare centres (TPA)
Chile, 10, 46, 212
China, 3, 4, 161, 162, 163, 169n, 172,
    186, 203, 229, 230, 231, 232, 233,
    246
Chinese Taipei, 46
civil service, 7, 8, 131–2, 161, 196
    see also teachers, civil service status
compulsory education, 15, 24, 26, 30,
    33, 48, 49, 70, 79
Constitution, 6, 45, 49, 164
Constitutional Court, 9, 74, 171, 176,
    178
corruption, 7, 8, 129, 131–2, 173
costs
    see expenditure; financial resources
CPA Australia, 227
curriculum
    Competency Based, 58–9, 60, 65
    Islamic schools, 69
    Local Content, 58, 59
    secondary education, 262, 263, 264
    schools, 263
    tertiary, 264
Czech Republic, 233

D

DCCS
    see Early Childhood Education and
    Development project, Dimensional
    Change Card Sort task
decentralization, 15, 16, 34, 35, 57–8,
    59, 69, 73, 109, 110, 117
    changes to architecture, 80
    effect on corruption, 131
    effect on district budgets, 117, 121,
    145
    effect on teachers, 59–60, 121
    governance at local level, 126–33
    Local Content Curriculum, 58, 59

DID
    see Regional Incentive Fund
Direct Cash Assistance (BLT), 147n
Dual Education System (PSG), 263

E

Early Childhood Education and
    Development (ECED) project,
    85–106
    child ability tasks, 99–100
    development domains, 94, 95
    developmental vulnerability, 95–6,
    97
    Dimensional Change Card Sort
    (DCCS) task, 98–9
    drawing tasks, 101–2
    Early Development Instrument
    (EDI), 94–5, 96
    early impacts, 103–6
    evaluation of initial impact, 90–103
    language skills, 102–3, 104, 105
    mothers' assessments, 100–101
    Strengths and Difficulties
    Questionnaire (SDQ), 97–8
early childhood sector, 12–13, 82–106
    census, 90
    childcare centres (TPA), 88, 89
    developmental outcomes, 83, 105
    ECED posts (Pos PAUD), 88, 89
    enrolments, 91, 103–4
    government expenditure, 114, 115
    health service units, 87, 88
    Islamic kindergartens (RA/TPQ),
    88, 89
    kindergartens (TK), 87, 88, 89, 104
    national standards, 89, 90
    playgroups (KB), 86, 87, 88, 89, 104
    policies, 89–90
    private sector, 13, 85, 87, 88
    rates of return on expenditure, 12,
    13, 82, 83, 86, 115
    rural areas, 90–103
    services, 87–9
    services by intended age group, 89
    services by ministry, 88
    toddler family groups, 87, 88, 89
East Timor, 167
economy, 9, 139
    export sector, 244, 246, 247–9
    growth, 5, 109, 139, 141, 178, 189,
    212, 236, 237

human resources, 3, 223
imports, 246
international competitiveness, 13, 237
productivity, 3, 5, 237
EDI
see Early Childhood Education and Development project, Early Development Instrument
Education for Youth Employment (EYE), 259, 265
Education Quality Assurance Institute (LPMP), 151–2
educational attainment, 18–23, 41–5, 83, 250
number of years of schooling, 18, 20, 21, 162
provincial comparisons, 20, 21, 42, 44
teachers, 37–41, 42, 49, 144, 157
see also learning outcomes
Egypt, 232, 233
employers
see industry; labour market
employment, 3, 174, 195, 198, 236–7, 246, 249–50, 253, 259, 261
school-to-work transition programs, 262, 265
teachers, 37, 56, 124, 132, 153
unemployment, 174, 249, 251, 256, 259
England, 10, 46, 212, 219
see also United Kingdom
enrolments, 23–6, 36, 57
age-specific rate, 24–5
by gender, 26
gross enrolment rate (GER), 3, 4, 23, 24, 139, 140, 142, 143, 163
junior secondary, 24, 26, 36
Malaysian universities, 221, 222, 229, 230, 231
net enrolment rate (NER), 23, 24, 26
primary, 2, 23, 24, 26, 36, 57, 83, 142, 143
secondary, 3, 4, 24, 26, 36, 57, 142, 143
senior secondary, 24, 25, 26, 36
tertiary, 9, 10–11, 26, 163, 168
equity of access
see access and equity

expenditure
family, 4, 24
household, 112
private, tertiary education sector, 121, 162, 164, 165, 167, 178
see also financial resources; government expenditure
EYE
see Education for Youth Employment

F

Fahmina Institute of Islamic Studies, 184, 187, 188, 189, 190, 192, 193, 194, 195, 199
vision, 196, 198
farmers, 3, 42
assistance from Nusa Cendana University, 197
females
access to education, 48, 68
completion rates, 31
early childhood sector, 104, 105, 106
enrolment rates, 26, 83
graduate earnings and repayment burden, 208, 209, 210
illiteracy rates, 21
teachers, 37, 41, 155
years of schooling, 18–20
financial resources, 6, 7, 45–8, 109–36, 203–5
early childhood sector, 114, 115
efficient use, 50, 58, 126, 129, 130, 134–5, 164
Islamic schools, 68, 70, 71, 72, 74, 75
loan systems, 10, 103–13
Malaysian tertiary sector, 219, 220–21, 228, 232
national education financing system, 75, 81
parental contribution, 61
primary education, 112, 113, 114
Regional Incentive Fund (DID), 134–5
Schools Operational Assistance (BOS) scheme, 70, 72, 74, 75, 76, 79, 116, 126, 132, 133, 135
secondary education, 6, 112, 113, 114, 115, 116

tertiary education, 9–10, 114, 115, 116, 162, 167, 175–6
university twinning partnerships, 219
see also expenditure; government expenditure; student loan schemes
Finland, 46, 64, 142
Flinders University, 224
France, 233
fuel subsidies, 175, 178
funding
   see financial resources

G

Gadjah Mada University, 177, 181n, 185
GDP, 9, 119, 139, 236, 246
   education budget proportion, 110, 111, 112, 113, 164, 178
   growth, 236
   per capita, 112, 113, 141, 203
   by sector, 140
gender equity, 4, 18, 19, 20, 21, 26, 31, 48, 68
Germany, 206, 233
Ghana, 9
Golkar, 57
governance
   schools, 58, 126, 153
   universities, 165, 169–71, 181, 182n, 185, 195
governance at local level, 110, 126–33
   indicators of quality, 129–30
   management systems, 130–31
government expenditure/funding, 5–6, 9, 45–8, 74, 109–10, 110–17, 133
   basic education, local and central government proportions, 127
   BOS grants program, 116, 132, 133, 135
   correlation with learning outcomes, 7, 127–8
   international comparisons, 47, 115
   local government, 47–8, 80, 127–8, 194–5
   Malaysia, 9, 47, 112, 115, 232
   non-basic education, 115, 125
   primary education, 112, 113, 114
   proportion of government budget, 110, 111, 112, 113, 116n, 124, 164, 178

provincial and district budgets, 47–8, 80, 127–8
relationship with education outcomes, 127–9
secondary education, 6, 112, 113, 114, 115, 116
sector of education, 114
teacher certification, 124–5, 127, 133, 147
tertiary education sector, 114, 115, 116, 162, 164, 167, 175–6, 178, 189
20 per cent rule, 6, 111, 115, 164
Grand Design for Basic Education, 70, 71, 79
grants
   local school, 135
   universities, 171, 186, 189, 190, 194

H

Harvard University, 190
HELP University, 224
higher education
   see tertiary education; tertiary education institutions, study; universities
higher education loan scheme, 206–13
   income-contingent loans (ICLs), 10, 179, 205, 212–13
   mortgage-type loans, 10, 204, 206, 210, 212
history of improvements, 15
Honduras, 141
Hong Kong, 46, 164
Human Development Index, 27
Hungary, 10, 46, 212

I

ICL
   see higher education loan scheme, income-contingent loans
IDI
   see Association of Indonesian Physicians
illiteracy, 2–3, 21–3, 48
   provincial comparisons, 22–3
India, 3, 4, 47, 141, 161, 231, 233
Indonesian Teachers Union (PGRI), 57
industry sector, 139, 140, 142, 197, 198, 200, 236, 246, 253–4, 256, 257, 259
   input to education and training, 260, 261, 262, 263, 264

inequality
  see access and equity; gender
  equity
Inpres SD
  see Presidential Primary School
  program
international comparisons, 161
  early childhood, 12, 96
  education systems, 64–5
  government expenditure, 9, 47,
  111n, 112
  government expenditure, tertiary
  sector, 164
  gross enrolment rates, 143
  middle-income trap, 141–2
  primary education, 5, 6
  student performance, 5, 45, 45n,
  46, 83, 85, 117–19, 142, 143, 169, 250
  student repayment burden, 206
  teachers' salaries, 6, 145
  teachers/teaching, 64–5
  university staff qualifications, 169
  universities, 186
  years of schooling, 162–3
international students, 11, 167, 217,
  219, 221–4
INTI University, 224
Iran, 46, 239
Iraq, 230, 231
Ireland, 142
Islamic kindergartens, 88, 89
Islamic scholars, 192, 198
Islamic schools (*madrasah*), 11–12, 33,
  68–81
  accreditation, 70, 71, 71n, 72, 73,
  73n, 76–7, 77, 78–9, 79
  administration, 12
  curriculum, 69, 79
  funding, 68, 70, 71, 74, 75, 80
  number, 68, 70, 77
  number of students, 68
  quality, 12, 68, 80
  registration, 72, 73, 78
  self-evaluation, 73
Italy, 46

J

Japan, 46, 47, 64, 65, 163, 164, 233
jobs
  see employment; labour market;
  workforce

Jordan, 231, 233
junior secondary education, 3, 24, 29
  demand for, 34
  graduates to senior secondary, 27,
  29
  number of schools, 32
  retention and transition rates, 26,
  27, 30, 31, 49, 83
  see also teachers

K

Kazakhstan, 231
KB
  see early childhood sector,
  playgroups
kindergartens
  see early childhood sector, Islamic
  kindergartens (TPQ); early
  childhood sector, kindergartens
  (TK)
KKG
  see Primary School Teachers
  Working Group
KPP
  see Para Professional Course

L

labour market, 13, 236–65
  changes in workplace
  organization, 244–5
  constraints affecting skill
  matching, 262
  employers' perceptions of quality
  of graduates, 252, 253
  employers' perceptions of skills,
  241–6, 251
  exporters, 247, 248, 260
  future needs, 246
  managerial/professional and
  skilled workers, 241, 242, 243, 245,
  247, 248, 260
  manufacturing sector, 245, 246,
  247, 250, 251, 256, 260, 263, 264
  non-education services sector, 245,
  247
  services sector, 246, 247, 250, 251,
  253, 256, 260
  skill acquisition, 240–41, 261
  skills in demand, 241–4, 246, 259
  skill gaps, 246–51, 261
  skill matching, 262, 264

skill measurement, 260–61
young people, 174, 249, 259, 261
see also employment; workforce
Lao PDR, 47, 112
Laos, 164
learning outcomes, 5, 7, 18–23, 41,
41–5, 117–20
    effect of local government
    expenditure, 127–30, 135
    effect of teacher absence, 154
    effect of teacher quality, 123–6
    effect of teacher supply, 134
    international comparisons, 5, 45,
    46, 83, 85, 117–19, 142, 143, 169
    mathematics, 5, 41, 42, 43, 44, 45,
    46, 83, 117–19, 120, 122
    national examination results, 42,
    43–4, 48
    parental factors, 42, 45
    reading skills, 5, 45, 45n, 83, 119,
    120
    school-level factors, 42, 45
    science, 42, 43, 45, 46, 83, 119
    see also educational attainment
legal issues, 9, 70, 74, 171, 176, 178
    see also legislation
legislation
    Anti Subversion Law, 56
    draft law on higher education, 10,
    171, 176–8
    Law 14/2005 on Teachers and
    Lecturers, 38, 41, 49, 144, 146, 148,
    150, 157
    Law 20/2003 on the National
    Education System, 6, 23n, 45, 47,
    70, 74, 90, 126, 135
    Law 22/1999 on Regional
    Government, 58
    Law 25/1999 on the Fiscal Balance
    between the Central Government
    and the Regions, 58
    Malaysia, 225
Libya, 231
lifelong learning, 239, 260, 261, 265
LPMP
    see Education Quality Assurance
    Institute

M

madrasah
    see Islamic schools

Mahidol University, 169
Malaysia, 5, 6, 47, 119, 162, 163, 176
    affirmative action in favour of
    Malays, 218
    cost of attending university,
    219–20
    double/joint degrees, 224
    foreign degree programs, 230
    foreign ownership, 224
    foreign universities, branch
    campuses, 11, 223–4
    funding of universities, 219, 220–
    21, 228, 232
    government expenditure, 9, 47,
    112, 115
    Indonesian students, 230, 231
    international students, 11, 167, 217,
    219, 221–4, 226, 229–32
    internationalization of higher
    education, 216–34
    Internationalization Policy for
    Higher Education, 229
    language of instruction, private
    universities, 11, 220, 230, 231, 234
    Merdeka University, 218
    Ministry of Higher Education, 225,
    226, 227
    New Economic Policy, 218, 229
    number of students studying
    abroad, 223n
    number of universities, 223, 232
    private education sector, 216, 218,
    220, 228, 230
    quality of higher education, 119,
    172, 226–9
    regulatory environment, 225–6
    students studying abroad, 167,
    232, 233
    teachers' salaries, 145
    tertiary education sector, 10–11,
    163, 164, 168, 174n, 176, 216–34
    Universities and University
    Colleges Act 1971, 218
    university courses, 221, 227
    university enrolments, 221, 222,
    229
    university twinning partnerships,
    168, 217–21, 227, 228, 232
    upgrading private colleges into
    university colleges, 223
Malaysian Qualifications Agency
    (MQA), 225, 226, 227

Maldives, 231
males
    completion rates, 31
    enrolment rates, 26
    graduate earnings, 208, 209, 210
    illiteracy rates, 21
    teachers, 37, 41
    years of schooling, 18–20
Manado State University, 185
Mexico, 112, 115
MGMP
    see Secondary School Subjects
    Teachers Working Group
middle-income trap, 141–2, 203
Millenium Development Goals, 70
Ministry of Education and Culture, 7,
    17, 18, 34, 37, 50, 54, 57, 60, 65, 68,
    71, 72, 73, 74, 75, 80, 81, 87, 89, 131,
    133, 148, 262
    Center for Education Data and
    Statistics, 16, 32
    strategic plan 2004–09, 90
    tertiary education sector, 160, 161,
    162, 175, 176, 177
Ministry of Finance, 72, 73, 76
Ministry of Home Affairs, 72, 73, 76,
    87
Ministry of Manpower and
    Transmigration, 260
Ministry of Religious Affairs, 12, 18,
    50, 68, 69, 70, 72, 73, 74, 75, 76, 79,
    80, 81, 87, 148, 160
    strategic plan, 71, 71n, 76–7, 78
    tertiary education sector, 160, 166,
    175
Mongolia, 169
Morocco, 46, 233
mortality rates, 83
Mozambique, 141
MQA
    see Malaysian Qualifications
    Agency
Mulawarman University, 185
Muslim students, 230
Myanmar, 47, 141

N

Nanyang Technological University,
    169
Nanyang University, 217–18

National Accreditation Agency for
    Universities (BAN-PT), 172–3
National Accreditation Board for
    Schools and Madrasah (BAN-
    S/M), 69, 71, 78–9, 80
    function, 71
National Coordination Forum for
    Education for All, 50
National Development Planning
    Agency (Bappenas), 16, 76
national education standards, 73, 73n,
    90, 126
national education system
    history, 55–7, 65
    integration of Islamic schools, 12,
    68–81
    Law 20/2003, 6, 23n, 45, 47, 70, 74,
    90, 126, 135
    prospects for full integration,
    79–81
National Family Planning
    Coordination Agency (BKKBN), 87
National Labour Force Survey
    (Sakernas), 207
national qualification framework, 241,
    260, 261, 265
National Socio-Economic Survey
    (Susenas), 12, 16, 17, 90, 92, 206,
    249n
National University of Singapore, 169
nationalism, 56, 57
New Order era, 57
New Zealand, 10, 46, 212, 233
Nigeria, 231
Norway, 112
Nusa Cendana University, 184, 185,
    187, 188, 189, 190, 192, 194, 195,
    196, 199
    vision, 196

O

OECD, 163, 170, 261
Oman, 231
Omega Schools, 9
Open University, 49, 163, 173
overseas students
    see international students

P

Padjadjaran University, 175
Pakistan, 141, 231, 233

Palestine, 231
Pancasila, 56, 56n
Papua, 153, 154–5
Para Professional Course (KPP), 259, 265
PGRI
    see Indonesian Teachers Union
Petronas, 221
Philippines, 6, 10, 47, 112, 115, 145, 162, 163, 164, 204
PISA
    see Programme for International Student Assessment
playgroups
    see early childhood sector, playgroups (KB)
Podes
    see Village Potential surveys
Poland, 233
policy implications, 133–6, 260–65
political stability, 55, 56, 65
population, education data, 6, 18–23, 25, 26, 30, 31, 139–40, 162, 163
Pos PAUD |
    see early childhood sector, ECED posts
poverty, 4, 5, 9, 10, 11, 12, 15, 21–2, 26, 27, 30, 31, 49, 68, 80, 83, 105, 106, 129, 154, 168
    access to education, 4, 10, 24–5, 34, 90, 117, 133, 168, 174–6
    decline, 109, 141
    learning outcomes, 117–19, 120
    higher education loan repayment burden, 212, 213
    tertiary education, 174–6, 178–9, 193–4
Preliminary Achievement Index, 175
Presidential Primary School (Inpres SD) program, 8, 33
primary education, 2–9
    incomplete, 2, 30, 162
    government expenditure, 112, 113, 114
    graduation from year 6, 2, 27, 28
    rate of return on investment, 2, 4
    retention rates, 3, 26, 27–8
    transition rates, 26–7, 28, 49, 83
    universal enrolment, 2, 57, 161
Primary School Teachers Working Group (KKG), 151

principals of schools, 8, 58, 130, 133, 152, 153, 155, 156
private sector
    early childhood services, 13, 85, 87, 88
    expenditure on education, 112
    Islamic schools, 68–9, 70, 71, 74, 76, 77, 81
    Malaysia, 216–34
    philanthropy, 176
    quality, 9, 32, 34, 265
    scholarships, 176
    schools, 8–9, 17, 32, 34, 38, 39, 42, 68, 74
    student performance, 42
    teacher training providers, 49
    teachers, 38–9, 146
    tertiary education, 160, 161, 163, 165, 166–7, 170, 173, 174, 175, 177, 178, 181, 189, 190, 198, 199, 216–34, 256, 264, 265
    tertiary graduates, remuneration, 146–7
    vocational training, 263
productivity, 3, 5, 237
professional societies, 174, 227
Programme for International Student Assessment (PISA), 5, 45, 83, 85
Programme for the International Assessment of Adult Competencies, 261
PSG
    see Dual Education System

Q

Qatar, 46
quality, 2, 5, 6, 7, 13, 49, 58, 61, 110, 117, 120, 121–2, 126, 132, 133, 134, 135, 136, 142, 144, 261
    education and training, 240, 250, 251–60, 261
    effect of increased government expenditure, 117–20
    local governance, 129–33
    madrasah, 12, 68, 73
    Malaysia, 226–9
    non-formal education, 256, 259–60, 265
    private sector, 9, 32, 34, 265
    schools, 4, 5, 8, 9, 32, 34, 71, 126, 136

secondary education, 3, 34, 252–3, 261
secondary graduates, 252, 253, 256
tertiary graduates, 253, 256
teachers and teaching, 7, 8, 15, 32, 34, 37–41, 49, 55–6, 57, 58, 59, 61, 64, 65, 110, 123–6, 132, 133, 144–57, 261
universities, 161, 162, 164, 166–7, 171–4, 187, 195, 196, 200, 203, 219, 224, 225, 226–9

R

RA
    see early childhood sector, Islamic kindergartens
rates of return on government investment in education
    early childhood sector, 12, 13, 82–3, 86, 115
    primary education, 2, 4
    vocational secondary schools, 256
Regional Incentive Fund (DID), 134–5
religious education, 69, 79
remote areas, 6, 7, 11, 30, 34, 37, 68, 150–51
    teacher absenteeism, 154
Romania, 233
rural areas, 3, 18, 20, 21–2, 34, 37, 83, 84
    early childhood services, 90–103
    urban comparisons, 18, 20, 21, 37, 83, 84, 155
Russia, 46
Russian Federation, 233

S

Sakernas
    see National Labour Force Survey
Saudi Arabia, 46, 231, 233
scholarships, 30, 176, 179, 193, 232
school committees, 8, 58, 132–3, 157
School Self-Evaluation, 73–4
Schools Operational Assistance scheme (BOS), 70, 72, 74, 75, 76, 79, 116, 126–7, 132, 133, 135
schools
    accountability mechanisms, 135–6
    accreditation, 69, 70, 71, 71n, 72, 73, 73n, 76–7
    curriculum development, 263
    infrastructure, 5, 7, 8, 156
    Islamic, 11–12, 33, 68–81
    junior secondary, 32, 33
    links with industry, 263
    local school grants, 135
    management, 8, 58, 58n, 132–3, 136, 156
    primary, 5, 15, 23, 32, 33
    private, 8–9, 17, 32, 34, 39, 42, 68, 74
    private *madrasah*, 68–9, 70, 71, 74, 76, 77, 81
    private vocational, 263
    registration, 72, 78
    secondary, 8, 32, 33, 34, 253, 254, 255
    senior secondary, 32, 33–4
    staffing standards, 134
    supply, 32–4
    vocational, 253–5, 256, 262, 263
    see also primary education; private sector; secondary education; teachers
secondary education, 2–9
    completion rates, 30, 162, 168
    demand for, 34
    employers' perception of quality of graduates, 252
    enrolments, 3, 4, 24, 35
    government expenditure, 6, 112, 113, 114, 115, 116
    graduates, 252, 263–4
    priorities, 262–3
    quality, 252–3, 261, 262–4
    retention rates, 26–7, 30
    transition rates, 27, 30, 83
    see also junior secondary education; schools; senior secondary education; teachers
Secondary School Subjects Teachers Working Group (MGMP), 151
senior secondary education, 24, 25
    government expenditure, 114, 115, 116
    number of schools, 32
    see also teachers
Singapore, 5, 6, 9, 12, 45, 46, 64, 65, 119, 164, 169, 217, 231, 233
skill sets, 239, 240
    see also labour market; workforce
SMAK
    see Chemical Analyst Vocational Schools

Social Science Citation Index, 172
socio-economic status, 4, 5, 12, 13,
    24–5, 27, 30, 45, 119, 120, 129, 168,
    175, 179
    see also poverty
Somalia, 231
South Korea, 4, 5, 6, 10, 45, 46, 47, 115,
    119, 142, 163, 164, 212, 231, 233
Sri Lanka, 231
SDQ
    see Early Childhood Education and
    Development project, Strengths
    and Difficulties Questionnaire
student
    scholarships, 176, 179
    subsidies, 4, 175, 176
student loan schemes, 176, 179, 203–13
    repayment burden, 204, 205–6,
    207, 208, 211, 210
student performance
    international comparisons, 5, 45,
    45n, 46, 83, 85, 117–19, 142, 143,
    169, 250
    public/private comparison, 42
students, international, 167
student–teacher ratios, 7, 35–6, 121–2,
    125–6, 134
subsidies
    government, 178
    schools, 30
    students, 4, 175, 176
Sudan, 231
Suharto, President, 33, 57, 177
Susenas
    see National Socio-Economic
    Survey
Sweden, 46
Syria, 233

T

Taiwan, 6, 45, 233
Tanzania, 231
tax system, 213
teacher training, 53–66, 197
    emergency programs, 55–6
    pre-service and in-service, 49, 61,
    66, 145
    providers, 49
teachers, 34–41, 139–57
    absenteeism, 5, 7, 8, 62, 152–6, 157
    certification, 6–7, 47, 116, 123–6,
    127, 133, 134, 146–7, 148–50, 156–7

certification process, 148–9
civil servant status, 8, 34n, 50, 54,
    55, 62, 63, 66, 76, 117, 124, 132, 145,
    155, 157
competency (testing), 7, 123, 124,
    133, 148, 149, 149n, 150, 157
deployment, 37, 134
by education sector, 35
educational attainment, 37–41, 42,
    49, 144, 157
expenditure on, 121–3
evaluation, 8, 66
gender, 37, 41
honorary, 34
intergovernmental resource
    transfer system, 7, 132, 134
oversupply, 7, 134, 145
private schools, 38, 39, 146
professional allowance, 123, 124n,
    133, 146, 157
professional development, 8, 41,
    61, 66, 136, 145
professional working groups,
    151–2
provincial comparisons, 39–41
quality, 5, 37–41, 123–6, 132,
    144–52
recertification, 133–4
recruitment, 7, 34, 50, 55, 121, 131,
    132, 133, 134, 145
remote area allowances, 6, 146,
    150–51, 155, 156, 157
retraining channel, 148, 149
salaries, 6, 8, 47, 48, 50, 63, 116–17,
    121, 125–6, 127, 134, 145, 146, 149,
    157
short-term contract (*guru kontrak*),
    34, 54
supply, 7, 34–7
unequal distribution, 134
vocational schools, 262, 263
working hours, 37, 49
    see also teacher training
teaching
    culture of, 61–3, 65
    modes of, 7–8, 53–4
    multigrade, 134
    need to strengthen, 262
    student-centred, 53, 54, 59, 60
technology, 144, 150, 199, 244, 246,
    263, 264
    transfer, 181, 256, 264, 264

Telekom Malaysia, 221
Tenaga Nasional, 221
tertiary education, 160–79
    autonomy, 10–11
    completion, 193
    design, 11
    enrolments, 3, 160, 162–3, 168
    foreign students, 11, 165, 167
    funding, 115, 162, 167, 175–6
    government expenditure, 114, 115,
    116, 164
    graduate earnings, 206, 207–9
    graduates, average remuneration,
    146
    gross enrolment rate, 163–4, 168
    institutions by type, 165
    internationalization, 162, 165, 167,
    171, 216–
    language of instruction, 11
    loan schemes, 10, 176, 203–13
    Malaysia, 216–34
    priorities, 264–5
    private sector, 11, 160, 161, 163,
    166–7, 170, 173, 174, 175, 177, 178,
    181, 189, 190, 198, 199, 256, 264–5
    provincial differences, 168
    scholarships, 168
    see also universities
tertiary education institutions, study,
    180–200
    alternative framework for high-
    quality small TEIs, 200
    institutions studied, 184
    methodology and limitations,
    183–5
    see also tertiary education;
    universities
Thailand, 3, 4, 5, 6, 10, 46, 47, 112, 115,
    119, 145, 162, 163, 164, 169, 204,
    206, 231
TIMSS
    see Trends in International
    Mathematics and Science Study
TK
    see early childhood sector,
    kindergartens
TPA
    see early childhood sector,
    childcare centres
TPQ
    see early childhood sector, Islamic
    kindergartens

Trends in International Mathematics
    and Science Study (TIMSS), 5, 41,
    45, 46, 117, 119, 142, 143

U

unemployment, 174, 249, 251, 256, 259
United Kingdom, 45, 47, 190, 218, 221,
    230, 230, 231, 232, 233
    Association of Chartered Certified
    Accountants (ACCA), 227
    degree programs in Malaysia, 223,
    230
    Law Society, 227
    Quality Assurance Association for
    Higher Education (QAA), 227
    see also England; universities,
    British
United Nations Children's Fund
    (UNICEF), 90n
United States, 10, 46, 47, 165, 186, 190,
    204, 206, 221, 228, 230, 233
    degree programs in Malaysia, 230
    Harvard University, 190
    Laureat group, 224
Universiti Sains Malaysia (USM), 234
universities, 11, 160–79
    academic mobility, 170
    academic publications, 172, 188
    academic quality, 171–4, 178, 196
    accreditation, 172–4, 225, 226
    autonomy, 161, 165, 176–8, 196
    British, 190, 218, 223
    business units, 194
    competitive grants, 171, 189, 190
    cost of attending, 206, 219–20
    dropout rate, 175
    employees' perceptions of main
    weaknesses, 258
    employers' perceptions of main
    strengths, 2578
    endowment funds, 190
    expenditure per student, 188
    funding, 114, 116, 167, 178, 181,
    188–91, 192, 194–5
    governance, 169–71
    graduate quality, 253
    industry links, 197, 198, 256, 261,
    264
    influence on policy making, 198–9
    international ranking, 161, 169,
    171, 180, 180n, 181, 185–6

international students, 167
Islamic, 167
leadership, 195–6
local community relevance, 191,
    196–7, 197–9
low-cost courses, 167
Malaysian, 216–34
number of, 160, 165
peer review work, 171
plagiarism, 173n
Preliminary Achievement Index,
    175
private, 10, 11, 160, 161, 163, 165,
    166–7, 169, 170, 171, 173, 174, 175,
    176, 177, 185, 194, 199
public/private partnerships, 189
research contracts, 189–90, 194
research grants, 171, 186, 189, 190,
    194
research-intensive, 11, 161, 170, 199
resource constraints, 181, 186,
    188–91, 195
scholarships, 193, 199
small/regional, 11, 181, 182, 186,
    187–97
staff qualifications, 169, 191, 192,
    219, 226
staff recruitment, 177, 187–8
staff salaries, 169–70, 171, 187–8,
    226
staff seniority, 170
state, 163, 166, 167, 169, 170
students, 61, 187, 193, 232
study programs, 10, 177
tuition fees, 183, 183n, 190–91, 192,
    194, 204, 230
twinning arrangements, 168,
    217–22
world-class, 180–82, 185–6, 234
see also Malaysia; name of
    university; tertiary education;
    tertiary education institutions,
    study
university graduates, earnings, 206,
    207–9
provincial comparisons, 208, 209,
    210, 215
University of Indonesia, 181, 181n,
    185, 189, 190, 194
urban/rural comparisons, 18, 20, 21,
    37, 83, 84, 155

USM
    see Universiti Sains Malaysia

V

Vietnam, 9, 112, 164, 169, 203, 106
Village Potential (Podes) surveys, 16,
    18, 32, 87
vocational training, 253–5, 256, 260,
    262, 264, 265
informal centres (BLK), 265
on-the-job training/experience,
    240, 241, 242, 243, 252, 256–60

W

Wiraraja University, 184, 187, 188, 189,
    190, 192, 193, 194, 195
vision, 195, 196
workforce
educational levels, 5, 6, 161
skills mismatch, 236–65
skills required in local economies,
    198
teaching, 7
young adults, 5, 6, 249, 260, 261,
    265
young children, 2, 24
see also labour market

Y

Yemen, 230, 231, 233
Yudhoyono administration, 162

Z

Zimbabwe, 231

INDONESIA UPDATE SERIES

1989
Indonesia Assessment 1988 (Regional Development)
edited by Hal Hill and Jamie Mackie

1990
Indonesia Assessment 1990 (Ownership)
edited by Hal Hill and Terry Hull

1991
Indonesia Assessment 1991 (Education)
edited by Hal Hill

1992
Indonesia Assessment 1992 (Political Perspectives)
edited by Harold Crouch

1993
Indonesia Assessment 1993 (Labour)
edited by Chris Manning and Joan Hardjono

1994
Indonesia Assessment 1994: Finance as a Key Sector in Indonesia's Development
edited by Ross McLeod

1996
Indonesia Assessment 1995: Development in Eastern Indonesia
edited by Colin Barlow and Joan Hardjono

1997
Indonesia Assessment: Population and Human Resources
edited by Gavin W. Jones and Terence H. Hull

1998
Indonesia's Technological Challenge
edited by Hal Hill and Thee Kian Wie

1999
Post-Soeharto Indonesia: Renewal or Chaos?
edited by Geoff Forrester

2000
Indonesia in Transition: Social Aspects of Reformasi and Crisis
edited by Chris Manning and Peter van Diermen

2001
Indonesia Today: Challenges of History
edited by Grayson J. Lloyd and Shannon L. Smith

2002
Women in Indonesia: Gender, Equity and Development
edited by Kathryn Robinson and Sharon Bessell

2003
Local Power and Politics in Indonesia: Decentralisation and Democratisation
edited by Edward Aspinall and Greg Fealy

2004
Business in Indonesia: New Challenges, Old Problems
edited by M. Chatib Basri and Pierre van der Eng

2005
The Politics and Economics of Indonesia's Natural Resources
edited by Budy P. Resosudarmo

2006
Different Societies, Shared Futures: Australia, Indonesia and the Region
edited by John Monfries

2007
Indonesia: Democracy and the Promise of Good Governance
edited by Ross H. McLeod and Andrew MacIntyre

2008
Expressing Islam: Religious Life and Politics in Indonesia
edited by Greg Fealy and Sally White

2009
Indonesia beyond the Water's Edge: Managing an Archipelagic State
edited by Robert Cribb and Michele Ford

2010
Problems of Democratisation in Indonesia: Elections, Institutions and Society
edited by Edward Aspinall and Marcus Mietzner

2011
Employment, Living Standards and Poverty in Contemporary Indonesia
edited by Chris Manning and Sudarno Sumarto

2012
Indonesia Rising: The Repositioning of Asia's Third Giant
edited by Anthony Reid

2013
Education in Indonesia
edited by Daniel Suryadarma and Gavin W. Jones

www.ingramcontent.com/pod-product-compliance
Lightning Source LLC
Chambersburg PA
CBHW060328100426
42812CB00003B/914